The Legacy of the Bolshevik Revolution

Forthcoming:

DAVID ROUSSET

The Legacy of the Bolshevik Revolution

Volume I of a Critical History of the
USSR

Translated by Alan Freeman

ALLISON & BUSBY
LONDON · NEW YORK

First published in Great Britain 1982 by
Allison & Busby Ltd,
6a Noel Street
London WIV 3RB.

Paperback edition distributed in the USA by
Schocken Books Inc, 200 Madison Avenue,
New York, NY 10016.

Original title: *La Société Éclatée* (part 1)

British Library Cataloguing in Publication Data

Rousset, David
    A critical history of the USSR
    Vol. 1: The legacy of the Bolshevik Revolution
    1. Russia – History – 20th century
    2. Russia – Politics and government – 20th century
    I. Title   II. Legacy of the Bolshevik Revolution
    947.084'1   DK266   80–49687

  ISBN 0–85031–160–8
  ISBN 0–85031–388–0 Pbk

Set in 10/11 Bembo by Alan Sutton Publishing Ltd
Printed and bound in Great Britain by
Biddles Ltd, Guildford & King's Lynn

SUMMARY OF CONTENTS

I

THE FIRST REVOLUTION AND ITS DISINTEGRATION

The technological threshold reached since the 50s puts the first world revolution in an entirely new light, revealing the decisive objective contradiction which governed the victory and destruction of the first revolution. It has defined the precondition of all forms of socialized production: the *degree* of development of scientific research and the *quality* of the technological system available. The first is of crucial importance. The second is no less essential: between the beginning of this century and the middle of it there has been no continued growth but a rupture, a qualitative *leap*. There has been no logical progression of growth but a discontinuity, an abrupt changeover to a higher level of integration, which has created its own original reality. The historical horizon has become a tangible limit. The third cardinal fact: marxists, who are intellectually speaking the best prepared, have not had the necessary experimental data at hand to develop a theory of the technological factor or to work out a technological programme for the revolution. Marx's axioms and basic theorems. The significance of the *world* concept of revolution (Lenin's strategy). The greatness and weakness of the theory of permanent revolution elaborated by Trotsky. Integrated science as the decisive factor in "the material conditions of production".

Its objectively necessary character. Its determinants in the production process. Its stages at the basic level of class conflict, 1920–29. The basic contradiction of this period of history takes place *institutionally* in Russia. The October revolution creates social relations which go beyond the technological capacity of the planet. The first effect of this contradiction is that property is concentrated, both in law and in fact, in the hands of the state. The technological immaturity can be verified by the "socialization of poverty" which was characteristic of war communism. NEP sanctions this state of affairs by re-establishing the capitalist mode of production. The capitalist mode of production produces its own constitutive social relations, which enter into conflict with the premature social relations introduced by the revolution. The conflict develops at the level of classes, and extends to the whole of society; its epicentre is the production process, and it develops as if it were a force of nature. NEP is an unstable socio-political compromise, dictated by the world balance of forces between the classes. The resistance of the revolutionary institution, anchored in the production process, is unable to stop or avoid the social destruction of the revolution — on the contrary, it determines the *social nature* of what follows. The stages of disintegration.

The October revolution constitutes the proletariat as the dominant class. The state which is created is, by its very nature, a working-class state. The working class fulfils two functions. One part of it, as the political *corps de l'état*, administers production. The other part, in the factories and places of work, assumes its role of a labour force. The same class takes on both functions in a *world* historical context which ensures that the two are antagonistic to each other. The result is a tension which necessarily leads to an organic break. This break is the matrix of a new class system. The division of labour is, objectively, the agent of this crucial transformation. The determining factors are world factors. The particular backwardness of Russia limits the selection of options. The party is at the heart of this disintegration: it is completely dominated by historical conditioning and by the class dynamic. Socially and politically, the proletariat is pressed back in stages from the advanced democracy of the councils to the rule of the single party. Its decomposition as the dominant class. The internal disintegration of the party is first of all the mechanical result of the division of labour.

The conflict between the party and the trade unions. The objective elimination of self-management narrows the functional *base* of the dominant class in its exercise of political control over the state and production. The appropriation of the means of production has been carried out by the state and, to a greater extent, directly by the working people. The political monopoly of the single party is the most precarious and restricting form of workers' control over the state. The proletariat can exercise some sort of compensatory social pressure through trade unions which are independent of the state. The cardinal and historically decisive problem of dual power.

The basic function of the revolutionary party and its verification in the experimental test of history. The dual role of democracy within the party. Democracy is the only structure which permits the essential function of the party, i.e. to elaborate operational knowledge. The revolutionary effectiveness of the party depends entirely on the quality of this knowledge; likewise its creative ability and power, and its real historical function. Internal democracy is the ultimate reserve for the proletariat's exercise of political control. The suppression of democracy within the party definitively removes the proletariat from the state. Workers' power has totally disintegrated.

The eviction of the proletariat from its function as the dominant class opens the problem of the succession. The result will depend on the conflict between classes. Since the proletariat has been forced back and the revolutionary institution has been tied down to production (through the nationalization of industry), the political *corps de l'état* has become an autonomous force. The party is the crucible of power, and thus becomes the arena where the antagonistic classes fight it out, either directly or through the mediation of particular people, and thus enslaved by the social conflict. The party's tendencies are the incarnation both of the scission with the proletariat and of its subjection to the other classes.

First crucial fact: the bureaucracy is the organic product of the October revolution; it is the reponse of the revolution to the historical conjuncture. This definition underlines the quite original character of the bureaucracy and explains its social power. Second equally crucial fact: the revolutionary institution is the natural support of the bureaucracy. Juridically speaking, it manages production as the agent of power, but in practice the exercise of this delegation in the absence of control creates real autonomous roots for it in the production process. This is the crucial mechanism in the first phase of the bureaucracy's emergence as a different class.

The political mechanisms of the succession. The civil war inside the party. The revolutionary institution is the natural base of the bureaucracy. The social composition of the bureaucracy results from the amalgam between proletarian managers and the traditional tsarist bureaucracy. The fusion takes place over a period of seven years. The political *corps de l'état* (the Thermidoreans) constitute themselves as the directing layer of the emerging *étatist* class, as the core of the high bureaucracy. The decisive factor is their convergence of interests in the personal activity of Stalin. The three major stages: 1923, 1925, 1927.

The armed clash between the classes. The directing intelligentsia. The large theoretical and political difficulties. The leninist concept of state monopoly. The important conceptual value of Rakovsky's ideas. The causes of the divorce between theoretical analysis and political practice. The theoretical and political foundations of the defeat of the Left Opposition.

The decomposition of classes and the society's regression into barbarism. What was at stake in the second world war. The balance of forces between the classes during the war. The nature of the scientific knowledge obtained: military violence as the catalysing agent. The new hierarchy of nations. Technological changes in the production process and the remodeling of its social armour. The premises of the second revolution in the process of productive forces.

II
BUREAUCRATIC SOCIETY AND STATE CAPITALISM

notebook"). The secrecy of the archives, the falsification of history and biographies, censorship of the eye-witness accounts — functional, technical necessities in the exercise of power. Continuity from Stalin to Brezhnev in the application of secrecy (the permanent explosive value of the texts: for example, the document of 31 December 1922 and national conflicts in Europe and Asia in the eary 70s).

Heightened efficiency. The functional reality of the state. The cardinal role of the party as the apparatus of renewal by co-option of the ruling class. Stalin as the most eminent strategist of the bureaucratic society.

I

THE FIRST REVOLUTION AND ITS DISINTEGRATION

1 The rebirth of a historical perspective

THE SECOND revolution is on the agenda in Europe and in the United States. The first revolution of 1917–29, catapulted into existence by the imperialist war, was destroyed in the savage undertow of the decomposition of world capitalism. The second revolution is being sparked by the most powerful scientific and industrial explosion of modern times.

With only a half-century between them, these two revolutions are situated within the same general perspective, but at two different thresholds. This difference is of fundamental importance.

The vista revealed by the Second World War affords a view of the revolution of 1917 which is basically new. No one could have anticipated it at the time, for the importance of the events, which turned out to be decisive, emerged only thirty years later. From our present viewpoint, the missing elements which determined the abortion of the first revolution can be clearly identified.

The social ruptures during the first twenty-five years of this century came about *before* the technology needed for socialized administration of the economy became available. Social and economic tensions developed *faster* than the operative capacities of scientific knowledge. The time lag of nearly fifty years between the effective realization of the conditions for the seizure of power and the elaboration of a technology of the socialized production process, defines the historical impasse of the October revolution.

The relative underdevelopment of world productive forces at the start of the century made it impossible to go beyond the capitalist relations of production, which were nevertheless no longer capable of ensuring the necessary growth or even maintenance of the economy. The radical calling into question of the monopoly system to which its own functioning gave rise came about in a situation where other solutions did not exist. The necessary advanced technology was not in sight, nor even the programme for its creation. In fact, no one could conceive of such a programme. The level attained by scientific research was not ready for the convergence of ideas

1

which the elaboration of this concept required. Scientific activity was intense, but at the level of the formation of fundamental theories (general relativity, quantum physics, wave mechanics) which were to stimulate and sustain the subsequent expansion of operative knowledge. But *subsequent*. It was to take more than thirty years of work (with the appearance of a generation of researchers born under the reign of these fundamental theories and formed by them) and large-scale upheavals before massive transfers of technology could finally occur. It would take until the crucial decade of 1950-60 for the apparatus of this programme to be established.

There is a discontinuity between the beginning of the century and its midpoint. The scientific-industrial expansion in the second stage of which we are now living does not comprise a logical extension of the technology of the early 1900s. It is not a simple exploitation of this technology. It does not result solely from an accumulation of facts and refinements in technique. It is characterized by the substitution of one integral system for another. A substitution such that if it had been possible in 1920 to carry out a forecasting study, as is done nowadays, it would still not have been possible to lay down a direction for research which could resolve the problems posed. At a clearly definable moment (the decade of 1940-50), the position of science in society changed abruptly and fundamentally. A new kind of integrality emerged from this mutation. This difference in the nature of the totality defines the relative underdevelopment of the first quarter of the twentieth century.

The capitalist mode of production could not be transcended, although the necessary political and social conditions were all present. It was as utopian in those times to want to build socialist relations on the existing infrastructure as it would have been to try and conduct space flights. The men of that time could easily have understood the impracticability of the latter, even though it was hardly possible to understand the real nature of the difficulties to be overcome. But they did not see, and did not know how to see, what blocked the way to socialism.

Marxists, however, entertained no overt illusions on this basic theme. Amid tendency struggles, polemics and a profusion of ideas, there is a number of general considerations on which they agreed. These are useful to recall, because they are indicative of an approach which marxists considered scientific and which marked them off, in effect, from utopians, anarchists and from the general confusion reigning today.

The socialist revolution is first of all a revolution: political, social and military confrontation. In order for military victory not to fall back into defeat, the satisfaction of certain defined economic and cultural preconditions is indispensable. The socialist revolution requires not simply a favourable balance of forces, but also a determinate organization of the forces of production. This necessary starting point did not exist in the East, but in Russia (in spite of all the grave distortions resulting from the weight of its backward sectors), in Western Europe, in the United States of America; England provided the best model yet achieved.

Socialist society is constructed on the basis of the highest world development achieved by capitalism. In our language we would say that the technology of socialism is, and cannot be other than, the most up-to-date.

The fundamental revolutionary value of socialism resides in its capacity to ensure, over a long period, a powerful growth of the productive forces which capitalism, in its time, has brought to a previously unequalled level but which it is completely incapable of maintaining.

The historical originality of the socialist mode of production derives from the fact that it should bring about in stages the elimination of classes: that it should lead to the advent of a free community, i.e. a community which is capable of controlling and directing its own development. This is an undertaking of a similar nature to the effort that is being pursued today to make a co-ordinated intervention in the genetic process.

These considerations must be refined with the utmost precision, for there are two spheres in which they have a big effect on strategy. The statement that capitalism is no longer capable of advancing the forces of production must be understood in a general sense. Obviously it may not be the case in certain particular branches and for certain nations. This has a precise meaning: world development is uneven. This unevenness becomes, in political, social and military action, a measurable factor that must be taken into consideration.

When we speak of the British model, and of the advanced character of Europe and of the United States, this does not mean that monopoly capitalism is a multiplication or aggregation of national economies. Monopoly capitalism has created an autonomous reality: the world market. It is at the level of the world market that the full realization of its potentialities occurs. It is also within the world market that its contradictions assume their greatest intensity. Because socialism is built on the basis of the highest level of development, the base of the socialist revolution is not and cannot be a national one. Socialist society is organized on a world scale. The socialist revolution aims, on the same basis and with the same violence, at the destruction of private ownership of the means of production and the break-up of national frontiers. Western Europe comprised the centre of the system which was to explode.

From this point, and since directives and programmes of action had to be defined, the divergences burst forth. The insurrection of December 1905 exacerbated them in Russia earlier than elsewhere. In Germany, they had already put the Lassalians in opposition to Marx. In the International they prepared the ground for the confrontation between Kautsky and Lenin. The war and revolution of October gave these divergences the breadth of a planet-wide split. This did not detract from the fact that the common basis nourished theoretical reflection and gave a direction to strategy.

Trotsky explains, for example, that around 1925-6 the conjuncture in China offered the Chinese proletariat the opportunity to seize power, but that the state of Chinese society did not enable it to carry out transformations of a socialist character, and that the impasse which would thus be created could only lead, if prolonged, to the destruction of the workers' state. Lenin constantly insisted that the overthrow of workers' power in Russia was inescapable unless the proletariat triumphed in Germany, France and Britain — into the advanced industrial countries. Taking up the common view that the socialist revolution could only be a world one, because the narrow national base was already a straitjacket even for monopoly capitalism and would therefore be incapable of leading to a higher growth of socialist production, he concluded that what was true for Britain and the United States was doubly true for Russia. This principle is the pivot of his writings and actions. There is no other legitimation for the conception of the Communist International as a world party.

In this sense, the October revolution was not, and could not have been, a "national" revolution. Its national tasks were only the application in particular conditions of its world task: the promotion of socialist relations of production. The Russian proletariat was fighting in the front line of a world revolution, a front which could not be maintained unless decisive victories were carried into Western Europe. This way of looking at things seemed so obvious to Lenin that he counted on decisive victories during the weeks following the Petrograd insurrection, and then in a few months' time; for the same reason, he began to speak afterwards of and organize a retreat. It is highly significant that it was precisely in this period of reflux, while Russia was dangerously vulnerable, that circumstances seemed to justify falling back on a "national" strategy, and that in November 1921 the Fourth World Congress judged it imperative to state: "The Fourth World Congress reminds workers of all countries that the proletarian revolution can never win inside a single country, but in an international framework and as a world revolution."[1]

This concept of a unified world strategy is at the core of the now classical "weakest link" interpretation of the fact that the revolution had its first breakthrough in Russia and not, as was predicted by Marx and Engels and was believed by the Bolsheviks, in England; an interpretation which after all takes up an old observation of Marx: "The most violent explosions are produced at the extremities of the bourgeois organism before having taken place in its heart, given that it is easier to regulate the centre than the extremities." It was the order of succession which changed, not the historical necessity. "Russia has commenced. Germany, France and England will complete the picture." This was Lenin's position at the Third Congress of Soviets. The same logic led Trotsky to envisage the uneven and combined development of socialism as an economic spiral, "Through the visitation of internal incompatibilities of such and such a country on a whole group of other countries, through reciprocal services between countries and through the mutual complementarity of their economies and culture, that is to say in the final account on a world scale."[2]

Rosa Luxemburg, the extent of whose differences of opinion on essential points is well known, completely agrees with Lenin here. She writes from prison: "The fact that the Bolsheviks have oriented their politics entirely in the direction of the world revolution is precisely the most vivid proof of their perspicacity, their firmness of principle, the audacious scope of their politics."

While it is an established fact that the world character of the socialist revolution occupies a central place in marxist theory and in the strategy of Lenin, it is important to grasp the full meaning of this fact.

Two notions are tightly bound together. The sphere of monopoly capitalism is the world sphere. This is its supreme reality. It is here that its full contradictions and its capacities as a mode of production are realized. Socialism is a higher mode of production. It constitutes the initial organization and the motor for a new stage of growth of the forces of production. Its base can only be the last stage of capitalism.

Saturn V could not have been built on the basis of rockets fuelled by gunpowder. It would be historically valid, but technologically absurd. The radical difference lies in the high skills of modern labour. Modern labour is the expression of a highly integrated system, which implies a mutation of the operative power behind society. In other words there is a discontinuity between capitalism and socialism, considered as systems of production. It could be termed a mutation. There is a jump from anarchic, blind growth to orderly development. The basic difference hinges on the qualitative level of social labour. It is evident that the springboard for such a forward jump can only be the most advanced product of existing technology.

In fact, this criterion does not suffice, as we have found out. It is also necessary to know exactly what *is* the current key technology; which of its capacities are not exploited by the capitalist mode of production; what can be produced and at what speed by the scientific principles which organize it and by the techniques which it possesses, once they are freed from external limitations (financial, economic ones, those due to the narrow confines of the market, in short, their social fetters).

Today we are in a position to proceed, up to a point, with such an enquiry. Fifty years ago, the means did not exist to take it anywhere useful. Basic scientific theories were only just becoming conceivable, and it was only their experimental repercussions which appeared. The transfer from basic research to industry was still heavily subject to chance, following indirect paths and subject to long delays. The system remained very loosely integrated.

We are touching here upon the unbridgable frontier of the historical horizon: the reality, by comparison with the present stage, of technological underdevelopment at the start of the century, and, more basically, the intellectual limitations inherent in this under-development.

Of course, we are subject to the same constraints. Clearly, when the technological conquest of the solar system has been achieved, world society will possess an intellectual and technical apparatus vastly superior to ours. It is no less certain that the knowledge thus acquired would be valuable for the solution of the problems which are now posed for us. In the absence of such knowledge, we are subjected to solutions which will later be shown as primitive, without being able to understand exactly in what way they are primitive. We are certainly capable, though, of knowing in what respects they are insufficient.

The marxists of the first quarter of the century found themselves forced to work out and set in motion an overall plan. From the moment that the market was detached from the economy, planning would become an absolute necessity. They had to invent everything and, without previous experience, to run everything themselves. They knew perfectly well that a concerted enterprise required accurate and complete statistical information. They also knew they did not have it. They were therefore quite capable of appreciating the insufficiency of their means. On the other hand, it was impossible for them to understand the indispensable contribution that electronics would make, and how it would constitute the irre-placeable foundation of any rational control of the productive forces. In this sense, they ran up against the primitive conditions of their attempt without seeing them. It was to take a half-century to over-come this blindness.

At this stage in the discussion, it is enough to point out the value which marxist analysis assigns to the *technological factor* in the process of production. That is, what Marx terms "the material conditions of production". Marx poses the following as an axiom in his *Critique of the Gotha Programme*: "Law can never be at a higher level than the economic situation and the degree of social civilization which corres-ponds to it." It is therefore, in the last resort, the "material conditions of production" which are decisive. It is not the "common ownership of the means of production". From the point of view of analysis (and from all points of view), this distinction is crucial.

Collective appropriation embodies the fundamental revolutionary act, the deliberate intervention of society. There exists a code for the process of production, as there exists a genetic code. Collective appropriation alters the social letter of this code. It therefore unleashes a far-reaching chain reaction. However, this appropriation cannot by itself produce a socialist society. The "material conditions" which make it possible are also necessary. This is the exact meaning of the value assigned to this factor.

Permitting himself some prudent speculation on the communist society, Marx envisages, as we know, two phases. In the course of the first phase, there will be extensive survivals from bourgeois law. "What we are concerned with here is a communist society, not as it has developed out of its own base, but on the contrary as it has *emerged* from capitalist society; and hence, it is a society which, in all its relations — economic, moral, intellectual — still carries the stigmata of the old society from whose womb it has emerged."

The first stage develops out of the material base of the old mode of production. The effects of the new juridical relations are therefore limited. They become social relations only partially and with difficulty. The contradiction between the material situation and law is expressed by the survival of bourgeois law in the organization of labour. The second phase opens when the material conditions of the socialist mode of production have been mastered and determine the process of development:

> In a higher phase of communist society, when the servile subordination of individuals by the division of labour has disappeared and with it the antagonism between intellectual and manual labour, when work has become not merely the means of life but also the principal need of

existence; when, with the all-round development of the individual, the forces of production continue to expand and all the sources of collective wealth flourish in abundance, only then can the narrow horizon of bourgeois right be completely overtaken and will society be able to write on its banners "from each according to his abilities, to each according to his needs".[3]

We have to pay the greatest attention possible to all these "whens" of Marx. They are not there by chance. They are presented as scientific criteria. Their common denominator defines "a gigantic development in the productive forces" as a basic obligation. Such a development presupposes, obviously, a corresponding technology. What emerges from this text is that the "material conditions of production" exert a continual and decisive influence. The role of this influence, its specificity and its permanence, are determined by the place which technology occupies in the process of production and by the general function of the latter in society. This function is clearly defined by what I would call the theorem of Marx: "Social relations of production change, and are transformed, *with the modification and development of the material means of production, of the forces of production.* In their totality, the relations of production form what are called social relations, the society and, notably, a society with a distinctive, unique character."[4] (My emphasis.) This theorem of Marx assumes a universal validity. In the same way as the laws of Mendel are the foundation of genetics, it is the foundation of the science of development of every society — and hence, necessarily, of socialist society. The value assigned to the "material conditions of production" finds its theoretical justification in this central concept of society.

There is no denying that if marxists did not discern the technological gap which prohibited the introduction of socialized production at the beginning of the century, then it was not for lack of any theoretical preparation, but in spite of this preparation. Marx provided the intellectual tools for the analysis; he did not possess the power to jump beyond the historical horizon of his era.

Hence — on this crucial question — there are no experimental data. Yet these data are all the more vital because one cannot embark on test-tube experiments in history.

Anyone wanting to conduct a critical analysis, from the point of view of the socially available motor forces, of the Levebvre-Desnouettes thesis on the new use of the yoke at the time of the first Capetians, would have no great difficulty in assembling the necessary references. In contrast, the libraries of 1900 or 1920 contained neither documents nor archives on socialist technology. The first result is that this absence of means of verification prevented the launching of any project: the first revolution did not possess a *technological programme*. It is remarkable that the growth of productive forces, which was so vital in theory and in all areas of interest for the revolution, was the only one where commentary remains general, imprecise, and did not go beyond a general statement of principles. Relative underdevelopment deflected the efforts of the thinkers.

Theses and polemics were exclusively devoted to social, economic and military factors of the revolution. Material abounded on these subjects. Two generations served their apprenticeship by living through 1848, the Paris Commune, and 1905. The French revolution was minutely examined. An autopsy was conducted on the peasant war in Germany. Bernstein, Kautsky, Lenin and Rosa Luxemburg disagreed as to the problem of the nature and role of the state, the dictatorship of the proletariat, insurrection, coalition government, and nationalization. These were all crucial questions because they involved a strategy for the seizure and exercise of power. There was nothing byzantine or academic in these disputes. However, the central feature, the "material conditions of production", escaped these controversies. On questions of technique, marxists entertained the normal optimism of their time: they believed that the progress then in hand was sufficient to guarantee progress to socialized production, that all that was needed was to break down the double obstacle of private property and the national straitjacket. This was clearly Lenin's position: "Seeing that at this moment capitalism presents an incredible block to progress, and how much advance may be made with already available techniques, we are correct to assert, with absolute certainty, that the expropriation of the capitalist will necessarily bring in its wake a gigantic development of the productive forces of human society."[5]

It did not occur to him to submit this position to the test of criticism, as he did with all others.

The second consequence of the absence of experimental data was that marxists, starting with Marx, had to rely on the experience of revolution itself. When the Germans wanted to know what the function of the state in a socialist society would be, Marx replied sharply: "This question can only be resolved on a scientific basis; you can couple the word 'people' with the word 'state' in a million ways, but the problem will not be advanced by so much as a flea's jump." True. But this is simply shifting the responsibility for finding solutions and inventions on to practice, while depriving oneself (and only in this particular case) of any theoretical orientation. Now practice cannot help altering fundamental data. In history, an experiment is never repeated. That which has occurred always creates new factors which change the entire conjuncture. This constant is particularly true during a revolutionary period, when powerful social forces are suddenly displaced, when the most solidly established institutions fall apart. The non-existence of theoretical forecasting (i.e. of guidelines, or indicators) carries, in a period of accelerating history, a very high risk of irreversible disaster. October is an ample demonstration of this.

The third consequence of the absence of experimental data is that it prevents the elaboration of a coherent theory of socialized production, so that under the pressure of events the marxist leadership will finally be reduced to a more and more narrowly empirical policy. From the end of the civil war, Lenin had to resort constantly to palliatives, through a series of setbacks. So much so that the destruction of the first revolution was accompanied by such a retrogression in theoretical work that our time still bears its imprint.

Nothing demonstrates more clearly what is irreplaceable about this theory of socialized production than the powerful synthesizing work undertaken by Trotsky in the years that preceded and followed October. The theory of permanent revolution represented the most rich and original contribution in the sphere of strategy. It was the most concerted work of interpretation, developed constantly for twenty-five years, and continually taken up again. Elaborated in 1905, it did not take its most advanced present form until 1930. It started out as an interpretation of the revolutionary process in a comparatively backward country, and became in its completed form a theory of world revolution. Setting out from national disparities, it developed into an integrated international strategy. It integrates, in effect, all the fundamental notions of marxism: uneven and combined development, the world division of labour, the essential autonomous reality of the world market and the uninterrupted character of the revolution. It must be classed among the most powerful unifying concepts of world history.

Marx formulated the principle of the uninterrupted growing over from the democratic stage to socialist measures, from socialism to a classless society, with each stage exploiting the possibilities created by the preceding one. Applying this principle to the bourgeois revolution of 1848, he foresaw its transformation into a proletarian revolution. This was a singular error on his part, since it amounted to an underestimation of capitalism's capacity for growth. It was a significant error: the revolutionary is perpetually obliged to make an appreciation of the situation he intervenes in, as it unfolds with his participation. But in addition, his appreciation is also action. It is easy enough to analyse past events such as the Empire, or the Alexandrian wars, or the use of armoured divisions in 1940, but another thing when you are engaged in the action. This is one of the reasons (but not the only one) why politics is an art and not a science.

This error in prognostication certainly contributed to the temporary eclipse of the principle of uninterrupted revolution. But even more so did the spectacular thrust of world capitalism: this was the golden era of reformism, its institutional phase. The passage from bourgeois democracy to socialism was obliged to conform to the predominant conception of slow stages, with reforms being given time to ripen through a process of continued expansion. Jaurès and Guesde might have disagreed on the ultimate use of violence, but they agreed on the rejection of the hypothesis of sudden leaps — admitting, within a linear perspective, that there were long time-lags between the accomplishment of democracy and the construction of socialism.

It took the approaching catastrophe and the sudden emergence of the first anomalies in the crisis of capitalism for the thesis of permanent revolution to assume a new vigour, which it then continued to display for thirty years. The explosion of 1905 in Russia was in a sense the first warning. It announced the most surprising anomaly: an upset in the predicted order of succession. The proletarian revolution erupted on the scene in Russia, not England, in spite of the general incredulity among marxists, including Bolsheviks. This unexpected detour posed the question of the revolutionary process in those countries where there was "retarded bourgeois development".

It is notable that in the first analysis Kautsky, Lenin and Trotsky were in agreement in recognizing that the Russian bourgeoisie was incapable of leading its own revolution to a conclusion. From this central fact, Trotsky draws a new, more precise and theoretically better articulated formulation, whose predictions were, in effect, verified in February and October 1917. It is really remarkable (and not just from the point of view of the history of ideas) that his thesis was, between 1905 and 1917, rejected not just by Plekhanov, the founder of Russian marxism, and by the Mensheviks, who when all is said and done were located on the left wing of the Second International, but also by most Bolsheviks. A good refutation of retrospective schematism.

The development of the theory at this stage principally concerned the dynamic of classes in the revolutionary process. The Russian bourgeoisie had to break the institutions of serfdom in order to open the way for industry. To reinforce this industry — to guarantee, as we would say nowadays, its competitiveness (i.e. in the last resort to consolidate and sanction its social domination) — the Russian bourgeoisie would have had to complete the agrarian reform and in this way sap the foundations of the Tsarist Empire. It was incapable of cutting the umbilical cord which linked it to large landed property. It was therefore powerless to carry out the democratic bourgeois revolution. This failure, which left the emancipation of the Russian bourgeoisie unfinished, stimulated the proletarian revolution to take charge of radical agrarian reform. It was the thesis of the leap which prevailed (and prevailed in a factual sense). History contracted. If, in February 1917, Kerensky had gone through with the distribution of the land, the October revolution would never have taken place. The peasant revolt hoisted the workers' insurrection on to its back.

The class basis of the strategy was clearly defined from then on. The proletariat needed the support of the peasantry in order to seize state power: the peasantry found, in the workers, the strength it needed to attain its own social objectives. In this coalition, the proletariat took the helm. Not necessarily because it was better prepared, or because it possessed wider perspectives (both of which are true), but because it was the expression of the labour-power of industry, because it embodied advanced technology.

After the revolution of October 1917 and the setbacks suffered by revolutionary initiatives in Western Europe, the second stage was entered. In the first phase, the theory of permanent revolution was an incisive criticism of reformism, borne out by events. In the second, it became violently opposed to the ideology of socialism in one country, the ideology of the dominant bureaucracy. Its field of application became planetary.

1917 to 1923 was a waiting period. Nothing could as yet be considered definite in Europe. Lenin carried out a succession of retreats and prepared, as far as he could, to relaunch the revolution in the West. After 1923, the die was cast. Hamburg and the crushing of the German proletariat marked the turning point. The prolonged isolation of the Russian revolution became a predominant factor in the international arena. Social troubles in India and the workers' insurrections in China placed the colonial and semi-colonial countries in the forefront.

In its new form, the theory of permanent revolution made the foundation of its international strategy the principle of inter-dependence between the revolution in these countries and the revolution in the metropolitan industrial centres. The Chinese and Indian revolutions would create new premises for the revolution in England, and the English revolution would open the second revolutionary crisis in Europe — which would use its enormous technological potential to snatch the Asian revolution out of its inescapable slide into bankruptcy and failure. The theory of permanent revolution became the theory of world revolution.

The intellectual richness of the theory of permanent revolution is revealed in the explanatory power it retains today, sixty years after it was first elaborated. In essence, it affords a correct interpretation of the successes and reverses which revolution has met in Asia, Africa and Latin America. It reveals the hidden causes of the repeated defeats of the revolution in Eastern Europe, particularly in Czechoslovakia. More profoundly, it is fundamentally confirmed by the advent of the second world revolution.

But in spite of its powerful creative capacity, this theory has not been able to account for the failure of the first revolution. To some extent a theory is like a computer: the efficiency of its analyses depends on what you put into it. If the user misconstrues or is unaware of important data, the logical instrument, no matter what its value, cannot furnish a valid account of the facts. It is striking that, faced with such a brutal setback, Lenin, and with and after him Trotsky, always considered the problem of leadership to be central — that is, the subjective factor. From 1918 to 1923, errors were imputed to the youth and inexperience of communist cadres in Europe. In the following ten years the faults were due to the thermidorean course pursued in Russia. Certainly, each error produced a change in the balance of forces, a displacement of classes in the national and international arena. The ebb of the revolution enabled the bourgeoisie to restabilize the situation, and relative economic stabilization in turn strengthened the position of social democracy, to the detriment of the communist parties. The Anglo-Russian committee was one error, the alliance with the Kuomintang another; the first led to the strangling of the General Strike of 1926, the second to the massacre of the Chinese communists. Stalinist centrism zigzagged between crass reformism and ultra-left adventures. These zigzags were continual. Trotsky spoke of "the third period of mistakes". And all these accumulated mistakes opened the way for the triumph of fascism in Europe. Trotsky devoted an enormous quantity of detailed argument to these errors. It is all true; Trotsky's culture was broad, his practical experience considerable and his pedagogy needle-sharp, and each demonstration is therefore undeniably rich in lessons. He nevertheless failed to penetrate beyond the surface. However great and, in certain limited cases, however decisive a subjective intervention may be, it still cannot on its own provide the key to a historical period. As long as one remains in the sphere of the dynamic of classes, theoretical analysis yields positive results. Once one starts on the material basis for this dynamic, one enters the realm of speculation. This explains why these events, from Hamburg to

Canton, from Madrid to Berlin, were confirmations in a negative sense. Defeat was always the proof. There is only one conclusion which can be drawn from this: that the analysis of capitalism must be taken up once again and deepened.

One of Trotsky's remarks reveals the stumbling-block clearly: "But do you really believe that Russia is ripe for a socialist revolution? This is what the Stalins, Rykovs and Molotovs objected many times between 1915 and 1917. I always replied: no, I don't believe it, *but the world economy and the European economy in particular are perfectly ripe for this revolution.*"[6] (My emphasis.) His adversaries remained silent, for the good reason that everyone agreed with him, as with Lenin and Marx, that the European economy was ripe for socialism. To be precise, they thought that starting from the present level, it was possible to bring about socialized production.

Events have shown that this was not the case, and we know today the basic reason why. The most significant point was not so much the lack of critical tools which would have made it possible to define, even in summary fashion, the theoretical basis of a technology of socialized production; the key factor was rather that marxists, who were intellectually best-prepared to study these questions, had never entertained the least doubt as to the quality of the tools available to them. Individually and collectively, they put on a show of the same blind confidence.

Marx elaborated the fundamental concept of a science of society. He defined the critical apparatus of historical analysis. He made a decisive contribution to the formulation of the laws of the social dynamic. He proceeded to verify them experimentally in the fields of economics and history. He made predictions which could be checked against reality — the most important was to have brought out the general tendency of the productive forces towards the world integration of the economy and to the socialization of the means of production. This prediction has been confirmed today, on a scale and in conditions which Marx could not have imagined. To take issue with what remains in his work of the philosophical heritage of his youth, or to accuse him of hasty conclusions or excessive schematism in his representation of the distant past, would be like denying all value in the work of Lamarck under the pretext that it remains impregnated with metaphysics, or the scientific quality of Darwin because today we have a more accurate and precise concept of the evolution of the species. In a sense, it would be to condemn him because he was not able to be a man of our century: like rejecting Newton for not having introduced relativity.

But it is precisely because Marx was a scientist that he did not develop the theory of the transition to socialism. His reply to the Germans is clear: science will settle the question. Without experimental data, no science is possible. Science is not possible for two reasons. One, because there is no continuity between capitalism and socialism but a break, a break between levels. A planned economy is a totally different thing from an anarchic economy, even if this anarchy is up to a point controlled and regulated (a control and regulation which, in their turn, will generate new complications). *Capital* deals with the analysis and synthesis of the capitalist economy, grasped in one phase of its development — that is, using the only material which Marx had available. Trotsky is perfectly justified in submitting that those who have any conception of what *Capital* is about understand perfectly well that neither in the first, nor the second, nor the third volume of this work, will they find the reply to the question: how, and at what speed, must the dictatorship of the proletariat carry out the collectivization of the rural economy?

The second reason concerns the social dynamic. While it is already adventurous to claim an ability to extrapolate from the functioning of an economy in order to understand what are fundamentally different processes, to predict class relationships in the same way is completely impossible. Theory indicates that, in its particular phase of growth, the process of socialization of the means of production brings about the disappearance of classes; but theory also indicates that this suppression cannot be immediate. Nothing more. Classes are not entities fixed for eternity. Their interrelations change: that is, their reciprocal positions in the social structure change. Equally, their internal composition changes. The production process is at the root of these changes. It is therefore certain that socialist production will modify the decisive components of the class struggle. It cannot fail to bring about considerable transformations in the composition of, and relations between, classes. The inevitable resultant conflicts will in turn create new social and political relationships. It would be utopian to try to envisage their outlines.

For lack of real data the theory of the transition to socialism has not got beyond some very general considerations. To put it another way, there has been no theory. This absence of data and the illusions which have been held concerning the adequacy of the available technology (due to ignorance, even at the theoretical level, of the necessary technical conditions) led marxists to a total misunderstanding of the nature and historical breadth of the period of transition. This error could not fail to bring about the ruin of the first revolution.

In order to understand the nature of this period of transition, it would have been necessary to take up again and deepen the understanding of the capitalist system. It is clear today that capitalism's capacity to tolerate a gigantic growth of its own internal contradictions was greatly underestimated. Many things which to Lenin and his generation were inconceivable have actually occurred. When I say "sustain", I understand by this (among other things) that the present acolytes of neo-capitalism are the historical equivalents of the reformists of yesterday.

This necessary deepening of marxist analysis is possible precisely because Marx worked scientifically. In order to understand the laws of capitalist society, he constructed a model, thus inaugurating a method which today is employed in all spheres of science. This procedure enabled him to determine the tendencies of the system and their reciprocal relations. But because a model is an abstract representation which is true for a complex reality, it has to be altered whenever the complexity of the transformations of the real has repercussions on those tendencies, or whenever it activates certain potentialities. Trotsky is one of the few to have understood this scientific approach of Marx. In relation to the third volume of *Capital*, he wrote in 1930: "Marx's formulations construct a form of 'chemically pure' capitalism which never existed and which does not exist now. This is precisely why they demonstrate the essential tendencies of capitalism *in general*, but they are only the tendencies *of capitalism* and nothing more." This deepening of the theory might have been made on the basis of the development of monopolies. Circumstances, accelerating the social crisis, decided otherwise.

In order to establish a programme for the period of transition, it would have been necessary to understand science (basic research in physics and chemistry) as the most important factor, the most decisive in its effects, of "the material conditions of production", and to foresee that its intervention would lead to high-level integration of all the aspects of development. At this time such views, even if they had been held by some, could not have been articulated around precise propositions.

Historical circumstances thus imposed a considerable time-lag on the development of theory. The social crisis arrived first. The logic of the revolution was with Lenin against the reformists.

It now became patently obvious that the first revolution was at one and the same time inevitable and premature and that, as a consequence, it could not survive.

2 The disintegration of the first world revolution

THE OBJECTIVE impossibility of going beyond the capitalist mode of production did not merely pronounce the doom of the first revolution; it also determined the means by which it would be destroyed.

To understand this best, we should start from a clear definition of the October revolution and recall the essential nature of the capitalist relations of production.

The Russian bourgeoisie lost political power in 1917. Its economic roots had gone. It suffered a complete social expropriation. The nationalization of industry, land, transport and credit and the monopoly of external trade concentrated the ownership of the means of production and the power of command in the hands of the state. The insurrection handed the state to the proletariat. Of course, it was only one part of the proletariat which constituted the political corps of the state. But it is never any more than a fraction of the bourgeoisie which administers the bourgeois state. It is therefore legitimate and necessary to characterize the state produced by the revolution as a workers' state. Such are the real dimensions of the October revolution.

The revolution gave a foundation in law to the collective appropriation by the workers of "the material conditions of production". This collective appropriation, after a brief attempt at direct control, assumed during this first stage the juridical form of state ownership.

The capitalist mode of production maintains and diversifies the division of labour; it sharpens the antagonism between manual labour and intellectual labour, between the tasks of management and the tasks of production; in consequence it develops appropriate social relations. The juridical aspect of these relations can certainly vary, but their real content cannot change as long as the mode of production does not change — a change which can only occur as a result of a high level of development of the forces of production.

"The development of the forces of production", writes Marx, "is in practice the first absolutely necessary condition, for the *further* reason that without it it would be poverty which was socialized *and that poverty would bring about anew the struggle for the necessities of life, and would as a consequence resuscitate all the old mess. . .*" (my emphasis). There is no room in this domain for freedom. A given

17

mode of production generates social relations of a precise type and can tolerate only these social relations. The code of production and the genetic code produce rigorously determined relations, with the difference that in genetics there is an extraordinarily large number of possible combinations.

In particular, the capitalist mode of production determines the processes of circulation and distribution of specific commodities.

> In every epoch, the distribution of objects of consumption is only the consequence of the way in which the conditions of production are themselves distributed. But this last distribution is a feature of the mode of production itself. The capitalist mode of production, for example, determines that the material conditions of production are in the hands of non-workers in the form of capitalist and landed property, whilst the masses possess no more than the individual means of production: their labour power.[7]

Finally: "Any division of labour which is developed and which organizes itself through the intermediary of the exchange of commodities is based fundamentally on the separation between town and country."[8]

The principal contradiction of the October revolution consists in the fact that it established social relations *in advance* of the relations of production, which therefore entered into conflict with the real level of the forces of production. It thus created a situation of extreme instability which could not in any way be prolonged.

It was this *real level* which prevented war communism from being transformed into a higher stage of collective control, and which forced Lenin to adopt the New Economic Policy (NEP).

NEP re-established freedom of commerce, opened the way to a new growth of the market, resorted to monetary calculation, substituted a tax in kind for requisitions, and freed small and middle industry. The monopoly of foreign trade was safeguarded. Heavy industry, transport, and large-scale credit remained the property of the state.

NEP registered the failure of war communism. The existing technology had rejected direct administration of the economy. The incompatibility was so insurmountable that it brought about generalized regression. War communism accomplished what Marx had envisaged as an unlikely eventuality: the socialization of poverty. It revived the struggle for the necessities of life and all "the old mess". In real life what occurred was Kronstadt, strikes, and revolt in the countryside — all of which, in 1921, was paving the way for a struggle against state power "of large masses comprising not only peasants but also workers".[9]

NEP was based on the necessity to resort to capitalism in order to save the economy from suffocation, to uproot agriculture from the village autarchy, to put a broken down industry on its feet, to fill the holes made by the civil war, and to put basic goods back into circulation: in other words, to recreate a dynamic of production — NEP therefore took over the fundamental tasks. This fact indicates that the capitalist mode of production *was the motor* of the development of the forces of production, and hence the dominant mode of production. It was not possible to re-establish this or that particular function of the process of capitalist production. The integral totality of the system had to be re-established. It was not possible to liberate small and medium industry, to choose state capitalism, and to maintain an administrative system of exchange. The restitution of the market became necessary.

NEP reconstituted the economic base for a rebirth of the bourgeoisie which had been expropriated in 1917. The market gave rise to it as an apple-tree bears apples. This was recognized by the "Thesis on the Tactics of the Russian Communist party" adopted by the Third Congress of the Communist International (June 1921):

> The tax on food, by its very essence, is equivalent, for the peasant, to the freedom to dispose of what is left of it after his payment of tax. To the extent that the state is not capable of offering the peasants the produce of socialist industry in exchange for the total of this remainder, to the same extent the resultant freedom of commerce inevitably becomes equivalent to the freedom of development of capitalism.

Lenin called a spade a spade. Hence the way in which he presented NEP laid bare the nature of the compromise. Thus, the recourse to monetary calculation: "if we succeed in stabilizing the rouble, firstly for a period, and then for the foreseeable future, we shall have won." The re-establishment of the market: "we need commerce, bourgeois traffic." The freedom of small industry: "a prosperous small industry will provide the peasants with articles of current usage." The open door to foreign capital: "our policy in relation to concessions seems excellent to me." The thesis adopted by the Third World Congress: "without carrying out any denationalization, the workers' state releases certain mines, certain sectors of forest land, certain oil rights, etc., to foreign capitalists, in order to get from them the means to create large scale Soviet industry".

NEP was a bridge between Russian capitalism and world capitalism. It was nevertheless a bridge with controlled traffic. The monopoly of foreign trade opened only one lane. With the mixed societies acting as go-betweens, the Soviet state was the only client which made itself available to the outside world. World capitalism and state capitalism joined hands.

NEP was a *political* accommodation between collective property and private property. This accommodation was a recognition of an actual situation. The development of state industry became entirely shackled to capitalist relations of production. The only safeguard remaining was the juridical form of property. It was linked exclusively to the centralization of command structures. In another historical context, state property would gradually have dissolved into social property. The opposite phenomenon took place. State property took on the increasingly accentuated character of private property, sanctioning state capitalism in the sphere of law.

Lenin, in his comments, linked the two facts very tightly: "the direct passage to a purely socialist economic form, to the purely socialist distribution of wealth, was outside our powers." "State Capitalism, even though not a socialist form, will be for us and for Russia superior to that which exists now." Where is the demarcation line between capitalism and Lenin's state capitalism? Not in the objective process of the production of goods, not in the relations of production, but in the command structures. And only in the command structures.

The theses of the Third Congress already cited are crystal clear on this point: "the development of capitalism under the control and regulation of the state (that is to say the development of 'state' capitalism in the latter sense of the word) is advantageous and *indispensable*." (My emphasis.)

Lenin says: "Our state capitalism is distinct from other forms of capitalism in the literal sense of the word in that we possess, in the hands of the workers' state, not merely the land but also the most important parts of industry." The difference is undeniably of a *political nature*: the concentration of the power of decision in the hands of the state took on an enormous *economic* importance. He who possesses the state draws exceptional decision-making power from it. This is so important that it is impossible to understand the events which followed if this fact is not admitted. However this admittedly great power has a limit to it. It is incapable of altering the real level of technology. It is absolutely incapable of substituting itself in society for the socialized process of production. From this point on it was inevitable that the social personnel who incarnated the functions of the state were also caught up in the machinations of the capitalist mode of production, in the same way as the peasants, the commercial petty-bourgeoisie and the re-emerging industrialists. State property possessed no magic which could prevent an analogous phenomenon to the kulakization of the countryside from taking place within the state itself. The state personnel could become, in the strictly social sense, kulak, NEP-man and dominant industrialist at one and the same time. In other words, centralized command did not guarantee the state against the loss of its proletarian character.

NEP opened and closed the process of the destruction of the first revolution: a complex world process of which the USSR was the focal point. There could be no question here of following events in detail. These years were too crowded. It is sufficient to detach the most important processes.

NEP was a total defeat. To be sure, the catastrophe imminent in 1921 was delayed. In this sense, Lenin's tactical objectives were attained. But the means utilized to achieve this seven years' survival (the period of relative economic success of NEP) were fundamentally foreign and hostile to the proletarian revolution. As a result of this, the delayed catastrophe finally arrived. These seven years of grace, and of confrontation, prepared the ground for an unexpected consequence: a consequence which would not have happened if everything had foundered in 1923 under the counter-blows of the defeat in Germany.

The irrevocable downfall of the marxist leadership, tragic because of its victims and because of the intellectual regression which accompanied it, nevertheless provides a rigorous demonstration of the scientific validity of the principles on which the marxist theory of society is based. It is rare for history to provide such an example, such a powerful demonstration of the impossibility of revolutionary action prevailing in a lasting way over the real technological level. It also demonstrates the corollary of this fact: the impossibility of maintaining the juridical norms and hence the social structures which they legalize, which do not correspond to the real relations of production. The demonstration of the first fact took five years: of the second, seven years.

On the Russian terrain, the destruction of the October revolution came about in two clearly distinct stages. The first was from 1922 to 1929: the capitalist mode of production generated the relevant social antagonisms which were natural to it. There was nothing unpredictable about this. The second stage came in the period 1928 to 1929, when the alliance between the state bureaucracy, the kulak and the NEP-man was broken. It attained its full extent during the famine and the ravages of the second civil war, in the thirties. The predictable, which was in fact predicted (the return to monopoly capitalism), did not come about. But "a society of a distinctive original character" was established to put it in Marx's precise way.

Thus from 1922 to 1929, the re-established capitalist mode of production worked towards the re-establishment of bourgeois society. A combination of three sets of factors determined the conjuncture. These were: the enormous resistance of the revolutionary institutions, the increasing re-privatization of the means of production, and the growing gap between the slow progress of nationalized industry and the rapid resurgence of peripheral private industry and private agricultural cultivation.

In this period, while the working class was losing its position as ruling class, the *institutional gains* of the revolution were maintained. Those social classes which had been destroyed did not reconstitute themselves. The state which had been organized by the revolution remained the owner of heavy industry, of transport, and of credit. This extraordinary resistance of the institutions of the revolution confirmed the socially radical character of the October revolution. (It makes nonsense of interpretations which discern in the seizure of power nothing more than a coup d'état led by a well-prepared military party.) The resistance imposed two powerful constraints on the situation. The re-establishment of the bourgeoisie began with the *consolidation of the middle classes.* The tension between the proletariat's functions of management and control as a ruling class and its function as work-force *were carried to the point of rupture. This dual course of the crisis, which was impelled by the maintenance of revolutionary institutions, opened the way to the totally unforeseen outcome of the 1930s: the appearance of a society with a distinctive, original character.*

Big capital and the big bourgeoisie were suppressed. State capital, based on the act of expropriation, substituted itself for monopoly capital. Large landed property disappeared. But it was not the state which replaced it. In the countryside, once the administrative and egalitarian intervention of war communism had been broken, a well-to-do peasantry took the place of landed property. Its existence derived from the distribution of the land and the absenteeism of the state, which was industrially incapable of exploiting its juridical ownership of the land. This fundamental contradiction *with the revolutionary institutions* was an expression of the contradictory tasks accomplished by the October revolution. More profoundly, it is a striking embodiment of the technological obstacles which destroyed the revolution. It led to an impasse which was to lead the state to use repressive violence on problems which it could not resolve through industry. This internal contradiction was to be carried over, as was the totality of the revolutionary institutions, into the new society, and was to determine the relations within it which must still be taken into account today. (The proletarian revolution, in fact, took in tow the unfinished bourgeois revolution. It redistributed the land. It abolished tenant farming. The abolition of tenant farming and the reduction of taxes brought the peasants some 500 to 600 million roubles. This was the concrete, palpable, calculable reason for their alliance with the bolsheviks. When war communism took on the *socialist* task of collectivization, it went into reverse, and these same peasants turned against the communists. The October revolution, certainly, came up against the backwardness of the countryside and the weakness of its industry: but also it came up against the low level of world technology. Even today, England and the United States are the only areas where industry has reduced the antagonism between town and country, without completely suppressing it.)

The state, in the absence of indispensable industrial techniques, could overturn neither existing agricultural technology nor the social armour of the peasantry. The generalized re-establishment of the capitalist mode of production brought about a precipitate re-emergence of differentiation in the countryside. However, ownership of the land was not a dead letter. The monopoly of foreign trade gave it a powerful reality. Agricultural prices on the world market represented land rents. The state's monopoly turned it into the effective owner of the soil. It bartered the products of its own land. It was the state, and no one else, which fixed prices. It became the effective custodian of landed rent. This negotiator presented itself as the only intermediary between the well-to-do peasantry, which earned the major part of the harvest, and the world buyers. In this role (and also as the largest supplier of industry and of the town), it was the principal client in the national market. In this double role, it clashed openly with the interests of the capitalist village. The resistance of the revolutionary institution (the maintenance of the monopoly of foreign trade) became the essential point at issue between the kulak and the state bureaucracy. The normalization through prices (i.e. through the market) of the relations between town and country was arrested. This anomaly precipitated the crisis.

Private hoarding of the means of production and social differentiation went hand in hand. As early as 1926 the kulak owned 75 per cent of rented land, half of the livestock and more than half of the machinery, part of which it re-let, at high prices, to the middle peasant. Official statistics reveal that, in 1927, 6 per cent of the farms were responsible for 58 per cent of cereals harvested.

Anchored in this predominance, the kulak acquired the consistency of an economic force. When the harvest of 1927 was over, he had a reserve of 800 to 900 million poods of cereals. The state, a major stockpiler of corn but whose stocks were severely depleted, was looking for money to pay its way. The kulak lent at high rates of interest. The state bureaucracy, caught in the toils of commercial transactions, was being subsidized by the rich peasantry.

The kulak's economic position turned him into a social force. He seized local control of the co-operatives and of agricultural credit. In

1926 (four years were enough), 49.7 per cent of administrative posts in the milk co-operatives were held by owners who represented no more than 6.4 per cent of the population.

The rich peasantry's grip on the cereal market, their infiltration into the apparatus of control, and the concentration in their hands of most of the harvests and revenues, gave the rich peasantry a clear understanding, and gave rise to a realistic evaluation of its interests: it was led to follow its own demands, in pursuit of corporate objectives: the guaranteed right to property (denationalization of the land); complete freedom of trade (suppression of the "organizations of stock control", the base of support for state commerce); freedom in international transactions (abolition of the monopoly of foreign trade).

The same process, which concentrated ownership, wealth, and social pre-eminence in the hands of one pole of the peasantry, precipitated the middle peasantry into financial, commercial and technical dependence on the kulak, and reduced the poor peasants to agricultural workers or unemployed labourers. The change came about so quickly and on such a scale that, from 1925 onwards, the state had to legalize the employment of a wage-earning work-force and the renting out of land. This concession amounted to a defeat. The rise in prices, the raising of indirect taxes on tobacco, matches, sugar, sweets, vodka, and beer constituted a swingeing attack on the poor peasant. The revolution had proclaimed the poor peasant its ally, the spokesman of the peasantry. NEP replaced him pitilessly with the kulak, and put him under the yoke once more. His fate was all the more effectively sealed by the connivances between the rich peasantry and the functionaries. These connivances were fuelled by "services rendered". The intermission which opened in October 1917 and which NEP brought to a close left intact the ancestral passivity of the poor peasant: "the authorities want it, and you cannot go against the authorities."

The NEP-man was the true twin brother of the kulak. Between the two of them they held the reins. Light industry, organized in the private sector, produced 40 per cent of all goods on the market. 50 per cent of the commodities exchanged passed through the hands of private commerce. A section of the proletariat, growing every day, began to detach itself from nationalized industry and became integrated into the sphere of the expansion of private capital. Gosplan pointed out that the conditions of life were much more advantageous there. The rise in the price of corn weighed all the more heavily on the working class now that bread was replacing meat, fat, vegetables, fruit and sugar, which were all now hard to find. Wages were, and had been for a long time, by far the lowest in

Europe. The wages of women and children were even lower. There were nearly two million unemployed; there was an incessantly growing number of famished peasants pouring into the towns — a sufficient reserve army to discourage strike action. The obsessive desire to "keep one's job", exhaustion, and disillusion led away from politics and towards indifference.

The capitalist mode of production maintained a deep-seated opposition between the tasks of management and those of production. In the denuded state of the economy, with nationalized industry, given no rest by the market, this opposition took on an exceptional intensity. The state functionary, the factory manager, and the overseer, in violation of the law, turned management into a repressive function. Compulsion became the general rule in labour relations. The ten-hour day (instead of the eight-hour day) was decreed from on high, as was non-payment for overtime and the uninterrupted working week. The state loan became, in practice, a further form of taxation at the base: a swindle, because shares bought were automatically not negotiable for five years.

The functional separation between the worker who had become an industrial and administrative cadre and the worker at his machine at the work-place took on the dimensions of an open divorce and was transformed into social differentiation. The bureaucracy denationalized the state to its own advantage.

With the market restored at the heart of the economy, nationalized industry was stretched on the rack like all the rest. The question of prices thus became central. The close link between industrial and agricultural prices became the Gordian knot. World prices, that is to say prices on the world market, were the court of highest appeal. The persistent backwardness of state industry registered itself as a growing, double imbalance between industrial and agricultural prices and between world and national prices. The dynamic of private capital was more powerful than the dynamic of state capitalism.

A dilapidated infrastructure, the lack of financial resources, the exorbitant incidental expenses of the bureaucracy and the incompetence of the leadership provide a clear balance sheet of the weaknesses of state industry.

The production of pig iron was only 80 per cent of what it was in 1913. The whole of engineering and heavy industry were in a similar state. Textiles had scarcely improved on their 1912 level. The only exceptions were coal, petroleum and above all electricity. This retreat places the population statistics in stark perspective. In the same period population went up by 15 million — nearly 12 per cent.

Production can be re-started quite quickly after an interruption, provided a sufficiently qualified work-force is available. But Russia, from 1918 to 1922, lost an enormous proportion of its industrial proletariat. This is a striking phenomenon with very considerable effects, which continued into the middle of the thirties. In 1913, workers in industry numbered 2,552,000. In 1921 to 1922, there were no more than 1,243,000. This was a heavy loss: nearly a million and a half. In 1928, the level of the first world war at last just overtaken, at the figure *2,822,000.*[10]

Because of this brutal discontinuity, the Russian proletariat was structured in the fiery crucible of the 1930s, at the same time as the society "of a distinctive original character" was being formed. This was a heavy political and technical loss. The most combative, best-educated and most qualified workers were withdrawn from production to staff the state machine. They became professionals in the administration, the party, the unions, the police and the army. A good number of them had been killed in the civil war. Of those left behind, many fled the factory. The haemorrhage lasted four years. They flocked to the countryside. They vanished into the anonymity of the village family. So much so that, when this process was reversed, beginning in the summer of 1922, it was a new generation of peasants which arrived in the towns.

A growing proportion of the work-force in the state sector had not yet acquired the proletarian mentality, did not willingly accept industrial discipline, lacked specialization and hence qualification, was bereft of trade-union experience and remained politically uncouth.

The price was obvious. The quality of production was low, there was widespread wastage, and cost prices were high — two and a half times as high as on the world market.

Until 1925 the machinery being used dated from before the war. The inheritance had been reduced by the massive destruction of world war and civil war, and by foreign intervention. The equipment was old and worn out. It was never renewed. And indeed there was no way it could have been, since between 1926 and 1928 investments were just over a thousand million roubles (equivalent to 110m. roubles before the war) per year, whereas between 1909 and 1913 the average annual investment had been between 350m. and 400m. roubles.

This nationalized industry — under-equipped, patchily tooled, deficient in its work-force and mediocre in the quality and quantity of its products — also had to bear exorbitant administrative costs. In 1926 Rykov and Stalin admitted that "the economic and administrative apparatus devours about 2,000m. roubles per year." And this was only one part of the bureaucratic expenses. The occasion of a quarrel between the party and the trade unions allows us to discover that the trade union budget was 400m. roubles, of which 80m. were allocated to wages. The direct effect of these expenses was that prices in the public sector were higher than in the private sector.

Financial resources, by contrast, were miserable. Private saving was suppressed by the expropriation of landed property, capital, commerce and private industry. This removed an average investment of a thousand million gold francs per year (the average between 1909 and 1913). 200 million gold francs of foreign capital must also be subtracted. Through weakness and incompetence, the party leadership failed to embark on a policy of public saving. Hence there was neither private saving nor public saving. Investments from 1926 to 1928 were one-third of those before the war, although the need was far greater and infinitely more pressing.

Nationalized industry lived on expedients. Machinery was paid for through short-term borrowing. In 1928 loans accounted for a quarter of national revenue. An eighth of this was covered by the state bank and the rest by the kulak. The extensive use of short-term credit and loans, guaranteed by the issue of bank notes, fuelled inflation. In one year (October 1928 to September 1929), the price index (base 100 in 1913) went from 2,791 to 3,653. The buying power of the rouble did not cease to deteriorate, whereas Lenin had counted on NEP to re-establish it.

The state owed enormous debts to the kulak, but it was an insolvent debtor. Lacking money, machines and qualified workers, nationalized industry was incapable of furnishing the villages with the equipment which they drastically needed.

The scarcity of means of production had as a corollary a dearth of cereals. The area of land which was sown grew smaller (102.7 million hectares in 1913, 97.2 in 1928). The yield per hectare fell (8.5 quintals in 1913, 7.9 in 1928). Rural unemployment became a scourge. This reduction of the cultivated area, due to the weaknesses of industry, reacted by aggravating these weaknesses. It deprived nationalized industry of indispensable raw materials and foreign currency. Exports of cereal of 2 million tons in 1927 fell to not much more than 500,000 tons in 1928. The powerlessness of the state to ensure the proper development of its industry or to respond to the social needs of the country generated a growing shortage of commodities, calculated in 1929 at more than 1,000 million roubles.

Furthermore, state industry had no leadership. It was not state capitalism but a patching-up job. There was no plan. So much so that a centralized command made its appearance only through police measures or through taxation. Under conditions of state ownership, the absence of a plan prevented capital formation. Without a policy on savings, the state did not have available the development fund it needed, which would emancipate it from its debts to the rich peasantry, and would ensure the growth of productive forces starting with the renewal and modernization of fixed capital. As a result, nationalized industry "lagged behind itself", in Bukharin's powerfully descriptive phrase. It was incapable of resolving its own problems.

The market concentrated the totality of these tensions on prices. Industrial prices climbed faster than agricultural prices. To quote Trotsky's celebrated metaphor, the "scissors", instead of closing, opened wider and wider.

Statistics, with 1913 as the reference point, indicate that the purchase price of cereals did not reach a coefficient of 2, whereas industrial produce on the private market passed a coefficient of 3.6. Trotsky estimated that in 1926 this divergence in prices cost the peasant 2m. roubles. Rykov (at that time Commissar for Agriculture), replying to him during the plenary session of the central committee of 1927, calculated the loss suffered by the peasantry at 400m. roubles. In any case, the kulak concluded that the state was cheating him. He was losing in the transaction. He therefore refused to sell. He considered himself safe enough for this refusal to be both possible and profitable. The corn strike broke out in autumn 1927, after three years of good harvest. The political crisis had opened. Its basic causes were not political but economic.

Because the market expressed in the most intense and complete fashion the division between town and country, it was the infernal machine which destroyed the first revolution. Once the capitalist mode of production was re-established (and once again, this re-establishment was inevitable because of the real state of technology) it produced all its social and economic effects in seven years, in a classic accelerating process. Social differentiation came into being everywhere, as much in the town as in the village. The state was not spared. The bureaucracy acquired its functional independence gradually, but quickly. This took on a more and more accentuated social character; the authorities gave themselves privileges in a most empirical fashion. The forces of production progressed equally quickly, provided one takes into account the general impoverishment of the 1920s. And it was precisely this progress which provoked the crisis of 1928.

Economic growth came into conflict with the arbitrary nature of state privilege. The dominating industrial position of the state was a survival from the revolution. It had sprung from the act of expropriation. It was not the product of a natural development of the forces of production. On the contrary, the public sector showed a persistent backwardness on the private sector. This backwardness was in essence due to the incompetence of the bureaucracy and to the cost of its upkeep. It acted like a brake. This was brutally translated into the cost and scarcity of industrial commodities. Distortion of prices and scarcity of commodities held back the progress of agriculture which, in its turn, disturbed industrial growth. In the last instance, this was all reflected in a growing imbalance between internal prices and world prices. Thus the market exercised a powerful pressure against the arbitrary position of the state by trying to displace its keystone, the monopoly of foreign trade. It is clear that the liberalization of the internal market and the end of the monopoly of trade with the world market would have permitted more equal relations between town and country and the resumption of capitalist accumulation in the village. The crisis reached its culminating point in 1928.

The elementary, primitive character of state capitalism did not permit normal capitalist relations with the kulak. Such relations could only have been established if state industry had become the motor of the national economy. The historical impossibility of promoting socialized production prevented the emergence of socialist relations with the peasantry. The capitalist relations of *production*, confronted by these obstacles, operated so as to clear the way for the *social* relations which were inherent to them. The result of this was an accumulation of violence, an explosive situation.

These fundamental objective processes, which were completely independent of the deliberate actions of people, were put in a clear light by the development of NEP, by its *necessary* character and by the *blind* approach of the social groupings.

NEP certainly resulted from a conscious political act, but this act was a forced one. The conviction that any other path would lead to imminent catastrophe weighed on the initial decision like a diktat. Lenin admitted this at the 11th congress: "If we had not transformed our political economy, we would have lasted but a few months more." On 29 October 1921, after seven months' experience, he repeatedly insisted on the obligatory character of the new course. At the Provincial Party Conference in Moscow, he underlined the imperative nature of the conjuncture — its severity, definiteness and scope. "We have to state that the retreat has been insufficient, that it has to be accentuated, that we have to turn back yet further in order to pass from state capitalism to the creation of state regulation of commerce and monetary circulation . . . this is why we are in the situation of men who are obliged to step backwards, in order, later, to pass once more onto the offensive."[11]

When Lenin wanted to take the situation in hand, it eluded him. He was not wrong in his diagnosis of the obligation to re-establish the capitalist mode of production; but he failed to appreciate the cause, and for this reason he underestimated the extent of this necessity. He thought that there could be an ordered retreat — that is to say, the maintenance of a certain control over events — whereas he was actually drawing up a disastrous balance-sheet and filing the revolution's bankruptcy petition.

On 6 March 1922, he announced at a fraction meeting of metal-workers his firm decision to finish with NEP. "We can now definitely say that this retreat, in the sense of a concession which we made to the capitalists, is finished. . . . I hope, and I am certain, that the party congress will also say this, officially, in the name of the leading party in Russia."[12] And, as a categorical and official full-stop: "The Congress, recognizing that the totality of these measures applied during the course of last year comprised concessions which the party recognized as being indispensable to make to the private capitalist economy, considers that in this sense the retreat is ended." Events did not follow desires and, of course, it was reality which settled things.

On the contrary, NEP took on an unsuspected breadth and power. Its breadth was legally recognized in the spring of 1925, when the government had to acknowledge the right of rich peasants to rent manpower and land; that is, the right to exploit an external work-force. Its power was established inside the very party which yesterday wanted to strangle NEP, the strongest interests of the capitalist peasantry were duly represented. In 1925 the Commissar for Agriculture of Georgia, with Stalin's connivance, lodged a project for the abolition of the nationalization of land.

It is rare to be able to observe a historical experience from which all that is not essential has been so well decanted, which is so chemically pure, and which obeys with such clarity the constraining objective determination of the relations of production. NEP gave an exemplary demonstration of Marx's theorems about society. The blind displacement of social forces provided a complementary proof of the direct relationship between the mode of production and the composition and position of classes. The capitalist mode of production imposes capitalist social relations. If this condition is not satisfied, the growth of the forces of production is jammed; the system goes into crisis and is threatened with disintegration. In contrast, the juridical and hence the political expression of the fundamental capitalist relationship depends on circumstances; that is to say, on the various historical factors operating. In the case of Russia, the solution could have been a return to monopoly capitalism. It turned out to be a new form of state capitalism. State monopoly, as the dominant structure, reconciled the needs of the re-established capitalist mode of production with the social environment, the product of the destroyed proletarian revolution.

From 1927 to 1929, these internal contradictions arrived at the point of rupture. At the same time as the tension was growing, the absence on all sides of any strategy — that is to say of any deliberate preparation for the conflict — became extraordinarily obvious. Politics was not merely lagging behind economic pressure – it was out of phase with it. With hindsight, the year 1928 appears crucial.

The peasantry was driven into crisis not by political hostility but by the failures of state industry, which was incapable of supplying them with urgently needed goods in sufficient quantities or at advantageous prices. The peasantry dealt with the town speculator, because he paid more for corn and supplied them with products of higher quality. They turned against the state because it was behaving like an insolvent debtor. All they wanted was for business to become profitable once more. After all, this objective conformed perfectly with the political agreement reached between the kulaks and the leading bureaucracy in 1925, which no one had ever queried.

The alliance of 1925 sanctioned a state of fact. But this sanctioning clearly took on a distinct political significance. Bukharin, taking up one of Guizot's slogans, launched the famous expression, "Enrich yourselves." And he explained that this slogan corresponded to what one could call the politics of reciprocal interests. "We help the kulak, but he helps us too. In the final account, we shall perhaps have to thank him for having acted this way." And since Bukharin was given to theorizing, in an essay which he published at the time entitled "Remarks of an Economist" he presented this tactic as a strategy for the period of transition, that is to say a very long-term strategy. He maintained, as was current in leading circles, that industry "must face up to the countryside, drag it out of the back alley of history into the forefront of political economy."

This alliance between state capitalism (nationalized industry) and private capitalism (the 25 million agricultural holdings) was integrated into a new and general political course which the rising middle classes could only welcome with satisfaction. In 1924 the bureaucracy invented the theory of socialism in one country, which entailed a complete rupture with the revolutionary past. It sanctioned the national reality — that is (from the point of view of the petty bourgeoisie) a return to economic sanity, and a hope that the renunciation of world revolution would provide a solid basis for the politics of concessions and hence for a probable eventual return of foreign capital to the internal market. If the rich peasant had had any notion of European history, he would have spoken of Thermidor. In fact, he needed no such reference to understand the situation.

Nothing indicates better the fact that the renunciation of world revolution represented a real turning point than another of Bukharin's statements: "It is also necessary to pose the question of an alliance with bourgeois states. If there were a situation in which a bourgeois state, as a result of particular circumstances of upheaval went over to the side of the Soviet Union against the imperialists, the communist parties would have to support the imperialist war of this state." This declaration, made in 1927 to the party committee in Moscow, was explicitly contrary to the fundamental doctrine of Lenin, who always put the interests of the world revolution before the particular and immediate interests of Russia. It expressed the inverse principle: that the private interests of Russia would decide. The cornerstone of the new international policy.

The strategy of reciprocal interests found itself underwritten in general policy. The régime changed its face. It was applied by an apparently solid team; Stalin, Rykov, Tomsky, Bukharin. No one at the top strongly opposed the domination established by the rich peasant over the co-operatives, over agricultural credit, or even over the village councils.

This political line was not repudiated in 1927 or 1928. The 15th Party Congress, which was held in December 1927 with the corn strike already under way, still ratified it. The enormous majority of delegates repeatedly denounced the "super industrialists" and "the danger of involving too much capital in large-scale industrial construction". Rykov in his report accepted the principle of the plan only with extreme reticence. Molotov was even clearer: "It is not a question of leaping lightly from a régime of individual exploitation into large-scale enterprises. It is necessary to advance step by step. Only this gradual progression is reasonable. No fantasies. Any constraint in relation to the peasant would be inadmissable." It could not be clearer.

Their actions confirmed this in the most vivid and infamous fashion. The adversaries of the rich peasant were decimated. Thousands of leftists were imprisoned; Trotsky and Zinoviev were excluded from the Central Committee in October 1927, and from the party in November. The desperate situation of the Marxist left was dramatically underlined in the same month of November by the suicide of Joffe. The expulsions were ratified on 2 December by the 15th Congress. Those expelled were deported. The rich peasantry were satisfied — they had got much more than they could have counted on in 1925.

The crisis therefore burst within an alliance whose links had been politically sanctioned and strengthened. That is to say, *in spite of* the official, actual political line. The passage from peace to war functioned as a constraint *in spite of* all intentions and programmes, because the state did not have the means to implement its own politics, and because the political compromise did not provide a sufficient basis for the capitalist mode of production. It was these same obligations which at the same time provoked the kulak to breaking point, and armed him.

The rich peasant acquired his strength in the conflict, because he was the authentic representative, the real spokesman of the whole peasantry. Not that the middle peasantry gave their support to the kulak light-heartedly. But their existence too was threatened by the scarcity of industrial goods. If it had gone on, they would have become poor peasants, unemployed agricultural workers. The failings of state capitalism brought about solidarity of all the classes in the country against it.

The year 1928 brought with it the clearest possible demonstration that the leadership of the bureaucracy, for its part, was engaging in war without a war policy, without any preparation: to tell the truth, without wanting to. The ink of the 15th Congress was scarcely dry when, in reply to the kulaks' boycott, the period of so-called "exceptional measures" began. Searches, fines, and confiscation rained down on peasants suspected of hoarding corn, from January until June. It is striking that even the leading group had great hesitations. On 16 February, Stalin published a sensational article in *Pravda*. He discovered that the kulak was the central figure of the village, that he was starving the country and laying siege to the state. It was the exact opposite of what had been solemnly proclaimed a month and a half earlier at the 15th Congress. He had chosen to be firm. But on 9 March, Rykov now chose conciliation, peremptorily reaffirming that NEP would continue. "Gossip concerning the suppression of NEP . . . is counter-revolutionary rumour-mongering against which it is necessary to wage a resolute struggle. NEP is the base of our political economy and thus it will remain for a prolonged historical period."[13] The month of June put everyone's backs to the wall. The failure was obvious. The fall in stocks bordered on disaster. They had to choose. Either escalate police measures into acts of civil war, or retreat and compromise. Stalin chose compromise. The "exceptional measures" were abrogated. The price of corn was raised. The politics of reciprocal interests took its course once more. This course was officially confirmed on 24 November 1928 by the following declaration by Stalin to the Central Committee: "in order to accelerate the rhythm of development of the rural economy and, in particular, of the production of corn, it is necessary to augment the profit from the harvest and to extend the cultivated areas within the individual economies of the poor and middle peasants . . . we must give a more vigorous impulse to the individual economies of the poor and middle peasants."[14]

Meanwhile a crucial initiative was taken, of great importance for our analysis. In September, the government issued a decree authorizing *foreign capital investment in all branches of economy*. The extent of investment envisaged was to attain three billion roubles. In order to overcome the weaknesses of heavy industry, in order to mechanize agriculture, and in order to provide a solid basis for the alliance with the peasantry, Stalin proposed that the international bourgeoisie take up the baton. Never before had an arrangement of such scope been proposed to the United States or to Western Europe.

This serious offer took three factors into account: Russia could not generate the vital investments it needed from within; agriculture could not find the income it needed for the growth of industry; industry could not of itself provide the means for its own development. It was a serious offer, in a more profound sense, because it unhesitatingly recognized the reality: that the capitalist mode of production remained the only possible incentive for the economy. It was a serious offer, finally, because it faced frankly (official ideology aside) the crucial question of primitive accumulation.

Preobrazhensky, who was a leftist, dealt with the question in a much discussed essay of that period, "The New Economics". He explained how Marx had described the historical process of primitive capitalist accumulation. This description remained valid. It defined the inevitable stage which any socialist society, without colonies, must pass through in order to constitute an "accumulation fund". A forced levy was necessary for this, at the expense of the peasant producers.

It is remarkable that this theory refutes the fundamental thesis of marxism. If, as it is constantly necessary to point out, socialist society develops out of the highest level attained by capitalism, it is absurd to maintain that the process of accumulation should repeat the primitive history of capital. On the contrary, it is obvious that large-scale industry and its advanced technology will produce this fund of accumulation in ample quantity. Preobrazhensky's theory, in reality, is an admission of the real technological level. It is no less remarkable that neither Trotsky nor his adversaries were conscious of this major incompatibility.

The left thus intended to turn the kulak and the NEP-man into the forced sleeping partners of state industry. The whole of the bureaucracy was unanimous on this point. Differences hinged on what was possible and what was not. Stalin retorted: "Industry cannot be developed in a vacuum; industry cannot be developed unless there is agriculture, no matter how little developed, as the principal market for industry. We have a great liking for the construction of fantastic plans without counting our resources. People tend to forget that it is impossible to launch industrial plans or grandiose enterprises without a certain minimum of resources, without a certain minimum of reserves." And then, becoming demagogic for precise political ends, he denounced the "people who consider the toiling peasant masses as a foreign body, as an object of exploitation for industry, a sort of colony." Dzherzhinsky, in a reply to Kamenev, threatened his opponents personally (it was to be his last intervention — he died shortly after leaving the rostrum), and denied the existence of reserves in the countryside. "The muzhiks have hoarded 400m. roubles: that is, four each."

Russia was confronted with the classic dilemma: in order to obtain the necessary industrial expansion, a high agricultural revenue was necessary; to produce this revenue, an industry was necessary which was capable of mechanizing the countryside. There was only one *technically beneficial* solution: to appeal on a large scale to foreign capital. This is what lies behind the September decree. Such a compromise, if maintained, would in all likelihood have created definitive social conditions for the re-establishment of capitalist monopolies. The destruction of the revolution would have ended up in the only other predictable way: the reconstruction of a big bourgeoisie. Consulate and Empire would have followed Thermidor.

The foreign capitalists did not take up the offer of sale, doubtless because the harshness and growing violence of the internal struggle led them to estimate that in any case the régime was approaching its end, and because they saw no reason to accord it support *in extremis*. A further reason, without doubt, was that they did not think that the ruling group, even if it remained in power, was able to ensure the security of capital. These were certainly short-term motives. But they were secondary motives. In 1929, world capitalist society was trapped in its own process of decomposition. A crisis on a grand scale was paralysing capital.

The fact that this world disintegration of capitalism did not open up a socialist transformation, but that on the contrary, it contributed to the strengthening of the most barbaric and primitive traits of Russian society, was ample confirmation of the relative under-development of the era, a thesis today established by the emergence of the new technology. One cannot understand the "distinctive character" of the society which was replacing the destroyed proletarian state, if one does not take full account of the planetary environment which presided over its genesis.

The bureaucracy was thus driven into a civil war which it had not prepared for and which it did not want. For a whole year it had waited for capital that did not arrive. During this year the conjuncture deteriorated to such a point that it became clear even to the most blinkered minds that a general dissolution was imminent. In Moscow famine appeared, with the rationing of bread. Collusion between soldiers and striking workers was frequent. In the countryside the communal *izbas* and the kolkhoz barns were burnt, and the functionaries were shot down by angry peasants. Since the bureaucracy refused to disappear, it lost its freedom of choice. It had to settle by force of arms what it could not settle through industry. On 7 November 1929, Stalin's article "The Year of the Great Crisis" thundered from the pages of *Pravda*. And though he made no reference to it, it is in no way an accident that the Russian calendar coincided, this time, with the world calendar. On 27 December, *Pravda* confirmed him: "To the devil with the NEP." The second civil war began. The first world revolution was buried in its own debris. The bureaucracy only wanted to survive. The course of events compelled it to become a new ruling class.

The year 1929 thus appears as a breaking-point. The state bureaucracy ceased to be a privileged, parasitic, leading caste. It entered a second civil war, followed by the great famine of 1931. It reacted as it were by instinct. Its mutation into a state ruling class took place in this furnace. Its organic existence was reflected in the legal code from 1932 onwards. After 1936 (the period of the show trials) restructuring and consolidation took place. From 1930 right up until the middle of the second world war, the new society was working out its class relationships: the administrative management of labour fashioned a state proletariat in its constraints. An examination of the law enables us to define the stages and articulations of this process. The bureaucratic society which emerged from the war generated three kinds of concomitant and contradictory phenomena: bureaucratic imperialism, the international extension of bureaucratic state capitalism, and the growing contradiction between the productive forces of state capitalism and the primitive bureaucratic control of the thirties. The combined development of these three sectors, since the 1950s, has developed a violent and extreme aspect under the in-depth impact of the initial effects of world industrial and scientific upheaval. The contradictions between bureaucratic imperialism and national bureaucratic interests, between state capitalism and its administration, became fundamental.

3 The splitting and defeat of the proletariat

WE CAN NOW trace the general course of events as if on a graph. And this way of looking at things enables us to identify the most important and distinctive feature of the situation. The destruction of the first revolution appeared to come about within a continuous process. To be precise, the bourgeoisie had not recaptured power. Yet the proletariat no longer possessed it. This maintenance of revolutionary institutions after the social, economic and political defeat of the proletariat touches on all the preceding and subsequent experiences. Equally, it contrasts sharply with the real historical content of the French revolution: it is this which makes the question of Thermidor so difficult. After Thermidor the French bourgeoisie still remained the ruling class. It is true that in some respects the fact that another fraction of the class was in power is important, but fundamentally this made no difference. Bonaparte consolidated and structured bourgeois society. The persecution of the left wing of the world proletarian revolution, the mass deportation of its cadres, the execution of its leaders, and their systematic assassination in Russia and abroad did not constitute a decisive proof of a *change of class*. On the more modest scale of its own era, the bourgeois Thermidor saw comparable bloody purges. Furthermore the second, decisive, civil war triumphed over the bourgeois counter-offensive. However, the working class had lost all the attributes of a ruling class. The bourgeoisie has lived through situations in which political power has become the monopoly of a single faction. The most striking example is the dictatorship of Hitler's plebeian horde. But the bourgeoisie has never lost its outright ownership of the means of production. Even when Hitler's bureaucracy was sitting on the back of the German bourgeoisie, finance capital retained its pre-eminence, industrial capital retained a great measure of autonomy, and landed property retained its independence. In Russia, the proletariat was entirely bereft of its right to the means of production. It did not even exercise the most indirect control. It was entirely confined to its function as mere labour-power. We cannot throw light on this contrast without re-examining the complex factors which intervened in what was, strictly speaking, the phase of destruction of the first revolution — a phase which extended for approximately ten years, and then at the time of the second civil war.

Our starting point is the fundamental fact that capitalism, in the first quarter of the twentieth century, had not created the basis for a technology of socialized production. As a consequence, the capitalist mode of production could not be overtaken. It was in no sense a question of a particular backwardness in Russia, but of a relative underdevelopment of the most advanced sectors of world industry. Maintenance of capitalist production relations could not therefore have been temporary or transitory — short- or medium-term. This would certainly have been the case if the backwardness had been specific to Russia alone.

The second fundamental determining fact was that the proletariat seized power, destroyed capitalist ownership of the means of production and eliminated the big bourgeoisie and the landed proprietors from the economy. As a consequence the proletariat became a ruling class. The conjunction of these two factors created a totally original situation. The working class took on the functions of directing and managing production. The same class was both manager and work-force. In the framework of a socialized system of production these two roles are not irreconcilable. Abundance would set limits to the practical difficulties encountered, and would provide the means for solving them. It is another thing entirely when the dominant relations of production are capitalist. The tasks of production and management become antagonistic. It is clear that their execution by one and the same class rapidly leads to an intolerable situation.

Functional tension thus begins to operate within the proletariat. All classes are of heterogeneous composition. Their unity is dynamic: in a certain sense it is a unity of function. Tension aggravates this heterogeneity. It legitimizes it. To an ever greater extent it tends to separate the majority of the proletariat, which remains a work-force, from another part which manages and administers. As history shows, the work-force proletariat very soon lost control of the state. The management proletariat very quickly integrated itself into the body of traditional functionaries. As distinctions grew, differences which were initially functional became charged with social significance. This process continued until the moment of split.

It was out of this organic split in the proletariat that new social formations emerged — in the first instance as a privileged bureaucracy, and then as a new ruling class.

The organization of the managerial part of the proletariat as a bureaucracy resulted in its turn from the initial historical contradiction. Once the management and control functions had been *socially* separated, they were able to develop along entirely different lines. For example, they could have become a technostructure (to use the modern terminology). The proletarian revolution introduced its own management procedures, that is, administrative procedures in a conjuncture to which they were not adapted, and it was therefore necessary to use force. They ran up against the low level of available technology — and this led to the use of compulsion and the universal use of the functionary. The functionary occupied all the posts which machines have taken over today. Every area where electronics is now used (or at least could be) was the exclusive domain of the functionary — from the central administration through the trusts and combines, down to the smallest workshops, encompassing all stages of the various commercial circuits. So much so that every economic development was accompanied by a proliferation of the administrative apparatus. Of course this was an extremely top-heavy apparatus, which cost dearly and reduced efficiency. But it was also the material basis for the bureaucracy. This is why bureaucratic symptoms appeared as soon as they were no longer masked by the war measures, before the recourse to NEP had shown its first effects. However they were still only deformations. They ceased to be so immediately after the second civil war and became instead the substratum of the new society.

The genesis of this bureaucracy differentiates it fundamentally from all others. Most of its habits, its peculiarities and its behaviour bear a strong similarity to those of other bureaucracies, past and present. However these are only secondary resemblances. Bruno Rizzi's thesis, which assimilates the stalinist bureaucracy, the bureaucracy of the New Deal and the nazi and fascist bureaucracies, does not stand up to examination. Its historic origins, its social genesis and its functions, identify stalinist bureaucracy by its very nature as an original phenomenon.

The initiation of this process threw into flux the most important organic components of society: its mode of production, its property relations, and its class relations. And this occurred not only at the national level but at the level of their unity and dynamics on a world scale. The split of the Russian proletariat did not only have social consequences in Russia and political consequences in the international arena. It changed the balance of forces between classes, generally weakening the proletariat, and thus made a powerful contribution to the spread of the world-wide regression of capitalist society in the 1930s, and to the accentuation of its most barbaric traits. In no sense did this occur in a passive way, but as analysis of the rise of nazism in Germany and of the decomposition of the civil war in Spain has shown, in an active way. However, the profound structural changes in the world proletariat, hidden beneath the political surface, went much further than this. They were not to become apparent until immediately after the second world war, in the major transformations which occurred in Eastern Europe and in China.

The specific backwardness of Russia exercised its influence at the level of political forms of power, social differentiation, and administrative techniques. It gave an immediate and powerfully violent aspect to the tension between the tasks of management and production. It explains the brutal re-adoption, at a more advanced economic stage, of the elementary administrative measures of war communism between 1930 and 1932; the very low threshold at which privilege was triggered; the concentration of political activity and hence of power into extremely narrow circles; and the "asiatic" content of the dictatorship. In a deeper, more general way it moulded the administration of state capitalism. It throws light on its primitivism. *And it thus provides a partial definition of the persistent organic instability of the bureaucracy*. The bureaucracy is the social and political expression of state capitalism. But between the bureaucracy itself and its technological base, between its general paralysing effect and the dynamic of the productive forces, an uneven development appears, manifested as a permanent questioning of the state institutions by the economy. Since the 1950s this conflict has developed as a major contradiction, expressed as opposing layers differentiated by function, interest and formation within the state class. State capitalism, in order to ensure its utmost free development, searched for a more rational social basis. So we cannot give an exact account of events without recognizing the particular backwardness of Russia. But notwithstanding the importance of its role, and the breadth of the deformations which it brought in its wake, the backwardness due to the historical development of Russian society cannot be taken as the fundamental, determining cause. The stalinist bureaucracy was the product of a very specific world conjuncture.

The party was the crucible of power at the heart of this dynamic. The concentration of property and administrative control in the hands of the state transformed it, as the political corps of this state, into the managing director of society; it turned its apparatus into an organ of control and delegated to it considerable effective power. But no matter how extended this power was, it could not mutate the entire sphere of social relationships. On the contrary, the living reality and hence also the power of the party were the product of large-scale transformations which went beyond the party, which it submitted to and did not control. In this context, the thesis of Milovan Djilas, which characterized the party as the *deus ex machina* of the new class, is a superficial, false view.

The power of the party was not an initial datum. It was a consequence of the fundamental modification of the balance of class forces; of the expropriation of the large finance and industrial bourgeoisie; of the disappearance of landed property, the organic split of the proletariat and of the metamorphosis of the state caste into a ruling class. Its establishment had required twelve years of upheaval and civil war, and a divorce between state property from social property.

The power of the party — in as much as it was a direct and autonomous expression of the apparatus — was inversely proportional to the power of the proletariat. It reached its peak when the working class, wrenched from its position as ruling class, was organized as the work-force of the state. During the entire period of preparation for insurrection, the moment of insurrection, the seizure of the state and the civil war, the party's real power lay outside it. It was based entirely on the proletariat. In this first, proletarian phase, two series of factors acted as disruptive agents: the specific backwardness of Russian society, and the deep-seated contradiction between the tasks of management and of production.

Russian backwardness (with respect to Western Europe and the United States) acquired such importance that it became, as we know, one of Lenin's obsessions — he considered it a permanent threat to Soviet power. This emerges clearly from, amongst other statements his declaration of 23 April 1918: "The condition of our country as a backward country has pushed us forward, but we shall perish if we cannot hold on until we meet the powerful support of insurgent workers in other countries."

This remark reveals the key to Leninist strategy: to hold on until the proletariat of Western Europe provided revolutionary relief. But in order to hold on, it was necessary, as far as possible, to preserve freedom of manoeuvre and control over the instrument of political action. Now it is in this very area that the most immediate and direct danger lay. The effects of Russian backwardness were nowhere so extensive or so profound as on the party itself.

This backwardness was expressed first of all in the creation of a political impasse. Its terms are clear: a very concentrated but numerically weak proletariat; a ubiquitous peasantry, mainly illiterate, trapped in primitive techniques; a weighty bureaucracy, a hostile survival from Tsarism; and a secular tradition of oriental despotism. And as a common denominator, a very dense, very circumscribed political milieu, with a very narrow social base at its disposal. This consequence was inescapable: the proletariat did not contain enough human and political resources, in spite of the formidable pressure from the countryside and from the office workers, to support a plurality of parties which would express simultaneously the new juridical relations of production and the natural heterogeneity of the working class (i.e. its divergent interests). If this was impossible, so much more so was autonomous representation of social layers in the countryside who participated in their own way in the revolution. Russia's backwardness paved the way for the single party.

No possible outcome could be more pernicious. The political base of the revolution became, almost from its inception, very narrow and hence very fragile. The process of reduction to a single party was an objective phenomenon. It was the first and principal deformation due to the backwardness of Russian society. I am not arguing that the Bolsheviks did not commit errors, but that these errors were in reality secondary. It is notable that after a brief phase of co-existence, the proscriptions against the Mensheviks, the revolutionary socialists, and the anarchists, were not at all imposed in the name of a principle, but were always presented as necessary because of *exceptional* circumstances. In fact, Lenin's aim was precisely to preserve principles which were being refuted by reality. In spite of him, and against him, the exception became the rule.

The backwardness of Russia deepened the impasse by annihilating democracy in the soviets. The same mechanisms were involved. This democracy was destroyed almost as soon as it was born, in its two most important manifestations. Functionaries designated by the party apparatus were substituted for delegates elected by the soviets. Factory councils (i.e. self-management) were replaced by authoritarian one-man management (management by state administration).

The elimination of democracy from the soviets marked the first historically determining setback for the proletariat as ruling class. The working class was deprived of its direct control over the state and the means of production. It lost the political initiative.

Democracy in the soviets contained in embryo the most advanced form of socialist control. It set in motion the withering away of the state. It therefore implied a very advanced technology, far superior to the actual possibilities of world technology at the time. It presupposed the arrival of the era of abundance, i.e. the automatic satisfaction of primary needs. To have succeeded, it would have had to spread from the outset to the advanced industrial countries. That it appeared in spite of Russian conditions, and in spite of international conditions, shows to what point it is the organic product of the socialist revolution — its immediate reflex, its profound, spontaneous reaction. Workers' self-management *at this level* is the most advanced form of *socialized production*. It demands a very high level of automation and of culture. It was so far in advance of historical reality that it could only succumb almost immediately. Far from being a creative stimulant, in this historical context, it became a crippling shackle.

The plurality of socialist parties characterizes this initial phase, which Marx defined as the moment when socialist society emerges from the womb of capitalist society, when the state still assumes a pre-eminent role, because profound contradictions, "the stigmata of the old society", still remain. However, not even this stage can be reached within the suffocating constraints of national boundaries.

The domination of the single party represented one stage, theoretically by no means inevitable, but certainly the most primitive, unstable and imperilled stage. It was a possible episode in the armed struggle on a world scale, whose outcome was still uncertain. It was a *national* conjuncture and depended on an international opening. It was a short, chance-ridden period, because the reinforcement of the state, which was by now becoming clear, expressed a sharp tension between classes. The party did not initiate events but submitted reluctantly to objective phenomena, which in no way depended on the deliberate intervention of the Bolsheviks. Nothing demonstrates this more clearly than the fact that events followed a totally different course to the predictions, which had been duly published and could be confirmed by experience. On the eve of the insurrection, Lenin estimated that the state would begin to perish as soon as power had been seized. In *State and Revolution*, written in August and September 1917 he outlined clearly what proletarian democracy had to be even before the event. The slogan "All power to the soviets" was not in his view a propagandist slogan. He saw soviet democracy as the corner-stone of the revolution. "Power to the soviets: this is the only way to guarantee gradual, peaceful evolution, in tune with events — to make sure this evolution goes hand in hand with the development of consciousness, with the general mood, and with the experience of the majority of the popular masses." In his pamphlet *The Imminent Catastrophe and How to Deal with It* (written in September and published at the end of October 1917), his fundamental thesis relates to workers' control of production. He envisages *as immediate measures* the nationalization of the banks, the insurance companies and industry, and also at the same time the suppression of the police and the standing army and the replacement of civil servants by an elected administration subject to recall. "For socialism is no more than that stage immediately following the capitalist monopoly of the state." Or again: "Socialism is nothing more than state-capitalist monopoly *placed at the service of the whole people* and which, by this means, has ceased to be a capitalist monopoly." (Lenin's emphasis.) The first decrees bear witness to a will to apply these ideas. But within a few months, revolutionary democracy was to be annihilated.

The extent of the effects of Russian backwardness as a detonator triggering a chain-reaction of degeneration and destruction of the first revolution is an established fact. However, it is not possible to appreciate fully its real extent unless it is replaced in its historical context. Russian backwardness operated in a world situation dominated by the technological impossibility of transcending the capitalist mode of production. That is to say, relief could not have come from outside Russia. Western Europe did not possess the means to reverse the conjuncture. Lenin's waiting strategy therefore had no real foundation. From this point on a new course was inescapable. Experience was to confirm this. The major contradiction of this period — between the powerful revolutionary upsurge and the relative lack of technological growth — was expressed very clearly on the ground in Russia. The resistance of the world bourgeoisie was concretized in a military intervention and in the support given to the "White Russians". The pressure of the world proletariat was so strong that it held back the counter-offensive and forced governments to renounce it. Without this active support of workers outside Russia (that is, without a *generally* revolutionary conjuncture) the Bolsheviks would have been defeated in a few months and the régime would have foundered. On the other hand, the existing level of technology did not permit the Russian marxists to exploit military victory with economic consolidation (i.e. through the implantation of socialist methods). So much so that the revolutionary institutions which were preserved became emptied of their proletarian content. On the world scale the objective limits of the revolutionary enterprise were clearly demonstrated by the defeat of the German proletariat in 1923. The Russian communist party was at the heart of the insurrection and the civil war. It constituted the centre of polarization of the international working class. This conjunction of circumstances established the proletarian character of the party in that period.

The working class therefore exercised its ruling-class prerogative only with the party acting as its interpreter. Through the party it retained the effective ownership of the means of production and exchange, and the juridical ownership of the soil. Through the party it controlled the state. And it was the proletariat in arms which guaranteed the defence and security of the revolution.

The double defeat of soviet democracy and of the plurality of proletarian parties did not therefore put an end to the role of the working class as a ruling class. It caused a considerable weakening of its base. State property remained social property in a narrow and fragile sense — in that the single party in power remained integrated with the proletariat.

The *division of labour* reacted against this integration in a way that was all the more corrosive because it intervened as a necessary functional objective. And it was not in the division of labour itself that the main danger appeared, but in the effect it had within a society dominated by the fundamental contradiction between the tasks of management and production. It became at one and the same time the instrument and the incarnation of this contradiction, because it could not be otherwise. Furthermore, this antagonistic relation between functions introduced a factor of social constraints imposed by Russian backwardness and aggravated by the intolerable impoverishment caused by the war and the civil war. It was a question of the administration of penury, of a disintegrated and ruined society in the context of a military mobilization of town and countryside. Authoritarian procedures created a permanent infrastructure and tended as such to produce a rationalization, an acceptance of the situation as it was. Administrative violence was used not only against former property-holders and a recalcitrant or hostile section of the peasantry: it was applied within the proletariat. It separated the manager from the worker at the machine within the working class. This new relation was established through the *organization of labour* after workers' self-management was overturned and the implantation of one-man (i.e. state) management began.

The proletariat's loss to the party of its direct control was expressed as an initial separation of the producer from the means of production. This had a direct bearing on its status as the ruling class. The juridical value of this status depended entirely on its real value, that is, in the last resort, on the basic relations of labour. Because of the historical context, the functional division which gave rise to a *technical separation* between the producer and the means of production was rapidly transformed into a *social separation*. This initial divergence was to continue growing until the final break at the point where the capitalist mode of production was reintroduced. We can grasp the real nature of the fundamental mechanism (at the level of the relations of production) which overturned the position of the proletariat in society. This separation, at first technical, and later social, between the producer and the means of production opened a growing contradiction, first functional, then social, between the party and the working class. Their integration disintegrated.

The backwardness of Russia turned the Bolshevik party into the sole party. Proletarian military force constituted it as the political corps of the state. The effective and complete suppression of big private property concentrated military, economic and political power in the hands of this state. The integration of the economy into the state transformed the party into a superior organ of control.

The general historical situation (the impossibility of transcending the capitalist mode of production) was confirmed to a remarkable extent in the case of Russia, because of the limits of the Russian situation itself. The total defeat of workers' self-management and then of the coercive administrative measures of war communism prevented this party control from developing into socially exercised control. This happened in such a way that the activities of control were institutionalized as a monopoly, dominated by the sole political corps of the state: the party.

Thus, the division of labour as it developed in the context of Russian society changed the role of the party from top to bottom, and in doing so transformed its internal organization and the texture of its political life inexorably, long before transforming its social composition.

Functional separation had already provoked an organic weakening of the proletariat well before it became charged with its full social significance. The vanguard of the working class was concentrated in the ranks of the Bolshevik party. The party comprised the best-formed politically, the most resolute, the most devoted, the most capable and the most active militants. Circumstances like repression, clandestinity, detention, exile and tendency struggles within social democracy had led to a gruelling selection-process. The process was stronger and more exacting than any law could have imposed. These circumstances forced the homogeneity of a combative minority on the Bolshevik group, in contrast to the parties of Western Europe, and at the same time contributed to unifying intellectual and worker militants from very diverse social origins. It was in the key industrial enterprises that the party was most strongly implanted, for obvious strategic reasons. A large number of party activists were skilled workers. The rapid recruitment of the months preceding the insurrection took place in the same milieu. Joining for expediency was not yet possible. The risks remained high and the immediate benefits zero. In the army, the most highly-developed regiments contributed contingents. The Vyborg district, the machine-gun regiment from Peter and Paul Fortress and the cruiser *Aurora* are the classic examples. Now this vanguard was uprooted en bloc from the production process. It was wholly absorbed with administrative, economic and military tasks. Political implantation in the work-place was seriously weakened, in the very precise sense that the worker at the machine lost his natural political leadership to the state, and this leadership became the leadership of the state. It was a very substantial loss, which was later to prove irreparable in so far as the tasks of management and production remained antagonistic. This weakening was aggravated by the loss of skilled personnel. The numerical smallness of the proletariat, its low rate of self-reproduction, the dismantling of industry and the split between town and country did not allow these gulfs to be rapidly bridged. On the contrary, the flight of the most competent workers to the villages held back this restructuring still further. It finally took place only in 1925 to 1926 — and then in the form of the promotion of an uncultivated peasantry, that is, starting from a politically primitive base.

The tasks of management and control brought about a total change in the social milieu where the party worked. Workers who had become managers constituted the summit of the state, its central motor. They directed, initiated, controlled and managed. The traditional bureaucracy, a veritable foreign body in its origins and in its interests, became the inevitable transmission belt. The party became lodged in the bureaucracy, which was passively and perfidiously antagonistic to it. The bureaucracy insinuated itself into the ranks of power as soon as that power was sanctioned by force. It made use of unavoidable daily technical co-operation to practise an insidious and sometimes overt osmosis which in its turn precipitated the social modification of the party which its fundamental change in role had triggered.

In December 1922 Lenin described the state administration as "a bourgeois tsarist mechanism". He was to say to the Fourth Congress: "At the top we have I do not know how many, perhaps twelve thousand of our people; at the base there are hundreds of thousands of former Tsarist functionaries." As for the relationship between the summit and the base, in October 1922 he described it as an effective subordination of the communists to the administration: "The governing communist nucleus lacks general culture. If we consider Moscow, with 4,700 communists in positions of responsibility, and the whole bureaucratic machine, which of the two leads the other? I doubt very strongly that it is the communists. In truth, they do not lead, they are led."

It was a dependence which grew rather than lessened over the years. The triple and sufficient reason was that the party was integrated into the administration, that its social force — the proletariat in the factory — was scattered and weakened, and that the bureaucracy reproduced itself rapidly through a spontaneous generalization and extension of its powers. The defeats of the marxist leadership, beginning with Lenin, signposted this constant reinforcement of the state bureaucracy. Lenin first diagnosed the bureaucratic danger on 19 March at the Eighth Congress. He gave a broader analysis in 1921 in his intervention on "The tax in kind". He was never to give up denouncing it even in his final hours of lucidity. In vain. This struggle, lost over a period of four years, confirms the inexorable nature of the phenomenon.

However, the mechanism was basically determined by the transformation of the single party into a superior organ of control, obliged to exercise this essential role under the dominion of the tension between the tasks of management and of production, in a national conjuncture which introduced compulsion into labourorganization. All other factors are secondary.

In the internal life of the party, relationships of authority and military-style subordination replaced political relations. By the very nature of things (because there was no time, because tasks were too numerous, too pressing and necessitated an increasingly thorough specialization), political life became atomized, personalized and specialized with no contact between people. Organs of management became administration bureaux. Temporary personnel, their numbers inflated beyond measure, became more and more involved and acquired independence. Because of the long distances, regions had to have autonomous powers, but rendered all participation in political decision-making precarious, futile, and finally impossible. A gap developed between the party officials operating in the provinces and those who were living in Moscow because of their jobs. A gap also grew between those who found a place at the core of the central administration and those who were absorbed into the army or into industry.

From then on, personal relationships took on an unprecedented importance. They became charged with exorbitant political significance.

It was in this climate, under the decisive pressure of external forces, that the creation of an *apparatus* in the current sense of the term came about. It was the product of circumstances and in no way the logical expression of a particular Leninist concept of the party. The Political Bureau and the Secretariat, which were to become the highly effective and indispensable levers of bureaucratic power, were born of convenience. Bolshevik party statutes did not envisage a Political Bureau. It was created a few days before the insurrection, following a proposal from Dzherzhinsky, in order to facilitate essential but clandestine meetings. It was preceded by a "small Central Committee" of eleven members which met the same requirements. This was initially composed of six members (Lenin, Trotsky, Zinoviev, Sokolnikov, Stalin, Sverdlov), then of four (Lenin, Trotsky, Stalin, Sverdlov). The civil war normally kept Trotsky and Stalin at the front, so the Political Bureau became reduced in fact to Lenin and Sverdlov. At that time it was unimaginable and certainly not predictable that it would become a central institution. Its mutation was completely due to external causes, and in no way to the party itself. Everyone considered the Secretariat of the Central Committee to be a technical service, without the least political importance. This was still the case in 1921 when Stalin was designated secretary, succeeding Elena Stassova, Sverdlov and Kalinin. The Secretariat did not create the bureaucracy, it was used by it for other ends.

In 1919 the Organization Bureau, at the outset, was no more than a means to discharge the Political Bureau from its administrative tasks. Once more the increasing complexity of party activities and its proliferation of organs gave rise to a common secretariat for the Political Bureau and the Organization Bureau. Krestinsky, Preobrazhensky and Serebriakov were appointed as its members.

The political strengthening of personal relationships was equally fortuitous. Because Lenin could not call a meeting of the Central Committee as often as was necessary, he would consult, depending on circumstances, Krestinski, Kamenev, Bukharin, or Serebriakov, when they were in Moscow. Because it was impossible for everyone to answer all the questions, let alone deal with problems of implementation, reciprocal confidence became a factor of great importance for the stability of power, and hence a political factor of the highest significance. Nothing shows better what the exercise of power had become than the intimate co-operation which existed at that time between Lenin and Trotsky. This is shown by Lenin's famous blank cheque: "Knowing the carefulness of the orders of Comrade Trotsky, I am so persuaded, so absolutely convinced of the correctness, the expediency, and the necessity in the interests of the cause, of Comrade Trotsky's order, that I approve of it completely."

The filiation of *the party as a structure of the ruling bureaucracy* from the *proletarian party* now appeared with full clarity. The division of labour turned the party into the highest organ of control. The reversal of its functions overturned its structures and profoundly modified the technical infrastructure of its political life. The new *technical* complex failed to provide organic links with the proletariat in the factories, because it was a more or less distorted expression of those objective constraints inherent in the tasks of management in the historical context of Russia and the world. In this sense it was more favourable to bureaucratic intervention; it lent itself best to an authoritarian administrative manipulation. But it did not settle the problem. It did not determine the route from the proletariat to the bureaucracy. The forces acting on events were outside the party. The party was subject to, and dominated by, the displacement of classes. And these profound changes in the relationships of forces were themselves the social expression of labour organization dictated by the real level of society. But this does not mean that the party was passive. It appeared as an extra-ordinary echo chamber. Its position as single party, as the only legally recognized political organization, turned it into the crucible of power. Class confrontation was expressed within it as an intense political confrontation.

The speed and extent of this mutation, and its semblance of natural catastrophe, are thrown into sharp relief by the measures taken, and the interventions made, by Lenin or Trotsky from 1919 to 1921. The two great polemics on one-man management and on the role of the trade unions were the practical and ideological expression of this. At this stage the party felt itself *forced*, and refused to justify and thus validate these methods other than with reference to an exceptional and hence temporary situation (beginning with the resolution on the organization question adopted by the Tenth Congress).[15] The party had to accept.

4 The disintegration of workers' power, 1920-21

THOSE WHO provided authoritarian methods and initialized the militarization of labour were not the future agents of the bureaucracy, but its determined enemies, the leaders of the still dominant marxist fraction — Lenin and Trotsky.

The years 1920 to 1921 are of exceptional interest because the organization of power had become the major preoccupation. Military problems had eased. The restoration of the foundations of the economy seemed, even to the most narrow-minded, to be in the public interest. It was necessary to move as fast as possible from improvised measures to meet immediate demands to a co-ordinated policy. In a huge devastated country, which had been plunged into chaos, which was unevenly developed with extremely diverse levels of culture, and which had been uprooted from the capitalist market, the first priority was to initiate new labour-relationships which were determined by the choice of mode of production. The first task was to define and adopt the institutions of a working class which commanded the state in its functions of management and control and yet remained the force of production. The workers' state had to become an administrative reality. The reversal of the economy posed the crucial question of the organization of power.

Once recourse to the market had been decided against, the infrastructure and the mechanisms for gaining impetus were necessarily adminstrative. The complexity of the problems to be resolved was fantastic. Consider the actual state of the country, its size, its immediate needs, its cultural level, and the lack of experience of that personnel which was available. The problems were so great that planning, organizing property concentrated in the hands of the state and centralizing decision-making and administrative control could not be done immediately. The necessary preliminary census of available resources, the apparatus of analysis and statistics which this presupposes, did not exist. In that domain, improvisation was impossible. In such a desperate situation the structure of authority became the most important thing. This was ultimately the decisive factor.

The party had possession of the state. It tended to exercise a monopoly of control *de jure* and *de facto*. The trade unions were the social and corporate expression of the proletariat in the factories. Resolving the question of authority in the economy hinged on deciding whether to establish relationships of equality or subordination between the party and the trade unions. The trade unions had a living tradition separate from the party – they did not issue from it. The party was lodged in the administrative bureaucracy, the functional environment. The communist fraction in the trade unions was impregnated and surrounded by workers in their workplaces. It carried out its activity in the factories and its daily life was steeped in trade-union struggle. The trade unions considered themselves the direct representatives of that (largest) section of the proletariat which was not integrated into the state and which remained a workforce. As a consequence, it was the trade-union legislation which became the legal foundation of the real social power exercised by this decisive part of the working class. The rights and duties of the trade unions describe the real functioning of the institutions, the constitution in practice of the ruling class.

Thus after the plurality of socialist parties was eliminated, and direct proletarian democracy was abandoned, the relationship between the single party and the trade unions became fundamental. It was the linch-pin of the political régime.

The dictatorship of the proletariat defines the position of the working class in society distinctly from all other classes. In no way does it prejudice the manner in which the proletariat exercises its dictatorship, nor the organization of its power. These are in fact determined by the relationship of forces in a constantly changing national and world conjuncture.

After its overthrow the bourgeoisie can either be deprived or not of its political rights. This depends on the level of development. The peasantry can be associated or not with governmental responsibility. This depends on the relationship between town and country, i.e. on the productive capacity of nationalized industry. There may or may not be a plurality of parties, or direct workers' democracy: in the last instance it is the *world* level of technology which decides. Of all the possible régimes constituting dictatorship of the proletariat the monopoly of power of a single party is the most primitive, the most precarious and the most unstable. It can only be explained by the retarded condition of the forces of production and by a very great international insecurity. Even so, the role of the trade unions is not decided by these factors alone.

The position of the trade unions is fundamentally determined by the antagonistic character of the tasks of production and management and by the real heterogeneity of the working class. The *proletarian* state does not cease to be a *state* — with all the implications of tension and contradiction in a society that its very existence implies. This is why Lenin placed great emphasis on the possibility of embarking almost immediately on the withering away of the state. In his eyes, this was the objective test of the successful initiation of socialized production. In contrast, the reinforcement of the state indicated a low level of development, antagonistic to socialization, and hence full of dangers. The tensions underlying the state in everyday life shaped it into the real state of which Lenin spoke, a state full of bureaucratic deformations. It was with this state that the working class had to deal. It was indeed a workers' state, but impure and blemished. These impurities and blemishes by themselves already justified the proletariat organizing the defence of its interests against arbitrary or unacceptable demands of the state. The working class was not ultimately homogeneous. It contained large divergences of interests which began to express themselves from the moment they ceased to be suppressed in distinct political policies of control which demanded distinct representation. The proletarian character of this state accommodated itself perfectly to this reality. In the absence of direct democracy and of the plurality of parties, the trade unions were forced to become the means of expression and organization of the social interests of the proletariat at the point of production. They became the necessary interlocutor with the state. It was the indispensable counter-weight to the correct operation of the power mechanisms.

Every factor of importance was exposed to view in the years 1920 to 1921. It was a period which hardly encouraged serenity. Nevertheless, it is most illuminating for an understanding of the concrete conditions leading to that organic split of the proletariat which constituted the initial conflagration out of which emerged an unforeseen society "of a distinctive and original character".

The ensuing debates were all the more difficult and passionate because misery was on the increase in the country, the villages were seceding, the worker, deprived of work and of provisions was taking refuge once more in the peasant shack from which he came, and because the revolution abroad was marking time.

The Bolsheviks had to restore production and organize work without the expected massive import of products, services, machines and qualified cadre from Germany.

Lenin considered the German revolution as the corner-stone of workers' power in Russia. There was no immediate reason for him to think that the German proletariat had been defeated. There were powerful reasons for believing the opposite. Hence the Bolsheviks had to begin without German support, but with the assumption that it was soon to come.

These two parameters — the absence of external support, but a momentary absence — alone permit us to understand the political line which Lenin and Trotsky took: that is, the line followed by the party. The consciousness of Germany's decisive importance was so powerful that once the retreat of the German proletariat was clearly discerned, the Russians actually sought *on capitalist terrain* at Rapallo that co-operation which the aborted revolution would otherwise have granted in greater proportion.

The authors of the proposed political line assumed its limited duration; it was of an exceptional character which was abnormal from the point of view of proletarian law. To think of it otherwise would be a distortion of Lenin's clearly defined position, and would be to misunderstand the decisive constraining power of the real level of society as a whole.

Hence, in an exceptional conjuncture, extreme and temporary measures were necessary. The intention was to repeal them at the earliest opportunity. Effectively, for the Bolsheviks, the war was being pursued by other than military means. The civil war in Russia was no more than a fragment of the world civil war. Military victory on the internal front could only be consolidated by the military success of the European revolution. Political economy was hence one aspect of the armed struggle. For Lenin this was certainly not a formal, external analogy, but a profound identity.

The way Lenin and Trotsky elaborated their tactics, and their choice of methods was dictated by these intellectual parameters *to the same extent* as by the objective situation. When Lenin executed a complete about-turn at the end of 1921, it was for him a question of passing from active expectation to retreat. I have demonstrated this sufficiently clearly. He used the same critical apparatus and the same guidelines, and he proceeded with the same intellectual coherence. For the purposes of analysis this aspect of his policy is as objective a factor as Kronstadt.

Finally, by the yardstick of efficiency, military experience had become the fundamental reference-point common to all the Bolsheviks.

The army was able to snatch victory because Trotsky had imposed iron discipline upon it. Discipline was not only imposed in the field during military operations. Only iron discipline could facilitate the integration of disparate groups of partisans, the amalgamation of officers of the old régime and revolutionary militants, in brief the creation of an efficient, experienced army. The horizon was dominated by the experience of the army. It was hence natural to draw on this success, and to use its *method* (discipline), and its *means of execution* (military units) in the economy. Military discipline rests on compulsion. It implies hierarchical structure and obedience without discussion. It was such discipline that Trotsky made use of.

Transferring this method and its instruments into the economy necessarily introduced compulsion into the organization of labour. Trotsky's experiment, which had succeeded in the vital field of transport, was conclusive for Lenin: the railways worked. The railway workers had been militarized, and the desired result obtained.

Military command imposes its own logic. Its economic corollary is one-man management in the factories. One-man management cannot be elected. Those charged with responsibility are nominated and recallable only by those who have designated them. Military discipline in production — one-man management in the factories — and the principle of nomination constituted a coherent system which had to be accepted or rejected *en bloc*. Its bastardization would have killed its efficiency — and hence its *raison d'être*. Lenin accepted this, drawing the double lesson of the failure of the soviets and the success of authoritarian management. This choice of system ran up against social incompatibilities — obstacles which had to be bypassed or destroyed within a short space of time. The tremendous needs of the situation allowed only for brief delays. From the party's point of view, the difficulties ought to have been surmountable. To be sure, its ideological tradition made adaptation to its new role painful and costly up to a point – but its role prevailed: military orders were for it the key to managerial activity. From the point of view of the trade unions, things were different.

The existence of trade unions is predicated on the confidence of the wage-earners. This confidence is not obtained to order. The trade-union apparatus cannot be confused with workers at the point of production. It carries a certain independent weight. However, its independence is a great deal narrower than that of the party. The success of trade-union struggle is its Gordian knot. It ceases to be a trade union if the majority of wage-earners no longer recognize it as such. It is not the vanguard of the class. It is in the most profound sense *of* the working class. Its function is not to group a minority, but to lead into organized action the least politicized and least professional layers. In a *proletarian* state on the other hand, far from withering away, its real function is reinforced. It now has to awaken the social consciousness of the least evolved part of the proletariat. Its tasks of education and teaching, in the true sense of the word, become vital for the new society. It *alone* can do this because it is genuinely linked to all the heterogeneous components of the class. It cannot assume this role if it becomes separated from these parts; it must maintain living contact and exchange with them. Workers' democracy is its oxygen. Workers' democracy constitutes its indispensable technical apparatus. It cannot organize control without introducing democratic procedure into the apparatus of control. It carries in embryo the power to cause the state to wither away, and discovers that this power is limited; it is limited only by the prevailing technological level, but this is for it too an absolute limit. That is why collective management is consubstantial to it. The trade union cannot become the enforcer of work-discipline without destroying itself. It cannot isolate production from the quality of life and conditions of work. The proletarian nature of the state changes nothing of substance, in as much as the state as employer is dominated by the imperatives of production in a civilization where these imperatives conflict with the demands of the workers. The proletarian nature of the state modifies only the forms of action, by giving primacy to negotiation. But the proletarian state is obliged to enter into contracts with *its own* work-force, or risk a rupture: we know this has enormous consequences. In order for there to be negotiations, there must be negotiators. The trade union is the qualified negotiator for wage-earners in production. It cannot be so if it is integrated into the state. The proletarian state, precisely because it is proletarian, must have workers who can negotiate freely. The entire history of the first revolution verifies this. The primacy of negotiation cannot lead to the repudiation of strike action. The bourgeoisie has utilized and will utilize the power of capital against its own government, when it judges this necessary. The legal right to strike is a fundamental guarantee for wage-earners in a proletarian state too. In no way does it imply that the workers consider their state to be the apparatus of a class enemy. It signifies only that disagreement over the question of control has reached a high level. Failure to understand these practical truths led Trotsky, more than Lenin, to Kronstadt. This is why the trade unions could not freely accept military discipline at work.

Lenin objected that the trade unions, left to their own devices, would only express corporatist interests and that they were incapable of raising themselves to the level of the general interest. From this he concluded that it was necessary to subordinate the trade unions to the state, *because the conjuncture assigned absolute priority to the imperatives of production*. We might well ask why. The trade unions were grouped in a Pan-Russian federation which dominated all branches of production. From this view point, it is clear that they could have easily discerned the lines of general interest. Nothing prevented the trade unions from developing their own statistical instruments for information. These instruments are necessary for the unions to fulfil their functions properly. They can serve this goal all the better because the proletarian state does not engage in commercial secrecy. The Russian trade unions were not led by narrow-minded trade unionists, but by the communist fraction.

Lenin's political line was entirely dictated by the backwardness of Russia, which the European revolution had been unable to alter. The price was heavy. Skill does not fall out of the skies. The most competent personnel had left production. The capacity of the industrial proletariat had hence been severely weakened. So much so that orders were given for qualified workers to leave the civil service for the work-shop. Hence it was necessary to make the best possible use of administrators, engineers, technicians and foremen who had been trained under the old régime, and who were politically indifferent or hostile. There was no other way to establish links with them than to accord them material privileges, which were to be resented by the workers, and power. Hardship was so great and so widespread in the towns that the allocation of provisions became a means of discrimination and incentive. Such a situation removed any possibility of pay rises and eradicated the least desire to improve living conditions. On the contrary the situation demanded an extra effort — a greater proportion of work which was not paid for (the subbotniks).

Ultimately, the proletariat was attached to revolutionary power through its social interests, which in the first instance it conceived only in the form of its immediate needs. As long as the problem of stabilizing insurrectionary power through armed struggle remained, as long as there was an immense and clearly visible danger, it was possible to maintain a dynamic coherence between the political direction of the proletariat and the whole class. The sacrifices accepted found their justification in combat. This did not prevent their effects from accumulating. Military victory, once it had been achieved, brought on a lessening of tension, a wave of exhaustion, a heartfelt desire for improved conditions. There were two reactions: flight, and resistance to civil mobilization. The wage-earners exercised mass pressure on the state for better conditions. For its own motives, the peasantry also put heavy pressure on the administration. The double contingency of these events created a serious threat. Lenin could offer no concessions in the material sphere. Compulsion was therefore imposed simultaneously by *measures of administrative control and by the economic impasse*. The trade unions were gripped in this vice. In order for compulsion to become effective, that is for military discipline to embed itself properly in the process of production the worker who ran away had to be a deserter and the worker who made demands an adversary. Since the party did not possess the necessary close contact with the rank and file, its leadership calculated that it must *reverse the role of the trade unions*, change them into exclusive agents of the dictates of production, and to subject them to the state and to the political corps of the state. It was the politics of war.

Lenin and Trotsky opened the debate. It is precisely the fact that there was a debate which makes this period so interesting and productive. The political split came about while the party, the state, and the trade unions were still completely integrated into the proletariat. And because the communist fraction in the trade unions was in the party, the confrontation took place also inside the party. It was not the party which operated like a demiurge on society, but society which projected its own contradictions into the party.

Intervening at the Congress of railwaymen, Trotsky justified the principle of nominations thus: "to reject this method and to struggle indiscriminately against nominations, counterposing the principle of election, is to forget the nature of the proletarian state. It is to repeat, in relation to the proletarian state, that which applied to a state representing a class enemy, for example the Kerensky régime, but which does not apply when the working class itself is in government. Nevertheless there are elements who have declared war on nominations. This is trade unionism: and now trade unionism threatens to reduce the trade unions to nothing, in removing all the reasons for their existence. The old trade unions struggled to ensure that workers shared in the national wealth which they created. The trade unions of today can only struggle to raise the productivity of labour, because this is the only way to improve the situation of the working masses."

Trotsky took as axiomatic the principle of the indivisible unity of interest and action of the whole class. This is correct *in general,* in a global historical perspective, in a model of the workers' state which is "chemically pure", to use the term applied by Trotsky to Marx's formula in Volume III of *Capital.* It does not apply at the level of daily reality, first of all because the leadership of the state can be wrong. It is not infallible. Lenin never ceased to point out the mistakes which he and others made. Secondly, because the party is involved entirely in tasks of production, and is subordinated to their imperatives, and the trade unions must serve as a safeguard against mistakes. It is undeniable that in the last resort, the situation of the worker depends on productivity; it is no less undeniable that blind pulling on the cord will cause it to break and someone will still have to give the alarm. And finally this unity is not axiomatic because it cannot be assumed that equal sharing of social wealth will come of its own accord. Even before a bureaucratic régime was established, the apparatus of control was not without unwarranted excess costs nor privileges. Furthermore at this level society was full of contradictions, so that the proletarian state had also to cope with the peasantry and its technical cadre, and so it was absolutely necessary for the industrial workers to have their voices heard other than through interpreters who were too concerned with the interests of the party. Here Trotsky confuses theoretical considerations and arguments of circumstance, and this mixture was to constitute an ingredient of that "dry powder" with which he was to be threatened a few years later.

We can see that, under such historical conditions, for the first time the crucial theoretical and practical problem was posed of the *relations between the proletarian state and the working class in its role as work-force in the production-process.* This was a permanent major debate at the heart of the first revolution.

Because the party is a workers' party, because the state is proletarian, and because there cannot be fundamental differences between the leadership and the class, the party has the right, under exceptional circumstances, to suspend the exercise of workers' democracy. Now, no one denies that it was vital to set transport going again. On the other hand, the trade union was opposed to the militarization of the railway workers. This generated polemics, opposed tendencies, and heated argument. Such things waste time, and lead to further deterioration. Trotsky concluded that the party must order a halt to discussion and that the order must be carried out: "Among the leaders [of the trade unions] at all levels there are those who have not understood that production is the decisive criterion, who have not understood that in order to save not merely the professional movement, but the whole working class, it is necessary to transform the whole apparatus in accordance with the principle: everything for production. . . . The working class now declares in the person of its political representatives: at this point I intervene, I call a halt to this period of struggle between two groups, I economize, I cut down and command. To reject the principle of intervention is to deny that we have a workers' state."

This example is interesting because it demonstrates pure reason within practical expediency. Since it was taken by the political representatives of the *proletariat*, compelled by public need, this authoritarian measure against the free exercise of trade-union democracy did not carry with it an erosion of workers' democracy: "which plays a colossal role in the workers' movement, even more than in the Communist Party, because it can only be rescinded by the trade unions." This was certainly abnormal, but "necessitated by the danger in which our country finds itself". A danger which assimilated economic activity into a military operation: "I have stated to several workers' assemblies in Moscow that at the moment when the 30th and 51st divisions were in front of Perekov, it was no longer a question of arguing about whether or not to attack the fortifications – it was necessary to attack them. And the order was given."

Lenin did not argue otherwise, although he was less free with his use of algebraic formulae. In any case, the comparison with Perekov is hardly satisfactory. It was not in fact a question of a battle to win (for example – to re-establish the transport services), but of a political economy-measure, whose outcome remained uncertain because of its dependence on what would happen in Western Europe. It was hence a political economy-measure which was extended for an unpredictable period. It is one thing to call a halt to an excessively prolonged discussion; it is another to bring about a permanent change in the role of the trade union. Now, it is precisely this that Trotsky's thesis on the integration of the trade unions into the state implies. "It is necessary for the trade unions to become the apparatus which calls the masses to collaborate in the production-process. In order to achieve this, it is necessary not to place oneself on the terrain of heaven knows what external struggle against a foreign bureaucracy, but to strugge within against backward prejudices and against routinism."[16] Not only did Lenin draw the same lessons from the same military experience, base his ideas on the same principles, and define the same objectives in the same way. In fact, he deepened the differences with the trade unions still further. He belaboured the defenders of collective leadership: "Why are you talking about the participation of the broad masses when it is no more than a matter of three, five or seven workers going into the councils of management? . . . The domination of the working class *is in the constitution, in property and in the fact that it is we who have taken all the initiatives:* administration is another question, it is a question of skill and know-how."[17] (My emphasis).

In his view efficiency should be the deciding factor: "the passage to practical work is tied up with the quesiton of one-man management as the system ensuring the best utilization of human capacity and a real, not merely verbal; control of work accomplished. . . . In the best possible case, collective management would involve a tremendous expenditure of effort and would contribute nothing to the efficiency and clarity of the work necessary to run large centralized industry.[18] The course of events is well known. On 7 April 1920, at the third All-Russian Congress of trade unions, after the party congress had finally, and not without difficulty, accepted his position, Lenin passed to a frontal political attack on the question of the role of the trade unions in the workers' state.

Capitalism has been demolished, but socialism has not yet triumphed, and it will take time for final victory. The misunderstandings we are running up against are not fortuitous, but result from the historical role of the trade unions, as co-operative groupings in the capitalist régime, and as the organization of the working class as the masters of state power. In the second case, the workers consent to all sacrifices and institute a discipline obliging them to say and to feel confusedly that the interests of the whole class are superior to sectional interests. We consider those workers who cannot consent to these sacrifices to be profiteers and we drive them out of the proletarian family.[19]

The trade unions retorted that there was no efficiency without real participation in the responsibility of control, for the valid reason that there was no other way to train workers for these tasks; without this, management responsibilities woud fall, as a consequence, under the control of the administrators and technicians of the old régime. As for the basic principle at issue, they submitted that one-man management was "an attack on the principle of workers' democracy and a method of removing workers from the management of industry".

The communist fraction of the All-Russian central council of trade unions formed the bastion of resistance in the factories. It had a large constituency in the public sector soviets. In the party, the Moscow committee was the principal ally of the trade unions. In the Ukraine, the party divided. The polemic reached its culmination in March 1920. Lenin was defeated at the third congress of water transport workers. He was beaten once again, on 15 March, at the assembly of communists of the central soviet. He was to win a narrow victory at the Ninth Party Congress.

The decisively important fact for understanding these events, is that the workers at the point of production were massively against the policy advocated by Lenin and finally adopted by the Ninth Party Congress.

The communist fraction in the trade unions was intimately linked to the proletarian work-force. It interpreted in its own language, in political terminology, the obstinate rejection of Lenin's policy by the professional worker. Its vote hence has an exemplary social significance. The vote within the party is different. The party was integrated into the state. Its functional separation had been achieved. It is quite normal that the sovereign organ of control should approve the only policy for production which its leaders judge efficacious. On the contrary, it is the breadth of resistance which is surprising. It demonstrates that the party remained rooted in the class at the moment when, because of its decision, it was consummating the political split with the factory workers.

The political split occurred in relation to the crucial question of the organization of power. That is, on the question of the status of the ruling class. The defeat of the trade unions therefore takes on immense significance. In the short term, it aggravated the tension within the proletariat. The way was open for the first trial of strength — the hostile demonstrations and strikes of 1921, culminating in the armed uprising of Kronstadt. And after Kronstadt — NEP.

More profoundly, the defeat of the trade unions opened a breach between the working class and the state, between the workers and the means of production. Workers at the point of production no longer possessed *direct access* to power and to the running of society. The party appeared at the meeting-point of all roads. The question of relations between the working class and the party hence became decisive. Workers' democracy without a plurality of parties, without elected leadership, without trade-union democracy became dangerously reduced to *democracy within the party only*.

Lenin defined three criteria for "the domination of the working class" : the constitution, property, and "the fact that it is we who take all the initiatives". The constitution can be violated. Property was juridically in the hands of the state. Private property gives the bourgeoisie effective power, even when it is momentarily without direct control over political matters. The nazi plebeians could crack the whip over the German bourgeoisie, but it had to reckon with finance capital, landed property, and industrial capital. Between the working class (in the absence of the socialization of control) and the means of production that state was interposed. That is — in terms of occupation — the administrators, the controllers, the managers. We know that the division of labour had already introduced a differentiation, and that this differentiation tended to involve social privilege. By this stage, *proletarian property* had not become effective (in the way that bourgeois property is) except as a function of the *direct* control which the proletariat was able to assume *at the point of production*, over the administration and the economic apparatus. *The elective principle* of control hence became absolutely central. Collective management (once again, in the absence of socialized control) was the only direct means by which the proletariat could influence or control the means of production. It was through elected management committees that the proletariat concretely exercised its property rights. It was this which gave the defeat of the trade unions the historical dimension of the first *social* separation between the proletariat and the means of production.

One final point: "it is we who take all the initiatives." Now, we know how the tasks of control (functional activity) had already profoundly altered the technical infra-structure of political life in the party. This had led to the increasing fragility of internal party democracy. The threat of Kronstadt was to hasten its collapse. We can now gauge the nature and importance of the stage represented by the years 1920 to 1921.

Tomsky's theses were adopted by the trade unions but rejected by the majority of the party. Their implementation would undoubtedly have led to a dual structure of worker representation. The theses confirmed the trade unions as autonomous agents of the wage-earners, claiming the right to intervene directly at all levels of control. They would impose a system of elected, collective management, from the central administration down to the level of the factory: "Point 7: The fundamental principle involved in the construction of organs of regulation and management of industry, and the only principle capable of guaranteeing the participation of the broad working masses outside the party through the trade unions, is the vigorous application of the principle of management of industry through elected management committees from the bureau of the factory." In the very limited cases of one-man management (Sapronov proposed that this should be confined to the small factories), the individual administrators were to be vigorously controlled by the trade unions without right of appeal.

This concern to take on the legally recognized, autonomous representation of the workers at the place of production is constantly emphasized with respect to the social and occupational roots of the trade unions; the theses stated that "the factory committees must be effectively constituted as local cells of the trade union". This is also the case for methods of control (that is, political-economy measures): Point 14: "but long-term growth of the labour product and the rationalization of the work-process at the point of production cannot be secured without improving the material conditions of the labouring masses. The trade unions must pay the strictest possible attention to bettering the economic situation of the working class, to participating with the greatest possible energy in the activity of all bodies concerned with the maintenance of workers' living conditions. At the same time they must contribute to developing the general culture of the producers by eliminating illiteracy, organizing technical and occupational training, establishing elementary schools, creating special training courses, etc." In order to show that the differences do not hinge on goals but *on ways and means*, point 15 stipulates: "The trade unions must direct all their efforts towards increasing the labour-product":[20] but it is precisely "ways and means" that constitute political activity.

The trade unions therefore proposed to inaugurate authentic

institutions of control and supervision. From the confusions and weaknesses of this first brief period of soviet democracy they drew diametrically opposed conclusions to those of Lenin. They considered that if soviet democracy did not exist in the organization of work, it could not exist anywhere else; that its paralysis was not an inherent deficiency but a consequence of its lack of secure foundations. They concluded that, rather than rejecting it, soviet democracy should be given a proper structural basis. Hence the proposals for institutions based on the factory, with the trade unions and the elected committees as their framework. In this scheme the management committees would allow direct representation of workers engaged in production at all stages, so that the administration inherited from the old régime could be placed legally and effectively under the social supervision of the work-force. Of course, it was understood that the regulation of distribution would be integrated into this system, and that this supervision would be exercised not only during the execution but also during the elaboration of national plans and construction-programmes. The logical extension of these theses is thus the definition of basic principles and strategy of economic policy. Higher productivity and improvement in the living standards of the wage-earners went hand in hand in a cause-and-effect dynamic. Not even the slightest allusion is made to methods of compulsion. The letter and spirit of the proposals are hostile to such a conception.

The theses are hence concerned with a system for the organization of power which in concept guarantees the working class the technical wherewithal for a real management role. The party remains the political motor of the state. It loses the monopoly of management which it had assumed only because of the demands of the moment. The trade unions become the promoters of workers' democracy in management; this is their new social function in a workers' state. This amounts to the integration of trade-union struggle into a political policy of growth, steered and controlled by the workers. According to these proposals, the critique of Lenin and Trotsky, who accused trade unions of unduly prolonging their old functions in the new régime, has no foundation.

In this system (which from the trade unionists' point of view had the advantage of compatibility with the principles of the October revolution) the actual proletariat (those in the factories) retains effective collective ownership of the means of production (without having to go through an intermediate administrative layer), because it exercises direct control over the implementation of plans and settles questions of economic policy directly. Furthermore, through practising these responsibilities, it acquires the necessary qualification for running the economy and draws from its own ranks the future generations who will gradually replace the officials and technicians of the old régime.

Sapronov, whose tendency at that time was very close to the positions of the trade unions, makes a very clear definition in his thesis of the resources offered by collective management:

> From the social and political point of view, collective management presents many advantages which should make it the fundamental principle of the soviet method of organization and which necessitate its maintenance and re-affirmation in the present period of militant work. The management committee is the high school of the process of learning state administration. It alone teaches how to settle particular questions from the point of view of general interest. Work in the management committee is the best means of winning the old bourgeois specialists towards fraternal collaboration, of instilling in them a proletarian mentality. At the same time it constitutes the best control over them, in so far as they have not definitively rid themselves of their old habits and their old mentality. Finally, and most importantly, only the links with the management committees prevent those workers who have been given the important positions from becoming absorbed into particular and narrowly practical tasks, and from becoming narrow functional specialists. Collective management . . . constitutes the necessary base of democratic centralism and the most powerful weapon against the rebirth of administrative caste spirit and the infiltration of bureaucracy into the apparatus of the soviets.[21]

The theses rejected by the communist fraction in the trade unions and adopted by the majority of the party under pressure from Lenin, broke *with the Bolshevik tradition of the October revolution*. This is without doubt the most striking characteristic effect of the real overall level of society in the political sphere.

As we know, it brought on the bankruptcy of administrative methods of control.

Contrary to what many people think, Bolshevism (in essence, that is, Leninism as it started out) is a theory of revolutionary democracy. The democracy of the soviets is the creative force behind permanent revolution. Political action by the party, and the control of the economy, are situated within, and in no sense marginal to, or outside, the soviets. The essential dynamic lies not within the party but in the soviets. The most fundamental dominant fact is that the state withers as social democracy grows, and is accompanied by the withering away of the military and professional character of the party. Everything which counteracts this powerful social mutation, everything which tends to slow down the rhythm of its development, everything which disfigures it, works against the revolution and indicates a fundamentally unfavourable relation of forces.

We know that in 1920 nothing concrete remained of this revolutionary democracy. The soviets had become a juridical fiction. But after the Ninth Congress not much remained either in the sphere of *theoretical thought*. This must be considered one of the most significant symptoms of the progress of the malady in the revolutionary body politic, of the stage which had already been reached in the internal decay of the revolution.

The militarization of the party and of production could and should have been explained with reference to the concrete international and national situation; that is, by the historical conjuncture. And in effect some arguments of this nature were developed. But, at the same time, Lenin and Trotsky presented a theoretical justification. It was no longer a question of circumstances which imposed these accommodations, but of the application of *principles*. With this hurdle crossed, the way was more or less open for the bureaucracy to usurp the ideological terrain. The state was a soviet state in abstract principle; it was by no means any longer a soviet state in its concrete reality. However, the theses which were adopted affirmed this fact as a dogma. From an illusion in the democratic capacity of this state, they drew the conclusion, at a completely practical level, that trade-union democracy should be condemned. This formulation is in contrast to the more nuanced and much more realistic analysis of Lenin. Nevertheless these theses are the recognized official position. Above all there emerges from these debates a theory of the dictatorship of the proletariat which totally fails to understand its initial democratic content, its historically distinctive character. It is indubitable that these issues are presented with a greater complexity in the writings of Lenin and Trotsky, but this does not alter the fact that the congress resolutions embody the political actions of the party. Their schematism is not accidental. The finer points left aside for the purpose of the succinct definition reveal the choice of the authors. The militarization of labour evolved into the militarization of theoretical thought.

This inseparable and explosive mixture of conjunctural and principled considerations became the general method of argument. State monopoly of control is justified by the formula, "under the régime of the dictatorship of the proletariat, the trade unions, organs of struggle of the sellers of labour-power against the capitalist ruling class, become the apparatus of the governing working class. The tasks of the trade unions are principally concerned with economic organization and with education. The trade-union organization must accomplish these tasks not as an independent force, organized in an isolated way, but as one of the essential parts of the apparatus of the soviet state as directed by the communist party." In section two,

"The trade unions and Soviet state", which is entirely devoted to the subordination of the trade unions to the state, we find a remarkable illustration of how principles which have been reviewed and corrected are used to further the immediate interests of the conjunctural political line of the party.

The scale of the resistance, its strength in the working class, and the violence of the polemic did not permit the thesis writers to leave anything open to interpretation. Certainly, they are inclined to emphasize some point more harshly than they would otherwise have done. This too reveals their political line. Excessive though it might be to start from the banal statement that politics is "the quintessence of economics" in order to establish that only the party has the mission to govern, this sums up what must be said clearly enough:

> Politics is the quintessence of economics, its generalization and its highest form. To counterpose the trade unions, considered as the economic organization of the working class, to the soviets, the political organization of the working class, is hence absurd and constitutes a deviation from marxism towards bourgeois prejudice and particularly to trade-unionist prejudice.

Such simplifications, which carry remarks of Lenin or Trotsky to the point of caricature, bear witness to the fact that the average level of intellectual discrimination in the party was already not very high.

In practice, the subordination of the trade unions was becoming clear through the finely-imposed subordination of their leadership: "Any communist fraction belonging to a local organization is subordinate to the party committee; the communist fraction of the central All-Russian council of trade unions is subordinate to the Central Committee of the Russian communist party." The communist fraction hence ceased to be the elected leadership of the wage-earners at the point of production; it became the designated delegation of the state in the factory. *This was the first important measure which stripped the working class in the factories of its directly elected political leadership*. It was a profound manifestation of political rupture.

The principle of one-man management, which we know to be the cornerstone of administrative control, was categorically affirmed.

Making a summary distinction between the social and administrative, taking up once again the argument of technical efficiency, and further assuming that the double identification between state property and social property and between party and class was established, the writer of these theses did not see in one-man management anything which restricted the character of the proletariat as the ruling class.

One-man management in no way challenges the rights of the class or "trade-union rights", and furthermore does not limit them, since the class is capable of governing by any means, and the form of power is conditioned by technical utility; in any case it remains the ruling class in its entirety which "nominates" the administrative and managerial personnel.

The militarization of labour, as predicted, modified the essential function of the unions:

> The factory committee is the subordinate cell of the trade union. The factory committee, without interfering with the control of the factory, will discharge the following functions: improvement of labour discipline, using all means up to and including disciplinary tribunals (elected by the general assembly of the factory) . . . .

The generalization of the principle of compulsion appeared in the concept of sanctions and in their choice. The theses advocated: "the use of repression in relation to idlers, parasites, and disruptive elements". The allocation of provisions was to be brought into line with the bonus system: in so far as the Soviet public has insufficient provisions, the conscientious and diligent worker should be better-provisioned than the negligent worker.[22] "The congress considers one of the urgent tasks of soviet power and of the trade-union organizations to be the systematic, concerted, vocal and rigorous struggle against absenteeism, notably through the publication of blacklists of absentees, the formation of work detachments of absentees undergoing punishment and finally the internment of deserters in concentraton camps."[23]

For the analyst, these theses have a further, very lively interest. They describe clearly, in precise language, not as yet weighed down with what was soon to become bureaucratic jargon, the technical infrastructure of centralized administrative control. Sections 6, 7, 8, 9 and 10, which are devoted to this question, constitute a veritable x-ray photograph of the administrative skeleton of the economy. The very mechanisms of bureaucratic proliferation are illuminated:

> Whereas under a capitalist régime each industry had to acquire large amounts of raw materials, its work-force etc. in nearby markets, the same enterprises must today fulfil all their needs under the direction of the central organs of the unified economy. Now, the country is vast. The principal factors of production are extremely unstable and disorganized. The means of communication (post and telegraph) are extremely weak, and the methods and results of economic statistics still extraordinarily imprecise. Given all this, our methods of centralization, which result from the first phase of the expropriation of bourgeois industry and which have inevitably led to a fragmentation of enterprises (into towns, provinces, various regions and districts) have unleashed an avalanche of red tape which poses a direct threat to our economy.

What precedes is the equivalent of a good technical adviser's report, and is completed by this note. "On the organizational side the task comprises the maintenance and development of vertical centralism along the line of principal management bodies in industry combined with reciprocal horizontal subordination of factories on the line of economic sectors."

The apparatus just described allows us to appreciate the degree of subjection of nationalized industry and how much it was shackled after NEP put it under the sway of the market. Still more, it shows how these technical networks were in aid of themselves, without any conscious intent, totally incompatible with democratic workers' control. Like some natural product, they secreted a thick proliferation of officials. The technical infrastructure of the bureaucracy was in place, before the bureaucracy began to function as such — at least at the level of political decision-making.

The prevailing circumstances, and the acceleration of the crisis did not permit any real application of the Ninth Congress theses. They created a tradition. They represented the militarization of the revolution. Stripped of the revolutionary spirit which still animated them deep down, they were to become, in the hands of the bureaucracy, a murderous instrument directed against the revolution.

The condemned trade unions did not accept their sentence. The workers in industry and transport stepped up their resistance. The tide of blind flight toward the village was not stemmed. The peasants began to demonstrate their hostility more openly. The slump in the economy began to assume the dimensions of a natural catastrophe. Confusion and arbitrariness reigned throughout the provinces, in the administration, and in the party. In Moscow, political agitation was more widespread than ever. Maximovsky, a member of Sapronov's tendency, wrote "the whole fish is going bad, starting with the head". Trotsky and his team of administrators and technicians were demanding the translation of the Ninth Congress resolutions into action. Lenin manoeuvred and drew back. The party, in spite of its power, had lost its grip on society. Events had slipped from its grasp. The fact is that the party was a prisoner of circumstance. It no longer had any real control over events. It was riven with disorder and factional strife. The polemic on the role of trade unions started once more with fresh virulence and a newly acquired violence, as if nothing in principle had been changed; as if on this point the Ninth Congress had been null and void. Lenin observed: "production is always necessary, democracy only sometimes." Perhaps this is true; but there was democracy nowhere, and anarchy everywhere.

There are two striking phenomena in this chaos: the forces of production were paralysed, and the working-class base of the party was crumbling away. On the one hand administrative measures with no basis in reality, far from re-stimulating the economy, brought about the reverse effect: if possible, they made it worse. As for the rest, the political split with the trade unions induced the social isolation of the party.

More than anybody, Lenin sensed the danger. He had always possessed that rare facility of being able to decipher the *direction of movement of classes*, before the consequences of this movement became manifest. He was never the prisoner of abstract considerations, no matter how logically well-founded they appeared. Thus it was in 1917 that his intuition and the speed of his decision alone permitted insurrection. In 1921, he did not underestimate the significance of his repeated failure at the union conferences and he did not overestimate his success in the party. He knew that the communist fraction in the trade unions, in spite of its verbal violence, was interpreting the depth of the working-class response in muted terms. He knew that all the arbitrary measures, no matter how much they conformed to necessity, were not worth the paper they were written on if the party did not have the freely-given consent and the reasoned acceptance, of the most devoted, the most dynamic and the most conscious parts of the working class. A policy which is logically just, but not understood by those who are to implement it, is worse than the most serious error. He understood furthermore that the revolutionary leadership could not engage in open struggle against its own base without running the revolution into mortal danger. He saw that the party was in conflict with its social base, because it had gone too fast and too far, and that the medicine it had wished to administer was doing more harm than good. For these reasons, and in spite of their agreement on basics, he opposed Trotsky, who was going by the book.

As a first step, Lenin's objective was to suspend the application of the Ninth Congress theses, which Trotsky wanted set in motion without delay. At this point, it was only because the opportunity was not favourable. At the same time, he had to return to basics and replace the general formulations on the workers' state, envisaged in its "chemically pure" state, by a definition of the state as it actually was at this precise point in history. It is such things which count, when it comes to the formulation of strategy. But, in so doing, Lenin shows up the weakness of the analysis of the Ninth Congress. In his Testament, he was to single out Bukharin for criticism as a misguided scholastic; but this criticism was equally applicable to others.

So Lenin advanced the definition, subsequently much used, that "our state is not a workers' state, but a workers' and peasants' state with numerous bureaucratic deformations." He added: "this is the sad reality." The obvious conclusions of this sad reality, which he drew, was that the workers had something to defend in the face of this state, so that the traditional role of the trade unions had not lost its meaning. This major concession called into question the integration of the trade unions into the state, if not also the issue of one-man management of the factories and the use of military discipline in production. It was a concession which bore directly on basic questions of principle, but also and more keenly on the decrees for their application. As usual, Lenin recognized this openly: "There is no doubt that we have made many mistakes. Most of our decrees must be changed."

Lenin was defeated by one vote in the Central Committee. In order to win the battle with the workers, he had first of all to wage it within the party. The polemic which it gave rise to poisoned the climate in the party permanently by enhancing personal disagreements and provoking divisions. Furthermore, it took up so much time that the situation was left to rot. The harvest was reaped at Kronstadt. Lenin's victory in March 1921, at the Tenth Congress, arrived too late. The party was ailing. Famine was the measure of the extent of the administrative failure. This time, the retreat had to take on the dimension of a fundamental strategic turn, unimaginable a few months earlier. Further, since everything depended on production, and since adminstrative control had no real roots at either the technical or political level, and was on all the available evidence decisively rejected at the real level of society, nothing was left but to return to the market and to reintroduce the capitalist motor. Lenin was almost the only person capable of understanding the need for such a major change of policy and he was certainly the only one capable of getting it admitted.

It is certainly hard to appreciate the political choices which were genuinely possible in such a complex conjuncture without having lived through it. The fact that we know the outcome makes it all the more difficult to judge. The Bolshevik leadership was highly conscious, and always had been, of the enormous weight of Russian backwardness. We know that it lacked and could not have had a precise conception of the global historic conjuncture, and that its unfounded conviction of the possibility of transcending the capitalist mode of production on a world scale had led it into an impasse. With this reservation, it is still the case that the refusal of Lenin and Trotsky to accept the party/trade-union duality appears as an error; an error which finally precipitated the disintegration of the revolutionary movement. Collective management, it is true, never acquired any serious technical or cultural articulation. But it could not have been more inoperative than administrative methods; and it would have been less damaging socially. The autonomous existence of the trade unions, and their central economic role, in the context of a clear-cut contradiction between the tasks of management and control, provided the embryo of powerful political tensions. But these would not have created the fatal effects of the party's social isolation within the working class. And on top of all this, no strategy could have averted the inescapable recourse to NEP. Within this perspective, workers' democracy provided far superior resources. It would have guaranteed nationalized industry a less heavy administration and certainly a less costly one. Freed from the effects of a proliferation of officials, and from its paralysing excess costs, a more competitive heavy industry would have responded better to the needs of agriculture. Relations between town and country, in so many respects decisive, would probably not have given rise to the level of violence which actually took place.

Why should the richer peasantry have embarked on the corn strike if it could have found the machines and industrial products which it needed at reasonable prices? It seems undeniable that in a market economy, the trade unions, with their long experience, would have proved better qualified than the functionaries to negotiate collective agreements, to deal with marginal private industry, with the co-operatives and with the central administration and to establish a balance between the standard of living of the wage-earners and the social surplus product. Apprenticeship in the exercise of responsibilities would have allowed the work-force to acquire skill gradually. It would have enabled the direct promotion of cadres from the ranks of the proletariat and hence, in the last resort, a more solid political base in a working class caught up in the machinations of a society where the influence of the rural and urban petty-bourgeois was being reinforced naturally. In this system too, the return to the capitalist mode of production would have provoked social differentiation; but the negative effects of a labour-aristocracy in the factories would have been far less than those of bureaucratic parasitism. It seems to me indisputable that trade-union democracy offered the party the means of a more certain, a more flexible and a socially firmer control of state capitalism. Trade-union guarantees, linking the immediate interests of the wage-earners to expansion, would have ensured the active support of industrial workers for the régime, whereas the bureaucracy, for its own ends, was determined to reduce them relentlessly. This is in no way a utopian view, but a reasonable probability whch would have changed things in Russia and elsewhere.

The fact that the political base of this strategy existed in reality is plainly established by the depth of the resistance and the reaction to Lenin's actions in other directions. The means for implementing it could have been brought together. It suffices to observe that the paralysis of the productive forces was the principal cause of the ebb in the working-class movement. Everyone, at this time, agreed with the diagnosis which explains the turn towards NEP. Now, NEP achieved what was expected of it: a restoration of the economy, that is, of the necessary material base for the re-establishment of working-class action. This restoration was blocked, slowed down, and severely distorted by the slow growth of nationalized industry, to a large extent due to bureaucratic parasitism. Workers' democracy could have eliminated this parasitism so that the material base, instead of being reduced, would have been consolidated and enlarged.

This policy did not have to emerge as the application of a concerted, worked-out strategy on a long-term basis in order to be stabilized. It would have been sufficient to have rallied to the trade-union theses. No one at the time, in the party or the trade unions, had conceived state capitalism as the dominant form of a historical period. The failure to appreciate the world level of development made such a conception impossible. But Lenin, as we know, had never considered NEP to be a lasting compromise. In the event, it lasted.

5 The theory of the party and the political expropriation of the proletariat, 1922

IT IS IN no way idle speculation to look at how things might have turned out differently. 1920 to 1921 was an extraordinary period. It is as important and significant a part of the general picture of the decline of the revolution, as the year of the insurrection was for its victory. For the same reason: many paths remained open. Irreversible processes had not yet begun. Hence, it is also the point in time when the intervention of the party was of the greatest moment; when its importance and its limits can best be discerned. It was precisely because so many possible variants were inherent in the situation that political decision took on such centrality. Once an irreversible process is launched (as it was on the eve of NEP), the party becomes the slave of circumstance.

It is not a question of the elaboration of a theory of the *party as such*. Such a monstrosity does not exist. The problem is to examine what happened within the Bolshevik Party, considered as the brain of the first revolution. We might understand in what way, after having led the revolution to its triumph, it participated in its destruction. And from there we must follow the unique process of its destruction; a mutation into a bureaucratic organ of state power, which was also to change the role and function of the *world party*. In so doing, it projected inside the working class, conceived as an organic functional world–wide unity (which it in effect became in the epoch of imperialism), social interests which were completely foreign to it. This is not only a question of vital theoretical interest, but it has major practical implications for the perspectives of the second revolution too. Of course, we can only deal here with the most general feature of this mutation, linked as it was to the organic split of the proletariat. There are two key situations to examine: October 1917 and the impasse of 1920 to 1921.

Once power had been taken, the task of the day was to draw the most radical conclusions from the political expropriation of the bourgeoisie. That is to say, it had to be extended into a social expropriation. Elemental class confrontation could never have bridged this gap on its own. The fury of this confrontation only created the opportunity. Political action was still necessary to seize it. The tension in the balance of forces was so high that it sowed the seeds of retreat. Homeostatic mechanisms were tending to stabilize the situation.

A favourable moment always presents itself as a brief interval. Revolutionary leadership therefore becomes acutely aware of the short time at its disposal, the size of the risks involved, the complexity of the situation — and the power of the adversary. Real uncertainty, lived through with exceptional intensity, exacerbates hesitations, intensifies divergences in diagnosis, and encourages vacillation. *In this sense, the political act of insurrection is in no sense an inescapable continuation of violent confrontation of classes.* It is always a difficult choice, against the stream. To decide on insurrection implied, in the first instance, resistance to accumulated pressures. The general act of expropriation is implicit in insurrection, but it is not automatic.

Reaction almost always sets in when the decision has been taken to go ahead with the struggle. The whole question is to know whether it is the first or the seventh wave. The most important political acts are undertaken in spite of latent ambiguity and uncertainty. Fundamentally, it is a choice.

Once accomplished, the political act escapes its authors. It becomes an objective factor. It becomes an ingredient of society in combination with all others. And because the combination is highly complex, the reality which emerges also escapes prediction. With the bourgeoisie uprooted from production, the class-struggle took on such a radically unexpected course, that the immediate Bolshevik programme had to be abandoned chapter by chapter; and at each stage it was necessary to improvise the basic measures. In 1920, Lenin and Trotsky rejected trade-union democracy. They did it in order to consolidate the revolution by restoring the economy. In reality, this choice unleashed mechanisms for the destruction of revolutionary power. To the repeated defeats of Lenin were to be added the continued defeats of Trotsky. Lenin and Trotsky were anticipating the return in force of the bourgeoisie. One became prisoner of the bureaucracy, the other was killed by it.

The consequences of the choice were not controllable. They reacted back on to the party, changing its social composition, overturning its structures, changing its policy, and sometimes rupturing it. There is no identity between the Russian communist party of 1921 and the Stalinist party of 1930. They were created out of two different societies. They were two original products of the overthrow of two different class-systems. Stalinism did not emerge from Leninism according to a Hegelian dialectic.

The rupture is striking at the level of the fundamental role of the revolutionary party. Theory is not an adjunct to the other activities of the party. On the contrary, it is the precondition for them. Every-thing flows from theory — this is the basic methodological principle of marxism. Revolutionary action translates theoretical formulations into strategy.

Theory is hence not assimilable into an ideology or philosophical system, in the accepted sense of the term. Theory is here conceived as it is in the natural sciences. It interprets experimental data and extrapolates into predictions. It is an instrument of knowledge.

Marx conceived scientific research as active. In this sense, his conceptual elaboration prefigured the actual course of development of science — as it had not developed in his time, but as it has become today. The scientific orientation today of physics and biology — at one and the same time an object of and a procedure for research — is clearly expressed by the 11th Thesis on Feuerbach: "Philosophers have hitherto interpreted the world in different ways. The point, however, is to change it." The scientific–industrial mutation through which we are living has brought about a confirmation, on the largest possible scale, of the essential process of appropriation of knowledge which Marx defined as *praxis*: "The question of knowing if human thought can lead to objective truths is not a theoretical question, but a practical one. It is in practice that man will discover truth, that is to say reality and power, to be within the scope of his thinking." The revolution as *practice* is hence at the heart of the science of society. It is in this total sense, which today shows and in the future will show an even more extraordinary relevance to biology, that the following proposition, which situates theory as a fundamental activity, must be understood: "The coincidence between changes of circumstance and human activity cannot be considered or understood rationally otherwise than as subversive practice."

With theory playing this role, and with society constantly under-going a process of transformation, theoretical elaboration has to be a continuous basic activity. A theory which because of its great inter-pretative value, and its high capacity for prediction, was confirmed over a given period and survived in spite of changes or a new accumulation of experimental facts, would outlive its role and become a scholastic dogma, ceasing to be an instrument for knowledge and progress. A party which renounces its essential critical activity would become, from the point of view of the revolution, a dead organization. It might have a long career as a corpse, but it would be something other than the brain of the revolution.

The idea of a party playing a theoretical role as its fundamental activity is not an ideal model but historical reality. Theoretical activity, as it has just been defined, constituted the common value of all those tendencies nourished by marxist thought. The most profound disagreements, which developed into splits, violent polemics, and counterposed strategies, stemmed from divergences over their theoretical utilization of the available social and economic data: that is to say the facts of experience. The theory of "stages", of the "English" order of succession, and theories of monopoly, of finance capital, of imperialism and of uneven and combined development, were all attempts at *scientific* interpretation of the mode of growth and crises of capitalism, Bernstein, Kautsky, Hilferding, Lenin, Rosa Luxembourg, Trotsky and Plekhanov all based their divergent positions on the published results of basic research. The fact that the tendencies finally hinged on distinct social interests in no way contradicts the primacy of theoretical activity. What is important is that all were in the first instance preoccupied with authentic knowledge. Tendencies and parties were, to a certain extent, fashioned by theoretical elaboration. It impregnated their every action. It linked together the worker militant and the intellectual in the same enterprise. Conceptual activity was collective practice to the highest degree. It provided the foundaton for all political decision-making.

The 1930s ended this powerful creative epoch. They opened a long era of stupefying regression and sterility in marxist thought, which remained alive only in narrow circles, exhausted itself in the struggle against scholastic counterfeits, and ended up, apart from the work of Trotsky, producing no more than a few valuable works on military questions. Thus, marxist thought played no role in the prodigious intellectual explosion of the last twenty years. As a result, the science of society marked time. This has not been without its effects on the exploitation of the rich perspectives opened by cybernetics and by the theory of structural levels; biology being unable to find in the social sciences a conceptual apparatus to integrate its projections. The effect on *practical activity in society* is such that it has become an objective factor of the greatest significance.

Hence, it is legitimate (and scientific) to situate the rupture in continuity between the Bolshevik party and bureaucratic organization at the level of its most fundamental activity: theoretical activity. It would be superfluous to demonstrate the crucial role of the science of society as a science for Lenin and Trotsky, and in a general way for the first Bolshevik generation. In the published works of Lenin, Trotsky, Bukharin, Piatakov, Rakovsky and Preobrazhensky, theoretical reflection and action are consubstantial. When one considers the overwhelming national and international tasks which Lenin had to deal with between 1917 and 1923, the importance which he accorded theoretical research is highly significant. More profoundly still *theoretical comprehension,* in his eyes, was the criterion of the *political capability* of a party.

Among the many examples of this, one anecdote is particularly revealing. Lenin, speaking in 1921 at the All-Russian Congress of Transport, began thus:

> As I crossed the room I came across a card carrying the following inscription: "The reign of the workers and peasants will be without end." As I read this strange card, which I realized was not in its normal place, but in a corner – obviously someone had realized that it should not have been there and had removed it – I began to think: "So, even on the most elementary and fundamental questions, we still have misunderstandings and false ideas." And, in fact, if the reign of the workers and the peasants was without end this would signify that there would never be socialism, since socialism is the suppression of classes: now, in so far as there are workers, there are classes, and as a consequence, there cannot be true socialism. As I noticed that after three years since the October revolution we still have cards of this nature even, if you like, hidden in a corner, I began to think that there are still very deep misunderstandings in relation to our most widespread and most frequently-used positions and slogans.

The advent of the bureaucracy changed all this. Under Stalin's reign, the *material conditions for research* were destroyed. The past was completely falsified in the archives. Reference works became inaccessible. Doctrines and theses were systematically distorted according to the needs of the moment, which were constantly changing. Contemporary sources of information were decreed secret for reasons of state security. The very statistics were grossly manipulated for *tactical* reasons. The most flagrant contradictions were imposed as official truths. On 6 November 1918, Stalin wrote in *Pravda* (which is in principle accessible in all libraries): "All the practical work of organizing the insurrection was carried out under the immediate leadership of Trotsky, President of the Petrograd Soviet. We can certainly say that in relation to the rapid passage of the garrison to the side of the soviet and the organization of the work of the military revolutionary committee, the party is above all indebted to comrade Trotsky." A few years later, Stalin could assert that "Comrade Trotsky, a relatively new man in our party in the period of October, did not play and could not have played any particular role either in the party or in the October insurrection", without anyone demanding clarification. Yet this was only the beginning (Trotsky is still called a "comrade") of a long and tragic process of degeneration. Scientific work was run by the police. Theoretical research became impossible because its most elementary prerequisites were suppressed. Theoretical activity, for lack of data and also because there was no use for it, ceased to be a technique for the acquisition of knowledge. *It became a technique for administration.* Its goal was no longer to understand the real facts and to make predictions. Its aim was useful mystification. Duplicity in the presentation of ideas and the falsification of history brought ruin upon all science in its very principles. The theory of socialism in one country was presented as a tradition of leninist thought, whereas it was a counterfeit; the thesis of the necessary reinforcement of the state, projected backward into the past, supplanted that of its withering away. We do not even have to mention the gross absurdities perpetrated as regards the realization of socialism and Russia's entry "into a higher stage", that of communist society. What is important to understand is that, independently of everything else, *systematic police falsification destroyed the very basis of scientific activity.* With the full assent of stalinism, police control came to be extended over research in physics and in biology, there also imposing a state dogma. The final balance-sheet was to be catastrophic for Soviet society. Stalinism was not just a deformed continuation of leninism, but a rupture with the thought and practice of Lenin; a barbarous antidote to marxism. This brutal rupture necessarily took place also at the level of the party. It is always necessary that the material base, the technical foundation, coincide with fundamental social activity.

In order to define the position of the party and its role in society, it is certainly not sufficient to establish that marxist thought and its historical traditions create a fundamental link between the basic knowledge and subversive practice. The party, like all institutions, no matter how extensive its powers, is subordinated by society and does not subordinate it.

The free intervention of the party takes place under the constraint of a determinate historical complex. Our analysis of the first revolution shows this clearly enough. From one point of view, it is easier to grasp this essential relationship by examining Lenin's role during the October revolution. "Would we have taken power in October if Lenin had not arrived in Russia on time?" asked Trotsky, and he replies: "There are numerous indications that we would not have been able to conquer it."[24] There cannot be any doubt that Lenin had to use his personal ascendancy to the maximum in order to break the very strong resistance of the Bolshevik leadership. The insurrection had to be brought about through the most exacting and violent struggle. Trotsky alone would not have been able to convince and impose his line. It is highly probable that the Central Committee ceded more to Lenin as a result of his intellectual authority, their knowledge of him and the fact that the party was formed under his impact, than as a result of the most telling arguments. And then the arguments began again when the problem arose of deciding between a homogeneous government and a coalition with the Mensheviks and the Social Revolutionaries. Left to their own devices, the majority of the leadership would have followed the middle path of conciliation. Trotsky might have been unable to conquer this obstacle, but it was still in the first instance due to him that the insurrection was a success.

The fact that the October revolution could in effect be imputed to the personal action of Lenin, and the efficacy of his close co-operation with Trotsky, reveal the importance of political action and the immense field covered by the subjective factor. But the same Lenin who introduced such an upheaval into history, the consequences of which are still being felt half a century later, *was neither able to organize socialized production nor control the forces he had unleashed.*

There is hence an objective limit to the effects of political action. It cannot supplant the material conditions which structure each stage of history, and consequently cannot carry out as it wishes the social transformations which depend on this base. In the best cases the party must carry out a succession of adjustments to the course it is following in the same way that a rocket is guided by restarting its motors. In less favourable situations it runs behind events, which escape its control. In the worst cases it is destroyed.

Furthermore, even the internal life of the party is subject to the fluctuations of chance. The more the conjuncture lends importance to political decision, through concentrations of forces and the intensity of the tension this creates, the greater becomes the uncertainty created by the complexity of individual interactions. Referring to Lenin's illness in 1923, Trotsky notes this in his own way: "The whole historical process is a prism for the operation of natural law as a series of chance events. If we were to use the language of biology, we would say that the rational law of history is realized through a natural selection of accidental facts. Conscious human activity developed on this base submits chance events to a process of artificial selection."[25]

Finally, the party itself is a product of circumstance. This was the case at the level of the immediate conjuncture, as much as on a historical scale. Much has been written about *What Is To Be Done?* and the dispute between the advocates of "spontaneism" and the "professional revolutionaries" which by 1904 had already become a bone of contention among Lenin, Rosa Luxemburg, Plekhanov and Trotsky. In reality, the Bolshevik party provides a typical example of permanent structural adaptation to nationally and internationally changing situations. As for democratic centralism, it is no more nor less than what the relationship of forces in society makes of it.

Lenin never made the party into a fetish. The party is simply the best available instrument, but in no sense the best in any absolute sense. He said this on 3 November 1920, to teachers of politics: "We know of no other form [than the party] and no country has yet found an alternative. The party can correspond to a greater or lesser extent to the interests of its class, and it has to accept changes or re-adjustments, but we as yet know of no higher form of organization."[26] The party is itself dependent also on the technological level of society and the extent to which the organization of labour is integrated, on the social composition of antagonistic forces in it, and hence on the dynamic of society as a whole. It is obvious that the second revolution has not yet developed its appropriate form of political organization.

The party as it really is hence results from a more or less successful adaptation to a necessarily transitory national and international context. Its efficiency depended on its flexibility and its capacity for change, that is to say as with all institutions, on the relative weight of its inevitable scleroses, the heritage of its recent or distant past, and new techniques. Its vigour is closely dependent upon its political strategy. The value of its political strategy is the product of its more or less close organic relationships with the historically most dynamic section of society and of the quality of its theoretical elaboration. The "best" party is hence that which exercises the most lucid and constant self-criticism.

The mystification of the party was a social phenomenon, which made its appearance in the history of the first revolution at the moment when the separation of the Bolshevik party from the proletariat at the point of production was fully realized. It was one of the symptoms of the changeover to a political and administrative organ of the state bureaucracy. The momentary support of Trotsky and the Left Opposition for this mystification certainly heped to sterilize their other critiques, and left them open to repression by their adversaries; more profoundly it indicates the breadth and objective character of the circumstances. It reveals, finally, that the functional separation had completely integrated the marxist intelligentsia into the apparatus of control. This could not fail to have extremely broad consequences on a world scale.

If one accepts the marxist principle of knowledge as subversive practice, and recognizes the inerconnection of theoretical thought and revolutionary action; if as a consequence one accepts that theoretical elaboration is a fundamental activity from which everything else proceeds, it is clearly necessary that party organization should enable the exercise of this function. Absolutely no scientific research is possible without freedom to scrutinize. This freedom is an absolute precondition, and as with all sciences, it is totally indispensable in the science of society. Free scrutiny implies free access to all information (to all available experimental data) and the free confrontation of different theses for which a certain order in working methods and debates is needed. In the domain of the party the application of these principles leads to the existence of discussion groups, tendencies and of factions; to freedom of publication and to the democratic distribution of documents.

The revolutionary party is an irreducible product of theoretical and practical activity. Its efficiency in action is entirely determined by the value of its research and its results. *This dependence* necessitates both theoretical vigour and flexibility of execution at the same time. The predictions formulated by theory are embodied in a programme, and when the party takes power, in a plan. To put it another way, all factors converge on political acts which are choices. The margin of error is always necessarily very great. Discipline in execution is based on reasoned consent. Its guarantee is the seriousness, breadth, and freedom of the preceding discussion; but also and in no less measure an ongoing criticism of the process of execution itself. This is true for two vital reasons.

Any complex decision is always vitiated with errors which become clear in the process of applying them. They must thus be amenable to correction. Mistakes are in the first instance the result of the inadequacy and imprecision of the instruments of analysis, aggravated by the inevitable impact of emotion (a moving, complex society, full of dynamic contradictions, is no ordinary laboratory). Second, it is a consequence of the fact that any major political intervention creates an original reality which is never in strict conformity with prediction and which must in its turn be submitted to the test of criticism. More fundamentally, events as they actually happen are always ambiguous and leave the way open to the intervention of successive hazards. In society, far more than in nature, Laplace's postulate is without validity. "Any intelligence which, for a given instant, knows all the forces whereby nature is animated, and the respective situation of beings which compose it, if it were big enough to submit all this data to analysis, would be able to encompass in the same formula the movements of the largest body of the universe and those of the smallest atom: for it, nothing would be uncertain and the future, like the past, would be present before its eyes."

Finally, the critical application of decisions is the only effective pedagogic method for the party as a collective enterprise. It transforms action into a teaching process. It gives body and life to the study of texts. It gives rise to a far better and more rapid process of training. In the strictest sense, it turns experience into apprenticeship. It transforms the collectivity which by its origins, its aptitudes, and its knowledge, is heterogeneous, into a functional unity. It is hence indispensable for the elaboration of theory, and for the efficiency of political strategy.

Discussion groups and tendencies provide the necessary base of support for the freedom to criticize and for the organization of the work of the party. Factions express this at the level of power within the party, power being the executive centre of policy. Theses are the only precise, concentrated, and technically indispensable expression of different interpretations of the conjuncture. Voting on theses is the indispensable sanction which constitutes the first step of political decision-making and which prevents discussion from degenerating into anarchic squabbling.

Relationships between groups, tendencies, and factions cannot be rigidly laid down. They are living relations and, because of this are constantly modified depending on the growth, and state of health of the party. Factions always give rise to tensions, because they seek to change the leadership. The acuteness of these tensions is in no way due to the existence of factions. To believe this would be to take shadow for reality. *The epicentre of internal conflict is to be found not in the party itself but in society*. The projection of social struggles into the party cannot take place in a mechanistic way. The intensity of its political life amplifies and refines them. The violence of the confrontation between factions is a thermometer of the conjuncture.

The party was the invention of the first revolution, and, without doubt, its most characteristic creation. It is consubstantial with it. It is the product of the first revolution's most fundamental feature: the combination of the creative capacity of the proletariat with theoretical reflection. It arose from within the prodigiously creative institutional activity of the working class which, throughout the nineteenth century and the first quarter of the twentieth century turned the planet upside down with its innovations. The party emerged at the same time, in the same way and followed the same dynamic as the trade unions, social legislation, workers' organizations and their international secretariats: the International Association for Labour Legislation, the International Labour Organization, etc. The party was integral to this context. It cannot be detached from it without misconstruing its origins and distorting its real significance. Like all other insitutions which arose from the activity of the proletariat, it was from the outset an *international institution*. This was the same with the trade unions, the labour conventions and all supporting bodies. The essential feature of the great period of proletarian activity was that it took place at world level. The political International that is, the world regroupment of parties, was a *functional unity*. It was first of all a unity of political elaboration, the world debating–chamber of intellectual life. All discussions of the national party not only reverberated but were also nourished in the International. Failure to understand this will prevent us grasping the essential fact that the world sphere is the natural terrain of workers' action. (The proletariat being the dynamic social projection of the phase of growth and world integration of capitalism.) Such a misunderstanding would also result in failure to recognize the way in which theoretical relection affects party organization.

The question of the mode of historical and organic growth of capitalism has been at the heart of marxist thought and discussion. Every society (that is, every world social system) arises through a process of uneven development. The law of uneven development within capitalism has taken on exceptional importance due to its accelerated rhythm of growth and a tendency to a more and more advanced state of world integration. As soon as we want to elaborate a revolutionary strategy based on scientific analysis, we have to understand the modalities of this development. These in fact determine what is or is not possible in terms of the successive stages of the revolution and the social forces which correspond to them. Both the programme and the means to implement it are dependent on them. As, of course, with the internal organization of the party which is responsible for setting them in motion.

During the main period of Marx's active life capitalism remained, up to a point, the sum of national economies. England represents the most advanced case. On the other hand Marx, as we know, stated the axiom that "a social formation never disappears until all the social forces which it is capable of sustaining have developed". From this factual observation and this theoretical conclusion, he makes the prediction that "an industrially developed country shows a less developed country an image of its future". This means that a proletarian revolution in any given country is only possible if the bourgeois revolution has exhausted its potential. The failure of the insurrections in 1848 confirmed his judgement and Engels wrote in his 1895 preface to *The Class Struggle in France*: "It demonstrated clearly that the stage of economic development on the continent was still far from ripe for the suppression of capitalist production." Germany and France had to catch up with England. This was the schema of stages and of the English model. To a large extent this analysis provided the basis for the reformist politics of the European socialist parties, and for their structure.

The advent of monopoly and entry into the imperialist epoch brought about a complete change in the *factual data*. The new stage of integration of capitalism changed its dynamic. On a European scale, uneven development became *combined* development. Social determination, as a result, no longer followed a linear national logic but started with the highest world level of evolution of capitalism and its action on the least evolved sectors, with the effects of the global capitalist system considered as a functional unity. Consequently the proletarian revolution takes *this reality* into account. The schema of *linear* stages no longer applied since the underlying situation had changed. Of course, this new relation of forces had to lead to a break with the old polemics between the reformist wing of social democracy on the one hand, and Rosa Luxemburg and Kautsky on the other.

The resolution of the problem of uneven development gives us the key to a country like Russia where feudal and capitalist modes of production co-exist. The Mensheviks and Bolsheviks were in agreement on the schema of stages. In the 1907 preface to his *Development of Capitalism in Russia*, Lenin states: "Starting from this economic base, the revolution in Russia will necessarily be a bourgeois revolution." However, his analysis of the genesis of classes, and of bourgeois dependence under the yoke of landed feudal property, led him to the belief that this revolution could only be realized through a democratic alliance of the proletariat and the peasantry. While the Mensheviks held that *in this stage* the liberal bourgeoisie would constitute the social force which should be supported, Lenin counted on a political mobilization of the proletariat. Hence, starting from a common theoretical schema, but with a difference in their analysis of *Russian social development* (and hence also of the character, *mechanical or otherwise*, of the determination of the social superstructure by the economic infrastructure), the Mensheviks and Bolsheviks were not only in disagreement on the programme but also *on the organization* of the party. The disagreements between Lenin and Trotsky hinged on the process of formation of capital in Russia. For Trotsky, the intervention of foreign capital through the agency of the tsarist state was the decisive factor. Trotsky, extrapolating from 1905, changed the law of uneven development into a law of uneven and *combined* development and founded the revolutionary strategy on the theory of permanent revolution. This in fact found experimental confirmation in the October revolution. Hence we see, in spite of the excessive simplification of the preceding exposition, how the theoretical factor affected the organization of the party, by combining with the creative capacity of the proletariat. The crucial questions posed by uneven and combined development, in their original terms, are transcended in the second revolution, *but at the same time they are posed again in a completely different historical context*. They are now posed as the new equations of the historical future by the nature of technological mutation and by the highly integrated character of scientific industrial change. It is hence necessary to learn how to pose these terms in the equation and define their possible solution in order to conceive and bring into existence that *form of organization* which is least incapable of coping with the tasks of the second revolution — the one which will take the place of the party which developed in a different conjuncture of world history.

Bolshevism gradually came into being at the heart of this extraordinary and intense period of world activity — in the midst of occupational, trade-union, legislative,. and political ferment. Its growth took place entirely within the ranks of the Second International, which on the eve of the war boasted twelve million members from twenty-seven parties in twenty-two countries, in which Kautsky and Rosa Luxemburg were closer as partners to the Bolsheviks in Russian affairs than Martov and Plekhanov themselves. We must grasp the vigour and reality of theoretical thought at this time, the power which was contained in the free exercise of critical thought; the efficacy of the free rein given to tendencies and factions, and the true significance of the party as the crucible of thought and action. This grasp is necessary to understand the historical breadth of the collapse which occurred in the First World War. It is also necessary for an understanding of what the first Bolsheviks were and what they were attempting to do in the first congresses of the Third International.

This model for a revolutionary party collapsed in 1921. Bolshevism, first as a faction, then as a party, had existed (certainly not as a "chemically pure" entity, but with impurities that can be overlooked) since, let us say, 1903. It had survived *in spite of repression*, in spite of the conquest of power, the war and the civil war. The division of labour, following its seizure of control of the state and the economy, began to gnaw away at this edifice. A rapid acceleration of the crisis, the split with the trade unions, the withdrawal of the workers from the factories, the uprising of Kronstadt and of the government of Tambov, sapped its base. The Tenth Congress put a definitive end to internal democracy.

I would argue that the party, no matter how great its powers, was subjugated by outside events, and that the epicentre of the conflicts which racked it was not to be found within it, but in society itself. The year 1921 provides clear proof of this fact. On these grounds alone its furnishes a prime example. The course of events makes this even more clear.

The divorce between the party (including all its tendencies) and the proletariat in the factories, which was already apparent in 1920, became a definitive social reality. This split came to fruition in armed struggle. The arms aimed against the proletariat were in the hands of authentic proletarian revolutionaries. This crucial fact has a central historical significance.

Lenin and Trotsky were not thermidoreans. They never pursued power for power's sake. In their very actions they were the indomitable adversaries of parasitic bureaucracy. Their entire lives were not merely *devoted* to the proletarian revolution, but were *integrated* into it. In taking up arms against the sailors and workers of Kronstadt, they were persuaded that they were safeguarding the gains of the revolution. Nevertheless, through their military victory they definitively sapped workers' power. They accelerated the ruin of the workers' state. With their own hands they prepared their own defeat.

For an understanding of history, we must accept these apparently contradictory data as they stand. They establish at what point conscious actors came under the constraints posed by the material conditions of society. They reveal the real depth of the phenomenon which I have defined as the *organic splitting of the working class*.

As we know, the consequences were immense. Immediately Lenin was obliged, with NEP, to undertake a formidable retreat without the support of the most important social force involved. The party was, as it were, without cover. It offered less resistance to the pressures and penetration of hostile classes, the well-off peasant and the NEP-man. The separation of party and proletariat at the point of production reached its full extent.

The Tenth Congress was completely dominated by what was going on outside. The Kronstadt uprising was not an accident: it was only the culminating stage of a series of strikes, rebellions and pillagings. Before the armed repression Zinoviev, President of the Petrograd Soviet, replied to spontaneous hostile assemblies of workers with massive arrests and the closure of factories which had passed over to open opposition. Peasant agitation in the provinces fired this incendiary mixture. I have already quoted the diagnosis of Lenin: "We could not have lasted many months more." The congress, even before finishing its debates and proceeding to the vote, precipitately dispatched three hundred delegates to put down the revolt. At the beginning of March 1921, the crews and garrison of Kronstadt convened an impressive assembly and received Kalinin with the highest official honours. The resolution adopted after passionate discussion today has the significance of a historical document. It is remarkable that their essential demands *prefigured the present-day themes of the workers' and intellectuals' opposition in the Soviet Union and in Eastern Europe*. They demanded the return to the Soviet constitution and to the October programme of the Bolsheviks. Their demands included free election to the soviets, freedom of speech and of the press for workers and peasants, left socialists, anarchists, and the trade unions; the liberation of political prisoners, workers and peasants; the abolition of the privileges of the communist party; equal rations for workers; and the right of peasants and non-employing artisans to dispose themselves of the product of their labour.

The assembly hence aspired to establish a broad workers' democracy, such as Lenin had foreseen on the eve of the insurrection and such as he had judged necessary in the first months after the seizure of power. In this sense it went well beyond the demands of the trade unions. But precisely in this sense it revealed the breadth of the demands of the workers at the base, which the trade-union leaderships were containing and restraining. It is very likely that if a serious compromise had been arrived at with the trade unions, this bloody outburst would have been avoided. Socially, the resolution indicates the basis and orientation on which the militants at the grass roots envisaged the creation of their alliance with the poor peasants and artisans, at the moment when the Bolshevik leadership had been forced to seek co-operation with the kulak. The discrediting of party policy can be measured by the resurgence of the left socialists and the anarchists. But at the same time the *social frontiers* of the workers' opposition were clearly defined. There was no question of breaking with the Bolshevik party but of exercising upon it such pressure that it would renounce its political monopoly. The trade unions wanted to put an end to its monopoly of control. In this way too, the trade unions, if satisfied, would have been able to dam up the wave of wage demands. It was not a question of returning to the situation before the October revolution, but of rediscovering its initial democratic course. The sailors, soldiers, and workers of Kronstadt were the social heirs of the revolution. Many soldiers and sailors were the sons of poor peasants.

The initiative for the split was taken by Zinoviev. He arrested the delegation to Petrograd, which was charged with presenting and explaining the resolution adopted. In defence, a Provisional Revolutionary Committee was elected at Kronstadt. The majority of the communists took part in it. The decision from this point on was in Lenin's hands. He accepted the challenge and put Trotsky in charge of the operation. The Red Army refused to march against the forts. Trotsky, assisted by delegates from the Tenth Congress, had to purge, punish and re-staff. The battle was led by officer cadets selected for their obedience to orders. On 18 March, Kronstadt, which Trotsky had called "the pride of the revolution", was crushed.

It is obvious that the Provisional Revolutionary Committee had not premeditated military action. Otherwise it would have waited for the thaw, which made the fortress inaccessible, but which placed Petrograd under the guns of the fleet. The advantages of this were so obvious that even the most stupid could have seen them. Nevertheless, Lenin offered the Committee no opportunity for negotiation. The demand which Trotsky made before the bombardment was for total surrender. The break was clear.

There was no doubt that the Social Revolutionaries and the Mensheviks attempted to exploit popular discontent for their own ends. It is possible that agents of White reaction thought they could envenom matters and rub salt in the wound. In reality, none of this was of great importance. The real force of Kronstadt was workers and peasants, attached to the revolution, and highly representative of the proletariat in the factories. This was the central fact. It was so unquestionable that Lenin decreed NEP.

In fact, Kronstadt brought home the question of power in the long term. This was its real meaning. The Bolshevik party was paying for the utopianism of war communism. Trotsky wrote: "The régime of starvation rations was linked to growing troubles, which led in the final account to the Kronstadt insurrection." And Lenin concluded in favour of the urgent need "to abandon the immediate construction of socialism in order to fall back in many economic spheres towards state capitalism" since, he said, "we have been defeated in our attempt to bring about socialism by storm."

The key to Lenin's policies lies with the crucial question of power. He was convinced (with good reason) that a reversal of the relationship of forces would give power to the Mensheviks (of the left or of the right) and would after brief delays bring about the victorious return of the bourgeoisie. It was therefore necessary for the Bolsheviks to take firm control of the state. He was ready, and he showed it, to make the most extreme concession in all other fields; but not in this one. He estimated that many retreats were practicable, on condition that the capacity to make decisions was preserved intact. Lenin never thought in *Russian* terms. His strategy was always international. The loss of power and the return of the Bolsheviks to opposition would express themselves immediately in a *world* reinforcement of social democracy, which would be a disaster for the revolution and, in the final analysis, would result in a long-lasting consolidation of capitalism. Behind the trade unions he saw the shadow of the Kronstadt commune. And behind the immediate *conjunctural* hostility of the workers he saw the war-wagons of the White Guards. Any concession on the question of power would lead to catastrophe, because of the preponderant place the peasantry occupied in Russian society.[27] The weakness of the proletariat and the non-existence of nationalized industry left no room for political manoeuvre. It was necessary to preserve power *in order to win time*, because time was working in favour of the European revolution.

This brings us to the core of Lenin's thought. His conviction was unshakeable. It was based on theory and on practice. It remained steady until the moment of his death. It is the only touchstone which explains and justifies his tactical and strategical turns. On the occasion of the third anniversary of the October revolution, he affirmed yet again that *"it is impossible in a single country to accomplish such a work as the socialist revolution"*.[28] (My emphasis.) So that independently of the difficulties peculiar to Russia, the fate of the dictatorship of the proletariat depended in the last resort on what happened on a world scale: "Our victory will only be a half victory — *and perhaps less* — in so far as the revolution is not accomplished in every country, including the richest and the most civilized." This is the ABC of Leninism.

What was new (but of central importance) in 1921 was not that the backwardness was becoming more marked, *but that it was impossible to make serious predictions as to how long it would last*. For the first time Lenin concluded that henceforth it would be necessary to deal with internal matters as if the isolation were going to continue for several years. To be sure, he reaffirmed before the Tenth Congress: "Help is coming from the West. It is not coming as fast as we want it to but it is coming and it is growing greater." Nevertheless it is the "not so fast" which now *became the determining factor in internal policy*. "However, if we concluded from this that help will come to us after only a short delay, in the form of a solid proletarian revolution, we should simply be fools." Moreover, no one could say *when* help was going to arrive: "for the last three years we have learnt to understand that counting on the international revolution does not mean counting on its coming within a definite period, and that the increasingly rapid pace of events may lead to a revolution next spring, but also may not." The conduct of internal policy was fundamentally altered as a result. "This is why we must learn how to *adapt our actions* to the *social condition of our country* and of other countries in order to be in a position to maintain the dictatorship of the proletariat *for a long period of time*, and to cope progressively with all the calamities and crises which beset us."[29] (My emphasis.)

This is a key declaration. It opened up the new course. This

declaration ushered in not only NEP, but a new period. Lenin interpreted this in his own way. The team of old Bolsheviks were to
draw from it the justification for Thermidor. Here again, without
knowing that they were doing it and, of course without wanting it,
the proletarian revolutionaries were greasing the rifles of the
thermidoreans.

Lenin's hesitation in decreeing NEP, the abruptness of the
decision, and the timidity of the first measures taken, all flowed from
the ambiguity of the conjuncture in Europe. Lenin understood
precisely the risks which were being run with NEP. It would have
been dangerous to run them if external help were about to arrive at
last. Trotsky, drawing the lessons from his stay in the Urals,
proposed in 1920 to substitute a progressive tax in kind for requisitions. Lenin called him a free-trader. The Central Committee
rejected his project by eleven votes to four. Trotsky was later to
explain that, with this door closed, nothing remained but the
militarization of the economy. On the watch for Germany, Lenin
waited. This passivity allowed the situation to degenerate. It was *in
extremis* that he finally took his decision. He made it alone, without
consultation, without discussion, and amidst generalized stupor. He
had finally admitted that the crisis in Russia had developed faster
than the revolutionary upsurge in Europe. And if NEP was not a
genuinely concerted political strategy, it was constructed on a day-
to-day basis, and if Lenin thought he could put a time-limit to it, it
was simply because he hesitated to accept the inescapable logic of his
own diagnosis. He knew that in time this logic would lead to an
impasse. He was desperately looking out for a turn in the European
situation. It was left to others to draw the conclusion of "the
prolonged period".

For Lenin the workers' hostility was conjunctural. It was the
primitive expression of the economic catastrophe. Once production
had been restored it would have permitted a new political consolidation. On the other hand, ceding to immediate pressure would have
amounted to opening the way, whatever the political convictions of
the workers' opposition, to the Menshevik usurpers, allied to the
Social Revolutionaries. This would have given a huge advantage to
world social democracy and to the Russian peasantry. In other
words, to the petty-bourgeoisie. This political retreat combined with
a new economic policy, would bring about certain defeat for the
revolution in Russia and in Europe. For these reasons Lenin judged
any concession to be criminal. Within this perspective, military
repression was a lesser evil.

In fact, the impasse had already arrived. It had been forged of an
inextricable compound of errors (the trade-union question), procras-

tinations, and objective constraints — the last-mentioned being the most compelling and in fact the principal ingredient. Fundamentally, it expressed in the most dramatic possible fashion the inadequacy of theory (common to all the marxist tendencies) which had led to an erroneous appreciation of the historical conjuncture.

It hence represented the calling into question of the role of the working class as the ruling class. With the soviets reduced to powerless talking-shops, and their democracy rejected and with the failure to impose trade-union democracy, everything revolved around the links between the proletariat and the party. Party democracy became the decisive question. The party was shackled by the chains of society itself. It began to crack under the crashing blows of Kronstadt. There were no less than eight tendencies at the 10th Congress. Lenin said: "The party is ill. The party is trembling with fever." The political differences deepened into a social differentiation. Sapronov, of the "democratic centralism" bloc, grouped Trotsky and Lenin together in spite of their momentary disagreements as the adherents "of the same group and the only group which formerly sought to militarize the economy". Shlyapnikov, of the Workers' Opposition, made the same distinction. "Do not believe," he said, on 26 January 1921 to the communist fraction of the miners' congress, "in this disagreement between Trotsky and Lenin. They will soon reach agreement and then the struggle will be conducted solely against us." They were introducing into the party the same social distinctions which existed in the proletariat.

They were muzzled. They began to be run to earth. The violence of Kronstadt paralysed them. On the vote on trade-union policy, already an anachronism and completely by-passed by events, Lenin received 336 votes, Trotsky 50, and the Workers' Oposition 15. Without doubt a derisory demonstration, but indicative of the extreme weakness of those who considered themselves at that time legitimately, to be the spokesmen of the factories. The separation of the party and the working class at the point of production was refracted by the tendencies. In view of the exceptional circumstances, Lenin prohibited factions and groupings.

To be sure, the resolution was hedged round with reservations concerning the principle of democracy. But the principle was dead. With its indispensable structures prohibited, democracy in the party was emptied of all reality. The matter was to take several months more, but the turning point had been reached. Once more the revolutionaries had made the bed for the thermidoreans.[30]

The proletariat at the point of production had lost all means of control.

6 The decomposition of power and the party factions, 1922-8

ON THE EVE of the year 1922, irreversible mechanisms came into play. The factors which brought about the destruction of the workers' state, which had for some time been contained by the violence of the social crisis, were combined and revitalized by the re-establishment of the capitalist production process. Once more the relationship between classes in Russia and in the world was inescapably altered. The integration of Russia into the world market assumed its real significance. Its political and social isolation expressed the rejection by the world's technological infrastructure of the attempts being made to introduce socialized control of the productive forces into the existing level of civilization. For the time being, this barrier could not be crossed.

What was not determinate, on the other hand, was the nature of the society that was to follow. The solution was to depend first of all on the evolution of the social crisis of capitalism in Europe and in the United States, and then on the degree of resistance of the revolutionary *institution* of the USSR. That is to say, it was to depend on the "social bases" which arose from the October revolution: even though these were caught up in the mechanics of the decomposition of classes. It was to take six years, from 1922 to 1928, to settle the question. In certain respects, it could be maintained that the question is still posed today. But now it is posed in a historical context which is so fundamentally different that it is no longer the same question.

The accelerating differentiation between classes and the tension in the market, the widening gap between agricultural and industrial prices, and the resulting antagonisms, the extremely low output from nationalized industry, the crying demand for investments, and the enormous disparity between world and Russian productivity, in brief the economic and social dynamic of NEP which I have analysed, all dominated the Bolshevik party and completely determined the course and rhythm of its internal crisis.

The party was subjugated. Because it exercised an absolute monopoly of the state; because the power of political, military and economic decision-making was concentrated in the state; because the state was the juridical owner of nationalized industry, transport, and land; because the monopoly of foreign trade turned the state into the sole intermediary between the Russian market and the world market; because constitutional assemblies and institutions were replaced by the organs of the party; because without workers' democracy (whether that of the soviets or the trade unions): no autonomous institution could exist outside the state. The party was, at the heart of society, the unique centre of decision-making and execution, and because of this unique role *the party was enslaved.*

Normally a completely opposite conclusion is drawn from the same facts, namely that the party's powers were enormous. This is a fallacy. Given the relatively low scientific and material base of the period, particularly aggravated by Russian circumstances, it was of vital concern that certain ways out existed. The economy continued to develop in a wildcat fashion. The state possessed neither the technical means nor the technological base necessary to dam up, control and guide the tumultuous flow of the blind forces of production. From the moment when the state administration turned itself into a compact protective shell, society projected its tensions and contradictions into the state and necessarily, continuously, called into question the established régime. The organic stability of the bourgeoisie as a ruling class relies on the actual distinction (its relative weight depending on the historical period) between political administration and economic control. The obvious anarchy of this system, to be sure, gives rise to all the contradictions with which we are familiar. But finally, ways are found, primitively, sometimes barbarously, around impasses where no other solution exists, as long as basic technological conditions do not change. Once the October revolution had liquidated big capital and landed property, the party/ trade-union diarchy would have provided this necessary way out. Far from weakening the system, it would have given it a functional flexibility, and hence a security which it never knew.

When Trotsky submitted that all economic questions could be resolved entirely from the political point of view, he made a premature and hence a false prognostication, since it was not just an idle remark.[31] The material state of society would without doubt have allowed an organized intervention into the economy, albeit a limited one; and it would have been one marked by a series of corrections and adjustments. This fact is so indisputable that this tendency appeared at that time in the nerve-centres of world capitalism.

These are not at all academic considerations. They find constant confirmation in the history of the first revolution and in the crisis of the bureaucratic régime which supplanted it. NEP was precisely the recognition of the impossibility at the state of evolution then reached of preventing the wildcat development of the economy. Lenin and

Trotsky believed at the outset that nothing more was involved than a narrowly limited concession — limited in both time and space. This error flowed from a generalized lack of appreciation of the technological prerequisites necessary to any socialized process of production. In trying to integrate NEP into a state administration as rigid and widespread as the Ninth Congress theses showed it to be, the Bolsheviks were packing huge explosive charges under the state.

It was hence inside the party, because of its position and function, that all social tensions converged. The subjugated party, isolated and separated from the proletariat, could find no way out other than the use of systematic violence. In this sector, and in this sector alone, it had very considerable power at its disposal which derived from the political alienation of the classes concerned. State coercion (military and administrative) became an essential instrument for the running of the economy. Its widespread use tended to raise the state, and the political corps of the state, above society, and to give a privileged status to the repressive apparatus of the state. Beyond a certain weakening of antagonistic classes (over and above the consolidation of an administrative infrastructure controlling the production-process, a new mutation came about: the transformation of the bureaucratic ruling caste into a ruling class. This is exactly what happened in the 1930s. The fundamental contradictions, however, were not overcome by this means. The very high social cost of the operation burdened industry seriously; the administrative corset it imposed permanently disrupted the growth of state capitalism; and it resulted in a constant organic instability in the new hierarchy of classes which gave rise to an uninterrupted succession of political crises. This phenomenon in its totality assumes a character which is completely new and unique in the historical context of the second revolution. Between 1922 and 1928 the party, embroiled in NEP, became the closed courtroom for political confrontation between classes and social groups. Completely besieged, the Bolshevik party turned itself into a heterogeneous conglomeration of hostile factions, each one defending antagonistic external social interests.

This is a new and highly significant fact and an essential tendency of the six transitional years. Up until this point the party had been a homogeneous vanguard organization of the working class. The tendencies which were formed and dissolved expressed differences of opinion among the same social group in touch with the same reality; and on certain occasions the polemics reflected divergent currents in the heart of the proletariat. The prohibition of factions and groups pronounced at the Tenth Congress called a halt to this internal life and institutionalized the separation of the party from the proletariat at the point of production. From Lenin's point of view, it was a necessary measure for the public good which preserved unity. In reality this measure, which to be sure reflected a modification of forces in society as a whole, *broke* the Bolshevik party. In fact, the party ceased to act as a political organ of the working class *and transformed itself into an arena where social groups and classes fought for their antagonistic interests and struggled for power.*

This radical transformation was masked by appearances: by the continuity of political personnel and by the mystification of language. It is certain that the participants were not immediately aware of what was going on. They had their suspicions. They observed events as if through a broken mirror. The division into right, centre and left was a trap which was to cost the oppositionists very dearly. Trotsky's writings at this time sowed these illusions. So much so that even today this type of linguistic usage continues to exercise its distorting influence. The variations on Thermidor illustrate the problems in understanding the situation. And this lack of clarity in analysis (although passionate and anguished) explains, at least partly (besides many other forceful reasons) the political vacillations, the incessant compromises, the official abjurations, and even the ignominies of the Moscow trials. We could say, stretching the point as far as possible, that the lineaments of several parties were formed within the Bolshevik party in the course of these six years, their programmes expressing hostile and competitive social interests. The well-off peasantry intervened through what it is now seen in conventional terms as the right wing, with Bukharin as principal leader and with the celebrated slogan: "Enrich yourselves." The agents of the state, of public administration and of the economy, and most of the officials of the party apparatus were grouped behind Stalin and the platform of "socialism in one country". Trotsky designated this the centre — a false definition. The proletarian intelligentsia, another part of the same apparatus, constituted itself into a left opposition with the political objective of bringing about the accelerated growth of nationalized industry and planning, with the theory of permanent revolution as its theoretical foundation. In the form of small, exhausted groupuscules without influence, successive workers' oppositions were no more than political and trade-union survivals of the proletariat in the factories. Between these formations there is nothing in common, except their historical origin and momentary, short-lived cohabitation.

There is, however, no equivalence between the situation in which these groups found themselves. The well-off peasantry was not directly represented in the party. It was represented by spokesmen through the medium of an opportune alliance with one part of the Bolshevik political personnel. The kulaks succeeded bit by bit in penetrating the administration of the less important state services. But the ruling circles were inaccessible to them. By all accounts this was their Achilles' heel, but it was also the weakness of the Bukharinites. They drew their strength entirely from a precarious alliance with a social class which was alien to them. Their power was the weakness of the proletariat. The very success of their political line (the enrichment and hence the economic and political growth of the rural middle classes), in the long run threatened them. As soon as their co-operation had developed to the limit of a split, they fell of necessity, into the narrowest dependence on the central apparatus of the party. This enterprise, with its successes and failures, lasted seven years.

The Left Opposition, on its part, maintained very distant relations with the working class. It was proletarian in its past, its concepts, and its militant tradition. It remained associated with the low-ranking party cadres, the "little men" of the generation of October. It maintained an influence, though a narrow and restricted one, in the apparatus of the trade unions. Its actual contacts in the factories were limited and difficult. It appeared as a proletarian political formation with an aristocratic nature, becoming more and more marginal in its composition and function.

The majority of its militants comprised the most resolute and best-trained members of the revolutionary intelligentsia. In the main, it recruited the second generation of Bolsheviks. It drew the school youth, the specialists and the technicians in the army and in the economic administration, at least those of an independent spirit. Outside those former militants of the October revolution who had remained in minor posts deliberately or because they were demoted for being too stubborn, it had little presence in the factories.

The functions discharged by its members tended to be administrative and dictatorial. In the first place because, once power had been taken, the division of labour, as far as possible, had placed at the critical points of military, administrative and economic control those most suited by their training or general qualities, and those not absorbed in central political tasks. Given the speed of events, a few years were sufficient to turn them into specialists. It was therefore inevitable that they reacted as such, even more so because Trotsky had become, through force of circumstance in a totally disorganized situation, the theoretician and practitioner of state control. His reputation was very widely know, and so those who were most conscientious in method, in producing results and in creating new institutions, and those most inclined to follow a positive lead, sought to work under his direction. The commissariat of war was a model of discipline and efficiency. So much so that Trotsky and his collaborators were constantly urged to intervene in sectors far beyond the army. Trotsky spent the winter of 1919 to 1920 in the Urals, dealing with the problems of the economy. For a whole year, getting the railways going occupied him completely. Obviously this was a time-consuming process, but he also considered this year to be very important for his personal development, and thought it worthy of note. He observed in his biography: "For me personally, this was a great year of learning."

His managerial side is obscured by his later work, linked with his period in exile. At the time this aspect of his character was very clear, almost to the point of being a characteristic political trait. Lenin was a good judge of such things. On 25 December 1922, beset by illness, obsessed with the very visible dangers ripening within the party, he resolved to outline in several carefully-chosen phrases (death was to make this his Testament), what, according to him, were the most fearsome character-traits of the principal protagonists. He noted as the most worrying counterpart of Trotsky's "most eminent qualities" his tendency to conduct himself as an uncompromising organizer. "He is without doubt the most capable personality on the present Central Committee, but he is excessively given to self-assurance and too much taken up with the purely administrative side of things."

It is noteworthy that he says precisely the same things about Piatakov, one of the leaders of the Left Opposition. In Piatakov, however, this tendency was not compensated by a highly developed political sense. Piatakov, with Bukharin, was the only one of the "young" members of the Central Committee to be mentioned in the Testament. "Piatakov is undoubtedly a man of goodwill and is very capable but he inclines too much to administration and to the administrative side of things to be reliable on serious political questions."

This basic characterization of the Left Opposition *as a directorial and administrative political aristocracy is essentially in tune with events*. It clarifies fully the organic weakness of this group, its isolation from the workers, and its tactical mistakes. We find it hard to admit, because Trotsky's work and the whole of his historic action are situated in a very different ideological and political world perspective. Yet it would never occur to us to appraise Trotsky's role in the October revolution *in terms of* what he was and did in 1905 (although it would be easy to demonstrate certain constants), because it would be absurd. We cannot judge the Left Opposition between 1923 and 1928 according to Trotsky's activities as founder of the Fourth International, even though clear correlations can be discerned. The Left Opposition, just like the Bukharinist faction and the

Stalinist clique, must be resituated in its specific historical context.

Its managerial and administrative role, the logic of its professional conduct and a combination of overestimation of technique and theoretical abstraction became decisive factors. The Left Opposition was fundamentally *a proletarian political organization without support among the proletariat*. This separation was first and foremost the product of its managerial role. Secondarily, but in a way which cannot be ignored, it was a function of its methods of work, a reflection of its specialization and its ideology.

The tasks of control and production remained antagonistic. After October, this contradiction took on an exceptionally brutal form because of the profound disruption of the economy and its low technological level. As the theoreticians and practitioners of administrative control, Trotsky and his team, in the eyes of the workers, incarnated *the logic of management, and the logic of output*. Trotsky and his most eminent partisans (Rakovsky, Sokolnikov, Piatakov, Krestinsky, Preobrazhensky etc.) defended and applied *military discipline* in the process of labour. They were openly and vigorously opposed to trade-union democracy which they considered inefficient. They broke with the majority of trade-union leaders. It was not their arguments which lived on in the memory of the workers, but their actions, weighted with the bloody episode of Kronstadt. So much so that when they demanded the re-establishment of democracy in the party, Stalin, a gross but cunning demagogue, turned their past as administrators against them. In *Pravda* on 15 December he wrote: "On the side of the opposition we see such comrades as Beloborodov, whose support for democracy had not yet been forgotten by the workers of Rostov; Rosenglotz whose support for democracy has kept the Donetz basin in a state of agitation for so long; Alski whose support for democracy is widely know everywhere. . . ." Sapronov's complaint (that Lenin and Trotsky were the *militarizers* of the economy) expressed the generally distrustful attitude of the wage-earners, which amounted at worst to hostility. The Left Opposition was isolated in the factories where it should have been most strongly implanted. Its method, which flowed from its practice, hindered it from overcoming the obstacle posed by its policies. The Left Opposition acted like heads of staff. Trotsky, along with Lenin, reckoned that the main danger resulted from the late arrival of the revolution in the world arena. He concluded that the strategy of the International was becoming decisive. The affairs of the leaderships in Germany, England, and in China hence occupied a privileged position. But these were elevated questions. To pretend for a moment that it was possible to bring about a regroupment in the Russian working class on the question of

China or of the Anglo-Russian Committee goes against all common sense. Posing the problem of world strategy as the key question is certainly well-founded, but assumes as a starting-point that there exists a politically qualified apparatus, professionally and politically capable of maintaining the debate. If the head itself is rotten, it is obviously necessary to reconsider completely the order of priorities and the way to resolve them.

Burning differences of political economy were thus opened up only amongst and at the level of the leadership. Trotsky posed — in fact, he was the first to do so clearly — the crucial relationship between industrial prices and agricultural prices. It is unquestionable that the growing gap between the two prongs of the scissors enabled the precise statistical localization of disequilibria in production. But he deals with the question as a specialist who is discussing with well-informed people. It was a decisive question for the country; carrying out the debate between professionals restricted the real audience to experts only. Once more it assumed that the cadres would decide questions and that political conditions lent themselves to such a confrontation. Lenin wrote "The Coming Crisis and How to Solve It" in a totally different way.

It is true that the different platforms of the opposition recounted, with well-documented supporting detail, the everyday problems encountered by the workers. They examined wages, the cost of living and conditions of work. They denounced the administration's abuses an the parasitism of the trade-union apparatus. But at the same time these platforms are full of polemical attacks on groups, sub-groups, deviations and half-deviations, all completely esoteric. *They are directed not towards the factory, but towards the party.*

The exhausting and all-encompassing polemic around the thesis of permanent revolution had an extremely high theoretical value, but had a very limited audience because of its cultural assumptions. It was the product of an aristocracy of the revolution, including, of course, workers — on condition that their marxism was at a higher level than that of elementary formulae. To attach such importance to this discussion assumed not only its significance as such, but that a favourable milieu existed for this discussion: that is to say, that the party and the International were able to follow the debate. It was also an assumption that *the most important effort must be spent on the ruling circles.*

As a consequence the opposition's methods, which accurately reflected its nature, could not link it to the proletariat at the point of production. In fact, they aggravated its isolation.

I am in no way underestimating the Russian workers. But it must be said again that the most qualified and the best-formed had gone into the administration. The working class had lost its natural political cadre. Its real level in 1923 to 1928 was very low. It was lower than it had been before the war or immediately after October. Remember Lenin's disquieted remarks concerning a certain poster which was not where it should have been. Christian Rakovsky made the following acute observation in his "Letter to Valentinov":

> The workers who joined the party after the civil war entered mostly after 1923 (the Lenin levy); they had no idea before what the party régime was like. The majority had that class education which had been acquired in struggle, in life, and in conscious practice. In its time this class consciousness had been obtained in the struggle against capitalism. Now it was supposed to be developed through participation in the construction of socialism. But since our bureaucracy had reduced this participation to a hollow phrase, the workers could not acquire any of this education. I am excluding the fact that our bureaucracy, by lowering the real level of salaries, by worsening the conditions of labour, and by encouraging the development of unemployment, pushed the workers into struggle and raised their class consciousness; but this consciousness was now hostile to the socialist state.

In relation to this "Lenin levy" which consisted in recruiting *240,000 workers* at one go in 1924, Stalin revealed in his report on organization to the 13th Congress that in some regions 70 per cent of the worker members of the party were politically illiterate and that the average was in general 57 per cent. He qualified this shortly afterwards by indicating that 60 per cent of the workers in the party *before* the Lenin levy were politically illiterate, but after it the figure rose to 80 per cent.

Of course the criterion here is the ABC of communism and not a knowledge of marxist theory in all its complexity. In the course of its vanguard struggle, the opposition remained true to its character and method. It called on *the party* to eliminate the bureaucracy and re-establish an *internal* elective system. It did not propose to the factory-workers to constitute pressure groups *outside the party* which could carry on the *social* struggle against the bureaucracy. Hence, it lost every possibility of making itself heard by the proletariat. First, because it did not distinguish itself, on this publicly sensitive point, from the Bukharinites or the Stalinists. Dzherzhinsky declared to the Central Committee in April 1926: "When I look at all our apparatus, our leadership system, our revolting bureaucracy, the incredible disorder of every conceivable administrative formality, I am literally horrified." Everything Bukharin had already said at the 13th Congress, when referring to the internal régime, was echoed by the left: "In most cases elections have become pure formalities; not only are the votes taken without any preceding discussion, but they rest on one question only: *who is against?* And since you put yourself in a bad light by saying that you are *against* authority, the question is settled." And finally, because this confusion reinforced the workers' feeling that it was the *militarizers* who were fighting amongst themselves.

As a managerial and adminstrative political aristocracy, the Left Opposition was situated within the apparatus of the state and confined itself inside it. Its whole strategy was directed towards the interior of the party and not towards the working class outside the party.

At the 13th Congress (at the height of the battle between the factions), Trotsky affirmed: "None of us either wants to be considered, nor can be in opposition to his party. Definitively, the party is always right. . . . One cannot be right except with and through the party, because history has created no other path through which to make one's correct positions effective." An absurd proposition, that Trotsky in 1907 would have subjected to biting sarcasm. But it has a certain meaning: *the refusal to pose the question of a new party and an acknowledgement that, even if it was desirable, it would not be possible to construct it.* The Left Opposition was in a total impasse because of its social composition (its integration into the state apparatus) and hence separation from the proletariat, and because of its strategy.

This sharp consciousness of being a current within the apparatus, and of having no other possible base than ruling national and inter-national circles, was combined with theoretical reflection about an abstract model of the workers' state, and reinforced by a professional over-evaluation of the administrative and technical side of things. It led the Left Opposition into inconsequential positions and disastrous tactical errors *on the very terrain which it had chosen*: the party. The refusal to bring the question of the bureaucracy before the working class led the left, on the initiative of Preobrazhensky and Sapronov in December 1923, to demand of the party the *immediate* election or re-election of *all* its officials. Now, this party was made of officials. They were its marrow. Out of 351,000 members in 1923, only 54,000 were workers. Nearly 300,000 were officials. Furthermore, according to Stalin's report to the 13th Congress, 60 per cent of these workers were politically illiterate. As for Bukharin, he assures us that they were not prepared to vote against the "authorities" for fear of getting into trouble themselves. This was the real social composition of the party that the Left Opposition saw as muzzled and to which it wished to restore political rights. The only positive result was that the threat reinforced the bureaucracy's instinct for self-preservation and aroused its defences.

The managing intelligentsia underwent, as did all other groups, the effects of the organic split in the proletariat; but it was also subjugated through the profound disorganization of the party and the pulverization of its internal structure, a by-product of the multiplication and interpenetration of the tasks of management and control. The leading circles remained the only circles open to discussion and confrontation. The methods of the Left Opposition were characterized by its "strategy of summits". It is also this which made it objectively vulnerable. Since its professional prerogatives were dependent upon the state, it was like all bureaucratic bodies subject to the state's assignment of jobs and distribution of jobs; that is to say to the Secretariat which placed and displaced personnel.

In answer to a question at the Ninth Party Congress about Shlyapnikov's journey to Norway, Lenin replied: "A Central Committee which permitted itself to send Shlyapnikov, an oppositionist, away on the eve of the Congress, would incontestably commit an infamous act."[32] (Ureniev in his intervention had spoken of "system of exile and banishment".) It seems to have been established that Shlyapnikov had been sent to Norway by the trade unions and that the Central Committee had consented to this with his agreement. We can see how rapidly things were changing. This infamous act was already established practice by 1924. Sending people to be ambassadors became a means of decapitating the opposition. Yoffe, Krassin, Ureviev, Kollontai, Rakovsky, Krestinsky, Lutovinov and Osinsky were sent abroad. The mechanism was simple but effective: a prominent ambassador is needed in London — who is better qualified than Rakovsky? Particularly since Rakovsky is also Trotsky's principal political ally and the President of the Soviet of Commissars of the Ukrainian people.

The pulverization of the party into a complexity of functional apparatuses and the reduction of political life to the ruling circles transformed the confrontation between factions, whether secretly or openly organized, into summit operations. It was the *apparatus* of Leningrad which gave Zinoviev his strength. It was the *administrative secretariat* which furnished Stalin with the means for extended control over the whole party. It was *the posts of administration and control* which gave the Left Opposition its influence. It was the *technical supervision* over the administration of village affairs which constituted the solid infrastructure of Bukharin's faction. It was the division in the secretariat which gave the Troika (Stalin, Zinoviev, Kamenev) the ability to organize their clandestine network. It was the administrative commission which in 1925 comprised the lever for the Zinovievist reorganization of the International. Political analyses and theses were now no more than weapons for administrative conflicts.

Power, the only real power, lay in the weight of the various apparatuses, and depended on the more or less central position which they occupied in the state. The preponderant importance of the Secretariat arose exclusively from its principal function: through the nomination system it gained sovereign control over the material interests of the functionaries and cadres of nationalized industries. Thus it was that the Left Opposition elaborated a strategy *arising out of the managerial positions which it occupied*. The central slogan of Trotsky was the creation of a "grand general staff" of the economy, which would group the soviets of labour, of defence, and Gosplan and whose task would be the elaboration and application of a general plan. Piatakov and Smirnov got down to dealing with the most difficult financial questions. Preobrazhensky published his essay "The New Economics", on the necessity for primitive accumulation. And it is true that the economy was in "absolute chaos". It was certainly essential to know whether or not to give credits to agriculture; whether or not to make the peasants pay a forced contribution to the accumulation fund. If these problems of government were to be dealt with, some minimal agreement on the ogranization of power was required.

In practice, the Left Opposition acted as if the crisis was not related to the class foundation of the state, as if the party was subject to deviations but continued to exist, and as if its adversaries accepted the confrontation as the terrain of the real discussion. In other words, the Left Opposition proved totally unrealistic. However, as we shall see, it diagnosed at the same time that the bureaucratic outgrowth was becoming a social phenomenon. This is a characteristic contradiction. The Left Opposition, inasmuch as it was a revolutionary proletarian intelligentsia, was the prisoner of an apparatus which, in the social sense, had ceased to be proletarian and from which it could not disengage itself because of its functional role, its composition, its concepts and its strategy. It represented, at this moment in its history, a remarkable example of a formation paralysed by its own elevated theoretical qualities. So long as Trotsky and the principal leaders of the left did not provide a theoretical elucidation of the social process through which they were living, they were incapable of reacting effectively. They were not to escape this impasse without being destroyed.

The only path historically open to the marxist left would have been to split, to return to social opposition, and to form a new party. They were incapable of following such a course. They refused to split the party right up to the point of their own extermination. It seems almost inconceivable that after Trotsky was deported, his friends decimated and the repression institutionalized, he should persist in trying to persuade the very same people whose response and determination had taken the form of systematic executions. The myth of the party and the International, to be sure, have provided posterity with one of the most remarkable works of Trotsky: his "Letter to the Sixth Congress of Communist International" and his "Critique of the Programme of the Communist International". This myth is evidently no accident. It reveals the social and political impasse of the Left Opposition.

Its ambiguity and its lack of realism can be seen at the very heart of events. While Trotsky was deliberating on the economy, what were his enemies doing? They prepared a coup d'état of which he was to be the principal victim. They were doing this not in 1927 but already in 1923, even before Lenin's death. There was not one month in the course of these four years in which measures were not taken against members of the opposition. There was no meeting held which did not establish even to the least perspicacious that playing by the rules of the game was a trap because the dice were loaded. At the end of these four years expulsions from the party, deportations and the first executions sanctioned the coup d'état. What did Trotsky advocate? In a letter dated 12 September 1928, addressed from his place of exile, Alma-Ata, "to a well-wishing critic", he found nothing more opportune than this unbelievable advice:

> It is necessary to begin by reducing brutally (by a factor of about 20) the party budget, which has grown monstrously and which is becoming the financial base of the arbitrary bureaucracy dominating the party. . . . Secret revolutionary expenditure must be checked every year by a special Congress Commission. The 16th Congress must be prepared in such a way as to be distinguished from the 15th, the 14th, and the 13th, by being a Congress of the party and not of the party apparatus. Before the Congress, the party must listen to all those factions amongst which its members have been scattered thanks to the régime of the past few years. . . . Since the liberation of the party is a long way off, the secret vote must be introduced into all those elections which go into the preparation of the 16th congress.[33]

Those whom the gods would destroy they first make blind. Through an extraordinary turn of events the marxist faction, in spite of its culture, its eminent abilities, and its powers of theoretical analysis, committed errors as blind as those of the last of the Romanovs. The "motor forces" of history turned away from the first revolution. Stalin declared to his adversaries in 1927: "To get rid of the present majority *you will have to launch a civil war in the party.*" As one skilled at manoeuvre, he accused his adversaries not of what he intended to do, but of what he was already doing. The preliminaries had been completed by 1925. Stalin was organizing civil war in the party because he was able to do so.

In fact, Stalin was the only one to exercise direct control over a social force, a "motor force" of history. Much has been said about his methods (the use of tricks, corruption and armed violence) in manipulating the apparatus of the state and the party, which opened the way to his dictatorship. I do not think, however, that sufficient attention has been paid to this other decisive aspect.

Stalin's power rested in the social corps of the state. The large numbers of Tsarist functionaries had been structurally reinforced by the integration of proletarian managers. The apparatus of the Bolshevik party — a product of circumstances, for the most part the party's atomization through a differentiation of roles (a division of labour) — had become the central organ of management, administration, and control. It was hence subject to the apparatus of the state, on which its actions in all sectors of society was narrowly dependent. But at the same time it dominated it, because it was the only existing expression of the executive power in all spheres, from the allocation of administrative privilege (nominations, appointments, promotions) up to the exploitation of the economic monopoly of the state based on the juridical appropriation of the means of production.

The split consummated in 1921 between the proletarian managers and the mass of workers in production *tended* to emancipate the apparatus of the state from its dependence on the working class, a dependence established by the October revolution. In parallel, the antagonism between the tasks of management and production led to a progressive emergence in the state apparatus of consciousness of its social specificity which was translated into a desire for material privilege and political power. Stalin was first the catalyst of this crystallization and then the strategist of its emancipation. This role could only be assumed by a group within the political apparatus because of the position of the party in society.

By the beginning of 1923, the integration of the proletarian managers, the functional structuring of the apparatus of the state, the appointment of privilege and authority linked to task and rank, and the resulting pretensions already constituted, in essence, a social reality.

This new social corps, which emerged already well advanced in its internal constitution and in the organization of its power is commonly designated as a bureaucracy, without it being legitimately assimilable with other analogous formations. Bureaucracy as such is a pure abstraction. The phenomenon of bureaucracy is always, in its distinctive attributes, the expression of specific historical conditions.

The social emancipation of the state apparatus was violently challenged. The political struggles which shook Russia to its foundations from 1922 to 1928 comprise the history of this confrontation.

7 The emergence of the bureaucracy

THE SOVIET bureaucracy was an organic product of the October revolution. It constituted one of its social bases.

The proletarian revolution secures its victory with the economic expropriation of the financial and industrial bourgeoisie. This expropriation is necessarily expressed as a suppression of the private ownership of the means of production. This suppression is carried out through the socialized organization of the production-process, which takes the form of self-management: that is, rational administration of society by its members. This self-managed administration of society initiates the withering away of the state. This is the dynamic of the revolution, its theoretical model.

This theoretical model is a real one — it correctly interprets a concrete social logic. Decrees of expropriation are not arbitrary actions. On the contrary, they are a response to an internal necessity. The only way the proletariat can seize property is collectively. Without this collective seizure there can be no lasting proletarian political power. Of course, this process can take other forms, follow different courses, or take on different rhythms according to the impact of local and international conjunctures.

We know that the October revolution really drew all these logical inferences in the space of a few months. We also know that it was a premature revolution. To say that it was premature does not mean that it was accidental. The October revolution was the correct response to the social crisis of capitalism, as it developed out of the First World War. The *proletarian* revolution was undeniably on the agenda in Europe, as a predictable and possible outcome. It became very probable indeed in Germany at the end of the war and again in 1922. The challenge to capitalism in its *world* bases was expressed in the violent struggle between its institutions in Asia. No revolutionary marxist leadership worth its salt could fail to take these facts into account. In terms of tendencies within the world marxist movement, this meant that the Bolsheviks and the Spartacists were right on the basic issues, as against the Mensheviks and the social democratic reformists.

However, we know that the social crisis of capitalism had entered into an extremely sharp pre-revolutionary phase *before* technical development had attained a necessary level to produce a *material base* of society adequate to transcend the capitalist production-process. It is for this reason, *and only for this reason*, that the first revolution was premature: it was not that Kautsky had a better understanding of the real historical conjuncture than Lenin, but that neither was capable of grasping it. Their disagreement touched essentially on the dynamic of the social crisis, on its various stages and its international nature. In this exclusive domain Lenin's prognosis of imperialism turned out to approximate far closer to reality than Kautsky's theoretical analysis. So much so that Kautsky's justifiable criticisms of the circumstantial methods and measures could not be taken into consideration because they were used as arguments in favour of a general theory contradicted by the facts; whereas the analogous observations of Rosa Luxemburg should have been heeded. However, they lacked the power of persuasion which revolutionary practice in Germany would have given them.

The obstacle of technology was by its very nature insurmountable. The fundamental compromise between the concrete logic of the revolution, incarnated in its laws and in its institutions, and the real technological level was expressed as the mutation of social property into state property which was simultaneously public and private. This transfer was not at all superficial but, on the contrary, fundamental. It was not just technical, but social. The contradiction between the social crisis of the capitalist system and the level of civilization, in so far as it did not develop into a prolonged decomposition of capitalism, necessarily changed the social bases of the proletarian revolution into social bases of state capitalism of an advanced kind. This substitution of the state for direct workers' control, in the context of a determined resistance by revolutionary forces, was the only inescapable phenomenon. Everything else depended on *political* circumstances. These propositions possess definite theoretical interest: they situate and hence allow us to describe and define the historical function of the bureaucracy in the period of capitalist decline.

If the German revolution had been victorious, it would have confronted the same insurmountable barrier. It would also have been blocked in its attempt to socialize the production-process. The same would have been the case for all the advanced industrial states. Hence, a revolution in Germany would have produced the same phenomenon of rejection accompanied by a reflux on to the state. At the same time, Germany would have confronted this obstacle with superior cultural and technical capabilities; with a professionally well-qualified and politically cultivated proletariat; with well-formed managerial cadres; with an up-to-date industrial and commercial infrastructure and with a creative dynamism. In other words, state capitalism would have been constructed without the shackles which paralysed the Russians: using more flexible and productive methods. Hence, without entering the realm of science fiction, we can conclude *that the period of world transition* would not have suffered the barbarous regression which in fact marked it; that the stage of the second revolution (in its scientific-industrial context) would have been attained more rapidly and at a lower social cost; and hence that this second revolution would itself have followed a different course. From this perspective it emerges that if state capitalism was as such the inescapable outcome of the victorious proletarian revolution, then its concrete content, and the way it came into effect, was conditioned entirely by political factors. An inevitable ignorance of the technical capacities of the time, and hence of a possible technological programme, must certainly be considered the general and essential factor of political conditioning.

Bearing these observations in mind, the concrete form taken by state capitalism in Russia was fashioned entirely *by Russian backwardness*, whose deleterious effects could be neither limited nor contained because of the setback suffered by the revolution in Europe. The Soviet bureaucracy derived its specific traits from this fact.

State capitalism in Russia developed from the primitive state administration of extreme shortage (war communism). It came about in spite of the political leadership of the state and against its will. Its promoters considered it to be an imposed concession, limited and temporary. As a consequence its growth was disorderly, and took place in leaps and bounds, as an incoherent series of reflex adaptations. This absence of a co-ordinated plan and programme aggravated the fragility and poverty of its technical infrastructure, the more so because the real problems of its development could not be posed in the proper terms. The dominant, socially useful, ideology prevented it.

Hence there were no policies of state capitalism in Russia which corresponded to the real functioning of the economy. This contradiction between the ideological superstructure of the régime and the real relations of production introduced a permanent instability into the system. This contradiction takes on a new significance in the present, historically original, context of the second revolution. The polemics on the reform of structures and methods of control comprise the least deformed expression of this.

In the absence of an adequate technology, the administrative control of the economy necessarily generates bureaucracy. In its essential functioning the bureaucracy is the substitution of man, as a work-force, for a non-existent machine. The bureaucracy accomplishes the tasks which are nowadays accomplished through electronics and a complex administrative apparatus. In the past it was a necessity for the purposes of instrumental control. Today, because of the tremendous advances in technology, it is a regressive survival. From this it emerges that the appearance of the bureaucracy is neither accidental nor a parasitic growth. On the contrary, it fulfils a fundamental function. The moment society, incapable of self-management, hands over its attributes to the state, the bureaucracy becomes the obligatory vehicle of state control. It constitutes itself as a "motor force" of history.

The substitution of humans for machines produces markedly inferior results. The quality of work produced is poor. At the level of the global economy these defects, inherent in the bureaucratic functioning, become an extremely important *economic factor*. The inflated costs of maintenance, and the considerable incidental expenses resulting from work carried out by administrative methods and their repercussion on cost prices, bear witness to this. (Remember that at this time retail prices in nationalized industry were two and a half times as high as those of the world market). It is one of the reasons why administrative control is rejected as the technological level gets higher. Administrative control is *a permanent violation of the material conditions of the capitalist process of production in this phase of its technology*.

The bureaucratic substitute for the machine is not only a primitive technical articulation, but an indispensable one. A human labour-force is also necessarily a social force. Its technical function necessarily carries with it social attributes. Bureaucratic state administration *hence signifies the social implantation of the state into the production-process*. The social corps of the state becomes an autonomous element integrated in the production-process.

The bureaucracy exploits state ownership of the means of production like a sitting tenant. Constitutionally, juridical ownership of the state is public. The bureaucracy has permanent tenancy, as the social corps of the state. However, this tenancy gives it a *real* and *autonomous* implantation in the production-process.

The transfer of social property to state property is not a purely juridical operation. The law by this means reflects an existing state of society. The proletariat had been incapable of establishing institutions of direct control. Hence, it had to relinquish a large part of its attributes as a ruling class in favour of the state, which exercised them as its agent.

This trustee — by the exercising of his mandate — tends to emancipate himself from political tutelage. This emancipation has resulted from a process which is both blind and conscious. The key to this chain reaction lies in the two complementary and indissoluble component parts of its function: the technical and the social. Administrative procedures *cease to be socially neutral* from the moment they set in motion a specific human work-force. Furthermore, they are not applied at the level of production, but at that of control. They incorporate and initiate decision-making and direction: that is, everything which relates to the exercise of ownership. The bureaucracy tends to confuse usage and right and to substitute itself for the proletariat as the effective owner of the means of production, precisely because its task relates to the exercise of ownership, because it is not a system of computers but a social corps and because the division of labour has turned it into a specific category. The bureaucracy draws its power from its role as an autonomous agent in the production-process. As such, it is the direct product of the organic split of the proletariat. We have seen how the division of labour gives rise to a functional separation between the proletarian who has become a manager and the worker who has remained at the point of production in the factory. We have seen how the antagonistic character of the tasks of management and production give a social content to this separation. We shall now see how the bureaucracy, as a substitute for a non-existent technology, is integrated into the armour of the production-process. It becomes, objectively, an essential and dominant component in the organization of labour. The role of administrative relations as relations of production is inseparable from the bureaucracy's role as a social corps. In this way it loses all the attributes of a parasitic layer. It ceases to be marginal. With its independence, it acquires the characteristics of a motor-force in society.

Hence the bureaucracy arose from the very texture of this society. It was as natural a creation of it as the kulak and the NEP-man. As with any human group, it became little by little conscious of its position and the power that it exercised, and transferred this into a *demand for rights*. In the same way and at the same time the kulak and the NEP-man, under analogous pressures, sought to have their economic and social existence recognized as a political reality. And, along with the kulak and the NEP-man, the bureaucracy had first of all to conquer its political legitimacy against the proletariat, because the October revolution had given the proletariat a monopoly over political power and its exercise. Now we can see what constituted the fundamental objective basis for the alliance between the bureaucracy and the urban rural middle classes. But this alliance contained the essential motivation for a murderous struggle against the proletariat which lasted four years (1923 to 1927). After workers' democracy in the extended form of soviets and in its more restrained aspect of trade-union democracy had foundered, the confrontation had to be concentrated in the party, the crucible of power. This is why Stalin was justified in talking of civil war *inside* the party.

The concentration of property rights in the state modified the juridical character of property *by incorporating political rights into it*. Political exercise of right became confounded with real and juridical possession of the means of production. The result was that the proletariat's struggle to maintain its political control over the state was identified with the defence of its juridical right to the ownership of the means of production. The result was also that the bureaucracy, as the social corps of the state, did not need to modify the juridical form of property.

Revolutionary institutions were the bureaucracy's natural base of support. In this case too, it is necessary to avoid any ambiguity. The bureaucracy did not take up unjustified residence inside revolutionary institutions. It did not take possession there *arbitrarily*. It was placed in this position as a reaction to the rejection of the socialized process of production by the technological infrastructure. It represented at once a *deformation* and a *continuation* of the October revolution. The powers of the state became powers of the bureaucracy. It took on the monopoly of foreign trade, the ownership of land and the nationalization of transport and heavy industry. In order to survive and grow it was compelled to defend revolutionary institution to consolidate the institution in its own way and to extend its scope.

NEP fundamentally rejected the revolutionary institution and its social bases, and hence rejected the bureaucracy. Under the backward conditions in Russia, this rejection reflected the violation by administrative procedures of the material conditions of the capitalist production-relations. In class terms it signified an *irremediable* opposition between the rural and urban middle classes and the bureaucracy. The kulak and the NEP-man were working towards the restoration of the bourgeoisie, that is, the re-establishment of capitalist social relations founded on the private ownership of the means of production. In order to protect its own interests the bureaucracy was *forced* to triumph, to constitute itself *as a ruling class*. In other words it had to extend its field of ownership to the whole of the economy. The historical alternatives were not the proletariat or the bourgeoisie but the bureaucracy or the bourgeoisie. Proletarian power had been eliminated by the technological impasse. The social content of the compromise could have been different, as we know, if the proletarian revolution had seized political power in Germany. The failure of the revolution in Europe was an objective fact, characteristic of the situation; in which must also be included the strategic errors of the proletarian leadership.

In the first phase the bureaucracy did not have a clear understanding of the irreducible antagonism which placed it in opposition
to the middle classes. It was more sensitive to immediate common
interests. The middle classes appeared to it as an indispensable factor
in the restoration of the economy, as they unquestionably were. The
bureaucracy was learning on the job, its nose to the ground. The
support of the middle classes was also vital to it in the political and
social battle against the proletarian resistance. Only under immediate
threat was it to gain a real grasp of the danger. Up against the wall,
it sought to cut the Gordian knot by compromising with world
capital. In 1929, after its scheme of huge concessions had been
rejected, it became embroiled in one of the bloodiest civil wars in
history.

Even though the bureaucracy was victorious in the social sphere in
constituting itself as the dominant class, it was not able to overcome
the fundamental opposition between bureaucratic administrative
control and the capitalist production-process. The whole history of
bureaucratic society is dominated by this contradiction, which gives
rise to its permanent organic instability.

8 The triumph of Thermidor

THE COMPOSITION of the Soviet bureaucracy was originally a functional amalgam of officials of the old régime and of the managing corps drawn from the working class. These two component parts were socially and politically heterogeneous. Their fusion came about during seven years of violence, factional splits and class confrontations. As with all social mutations, it took place through a half-blind process of civil war.

Automatic mechanisms came into play at the level of the organization of labour and the emergence of material interests. The community of function created habits, gave rise to reflexes and fashioned its own mentality; rapidly acquired privileges converged into social solidarity. Lenin, as is known, deciphered these elementary mechanisms with lucidity.

The elaboration of a group ideology and the definition of a policy and strategy of group interests set in motion semi-conscious processes and led to ever more systematic and better-conceived interventions. The proletarian managerial corps was the theatre of profound changes. In relation to the October revolution the new course was thermidorean, and in it the anti-proletarian reaction was expressed in the most concentrated and violent fashion. There was the dislocation of the institutions, the party was isolated and destroyed internally, there was a rapid resurgence of hostile classes, growing political disintegration of the proletariat, the downturn of the European revolution and the extreme confusion of different tendencies. Despite all this, the resistance was stubborn. It lasted seven years, and the confrontation took the form of a civil war within the party. Thermidor in Russia expressed the way the bureaucracy came to consciousness.

From 1923 onwards the thermidoreans occupied a dominant position. From 1925 they had their own ideology — socialism in one country. In 1926 they undertook *on a grand scale* the physical and political elimination of the proletarian wing. The coup d'état reached its climax in 1927. By 1928 the bureaucracy had conquered political power. Its cadres and its leader held all the levers of control. Events, however, left it no respite. Once the danger from the proletarian side was removed, it had to face the onslaught of the coalescing middle classes. With its political rights acquired, it was to acquire its sovereign status through civil war. Hence there were three major phases: 1923, 1925 and 1927. The year 1923 appears as the launching-pad of the whole operation. The thermidorean course was sufficiently advanced to furnish the bureaucracy with the political cadre indispensable to it. The defeat of the German workers took on a world dimension. It isolated the proletarian revolutionary faction in the international arena. It ruined any prospect of a quick revolution-ary victory in Europe. In Russia, it provoked a massive retreat into national positions. It opened the way to the thermidorean ideology of falling back on the national state.

It is easy to establish that the thermidoreans held the upper hand in 1923. I shall only present two conclusive indices. Lenin's personal prestige was immense. In the normal climate of the party one could either adopt or reject his propositions: it was inconceivable that they should be censured. When Lenin was ill he became preoccupied with the Georgian question. Stalin and Dzherzhinsky were carrying out large-scale repression there. Lenin observed on 30 September 1922: "Stalin played a fatal role there." He dictated a letter-programme on the national question. His personal secretary, L. Fotieva stated on the 16 April 1923: "Vladimir Ilyich considered that this article should serve as a directive and attached great importance to it." Neverthe-less, the article did not appear. Stalin was to be designated to present the report on the Georgian question to the 12th Congress.

In 1923, the bureaucratic danger became an obsession for Lenin. He wrote an article on the radical reorganization of the workers' and peasants' inspection and insisted on its immediate publication. Bukharin refused. Stalin, Molotov, Kuibychev, Rykov and Kalinin were opposed to it. Kuibychev contemplated a stupefying deception which says a great deal about the moral and intellectual decay of the party cadres. He suggested that a single copy of *Pravda*, containing the article, should be brought out to fool Lenin. To add a humorous touch, the imaginative Kuibychev was nominated to the direction of the central Control Commission.

The degree of integration between officials and cadres of the party *before* the death of Lenin, is thrown into sharp relief by a brief exchange of views which Trotsky reported in his letter to the Historical Institute of the party, dated 21 October 1927. Lenin proposed that the Central Committee have a special commission attached to it, charged with purging the administration. He suggested that Trotsky should take it in hand. Trotsky declined and his reasons are illuminating:

> Vladimir Ilyich, I am convinced that we must not forget that in reality, in the struggle against the bureaucratism of the Soviet apparatus, in the provinces as at the centre, a gathering of officials and specialists, comprising members of the party, candidates and outsiders is forming

around certain groups and leading personalities of the party in the provinces, in the districts, in the regions, at the centre, that is, in the Central Committee, etc. In putting pressure on the official, one would confront the party leader, to whose camp the specialist belongs, and in the present situation, I should not like to take on this task.

The level of organization attained by the thermidoreans in 1923 was already well advanced, and better structured than either Lenin or Trotsky suspected. The secret Troika of Stalin, Zinoviev, and Kamenev which directed Thermidor, was enlarged in 1923 into a clandestine group of seven leaders, the Semiorka. This group included six members of the Political Bureau, Zinoviev, Kamenev, Stalin, Bukharin, Voroshilov and Kalinin, and the new president of the central Control Commission, Kuibychev. The conspirators agreed not to polemicize among themselves. They had a secret code by which they corresponded. They extended their network to the whole of the administration, penetrated all its organs and created a sort of closed order with agents, discipline, means to spread their ideas and abundant resources deriving from the funds of the state, the party and the trade unions. Zinoviev and Kamenev revealed these facts to the Central Committee in July 1926.

Lenin's Testament is a centre-piece in this dossier. Lenin knew that a split was a serious and fast-approaching danger. He believed that it was closer and more likely than the acute phase of the social crisis. But this also meant that he thought there was time to take preventive measures before the acute phase arrived. This text is very important for our understanding of events. "Our party rests on two classes and this is why its instability is possible, and why its disintegration is inevitable if agreement cannot be established between these classes. In such a case there would be no possible way to prevent the split." Lenin wrote these lines on 25 December 1922. He could appreciate neither the breadth of the consequences of NEP nor the extent of the defeat of the European revolution. In spite of this, his prognostications on the basic issue were remarkably clairvoyant.

He knew that the line of division would pass between Trotsky and Stalin. "In my opinion, the relations between them constitute a good half of the danger of this avoidable split." However, he did not see the two protagonists as being equivalent. He did not demand they should both be deprived of authority. Of Stalin he said first of all: "Comrade Stalin, in becoming General Secretary, has concentrated immense power in his hands, and I am not convinced that he will always be capable of using it with much prudence." He added on 4 January 1923: "I propose that the comrades reflect on the best means of replacing Stalin in this post and nominating a man who is different to Stalin in every respect. . . ." He concluded· "This situation may appear like an insignificant game of bagatelle, but I think that in order to guard against a split, and from the point of view of what I have written above concerning the mutual relations between Stalin and Trotsky, it is no bagatelle, in so far as it could acquire central importance." We know that, shortly afterwards, Lenin was to break off all relations with Stalin. He narrowed down the *immediate* danger to the person of Stalin, who would have to be removed as a matter of urgency, and to his role. He had discovered the strategic value of the general secretariat. That is to say that he had no illusions as to the real state of the party (in 1922); as to the atrophy of its political life; and as to its functionarization which *alone* gave so much power to a technical organism which, two years earlier, was of no political importance. The wherewithal of the split was hence contained within the apparatus.

Lenin constantly asserted in his public declarations that in order to fight against bureaucratization it would be necessary to appeal to the workers in the factories and organize a control by workers, external to the party, over the administration. Now, in the course of the decisive months, when the danger of a split and the bureaucratic danger were combined, Lenin in his discussions in his notes, in his articles and finally in the Testament, advocated *defensive measures within the apparatus only*. These comprised the remodelling of the workers' and peasants' inspection; a special commission attached to the Central Committee; increasing the number of members of the Central Committee by "up to 50 or 100 people"; and above all the departure of Stalin. He no longer spoke of resorting to direct worker intervention. This is an important piece of evidence, in view of the lucidity of the witness.

It was in no way accidental. To return to the request already mentioned, Trotsky was *implicitly* suggesting that if there were to be a purge in the state, it would have to begin in the party. Lenin noticed the implication: "so I say that it is necessary to combat Soviet bureaucratism, and you propose to include the Organization Bureau of the Central Committee?" Trotsky adds, "Vladimir Ilyich said to me then: 'Very well, I propose a bloc to you.' " Trotsky recounts a revealing detail: "Vladimir Ilyich told me that he proposed the creation of a commission of the Central Committee for the struggle against bureaucracy 'in general' *and that through this we should equally begin the attack on the Organization Bureau of the Central Committee*."

Lenin was a prisoner of the apparatus — an unwilling prisoner. The Russian proletariat had become politically distanced from the party. The peasantry was pressing harder. The equilibrium between the two classes was breaking down. But Lenin was also a prisoner voluntarily. An appeal to workers in the factories carried a high risk of precipitating the split. A split in the party which holds power poses the question of power. In the existing social relation of forces, the bourgoisie could slide into the breach. For these reasons, Lenin looked for ways out in the interior of the apparatus. And this was why he attached such great importance to the question of who controlled the general secretariat. We do not know how Lenin would have reacted later on. Once the form of the danger had become clear, he would perhaps have been capable of breaking publicly and appealing, against the degenerated party, to the workers in the factories, as he had threatened to do on the eve of the insurrection. In any case, he would have been firmly on the side of the proletariat. Without doubt, Zinoviev was the only other person to have understood, and very quickly, the strategic value of the secretariat. While Lenin concluded the necessity to eliminate Stalin, Zinoviev found it expedient to make an alliance with him. These are in no way tactical differences, but fundamental differences of policy. It is clear that the illness which eventually killed Lenin was a stroke of luck for the thermidoreans. Furthermore, I am convinced that Lenin's reasoning exercised a profound influence on Trotsky. First, because he agreed with the premises of this reasoning. Secondly, because the premonition of death gave these propositions and remarks, which were certainly hasty, but also scrupulously weighed, a sort of exceptional insistence. The fear of the split and its consequences, inherited from Lenin, was to paralyse Trotsky.

Hence the thermidoreans enjoyed an enormous strategic advantage: *their adversaries were obliged to do battle on the terrain which was least favourable to them, and could take no initiative which could directly jeopardize power.*

There is abundant information on Stalin's use of the Secretariat, on the efficacy of his tricks, his gross behaviour and his violence. The conjuncture in 1923 was highly favourable to the thermidoreans: they had yet to exploit it.

There is a remarkable constant in Stalin's actions. *He manoeuvred and shifted in every respect, except on the essential question of continuous reinforcement of the powers of the bureaucracy.* The political rights demanded by the social corps of the state coincided with the conditions for personal power on a sufficient number of points to merge into a single programme.

In 1925 Trotsky described Stalin as the most eminent mediocrity in the party. This was true, in the most profound fashion, from the point of view of the revolution. And this was not only the case because his aspirations to be a theoretician (revealed by Bukharin) did not rest on any real ability. It is also because he never really understood what the proletarian revolution was. But of all the thermidoreans he was the most eminent, the most capable, the most determined, and the most energetic. He was well served by his own serious defects. It was no accident that the bureaucracy quickly recognized him to be the leader capable of guaranteeing victory. His contempt for principle, his ignorance of theoretical preoccupations, his lack of scruples and his cruelty, his cunning perspicacity and his passion for power, which guided its analysis of events, allowed him to understand very early the value for his purposes of the aspiration to personal satisfaction and authority of the new controllers. These defects also gave him the means to decipher the latent force behind the social corps of the state. There was an astonishing conformity between this new class, with its awakening self-consciousness and this Old Bolshevik. This alliance, almost instinctive and clairvoyant in perceiving the interests of the state, was the linch-pin of the stalinist dictatorship. This connivance ended on the eve of the Second World War. Stalin was transformed into a major obstacle for the class which, until then, identified itself with him, although in terror of him. He appeared more and more to be the principal shackle on the necessary reorganization and expansion of state capitalism. His personal dictatorship became clearly incompatible with the stability of the régime, the growth of the productive forces and the security of its cadres. His death, the murder of Beria, and Khrushchev's report, proceeded from the same social logic, under the same historical constraints.

From 1922 to 1928 Stalin needed allies. This was because the disintegration of the party had created fiefs and because he had to reckon with them — the Leningrad apparatus was not under his control, but under Zinoviev's; and because he had to isolate Trotsky. He was forced to compromise. For a long time he had known all the leading cadres of the Bolshevik party intimately. He knew how to play on their hidden motives. The question of Lenin's succession offered him a unique opportunity to unite in a coalition the ambitions of all the others, by attacking the only person who appeared, to all those not in the leading circles and hence not candidates or supporters of candidates, the heir to Lenin.

The systematic, permanent offensive against the Left Opposition shows how the search for power and the defence of the social interests of the bureaucracy fused with each other in the most natural way. Stalin could not achieve the dictatorship without annihilating Trotsky. At the same time the bureaucracy felt its privilege and authority menaced by the left which was advocating large-scale dismissals and elected positions instead of nominations. Hence, it concentrated its forces in support of the one who most consistently and firmly attacked its enemies. In a general sense, for the thermidoreans and for the social corps of the state, Trotsky and the Left Opposition *represented the major permanent danger, a possible leadership for the proletariat.* The occasion for such a reversal could arise, either because the external situation deteriorated to the point where the war risk was obvious to all, or, on the contrary, if the conjuncture in Germany reversed to the extent that the workers went on the offensive again. In either case the credit of prestige could work effectively in Trotsky's favour. He was hence an enemy, with whom no reconciliation was possible; whose intellectual reputation had to be ruined, whose historical tradition, whose ascendancy conferred by his close co-operation with Lenin had to be destroyed; and whom it was finally necessary to isolate from his own friends and have physically placed at the bureaucracy's mercy. In consequence, Stalin could not tolerate the least reconciliation with Trotsky. When Kamenev and Zinoviev, disquieted by his growing power, wanted to recreate with Trotsky the pact that they had previously made with Stalin, he smashed them and took over the bastion of Leningrad. Because their final objective imposed it on them, the stalinists made simultaneous use of historical falsification, personal calumny, ideological offensives, the corruption of adversaries, and physical repression. These were the ingredients of the coup d'état. Because the uncertainties of the world situation created a permanent potential danger, it was vital for Stalin to gain control also over the apparatus of the International. The unity of his strategy, its internal coherence, and the permanence of his objectives were revealed with great clarity. His zigzags, which by this time had become perfectly obvious, were either tactical or related to questions which, however important they were, were secondary in relation to the social objectives of the bureaucracy and the central question of power.

Any revolution develops big internal tensions. Prolonged tensions sap the social forces which create the revolution and the individuals to carry it through. A moment of down-turn always occurs. This creates the basic premise for a Thermidor. We know what kind of role this exhaustion played in Russia. Its effects had been aggravated and amplified by NEP. However, *the determining political factor* was the defeat of the proletariat in Europe. Thermidor appeared to the majority of the Bolshevik cadres as a compromise imposed by history, a compromise which permitted them at one and the same time to conserve the benefits of power and to persuade themselves that they were still safeguarding the permanence of a revolutionary base. In other words, it was a satisfactory compromise. It was from this that the vital importance of the struggle against the theory of permanent revolution arose. What for a distant observer could appear as casuistry and abstruse quibbling was in fact the passionate heart of the conflict. A revolutionary who becomes a thermidorean after being schooled in marxism has to provide himself with a theoretical justification. It is as necessary as oxygen. This was the first and without doubt the essential function of the ideology of socialism in one country.

From the point of view of theory, the thesis of socialism in one country is devoid of any consistency. It is rather as if after Pasteur, the belief in the spontaneous generation of disease had been re-established as a dogma. An autarchic economy is impossible, and to the limited extent that it can exist, it can only be an enormous regression compared with capitalism. The historic virtue of capitalism has been to bring the productive forces up to the level of an organic world unity. National frontiers were challenged as much as the private character of the means of production. Socialist relations are based on a world technology and on its development as such. This is the ABC of marxism. But it matters little that the thesis of socialism in one country was an aberrant one. It was not a tool of knowledge. The reason for its existence was social. Its usefulness was that of persuasion. Its method was scholastic. It legitimized Thermidor. It legitimated the national state and its servitors. It provided an ideological wrapping to the social interests of the bureaucracy, in the national framework and in the world arena. In effect, the thermidoreans carried out a fundamental modification of the strategy of the International. They turned it into an apparatus of the Russian national state. They did it in the most constrictive fashion possible: by permanently subjugating it to the economic political and diplomatic objectives of national soviet power. The thesis of socialism in one country had the task of turning this servitude into a revolutionary obligation. On this question, I have cited Bukharin's clear definition. The appearance of this thesis, as a body of doctrine, in 1925, established that the self-consciousness of the state held a powerful strategic position. It possessed an ideology. It had a more homogeneous general staff, a general political staff which was better suited to its task, than in 1923. It was ready to take a general offensive.

The decisive blows were delivered in 1927. They had been prepared for a long time, and in minute detail. The decision to eliminate Trotsky had been taken in 1922. It was carried out five years later. It was the end result of a vast, systematic operation, which replaced all the cadres of the party and the International; which subordinated the whole administration to the general secretariat; which fundamentally altered the historic tradition of Bolshevism, through the falsification of texts and biographies; which combined the action of the Cheka and shock troops at the base of the party, in its periphery and in the factories. The opposition which had been mercilessly hunted down was crushed during the winter of 1927.

The split-up of the Troika in 1925 provided Stalin with the occasion to get rid of the fiefs which he had up to this point not directly controlled, and to eliminate or domesticate the Zinovievists in the International. The 15th Congress, in December 1927, reveals, in the most flagrant fashion, that the political apparatus was entirely subordinate to him. The bureaucracy had conquered its political rights on the back of the proletariat. It placed Stalin's personal dictatorship in power.

The procedures followed in this last year of direct confrontation with the revolutionary intelligentsia were nevertheless slow and circumspect. The decisions had been taken: but they were slow to be pronounced and put into effect This fact is highly significant. Although Dzherzhinsky had turned the Cheka into a docile instrument of the dictatorship the army remained restive. There is no other explanation for the last-minute care which Stalin took. He purged the military inspection before finally taking on Trotsky. The most eminent leaders and military councillors, all profoundly influenced by the thought and action of Trotsky, were relieved of their posts. Smilga was sent to oriental Siberia, to Khabaravsk. Muralov, Mrachkovsky, Lachevich and Bakayev were all removed, expelled and deported. The army remained the weakest link of the dictatorship.

In June, the praesidium of the Central Control Commission examined, without coming to any conclusion, the demand for expulsion laid against Trotsky and Zinoviev. From the end of July to the begining of August, the plenary assembly of the Central Committee and of the Control Commission took up the question again without reaching a decision. In October, Trotsky and Zinoviev were expelled from the Central Committee. In November, they were expelled from the party. On the 16th of the same month, Yoffe killed himself in Moscow after writing a letter to Trotsky — an act of great significance. On 2 December, at the 15th Congress, expulsion orders were announced against every Trotskyist, Zinovievist, and member of Sapronov's group. Thousands of arrests and deportations followed. In January 1938, Trotsky was exiled to Alma-Ata in central Asia. A new historical conjuncture had begun. Blumkin was shot in 1929.

9 The defeat of the Left Opposition, 1928–30

STALIN HAD WON the civil war in the party during the winter of 1927 to 1928. The success of the coup d'état provides us, in a way publicly, with the immediate social, political and military data of Thermidor. Two questions, however, had not been resolved: the succession of the régime, and the historical breadth of the political defeat of the Left Opposition.

The social suppression of the proletariat and its political and economic expropriation completely deprived it of all the attributes of a ruling class. It also lost its position as the proprietor of the state and the means of production, just as immediately after October 1917 the big bourgeoisie and the landed property owners were expropriated. This lapse into the role of pure subjugated labour-power was in no way a consequence of the defeat of the Left Opposition. The reverse is true. The oppositionists could be annihilated because the proletarian infrastructure of the state was already destroyed. Their complete and irreversible rout only signified that the working class had lost the last ally on which it could count within the state apparatus: the left wing of the leading intelligentsia.

The fact that the workers' state had ceased to exist did not determine the class nature of its successor. It was not at all the newly-rising bourgeoisie which broke the neck of the dominant proletarian class. It was the state bureaucracy which arose out of the October revolution: the exclusive proprietors of the revolutionary institution, constituted as an autonomous social force in the process of production by the organic split within the proletariat. The extermination of the Left Opposition signified to the bureaucracy a decisive stage in the establishment of its sovereignty over the state and over the means of production: however, it was only a stage. Its grasp extended over everything which was nationalized — and no further. Peripheral industry, private commerce, whether legal or clandestine, and the immense majority of farms escaped it. Caught within the internal and global constraints of the market, the state sector progressed more slowly than private enterprise. Its financial dependence was growing. The bureaucracy had supplanted the proletariat in the sphere of the state — it had not mastered the dynamic of the national economy. In the social arena the dominant position of the bureaucracy was contested by a coalition of middle classes, pregnant with a new big bourgeoisie.

Hence, it appeared clearly that the class nature of the succession had not been settled and that it was to be settled in and through this confrontation. It was this question which was now at stake in the three years 1928, 1929 and 1930, and in the civil war which now broke out. The state bureaucracy, which had emerged as an autonomous force in the process of production, that is, had become a differentiated class (and which was hence already entirely different from the privileged caste which existed during war communism), could only establish itself as a ruling class through the appropriation of the whole economic process. This could not come about, because of the relative weakness of its economic base, other than through the military expropriation of the middle classes. And of course, this second civil war was being prepared by the eviction of their allies in the state apparatus: the right wing of the leading intelligentsia, the Bukharinist faction.

At the start of 1928, nothing could justify the assertion that the bureaucracy was going to succeed in its mutation into a ruling class. It was not working scientifically towards this goal. Its leaders remained attached to a policy of co-existence and co-operation with the kulak and the NEP-man. It was reluctantly that they engaged in warfare. Stalin kept his guns at the ready and at the same time sought, through proposing a vast programme of concessions to foreign capital, a long-term solution of peaceful compromise. This process was fundamentally blind. It came about as a series of reflex actions. Hence, in 1928, a basic objective ambiguity existed. The real danger of a return in force of the bourgeoisie masked the historic role of the bureaucracy to the protagonists. So much the more because Lenin and Trotsky had always interpreted Thermidor as the triumph of bourgeois reaction. For the Left Opposition, the Bukharinist right represented the main enemy: the trojan horse of the kulak and the NEP-man in the party. The main accusation that they made against Stalin was that through his support for Bukharin and still more through his systematic and ferocious repression against the revolutionary marxist wing of the party he was facilitating the return of the bourgeoisie to power. It was in this sense, but in this sense only, that they regarded him as thermidorean number one. They were persuaded that, in so doing, Stalin was working towards his own downfall, and that the bureaucracy would not and could not survive Thermidor. This confusion on the social nature of the forces in play transformed their political defeat into a catastrophe of historic breadth. It led first of all to the disintegration of the Left Opposition. From the moment that events failed to confirm their prognosis, the oppositionists were completely disarmed. Their theoretical analysis floundered. Their political programme was emasculated. Even more than persecution, the brutality of the prison guards and the conditions in the camps, it was this impasse which numbed theoretical thought, nullified the political demands and which explains the retractions and abjurations. It was this same inability to grasp the social originality of the phenomenon which was taking place under his eyes, and of which they were the victims, which entirely ruined their historical future on the world arena. It was the objective limit to Trotsky's greatness.

This provides us with a vivid illustration of the absolutely unique central role of theoretical thought in revolutionary action. It shows also the extraordinary difficulties we meet in analysing an event once we get to the heart of it. With hindsight (which is not a matter of the number of years, but of the level which society has reached today), it has become clear that the initial lack of understanding of the technological conditions necessary for the establishment of a socialized production–process, accounts for the impasse in which marxist thought found itself then. It is because neither Lenin nor Trotsky understood the fundamental data of the world conjuncture of the first revolution (and, to repeat, they could not have done so), and they were thus blocked in their attempt to master the social nature and historic function of the bureaucracy. The bureaucracy was the fundamental expression of the social victory of October 1917 in a world conjuncture that did not allow capitalism to be superseded on the technological level.

Nothing illuminates this better than the question of state capitalism, which was crucial at the time. State capitalism was called into question by the kulak and the NEP-man. The defence of state capitalism was, according to Lenin's teaching, a vital necessity for the revolution. Now, the bureaucracy genuinely defended the state capitalist monopoly. Politically decisive confusion about the state capitalist monopoly was revealed clearly.

In Lenin's view *revolutionary democracy* became the *essential* criterion which drew the line between capitalist monopoly and socialism. He explained this very clearly in September 1917, in *The Imminent Catastrophe and How to Deal with It*.

This text, of considerable interest (and, indeed, the whole pamphlet should be re-read) is unambiguous. For Lenin the state capitalist monopoly provided the technical instrument necessary for the passage to socialism: that is to say, to socialized control. He considered that the concentration of control and power was indispensable to a rational administration, that is to say a planned one. The chapter on the nationalization of the banks provides a concrete demonstration of this. It is no mere academic reference: this instrument must be placed under the control of the whole people. It is this control, revolutionary democracy, and fundamentally this alone, which provides the distinction between state capitalism and socialism. He repeats this as if hammering in a nail. *The state monopoly provides the technological foundation for a socialized production-process.* This is so true, so revealing and so illuminating for what follows, that each word must be carefully weighed in this affirmation: "the objective course of development is such that there is no way forward after the *monopolies* without progressing to socialism."

It is striking to note that Lenin carried out only the technical objectives of his programme. He had established the foundation of the economic monopoly of the state. He failed totally in his attempt to organize revolutionary democracy. Technical concentration plus withering away of the state equals socialism — in this equation the decisive term is a political one. Without revolutionary democracy (workers' self-management), the state monopoly necessarily remains a capitalist monopoly. But the withering away of the state is not a uniquely political question, in the sense that political measures are inoperative if the necessary technological support is not available. We are constantly forced to return to the fundamental impasse of the first revolution, which is the key to all the rest.

Lenin's teaching and practice played a major role in the formation of the new generation of Bolshevik middle cadre. He returned constantly to the theme of the economic monopoly of the state. He took on Larin as adviser, because he had studied at close quarters the forms of state capitalism which existed in the German war economy. And it was no accident that his book *State Capitalism During the War in Germany* was published in Moscow in 1928. In 1921, in "The tax in kind", Lenin explicitly reaffirmed (and quoted numerous passages of) his thesis of 1917. He denounced the offensive of the urban and rural middle classes against state capitalism and socialism and insisted that it was necessary to defend them against the encroachments of the small producers. In working towards concentration and centralization in the technological context of that epoch, Lenin was preparing the way to a bureaucratic society, even though he was consciously struggling against it.

Lenin's teaching on the technical importance of state capitalism had such a hold on the managerial intelligentsia because its best representatives were inclined, as Lenin himself observed, to overestimate the administrative side of things, and because the situation lent itself to this: leaving all theory aside, to speak totally empirically, there was no other way out of the prevailing chaos. And so the pre-eminent role of the economic monopoly of the state was part of the common convictions of the Bukharinists, the Trotskyists, and the Stalinists. Their disagreements touched only on the methods and procedures used, and there again on the question of techniques. Preobrazhensky's study, "The New Economics", is very revealing in this respect. It is remarkable that the criteria which, according to him, define the socialist character of the public sector are essentially *technical* and converge in the regulation and rationalization which depend on systematic state intervention. Mechanisms of control and orientation become the determining factors of the passage to socialism. It is a manager who is writing. The context of revolutionary democracy, decisive for Lenin, has become blurred: notwithstanding that Preobrazhensky was a member of the left intelligentsia. The differences with the Bukharinists and the Stalinists emerged on methods of accumulation, that is to say, above all about methods of levying taxes on agriculture. Yet on the social question — which, however, is primordial — there was a common principle. Preobrazhensky took up in his turn Stalin's sophism: "the working class cannot exploit itself". Bukharin wrote in the *ABC of Communism:* "The proletarian state, an organization of the proletariat, cannot exploit the working class: one cannot exploit oneself." Under the domination of state capitalism, the bourgeoisie loses nothing through the fact that certain private enterprises cease to exist in an isolated way, since in being associated together they exploit the public *jointly* as well as they did before individually. In the same way, through proletarian nationalization, the workers lose nothing from the fact that they are not the individual owners of their factories, since the factories belong to the working class which is called the Soviet state."

I have shown how through such concessions, the political and social expropriation of the proletariat came about. The powerful intellectual traditions which conspired in the political defeat of the Left Opposition are now visible. It is all the more remarkable, and instructively so, that in spite of the weight of this tradition and the violence of the repression, the theoretical analysis carried out during the years 1928-30 did in fact elaborate a new and more exact interpretation of events.

Political life was now confined to the isolators, to faraway enforced residences and to the prison camps. It was intense. Theses circulated along strange and subterranean channels. Discussions were passionate. Physical and moral extermination was to put an end to this. The camps, which were to undergo such a major extension during the 1930s, and in fact change their very nature, were silenced. This silence was not to be broken until after the Second World War.

The effort of conceptualization which was pursued under such tragic conditions from 1928 to 1930 was the last expression of marxist thought in the Soviet Union. The intellectual rebirth in Russia brought on by the disasters of the Second World War was oriented according to other criteria, in a fundamentally different reference frame, and even then remained at an elementary political and social level. Thus the barbarous regression of stalinism took the form of a historical rupture. The living continuity of marxist thought was not simply disturbed but broken. There was no passing on of political thought, even through a slow, clandestine process. Documents remained inaccessible and the stalinist terror had destroyed the men and their teaching. The works of the post-stalinist generation, which demonstrates its non-acceptance of bureaucratic society so clearly, also reveal this hiatus in a striking fashion. The discontinuity appeared so profound at this point that we have to consider it as a major trait in the post-war period in Russia. It is not possible to grasp the dimension of the phenomenon, nor grasp the nature of new oppositions, and even less to make a full evaluation of their capacity, without making reference in some way to the methods, criteria and quality of conceptual work operating in the very period when present-day society was being constituted. It is because these three years show us how Russian marxists initiated the study of this emerging society — which was organically different to their predictions — that comparison with the present-day opposition, the product of this society, is instructive. Furthermore the difficulties on which this effort of conceptualization stumbled throw light on the intellectual shackles which amplified, in the domain of theoretical interpretation and hence of strategic elaboration, the political and social defeat which the Left Opposition suffered. This amplification had such enormous and lasting consequences in the international arena that its effects are still with us today.

To appreciate the value and comprehend the limits of the attempt at understanding which was made at that time, we must certainly take into account the immediate situation. The speed at which events were building up gave no time for reflection. On the part of the leading group, between the expulsions of December 1927 and the military decisions of 1929 hesitations, zigzags and tactical turns multiplied, and masked the basic line of force all the more because their successive approaches were in effect blind and followed each other as uncoordinated reflex actions.

Confusion, internal contradictions and splits in the ruling coalition, maintained the illusion that nothing that had yet happened was irreversible. The role of Stalin's intervention at the social chessboard was still ambiguous because of uncertainty about the fate of Bukharin and his faction, the social danger which he represented due to the undeniable reinforcement of the offensive of the middle classes, and the possibility — correctly regarded as serious — of the political victory of the neo-bourgeoisie. This ambiguity was all the harder to resolve because the most influential marxist theoreticians had never envisaged the mutation of the state bureaucracy into a social class and because their conceptual apparatus did not prepare them to identify the appearance of such a phenomenon in real life (that is, to discern it among a rapid and apparently incoherent succession of daily events). These already considerable difficulties were aggravated by the scale of the repression. The analyses were therefore carried out on the spot, by militants caught up in the conflict, subjected to extraordinary social, moral, political, and physical pressures. Furthermore the opposition was profoundly heterogeneous. Splits appeared, which were due at one and the same time, but in an inextricable way, to circumstances and to fundamental differences — and hence to strategic differences. Zinoviev and Kamenev had taken part in Stalin's coup d'état. They prepared it against Trotsky before seeking to mount it against Stalin. Kamenev recognized this clearly when, replying to those who reproached Zinoviev and himself with having broken with their allies on the left, he remarked: "We need Trotsky to govern; but if we need to get back into the party, he is a dead weight." It is undeniable that the men behind the coup d'état had neither the same conceptions nor the same perspectives as the leading nucleus of the Left Opposition. The struggle was hence conducted of necessity on all fronts at once. The high political value of the marxist intelligentsia is confirmed by the fact that in such a conjuncture the effort of conceptualization was pursued and still led to positive results. It is still more striking that the stalinist and nazi eras provoked a generalized and lasting political illiteracy.

Only a limited amount of material, unfortunately, has come to us from this period of rapid change: the documents which clandestine oppositionists succeeded in smuggling out of Russia. It is clear that a large number of texts were destroyed or are still locked in police archives. When these archives become accessible (and one day they will) theoretical and historical teaching will benefit greatly from it. Up until now the important collections which exist in the United States and Europe are far from having been entirely and systematically utilized.

I will only cite two texts, both from the pen of Christian Rakovsky. The first is a letter which he sent in 1928 to Valentinov, an oppositionist Old Bolshevik deported with him. The second is a declaration which he issued in April 1930, and which was signed with Muralov, Kossior and Kasparova, which was addressed to the

Central Committee, to the Central Control Commission "and to all members of the party".

These texts are good examples of this confrontation of ideas at the heart of the social violence. They permit us a clear grasp of the processes through which the effort of conceptualization passed. Given the fact that their author was one of the most eminent leaders of the Left Opposition, they also illuminate in great depth the theoretical background to the political and social defeat of trotskyism.

In his letter to Valentinov — written in 1928 — Rakovsky attempted to decipher what I shall call the molecular process of disintegration of the proletariat as ruling class. The facts which he quotes had been known already for many years. They were occurring on a growing scale, however, and so could no longer be ignored. Rakovsky's originality was to submit their analysis to functional criteria, which from the methodological point of view was essential. He takes as a working hypothesis the assumption that the proletariat's function as ruling class constitutes the decisive factor in its social mutations and hence in the political crisis. To give himself a broader perspective he refers, in common with the whole Russian marxist school of the period, to the French revolution. Finally, he respects the terms of experience and refuses to resort to empty syllogisms, even those of the left.

"Up until now", he writes, "we knew what could happen to the proletariat, what could be the oscillations in its moral condition, when it was an oppressed and exploited class: but it is only now that we can evaluate on the basis of facts, the changes in its moral state when it takes *management* in hand. This political position (that of being a ruling class) is not without danger; on the contrary the dangers are very great." He makes it clear that "it is a question of inherent difficulties for any new ruling class, which are a consequence of the seizure and exercise of power itself, of the capacity or inability to make use of it". He takes as his fundamental starting-point that "When a class takes power, one part of it becomes the agent of this power. Thus the bureaucracy arises." Hence, the bureaucracy is not an accident. It is a functional consequence of events. This division of labour is not purely technical: it assumes the character of a social diversification. This is why, in opposition to Preobrazhensky who maintained that the crying inequalities of Soviet society "in no way resulted from the monopoly of a small fraction of the proletariat over the instruments of production", he stressed on the contrary the social significance of this phenomenon: "Certain of the functions which are otherwise fulfilled by the whole party, or by the whole class, have now become attributes of power, that is, of only a certain number of persons within this party and within this class." In order to clarify the nature of this dispossession, he recalls how the Third Estate, which by 1792 had acquired "the legal possibility of participation in the administration of the country", saw itself eliminated from the government through the passage of formal and effective authority, "into the hands of a narrower and narrower group of citizens". This leads him to reject Bukharin's sophism that "the working class cannot exploit itself". He says that the difference between "the social position of a communist who has at his disposal a car, a good apartment and regular holidays, and receives the maximum salary authorized by the party" and that of a communist "working in the coalmines and receiving a salary of 50 to 60 roubles a month", does not just shock proletarian morality, but constitutes a major social and political factor. His direct, intimate experience of ruling circles enables him to appreciate the depth of the split brought about by functional differentiation. "The psychology of those who are charged with diverse tasks of management in the administration and the economy of the state has changed to such a point that not only objectively but also subjectively, not only materially but also morally, they have ceased to be part of this same working class."

As a result, the latent heterogeneity of the working class explodes under the pressure of new functions, so that its organic unity can no longer be the result of anything but *political decisions*. From this, political struggles take on a new dimension. "The unity and cohesion which up till now have been the natural consequence of the revolutionary class struggle cannot now be conserved except through an entire system of measures whose aim is to preserve the equilibrium between different groups of this class and this party, and to subordinate these groups to a fundamental goal." Now it was precisely inside the party that there also appeared "tie-ups between different social layers". He concludes: "Its function has modified the organism itself." This is the culminating point of the letter to Valentinov. The second text — the declaration of 1930 — shows clear progress in this effort of conceptualization. After stressing the molecular processes of dissociation and rupture, Rakovsky attempts a global, dynamic interpretation of the historical conjuncture, which he defines as the matrix of a social ruling class and an original organic structure:

> In front of our eyes *there has formed* and is forming a large *class of rulers* which possesses growing internal subdivisions, which multiplies itself through co-optation, through direct and indirect nomination (bureaucratic advancement, and a fictitious electoral system). As a base of support of this new class we find also a new kind of private property —

the possession of state power. The bureaucracy "possesses the state as private property", wrote Marx *(Critique of Hegel's Philosophy of Right)*. This proposition nuances the formula: *"A proletarian state with bureaucratic deformations"*, as Lenin defined the political form of our state. *We are developing a bureaucratic state with communist proletarian survivals.* [Rakovsky's emphasis.]

Rakovsky was expelled from the party, relieved of his state functions, and exiled. The whole Left Opposition, (that is, the ruling fraction of the marxist intelligentsia) was eliminated from the state administration and hounded out of the party. It was hunted, exiled, and finally joined the cadres of the old workers' oppositions in the isolators. The Bukharinist right was annihilated and the worker dispossessed of his theoretical and practical rights of control, confined in his factory and compelled to play a role, purely as a member of the work-force. The war against the middle classes which in 1928 was merely threatening, was openly declared. It was conducted with unparalleled violence, by the military forces of the state *alone*, that is, without any direct participation by a disarmed working class. The people were not armed. On the contrary, it was the social passivity of the proletariat which gave the state bureaucracy its freedom of action. The military methods of the middle classes in the countryside and in the towns never went beyond random murder, the destruction of property and the scorched-earth tactic. Their principal weapon was economic disaster and famine. In these conditions, the probability of a victory for state terror was increased greatly. Such were the salient facts of the new conjuncture, for which Trotsky's habitual analysis, until now generally accepted, cannot completely account. Trotsky's basic strategy assumed an elevated capacity for autonomous intervention by the working class which events were to remove, and an implantation of the Left Opposition in the factories from which in principle it expected to exert its influence. This was brutally exposed as a myth. The tactic which Trotsky elaborated was based on a definition of tendencies centred on the crucial notion of *centrism* (Stalin's faction equals centrism. The opening of the civil war reduced this to shreds). Furthermore the party had ceased to be an accessible terrain of struggle. Massive expulsions and exile had put a definitive end to this kind of action. Rakovsky hence attempted to formulate a new interpretation, consistent with the facts.

It is sufficient to look at the 1930 formulation (a first approximation, but the only one to have come down to us) for the inadequacies and errors in the progress made to reveal themselves. The "proletarian communist survivals" in the state no longer corresponded to anything real. At least, unless the isolation were to be considered as a political structure of this state. On the contrary, the notion of "a large class of rulers" based on "a new kind of private property: the possession of state power", in spite of its ambiguity, provides a powerful interpretation of the facts and, because it fits with experience, an operatively useful concept which would have permitted, both theoretically and practically (politically) a way out of the open impasse resulting from the absence of a coherent conceptual system in line with reality.

Rakovsky had at his disposal a sure method for confirming the validity of his thesis and for deducing an exact prediction from his thesis. And that is what he did. He predicted that forced collectivization and the launching of the five-year industrial plan would consolidate and reinforce the ruling bureaucratic class. "The temptation," he writes, "presented to the bureaucracy by complete collectivization and an accelerated rhythm of industrialization, is not hard to guess at. It would enlarge the army of bureaucrats, augment its share of national revenue and reinforce its power over the masses."

This was a remarkable prognosis which was completely vindicated and which, in fact, provided the concept of bureaucratic ruling class with its first experimental confirmation. We can see the accuracy of its predictions because we are familiar with events as they finally turned out. In 1930, however, it was nothing but a contestable and controversial hypothesis.

This thesis and prediction run completely counter to the ideas which were accepted up to this point. It is interesting to note that from 1929, Rakovsky distinguished himself from Trotsky on the interpretation of Stalin's industrial turn. Almost all the oppositionists considered the effective struggle against the kulak and the inauguration of the five-year plan as a left turn of the stalinist faction, a turn which confirmed the centrist content of its politics. To this judgement, "correct in principle", Rakovsky made major corrections in complete opposition to the tactical concept of centrism. He underlined the fact that these measures, "under bureaucratic direction", that is to say when the class is replaced by officials who transform themselves into an isolated ruling class, lead *not to development but to the failure of socialist construction.*" This is in relation to the analysis put forward in the letter to Valentinov. In 1930 he substituted the notion of class for the notion of caste, and as a consequence gave a new social dimension to his prognosis. It was not any more a question of a failure of socialism which would bring about a return to the régime of capitalist monopolies, but of the consolidation of a class society with a new structure.

Trotsky, starting from the concept that the bureaucracy comprised a differentiation which was at once functional and political, but located within the proletariat and historically dependent on it, had predicted in *The New Course* that "notable economic progress", that a "powerful impulse given to industrial life", would create the fundamental conditions for the liquidation of the bureaucracy; then in 1930, in *Towards Capitalism or Towards Socialism*, he put forward the thesis that "The crisis cannot be resolved except through a rediscovery of the revolution on a more elevated basis, or through a restoration of bourgeois society." The value of a theoretical concept in social science is established, as in all other sciences, by its power of elucidation confirmed by experience. Experience did not confirm either of Trotsky's predictions. It is necessary to underline the fact that the concept which permitted Rakovsky to formulate an exact prediction was not the general definition of a class "of rulers", but the precise notion that this class held the state as private property. On condition, however, that it gave this private possession its real content: private appropriation of the means of production via the state's intermediary role in the production-process.

The definition of a class "of rulers", while it correctly interprets the obvious fact that the corps of the state was constituted as a class, leads nevertheless to confusion. Trotksy introduced a fundamental distinction between a political class and a social class. He recognized in 1930 that "the bureaucracy had reconstituted numerous characteristics of the ruling class", but he denied it any autonomous roots in the production-process. Rakovsky hence differentiates himself fundamentally from this position by including the notion of a new form of ownership. Now it is precisely because Trotsky reckoned that ownership of the means of production remained collective appropriation by the proletariat (and that the parasitic bureaucracy was no more than a sitting tenant) that he concluded that the growth of productive forces must inevitably lead to a liquidation of bureaucratic parasitism and to confirmation of the proletarian revolution, "at a higher level." If experience refuted this prognosis, it is obvious that the validity of his premises is questionable. If historical development establishes that forced collectivization and industrialization provoked a social growth of the bureaucracy, an enlargement of its itervention in the economy and an enormous extension of its political and military powers, then experience confirms fully that the bureaucracy effectively and genuinely possessed the means of production (and not at all through usurpation, as an agent of a proletarian master). It confirms also that it intervened in the social process as an autonomous force and not as a technical and abusive instrument of the working class and that it was hence, in effect, constituted as a class and as a ruling class.

This confirmation relates to the essential question, the operative validity of the concept — it still does not resolve the fundamental questions which are raised by the emergence and functioning of the state bureaucracy as a class. In the same way, when the principle of evolution had been formulated and confirmed, it did not elucidate those problems which are now resolved through molecular genetics, but it created the ability to understand and the operative power which permitted identification of the genetic code and its mechanisms.

It is clear that this first version of Rakovsky's thesis leaves too many crucial questions unexplored and not even posed. It was more of a coherent reading of events than a search for their causes. Already, with the letter to Valentinov, Rakovsky — even if he saw that control of the state and economy had become the exclusive affair of a narrow group — did not ask himself why workers' democracy (an essential component of the Bolshevik programme) could not be instituted. In the same way he sees that in 1930 the bureaucracy had constituted itself into a ruling class and that from this it had drawn its capacity for the private ownership of the state: but he did not pose the central problem of the dynamic of classes which is entailed in a mutation on such a grand scale, nor how the proletarian October revolution had been able to generate such a manifestly foreign progeny. In other words, he did not question accepted ideas about the world historical conjuncture. So that though he saw the facts, the facts remained an apparent aberration. In the same way he saw that the bureaucracy was laying hold of a growing portion of the national income, and did not explore the structures through which they were doing it or the mechanisms which governed the seizure of surplus value. In other words, he did not explain the new processes of exploitation of the work-force. Rakovsky disappeared into the camps and we know no more of the eventual line of development of his research. The essential point is that he was a witness of his time and from what he witnessed he drew logical and *verified* predictions. Trotsky, because the new mechanisms of exploitation of the work-force were not elucidated, obstinately refused to recognize the lesson of experience, the duly confirmed facts. In the same way, capitalism existed well before Marx had formulated a theory of it.

A theory is not elaborated for the purpose of intellectual satisfaction. A theory in line with the facts must produce an effective strategy. In 1930, Rakovsky did not draw a general political perspective from his coherent concept of a state ruling class and from his precise and verified prediction. I do not use the term "programme", which necessitates a more extended collective elaboration, but refer to lines of advance which would structure a new orientation. He simply took up the standard slogans of the Left Opposition, which his own analysis of the historical conjuncture totally refuted. The contradiction is so flagrant that it has the value of a test case.

The major political fact at the beginning of the 1930s was the political split in the party. Rakovsky interpreted it in its real social context as a class antagonism. The process of dissociation and organic splitting of the working class was consummated. The party had become the organ of administration and combat of a new aggressive ruling class, the state bureaucracy. The social split hence appeared as the salient objective fact in the situation, and in consequence heralded a fundamental change in the balance of forces, ushering in at this level a new and lasting period. It is furthermore obvious that such a reversal could not fail to radically alter the balance of class forces in the international arena, helped by substantial transformations in the structure of the world proletariat. It is hence necessary to translate the objective fact of the split *into political terms*.

The split which Lenin had foreseen came about. The dynamic of class struggle amplified it into a social discontinuity. The first crucial political term of this discontinuity was the definitive liquidation of the workers' state. The second political term of equal importance was the social nature of the succession. The real heir — no longer the presumptive one — was not the bourgeoisie but the social corps of the state, elevated to the level of a class. The third political term corresponds to the process which it went through. The mutation into a class did not result from a deliberate (conscious) plan but from a blind interaction of forces (and hence a process which, beyond strictly national circumstances, was objectively conditioned by the developmental level of world society. These three *political* facts necessitated a radical revision of all strategic, tactical and programmatic data. Rakovsky and his co-signatories addressed the declaration of April 1930 to the Central Committee, to the Central Control Commission, and to all members of the party — that is to say, not only the fraction which had been expelled and exiled to Siberia, but to those leading organs which, in their own words, assumed the social interests of *the class enemy*. What did they demand from the leaders of this "large class of rulers"? The restoration of the prerogatives of the party congress and the re-establishment of democracy in the party through free elections. In short, they took up the rehashed slogan of the Left Opposition. Such a flagrant contradiction between conceptual analysis and political demands must be considered as one of the powerful factors which led to the rapid disintegration of the left intelligentsia.

The partisans of the coup d'état — Zinoviev, Kamenev and their friends — had a cynical and more accurate view. The surprising inconsistency of such experienced militants as Rakovsky, Muralov, Kossior and Kasparova has its roots in contingency, to be sure, but also in political antecedents, which were the more essential factor.

From the point of view of contingency their passionate, political attachment to the past of Bolshevism, the long period spent in the same milieu (they had always been the intelligentsia of the party), and the attraction exercised by the intellectual prestige and revolutionary tradition incarnated in Trotsky certainly appeared as a shackle and acted as a brake. The affective ambiance of the revolutionary entourage also intervened strongly. When the representatives of another colony of exiles objected with some pertinence that "if the party, the principal instrument of the revolution, is liquidated, if it is an opportunist party, how in this case can it be that the state remains a proletarian state, and how can we propose that it undertake reformist tasks?", they were throwing light on an obstacle which was not purely intellectual but much more emotional. It is easy to resist the class enemy. It is far harder to identify in one's erstwhile companion a social enemy, even if his police are beating you up. It is less painful to see in these confrontations a fratricidal struggle. It is easier to speak of reform than to admit that the revolution is dead and that everything must begin again. This unhappy subjectivity plays an undeniable role in this period of the great turning-point. However, the political question remains essential. Rakovsky concludes his April declaration with this clear capitulation: "We do not propose any new programme to the party, we are struggling only for the re-establishment of the old programme confirmed during the hard struggles and glorious victories, and of the tactical line of the Bolshevik communist party."

Thus, to respond to the demands of a situation entirely new in its basic outlines, Rakovsky's group (the most clairvoyant and the most convinced of the originality of the historical conjuncture), could think of nothing better than a return to the initial Leninist programme. It can be seen how an intelligent reading of events, even when it gives rise to well-founded predictions, is not sufficient to provide conceptual interpretation with the necessary rigour; and that the absence of a theory of the causal dynamic of the new society paralysed attempts at strategic elaboration. More fully, from the point of view of history, it was an indication of the weakening of a political formation whose creative role had been considerable.

"We do not propose any new programme to the party" provides a very correct definition of the attitude which the whole of the Left Opposition took during the early 1930s, which above all considers still valid the classical conception of the workers' state with powerful bureaucratic deformations. It was the basis of its rapid disintegration.

For this left intelligentsia, the decisive factor was the common conviction that the state from which it had been excluded remained, for all its blemishes, the only lever of the revolution. If Stalin (like Bonaparte) was continuing the work of the revolution — with barbarous methods bringing great perils in their train — was it not better finally to submit to him than to languish in the isolators since the balance of forces did not permit a change in leadership? For this aristocracy of managers, above all sensitive to the administrative side of things, was the basis of the opposition platform not the programme of industrialization and planning? So shouldn't an agreement be possible with Stalin after his break with the Bukharinists? Did he not defend the state monopoly in his war against the kulaks, doubtless by barbarous methods involving enormous cost, but in the last analysis was this not a method of guaranteeing the heritage of October? As important as democracy in the party was, as disquieting as were the strategic errors committed in China and in Europe, would it not safeguard the revolution in a period of world retreat and internal reaction to ensure the solidity of its economic base, even if in the momentary abandonment of the struggle on other fronts?

Piatakov, confirming Lenin's judgement of him, Krestinsky and Antonov-Ovseenko had joined Stalin in 1928. Now Piatakov was certainly, after Trotsky, the one who enjoyed the widest popularity. As early as July 1929 Radek, Preobrazhensky, Smilga, Serebriakov and Drobnis had crossed the Rubicon, in the company of hundreds of more obscure militants, or in some cases better-known militants like I. Smirnov and Beloboradov. Rakovsky, Muralov, Sosnovski, Kossior and a few other small groupings formed the last square around Trotsky. It was to take long years of suffering, of intellectual and moral despair to defeat them. However, their refusal, in 1930, to pay allegiance to Stalin, was not articulated around any political programme. How then could they have escaped from their isolation?

The Russian Left Opposition incorporated the marxist intellectual élite. It had been anchored in the state by the October revolution. By its functions it had become managerial. The growing and then con-summated divorce between the state and the proletarian work-force had uprooted it from the factories. Excluded from the state, it no longer had its feet on solid ground. It had to carry out a conversion on an extremely broad scale without having at its disposal instru-ments of analysis, conceptual system, general perspective, or the programme of action, which might have furnished it with the theoretical justification and the practical means for political rearmament. This obstacle broke the majority of its cadres. Confined in exile and in the isolators they remained a highly qualified, unemployed professional cadre force. The Stalinist bureaucracy which was now dominant needed this technical qualification deprived of its political bite. It was hence possible to bargain, and this was achieved. Stalin bought and sold. Then, once the task was completed, he destroyed morally and exterminated physically.

These first capitulations were hence the immediate, tangible product of the absence of any political perspectives. The Left Opposition found itself historically isolated in an impasse. Trotsky's rejection of the theoretical propositions advanced by Rakovsky set the seal on the impasse. Political ambiguity facilitated the capitulations, but under conditions of terror, constant repression and police blackmail which were the counterpoint. Moral decomposition could already be felt in the shady and compromising affair in which Radek was involved, leading to the arrest and execution of Blumkin. Other capitulations were already appearing on the horizon, preceding, preparing, and accompanying the show-trials, and the solitude and putrefaction of the concentration camp.

The consequences on a world scale were to be immense. The destruction of the first revolution took on a planetary breadth. The proletariat — considered as a world class — was profoundly disturbed in its organic composition. The barbarous decomposition of capitalist society became the dominant factor of the historical conjuncture.

10 The world disintegration of the first revolution

AT THE beginning of the 1930s the first revolution, its internal resources exhausted, disintegrated completely. It was no longer a question of a retreat on the international arena, but of a social regression which, from Europe to China, decomposed the political forces of the proletariat right down to the foundations which had been slowly constructed during the nineteenth century. In the heart of Europe the German working class, politically defeated in 1923, was physically annihilated in 1933. Social democracy was as completely eliminated from the scene as the KPD. The trade unions were destroyed. The Austrian Schutzbunder were crushed. National and international institutions, founded over the course of a century of workers' struggles, were in ruins. The Chinese workers, politically strangled in 1925, ceased to be a social force of any importance after the Canton disaster. They vanished from the Asiatic arena: the Chinese communist party was eliminated from the towns, to such an extent that even in 1950 it had not regained its implantation in the working class. The violent proletarian counter-offensive of 1936, in France and Spain, floundered in defeat. The socialist and communist parties in France were isolated from the working class and so weakened that socialists there are still today without any real working-class base. The Trotkyists, who had begun their implantation in the factories, were relegated to the status of a sect. The military disaster in Spain totally destroyed the socialist, communist, POUMist and anarchist forces, and annihilated the trade unions. The breadth of this political loss of influence can also be measured by the historically significant fact that the European revolutionary proletariat definitively ceased to be the point of attraction, the initiator and the co-ordinator of the national and social struggles of Africa and in Asia. The consequences were extra-ordinary. Revolutionary strategy in the colonies and in the semi-colonial countries was completely upset. The urban middle classes and their intelligentsia took the place of the proletariat in Latin America and Africa. The peasantry became the main force in Asia. The convergence of these substitutions and this separation from Europe led to an actual split from the industrially advanced countries. This split was at the base of the military theories of the

141

Chinese and the Cubans. This planetary break-up, comparable to those volcanic belts which are in a permanent state of near-eruption, provoked one of the most explosive tensions of world society. In Europe, we will have to await the approach of the 1980s before the new basis of revolutionary growth appears — but in a fundamentally new historical context.

The recession of the world proletariat had a contradictory effect on capitalist society. The bourgeoisie was consolidated in its position as ruling class. But at the same time, the abortion of the revolution accelerated the decomposition of the productive forces. The proletarian revolution in Europe, even though incapable of promoting a socialist organization of the economy, could nevertheless have cleared the way for an enlargement of the field of operation of the forces of production and enabled a more advanced rationalization of their control, though the concentration of the means of production in the hands of the state and through inter-state associations. In other words, a common market and a relative integration of political economies, could without doubt have been possible. But this way out was no longer in question. The political consolidation of the bourgeoisie was taking place above a powder keg. Capitalism was entering the sharpest phase of its organic degeneration.

The 1930s permit us to grasp one of the most complex mechanisms of the historical process — how it is determined — while maintaining a wide margin of indetermination. I call this the co-existence of potentially divergent actions. The existing technological level completely inhibited the transcendence of the inherent contradictions in monopoly capitalism through the establishment of socialized production relations. But at the same time, existing technology created a productive capacity incompatible with the market's absorptive capacities. This was in no way a new feature: it is on the contrary a constant symptom of capitalist growth. So far the conjunctural crises resulting from it had found temporary, partial solutions in a more advanced international integration. For the first time, because of the level now attained, a more integrated organization of the world market implied rationalization, that is to say planning, which more than ever before calls into question national frontiers and the private ownership of the means of production, and hence the structure and function of the monopolies; and which directly confronts the collective interests of the national bourgeoisies as well as the existence of the market as a regulator. The stability of national bourgeoisies expresses at the same time the uneven development of society and the mode of formation of capital. This is the unique character of the impasse which opened with the First World

War and which became aggravated on the eve of the 1930s. Its determining mechanisms now appear clearly illuminated.

However, it does not follow that the organic degeneration of capitalist society was inevitable. The development of the social crisis brings with it a choice between the possible options, blind though the choice may be. Through this blind process of selection, factors of indeterminacy interfere in the historical course of events. We know that the proletarian revolution is possible. We know also that to consolidate its political and social power it has to concentrate the private ownership of the means of production in the hands of the state. This concentration creates the technical and political infra-structure which is indispensable to the planning of the national economy. This makes possible, through a more organic rationaliz-ation, the solution of a certain number of problems of growth. The success of the proletarian revolution in several industrial countries does not allow all national antagonisms to be overcome but it never-theless creates the social, political and technical conditions for a common market. Thus the role of consciousness in history is circumscribed at a given level of civilization. The conscious objective of the proletariat is altogether another matter. It pursues a temporarily utopian goal, socialization. Even though diverted by insurmountable constraints, the proletarian revolution can neverthe-less lead towards a relatively positive solution. Through the inter-mediary of state capitalism and the inter-state common market, it brings about a new and superior integration of the world market. Global regression is avoided. The terrain, once consolidated, lends itself to an expansion of the forces of production. Now this solution really existed, as a potential option, for several years. It could not have been imposed without conflicts, but it was a possibility.

The first abortive revolution in Europe and the defeat in Russia modified the social terms of the fundamental dilemma, without however suppressing it. To escape from organic degeneration, the creation of a more strongly integrated world market remained an absolute necessity. But the bourgeoisie remained the only available social force to bring it about. It could not pretend to this goal except by submitting to the most violent distortion. Capitalism had been constituted on a national basis and its expansion had been uneven, not only as regards its internal components, but in its territorial implantation. The bourgeoisie, the ruling class, was hence sub-servient to the national economy; the growth of national bourgeoisies was therefore uneven. Capitalism ceased to be a combination of national economies and developed as a world functional unity, through the extension of finance — capital and the advent of the monopolies. Imperialism was the political and social process of this mutation. Imperialism is not only the blind, ferocious exploitation of two-thirds of the planet, but also the sharpest phase of conflicts between national bourgeoisies. Hence the First World War. The new integration of the market implied a rationalization, and thus a certain degree of international planning, which assumed a social class sufficiently coherent on a world scale to promote the institutions and mode of production of this new integration. The bourgeoisie was historically, and in a certain sense genetically incapable of this transmutation. The only — theoretically — possible way out was for the most powerful bourgeoisie to take temporary advantage of its power to impose coercion on all other national bourgeoisies: to fix uneven real relations to its own profit. In other words, the only way out for this imperialism was to produce a super-imperialism. The solution would still only be partial and provisional, but could be sufficient to bring about a transitory regulation of the contradictions of the system. At the time Kautsky envisaged the possibility of this type of perspective. It is clear that such a modification in the disposition of states could not be obtained without an extremely violent world conflagration accompanied by massive destruction. The difficulty is so much the greater because the dislocation of the world market provokes a reflux of the forces of production into national frontiers: that is to say, a new aggravation of national antagonisms. This, in effect, is what came about. And this explains our present splintered society: a new hierarchy of states, the links of subordination and dependence between industrial bourgeoisies, the character — both rational and yet profoundly chaotic and contradictory — of the prodigious upsurge in the forces of production, and the unprecedented role of permanent military terror. In the end this explains the explosive historical charge and the high level of planetary tensions: the crucible of the scientific, technological mutation of our time.

The decade 1930 to 1940 was supremely determined by the blind and wildcat combination of the organic degeneration of capitalism and of exacerbated national antagonisms. Once this is made clear, the mechanisms at work can easily be elucidated.

The breakdown of the automatic regulating mechanisms of the market, and the total blockage of the first revolution, constituted the basic elements which through their interactions created the historic impasse of the 1930s. The disintegration of the world market turned into a regression of the whole of society. The curve of development was an involution.

Two very visible symptoms show that it was the mode of production of the system which had been affected. The retreat of the productive forces behind national frontiers extended into a falling-back on the state by the bourgeoisie. This was a generalized phenomenon: the New Deal in the United States, nationalization in France, statification of the economies of Germany, Japan and Italy, public control and nationalization in England. The intrusion of the state brought about a structural modification of monopoly capitalism through the introduction of a state monopoly. The state monopoly disrupted the financial and managerial framework of the production process, and as a consequence inhibited the re-restablishment of the mechanisms of the market in a pure and simple form.

The rapid appearance and extension of relations of administrative compulsion in the organization of labour became the major feature of the most affected national economies: particularly in the heart of Europe, Germany. From the moment that administrative compulsion became an integrated factor in the process of production it tended to fashion all social relations. Current usage gives this the name "totalitarian dictatorship".

"National" recession of the world economy was accomplished by an immense wastage of productive capacity. The brutal and generalized halt to technological innovation was accompanied by a return to technical and social forms of primitive exploitation, associated with a critical fall in the standard of life. The result was that the disintegration of the world market was expressed in the disintegration of society.

Permanent unemployment took on such proportions that it engendered a decomposition of the working class, as revealed by the continuous growth of a lumpenproletariat. Embroiled in bankruptcy, the urban and agricultural middle classes became proletarianized. Their proletarianization unleashed an immense emotional reaction, which became in its turn an objective factor in the situation. With no possibility of their re-employment in production, which was already laying off a growing proportion of skilled workers, they formed an unstable plebeian mass at the base of the bourgeois pyramid. Under their steadily increasing pressure the big bourgeoisie, organically weakened by the violent crisis demands of the economy, took refuge in the state, transferring its own debts to the public purse and ceding the initiative of management of political economy to the state. The state monopoly was born of this wild abandonment. It was an indication of its depth and its irreversible course: the instititional expression of the regression of the whole of society.

With the decomposition of the proletariat — a great part of it thrown out of the production-process — annihilating it, the middle classes — enraged, uprooted from their traditional foundations, searching in vain for a way out — became the most unstable, the most mobile and the most violent social force. Fascism was the ideological military and political expression of the social despair of the middle classes. Through a succession of military actions and compromises with the big bourgeoisie, the plebeians took hold of the political levers of state monopoly.

The only way the plebeian leadership of the state could halt the disintegration of society was to generalize compulsion and bring it into the heart of the production-process. Systematic and permanent repression created a mass of generally available ex-victims of repression, which became a large fraction of the operatives of the state in production. The disintegrated professional layers were transformed, in part, into a subservient administrative work-force. From the moment that prisoners were introduced into the process of production, they ceased to be an inert social mass and became an active force which brought about new administrative relations of production. The general social effect was a double one. The state, in effect, owned the prisoners; but this possession was effectively and juridically exercised through a specific apparatus — the repressive apparatus. In Germany, the SS became the real owner of the concentration-camp work-force, even if it only exercised this right of property via delegation. Having discretion over the disposition of a subservient work-force which was not numerically limited, the SS, whether through direct implantation of its factories, or through the location to its profit of its work-force to private trusts, became rooted in the production-process in an autonomous fashion. This gave the repressive apparatus a considerable independence and created the basis for privileged control over the state. At the same time, the repressive apparatus became, after the manner of things, the active agent of the extension of forced labour and hence of coercive relations in the production-process. So much so that within this decomposed society a new system of social relations emerged: the concentration-camp society. It can be seen that the extortions, tortures, and inhuman treatments which in the first instance, and justly so, horrified international opinion were from the historical point of view not the most important nor the most significant feature. The essential feature, on the contrary (and in truth the most horrifying), was that the concentration-camp society was without doubt a functional society; that is, a historically realizable human condition. My generation truly lived through the prolegomena of a particular kind of barbarism: the barbarism of disintegrated industrial society. In the global perspective which can be mapped out for the human species, this is in fact the greatest risk. As soon as I returned from the camps, I undertook to define the organizing principle and to decipher the mechanism of concentration-camp society. Since then, other works have shed notable light on the impact of the enslaved work-force on the national economy. It is still the case that the sociology of concentration–camp society has not been system-atically formulated or taught. The concentration-camp phenomenon is the most characteristic of the phase of organic degeneration of world capitalism. Among all others, it has the highest and most immediately historical significance. The use of compulsion reached limits which, at a certain time and under the conditions of an extended integration of the advanced areas of civilization, could have reduced and atrophied the creative capacities of the species. Social involution could perhaps to this extent have reacted on biological evolution itself. At least for a long historical period, the danger would not have been without some stability. It is obvious that repression would not have been capable of taking on a concentration-camp scale if the infrastructure of the world economy had not crumbled away. The concentration–camp phenomenon was the projection of a possible future into the present. It nevertheless reached such dimensions that it overthrew the cultural basis of society to the extent that, just as an earthquake causes long-buried terrain to emerge, intellectual life was sterilized and scientific progress halted by the resurgence of ancient myths, methods of conduct and primitive mentalities under the veil of official dogmas embodied in the political corps of the state. The co-existence in the same society of very different mental ages and the survival within an advanced culture of previously antagonistic stages of development, constituted the break-up of a civilization. Social regression brought matters to a breaking point.

The continuity of a culture is not in any way a question of genetics. Its transmission is functional, institutional, written and oral. It can be interrupted easily. Up until now the active agents of civilization have not been numerous. They represent a thin social tissue vulnerable to destruction. Concentration-camp society is the highest form of this process of destruction.

The present world-wide scientific expansion and the high level and global integration of fundamental research, together with the increase and extension of that human milieu engaged in intellectual activity and the transmission of science, and the very dynamic of our society, all still constitute guarantees which are offset, it is true, by the scale — as yet unattained — of possible future catastrophes which, if they occur, will be precisely described as universal.

When the crisis of monopoly capitalism entered its sharpest phase, it had attained its highest level of development. It is precisely because its growth posed, as a permanent reality, the problem of its next stage, because it could not progress without modifying its mode of production, that the vital organs of the system were called into question, and a rapid regression began: the pathological retreat to national terrain. But this negative course was only just beginning, even though it immediately assumed an explosive breadth and its rhythms of development started to accelerate. The capacity of the productive apparatus remained enormous. It was certainly out of proportion with the possibilty of absorption into a national market which was too narrow and which was still being squeezed by general social decomposition. The contradiction between this productive capacity and the critical absence of outlets became decisive in its turn. It determined the dynamic of the regression, its rhythm and its violence. It is at this level that the blockage of the proletarian revolution produced its most potent ill effects. It closed the door to any rational outcome, to any possibility of a planned regulation and an extension, even a relative one, of the market. In this way also, technological backwardness was transformed into historical impasse. Technological innovation is vital for a new mode of production. Now, any innovation necessarily augments productive capacity and immediately aggravates the fundamental contradiction between the productive apparatus and the market. Research hence comes up against a prohibition. It is sterilized at source. In these conditions, the system tended to seek a new equilibrium, not through progress, but through a massive destruction of parts of the productive stock of the planet. What was involved was an objective tendency, totally external to intervention by man and which, on the contrary, subjugated man. War became a necessity: of the same order as a chemical reaction, war was destructive. Because of the potential capacity of the system, it had to operate on a planetary scale in order to fulfil its role. The new war had to be worldwide in a much more real fashion than the conflict of 1914–18. At one go, in order to realize its objective of destruction, it had to mobilize means of destruction of equivalent scope. That is to say, it had to exploit to the full all productive potential. So much so that new conditions were created for a technological resurgence which was scientifically and technically possible because general regression had not yet taken on such an irreversible character that concentration–camp relations dominated other than in a temporarily limited and marginal structure. This is why concentration–camp society was still only the projection of a possible future into the present. This global enslavement was inherent in the historical conditions of the time. There was no deliberate action which could have modified this necessity in this context. The war, at this stage, was unavoidable.

The mechanisms which came into operation were completely determinate. At a given moment, all other possible options were thrust aside. From this point, men and their passions became the agents of forces of which they were no more masters. The chain reaction could not be stopped as long as the conditions which launched it continued to exist. On the contrary, it reacted on these conditions and modified them, thus opening the way to new eventualities which, in their turn, re-established the possibility of choice. In so far as the proletarian revolution had not been completely destroyed, conscious action still had great scope to intervene. Problems of direction, of organization and of strategy remained major ones. There was an ambiguity in the situation. Deliberate action could resolve it. With the irrevocable defeat, this indeterminacy ended. The process was irreversible, but only to the extent that in accomplishing its goal it had itself modified its own conditions of existence. It is, certainly, very difficult to fix in time this passage from one state to another. The crushing of the Hamburg insurrection in 1923 was certainly a turning-point, and started the decline. It is very probable that in 1936, when the proletariat had retaken the offensive in France and in Spain, possibilities for success still existed, although without doubt they were weak. It would be necessary, for a correct understanding, to take full account of the world consequences of the destruction of the workers' state in Russia. In any case, the Spanish Civil War, isolated by the retreat of the workers' movement in France, faced irrevocable defeat from the moment of its first setback.

Given the combination of factors which characterizes the impasse of the 1930s, the war was inescapable. However, the war as an economic, political and military process carries with it, as does any historical event, a degree of indeterminacy. Conscious action re-entered decision-making processes in all domains and at all levels.

The Second World War was the second imperialist war, but the first one to incorporate so many national and civil wars (class confrontation) at such a level. In contrast to what happened between 1914 and 1918, civil war did not arise from defeat, and military rebellion did not arise from a slow attrition of the front line. Civil war was this time consubstantial with imperialist war. It was one of its fundamental expressions. It was the most striking symptom of the depth and nature of the capitalist crisis. German capitalism led at the same time and indissolubly an imperialist war and a civil war. The Anschluss, the occupation of Czechoslovakia and the colonization of Poland brought about at one and the same time the subjugation and subordination of the productive capacities of these regions and the incorporation of their markets; and the destruction of their workers' parties, their trade unions and the institutions of bourgeois democracy. The first major German defeats in Russia were in no way due, in essence, to the chosen military strategy of the Russians, but to the conduct of the parallel civil war and its ferocity. The Nazis' strong grip on Europe subsisted on the transformation of the European wage-earning classes into a subjugated work-force. Each new conquest became an enlargement of the base of concentration-camp society. This became, in the end, the infrastructure of Europe. The explosion of Japanese capitalism set Asia ablaze. But while its imperialist expansion directly opposed it to powerful English, American, French and Dutch interests, it is also true that the brutal exploitation of resources and work-forces raised up against it national bourgeois and popular masses and brought about a con-siderable reinforcement of national war and a general extension of civil wars. The confrontation of the Germans, the Italians, the English and the French in Africa engendered and nourished, politically and militarily, active national resistance groups against undifferentiated imperialist implantation in these regions.

In the global theatre of its operations, imperialist war provoked an unprecedented calling into question of world capitalism, up to the rupture of one of its most fundamental institutions: the colonial infrastructure was destroyed. At the same time there was a violent redistribution of forces, effected on a planetary scale, which took no account of diplomatic and military alliances. Britain and France were eliminated from Asia, Great Britain was expelled from Latin America; the whole of Europe was squeezed back into a continent whose economic foundations had been weakened and disorganized. The national unity of Germany, the most powerful European industrial complex, was shattered. Japan was reduced to the islands. The imperialist war opened the way to super-imperialism.

Following the First World War, the United States already occupied a strategic position in the world capitalist system. This was clearly enough demonstrated by the devastating effect of the Wall Street crash on Europe. The genuine weakening of England and France through the dynamic of their productive forces was not transferred mechanically through the sphere of political power. The colonial empires masked the retreat and through their exploitation (their super-profits) constituted very effective reserves of strength. The superior capacity of German and Japanese capitalism mobilized serious and aggressive forces in the world market. Although in an advanced position, the United States was not then ready to impose their leadership either technically or politically. However the high profitability of productive apparatus of the USA, the solidity of its technical base, the continental scale of its internal market, the quality of its cadre force, and the connections it had already established between manufacture and research (although eccentric and weak) allowed it to hold out against the tidal wave which carried away financial superstructures, blockaded external outlets, bankrupted enterprises, ruined farmers, and put whole towns out of work. American society was traumatized: even today, the ghost of the great depression is not dead. Resort to the state came about, in the heart of this peril, as a measure for the public good. The exceptional quality of its technological resources, the existence of immense reserves of accumulated wealth, the value of the available cadre, were a sufficient basis for a state monopoly without introducing coercive administrative relations into the organization of labour. It is still the case, however, that state monopoly was implanted in the world nerve-centre of monopoly capitalism, bringing about a worldwide structural cleavage. But it is not likely that the United States could have resisted the profound effects of the disintegration of the world market for any great length of time if the forces of production had not found an outlet in the war.

On a world scale, the respite gained has proved to be decisive. The implantation of administrative constraint into the American economy, and the appearance within American society of a concentration-camp sector, would in all likelihood have made irreversible the global social regression already launched in Europe. Technical and human resources, and reserves of wealth, furnished the indispensable margin of manoeuvre for the strategy of the New Deal. In the context of American history the workers' trades unions took on, in relation to the state, the role which before fascism was assumed by social democracy in Europe. The policy of social reform in the place of the physical destruction of proletarian organizations guaranteed, in essence, the exercise of elementary democratic freedom: an absolutely necessary precondition for the advancement of science. As a result of its economic base, the American bourgeoisie maintained a potential creative capacity in the heart of the organic degeneration of capitalism. These exceptional conditions resulted in two fundamental departures. They allowed the American bourgeoisie to open the road to its hegemony via the war, and to develop, to its benefit, a kind of super-imperialism. They made the United States the birthplace of a technological mutation.

As we know, the planetary scope of the war necessitated the complete exploitation of all productive capacity, which recreated the requisite starting-point for a new growth of technological innovation. This process was an absolutely blind one; it was, in a way, objective. Military exigencies saved society. Consciousness only intervened as a consciousness of the needs imposed by the war: survival. It took the terrifying perspective of destruction before the obstacle of the private interests of the national bourgeoisies could be partially set aside and organic co-operation between the United States and Britain could be improvised little by little. It also took the understanding that potential material superiority was not sufficient to win through, but that this superiority had to be translated into operational terms and that time played a crucial role. It was hence imperative to accelerate the pace of research, to concentrate and plan it in order to increase its yield; it was no less imperative to minimize the delay between laboratory results and their industrial exploitation. These imperatives overturned the basics of a system of production defined by the market and its criteria. It was hence obligatory for a state monopoly to take charge of the programme. The problems to be dealt with were posed by developments in the techniques of warfare. As we can see, the advances which were to carry humanity to the most elevated threshold yet attained were entirely empirical.

Military necessity and an understanding of possible pitfalls were in no way to be sufficient, however. Basic preconditions had to be fulfilled. World scientific research had to be at a level which would permit a technological transformation. The level attained in the first decade of the century was in no way sufficient. In the first instance, an international mobilization of scientific workers was necessary. Nazi regression eliminated Germany from this competition, in spite of the high quality of its researchers. It was the maintenance of democratic rights and liberties in the United States which made it possible there. Finally, there had to be a concentration of financial and industrial resources, of co-ordination and planning, which only a state monopoly could authorize. At the heart of the techno-structure of capitalism in decomposition, the violence of the war created the premises for the capitalist mode of production to be transcended for the first time.

During the war the general regression of the proletariat on the world scene engendered effects whose political and hence social significance was immense. They affected the objective conditions which underlay the peace and intervened as an important factor in the historic context of the second revolution.

The revolutionary proletariat ceased to exist as an international political force. Its unified world organization was destroyed. Ideological regression was even more profound: internationalism — as a theory and programme of action — found itself brutally restricted to narrow circles of isolated oppositional cadres, without links outside their own ranks. At the same time — and this is neither accident nor chance, but part of the inevitable logic of the retreat — the proletariat was displaced from the leadership of civil wars and wars of national liberation which spread throughout the world. It constituted no more than a supportive force, certainly important in

Europe, but nevertheless supportive. National resistance took precedence over class confrontation. The petty-bourgeoisie and its liberal intelligentsia took the initiative in Western Europe, Latin America, Asia and Africa; so that the peasantry formed the principal combat force in the semi-colonial and colonial countries. National ideology became the most powerful political arm in the struggle against nazi or Japanese oppression. It is on this platform that the proletariat itself entered into action. The railway workers, who in Europe gave one of the most remarkable displays of the combative strength of the working class, provide us with a constant confirmation of this fact.

The enforced social exploitation of nazism and its national oppression are the inseparable products of the organic decomposition of monopoly capitalism. The suppression of the revolutionary proletariat was expressed in the fact that national resistance supplanted social resistance, that it incorporated it and dominated it. In Europe this substitution became an impasse of historic breadth.

On the global scale, these were the syndromes of the splits between the industrial metropolises and the rest of the world. These splits brought about a discontinuity in modalities of growth, so much so that uneven development took on an entirely new significance when the new technological mutation determined the dynamics of the forces of production. This significance became a fact of fundamental importance in the splintered society.

On a European scale the predominance of wars of liberation over class conflict, of national ideology over fundamental justification and of political leadership in the hands of the liberal petty-bourgeoisie, prolonged and amplified the disaggregative effects of the retreat of the forces of production to a national terrain. They led to the internal break-up of Germany and confirmed the Balkanization of Europe, and hence its economic and strategic subordination. It also opened political, social and technological avenues to the establishment of a super-imperialism, so that until the 1960s the American state monopoly was, within limits imposed by its own strong contradictions, the only integrative force in Western Europe.

The national deviation in the conduct of civil war was the direct result of the floundering of the first revolution. The fact that the national question was in effect posed in Europe; that there existed undeniably a national oppression to the point of calling into question the existence of the national state; that the partition of Poland threatened to prefigure the same in France and was the prelude to the partitioning of Germany; that all this came about on a continent where the nation for the first time became a historical reality, and which was also the earliest to industrialize and the most strongly structured birthplace of a grand culture — establishes the experimental proof, the most irrefutable and in a certain sense the most vivid illustration, of the fundamental organic character of the crisis of world capitalist society. It shows the true breadth of the regression — a truly fantastic one. It confirms the exact historical significance and the fundamental original traits of the 1930s; it underlines how the crisis was without precedent. Between the first and second imperialist wars, a catastrophic collapse took place. Nowhere has the previous level been regained. National dismemberment has become one of the real factors in military operations, as much for the USSR, Central and Balkan Europe, as for Western Europe. At the heart of the most highly and powerfully industrialized system, a process of barbarous colonization was born, and hence a process of massive destruction, primitive exploitation, an unparalleled fall in living-standards and a cultural regression of planetary scope. Such a profound shake-up of the historical foundations of Europe provoked shock-waves of a more and more extended character in European society. Internal conflicts were submerged by the external threat to the traditional collectivity. National ideology, re-activiated by the real danger of dismemberment, froze class confrontation. The liberal petty-bourgeoisie imposed a holy union against the occupying forces, in the name of military efficiency. Reality was overturned: social subjugation became the consequence of national oppression.

However, reality cannot be totally inverted by the facts. National dismemberment is not the result of military necessity. On the contrary it hinders military operations. Creating an active resistance out of an opposition which is diffused but nevertheless generalized among the population, it solidifies numerous contingents who will later find their role in battle; it aggravates, as a result of the hostile isolation which surrounds the army, the internal conditions for the demoralization of the troops. It provokes an excessive multiplication of security services. It imposes direct control of the administration of subjugated nations. It hence engenders an extreme tension of forces. These effects appear to be constant both in Asia and in Europe, and hence independent of the specific situation of the various theatres of operation. National dismemberment demonstrates the fall in the level of the forces of production. Fundamentally it was an economic necessity. The German and Japanese bourgeoisies did not have the vital material resources to hold together the militarily defeated bourgeoisies in their enterprise. On the contrary, Berlin and Tokyo were obliged to carry out a direct and brutal despoliation. Existing reserves were pillaged and the exploitation of the industrial and agricultural productive apparatus passed into the hands of the occupying forces, for their immediate profit. National states were transformed into administrative adjuncts of the dominant military state. German and Japanese state control were established at all the strategic points of the subjugated national economies. Whilst bringing about necessary technical concentration, this in fact opened the way to the expropriation of enterprises and exploitation of those which were most important and vital. Plans for total absorption were elaborated, prefiguring the pure and simple integration of an immense part of China and Europe. For the first time in history a considerable portion of the European bourgeoisie was reduced to the role of comprador. Tightly controlled commercial transactions squeezed out native producers into parasitic circuits. Administrative constraint regimented the organization of labour and transformed the workers into a subjugated labour-force. Compulsory labour transferred European workers en masse into German industry, in order to fill the gaps created by military mobilization. The concentration-camp infrastructure became a European institution. National oppression became profound social exploitation.

These were not at all episodic symptoms. They were manifested for a long time before the opening of hostility. All the war did was to generalize them. They were the projection into civil life of the catastrophic collapse of the world capitalist system characteristic of the 1930s. The diagnosis revealed by the facts is unambiguous: the threat to established nationalities was essentially conditioned by social regression. National resistance was incapable of resolving the problems posed. Its ideology masked the real facts. Its national objectives stopped it organizing a unified European strategy, with an integrated European programme. Together with the political, social and military domination of nazism this would have created the premises for organically united revolutionary action on a European scale. Perhaps even more seriously, national resistance could not and did not want to dissociate the German people from nazism and thus condemned itself to seeking the disintegration of the Reich as the only possible outcome.

Germany is the linch-pin of Europe. It is a constant of European capitalism. It would also be a fundamental reality in a United Socialist states of Europe. German industry represents the most technically qualified and most integrated continental ensemble, to such an extent that its productive capacity is of a planetary character. This resulted from the inescapable effects of an accidental historic conjunction: the combination of a high and ancient culture and an economic and nationally retarded development. Entering later than Britain and France into the capitalist orbit, but rich with cadres and skilled workers, Germany had available from the outset an internationally better elaborated technology. It was hence able to realize an industrial infrastructure which was more modern, more complete, and of higher productivity. It became the principal and best-equipped factory-laboratory of the continent. In consequence Europe was and could not fail to be other than a sort of tributary of German industry.

Germany attained this industrial power at the moment when monopoly capitalism was no longer capable of enlarging the world market without resorting to violent internal modification. It was hence inevitable that German capitalism should become the most dynamic historical, political and military expression of the contradictions of the system. The German productive forces intervened like a powerfully armed troop risking a decisive sortie from a besieged keep. The war was nothing more than an attempt to resolve a problem which would no longer yield to economic regulation. Incapable of finding its own successor through its own mechanisms, capitalism searched for a provisional solution, through the partial distraction of its vital forces. This was the meaning of Versailles and is confirmed in an explosive way by the military occupation of the Ruhr. It was nothing more than the repetition of the war on a reduced scale. France, industrially weaker, used its temporary military superiority to contain the German productive forces through armed violence. In this way it endangered the bourgeoisie not just in Germany, but also in Europe. Under the double impact of Versailles and the Ruhr, Germany became the crucible of the European proletarian revolution. For the same reasons, when the social relationship of forces was reversed on a world scale, the process of decomposition of German society determined the dynamic of the barbarous suppression of the whole of European society.

The petty-bourgeoisie, tied to marginal economic functions, and at least one part of it to archaic structures, was carried along by a misunderstanding of the real factors conditioning society. At the very moment when the desperate German middle classes blamed their misfortune on the diktat of Versailles, the French petty-bourgeoisie reckoned that it was the conduct of the German people which gave rise to all evil. This misunderstanding of historical reality led to a failure to appreciate the genuine role of Germany and its place in Europe. The disintegration of the German nation — as an objective of the war — reflected the past and carried its own poisons with it, with a toxicity intensified by the catastrophic collapse of world society. Through the partition of Germany, Europe was working towards its own downfall. So much so that every success in arms brought on economic defeat at the hands of the economically strongest bourgeoisie in the world, the American bourgeoisie. The decline of Europe, which rapidly destroyed its imperialist status, facilitated the advent of a dominant imperialism.

Is this to say that the national deviations in the military resistance produced only negative effects? This would be an incorrect conclusion with dangerous implications, based above all on a total misunderstanding of the social functions of nazism. The Nazis did not only destroy physically the political and trade-union organizations of the proletariat and the institutions of parliamentary democracy. They constructed a concentration-camp administration, a coherent ensemble of social relations which introduced a subservient organization of labour and brought about a fantastic cultural retrogression. Compulsion, carried to these lengths, stopped scientific progress. It sterilized technological innovation at source. Hence, it tended to institutionalize a degenerated society which, deprived of indispensable technical and intellectual resources, engaged itself in the liquidation of its economies; a liquidation which in its turn led to continued degeneration. With the Nazis the barbarism of degenerating industrial society was fuly exposed. The world military victory of nazism could not have unleashed anything but a regression of world civilization. A failure to understand this is a failure to grasp both the necessary technological preconditions for any transcending of the capitalist production-process, and the real scale of the concentration-camp phenomenon. The national resistance, to the extent that it led to the military defeat of nazism, played a pre-eminently positive role. Its limit was elsewhere: it was not able to bring about a renewal of revolutionary initiative. Its victory and its failure were two historical components of today's splintered society.

The elimination of the proletarian revolutionary forces was expressed, perhaps in the most striking way, in the fates of the German armies. During the war the Wehrmacht was the Achilles' heel of the nazi régime. The great mass of the army was composed of peasants and workers, of those who had suffered the hardest repression before the war and who were sustaining the highest sacrifices during the war. Their links with the régime were ambiguous. They feared it: but their fear of the SS was mingled with latent hostility. The physical elimination of the social democrats and the communists was not so far-removed that it could be forgotten. The errors and failures of the leadership of the working class had demoralized the old generation as much as fear, and in its eyes these errors had removed the credibility from the possibility of a revolutionary outcome. The young generation was captured by the régime's slogans as a result of the break in continuity in political teaching (the massive destruction of writings and of cadres), and an intensive and constant propaganda campaign. In contrast, the reality as lived in the factory acted as an antidote. If the SS was the strike force of the régime, if it composed its general staff, its administrators and social armour, its economic cadre-force and its power in the civil war in Europe, the army in the war was the weak link of the edifice. Only an indispensable minority of workers remained in the production-process in Germany: all the rest was of European origin. Hence it was only the army which could launch a new revolutionary German generation. For this two conditions had to be satisfied: that the mass of workers and peasants ceased to believe in military victory and that another outcome should appear sufficiently likely to them. The first bloody reverse on the front opened the breach between the army and the régime. When the army in Europe encountered social isolation and the growing certainty of collective disaster, opposition was paralysed within its ranks. The troops were to continue to fight to the last ditch because, in terrible isolation, they saw no other path to take. The feeble attempts at opposition which took place at the summit of the military apparatus were aborted into a puerile murder attempt and a futile suicide. The officers who were hanged represented the remorse of a degraded bourgeoisie. The workers and peasants remained cloaked in silence and buried under the debris. The effect was terrifying: a social abyss was dug in the heart of Europe. The absence of any revolutionary upsurge in Germany immediately after the war enhanced the revolutionary ebb of the 1930s throughout Europe. It was to take a new society and a new generation in order that, with the approach of the 1970s, a new course should be set in motion.

The débâcles of the Russian front, the retreat in Africa, the ignominious fall of the fascist axis were powerful levers for detaching the army from its nazi masters. These levers were not grasped. To be sure, a handful of revolutionaries were exterminated or deported for trying to accomplish a task whose accomplishment should have been the first strategic object of a co-ordinated European resistance. It would also have necessitated a programme which did not exist; the programme of an economically integrated and socially revolutionary Europe — obviously incompatible with the platform of national resistance. Thus, at the moment when the powerful constraints of the war worked towards the elaboration of a superior technology which, in its empirical logic, posed the necessity and the possibility of a more organic planetary unification, the regression of class confrontation to within national horizons brought about a Balkanization of political forces.

This irrefutable diagnosis of the elimination of the proletariat as a preponderant international force on the eve of the 1940s is central for understanding the world social milieu at the outset of the great technological changes. This is not a question of a fortuitous phenomenon or even of a temporary self-effacement but of a political disintegration without precedent in the history of the working class. In the very heart of the failure of the Second International, a new revolutionary growth was taking place on a worldwide scale. Nothing of this type occurred this time. The national division of the proletariat was perpetuated, in striking contrast with the superior level of organization of the forces of production. Its regression in three domains — theory, organization and strategy — became a constant feature in flagrant contradiction to the extraordinary creative power which the proletariat demonstrated during the whole of the nineteenth century and the first quarter of the twentieth. It was a politically disintegrated class, before the fundamental modifications of technology could overcome the ruin of its material base in the production-process. Political data alone cannot provide a satisfactory account of a process on such a scale. It implies more organic splits: social modifications. The mode in which the first revolution withered away appeared as a decisive factor; but at the same time it was itself profoundly deflected by the catastrophic collapse of capitalism. The world conjuncture of the 1930s exercised sovereign domination over the appearance of the new society in Russia and determined its fundamental traits.

II

BUREAUCRATIC SOCIETY AND STATE CAPITALISM

11 At the threshold of bureaucratic society

IN THE USSR the dominant feature of the decade which opened in 1930 was the establishment and internal organization of a bureaucratic society. The world conjuncture determined its specific fundamental traits. This was done in such a way that it made its appearance as a state-capitalist bureaucratic society containing powerful concentration-camp deformations.

Hence, we are talking about a *specific society*. This is the inescapable consequence of the transformation from a state-capitalist bureaucracy which is functionally differentiated into a ruling class exploiting the work-force. A class is never an autonomous body without even narrow connections with other classes. There are functional organic relations between classes. The appearance of a new type of class was necessarily accompanied by the internal modification of other classes. The arrival of a new ruling class signified a historical structural change in society. These major changes were, in effect, the product of a mutation in the relations of production; the process of production was the matrix of the new society. The existence of a new ruling class follows from an examination of the totality of functional relations of society. The establishment of the state bureaucracy as a ruling class was combined with the simultaneous development of an agrarian bureaucracy, with its own roots in the economy, which substituted itself for the former middle classes; with the organic constitution of a professional work-force of the state which assumed the role of the classical industrial proletariat; and with a diversification of the state bureaucracy which was not at all purely functional, but which demonstrated a great heterogeneity of roles in the organization of labour and hence also of divergent social interests.

We are therefore dealing with a *bureaucratic* state capitalism. State capitalism has appeared in the past and will appear in the future in very different social forms. The *bureaucratic* character of this specific society was, in the event, a direct effect of the October revolution: of the fundamental fact that the big financial and industrial bourgeoisie, and the landed proprietors, had been wrenched from the production process, with the result that the state had been substituted for them as the private owner of the means of production; and of the fact that, lacking the necessary technology, this appropriation came about as a social substitution to the benefit of the social corps of the state. Hence, the bureaucracy constituted itself as a class which became differentiated in the process of acquiring autonomy within the production process, and it became a ruling class after the complete expropriation of the middle classes. So the bureaucracy, the creature of the first world revolution, appeared as a new, original phenomenon. To be sure, it is possible to discern analogies in its behaviour or existence with all past or present bureaucracies, but these are marginal analogies which are in no way of any fundamental historical value. Such analogies can illuminate certain features, but they would not lend themselves to a global functional interpretation.

The mode of production remained *capitalist*. The state monopoly no more possessed the power to modify the mode of production than did the private monopolies. Like them, it brought about considerable changes in property relations, in the division of property and the mechanisms of the market. The techniques of prediction, of control, and of planning which were a response to a certain stage of growth of the productive forces broadened the contradictions of the system, but did not go beyond it. The state monopoly in no way launched an automatic socialization of the process of production. Socialization implies an advanced level of rational integration of the world economy, a very high level of production, a consequential abundance of consumer goods, and fundamentally, the substitution for a human work-force of automatic circuits in the processes of construction, control, and circulation of products. These are the necessary material and cultural conditions which are the preconditions, but only the preconditions, for the socialization of the production-process. That is, they are the most advanced form of workers' self-management, which would be expressed through the withering away of the state and the transformation of social classes into occupational categories which would do away with the separation between manual labour and intellectual labour as a social antagonism, and which would eliminate the market in all its functions. The state monopoly in itself does not create a specific mode of production, at once different to both the capitalist and the socialized systems. It remains under the yoke of the same technological conditioning as the private monopolies. All it does is to bring about a higher degree of concentration of property. But this property remains private property, even if it brings with it a certain dilution of the entitlements of property, even if the exercise of ownership is carried out through a process of delegation and under the growing form of the social services. This was in no way a new phenomenon. In China, since very ancient times, state property had been a dominant form of appropriation. The development of capitalism created more and more services which were assigned to various functions. The concentration of property in the state authorized a more extended rationalization of those techniques of control which were already inherent to the classic monopoly-capitalist phase.

In spite of these advantages, the state monopoly is not necessarily in itself an instrument for the expansion of the productive forces. It could have been, on the contrary, the form taken by a retreat of these productive forces behind national frontiers. This in effect was its form in the 1930s. It is not so today. The state monopoly, finally, does not represent an inevitable, historically necessary stage in a transcending capitalism. Structures of co-management and self-management can evolve without society first passing through the stage of a generalized state monopoly. Furthermore, the socialization of production-process is not an inescapable stage of human history. Nothing in history has ever been inescapable and nothing ever will be. The very existence of the human species is in the last resort totally dependent on conditions over which it exercises no control, and its permanence is in no way absolutely guaranteed. Technological advance and its internal logic reacts on society which, in its turn can either halt the process, deform it, or permit it to realize its full potential. Socialization is, like everything else, an option — without doubt highly probable, but only probable. During the 1930s, the state monopoly in Russia and in Germany was the basis of a regression of historical breadth. During the course of the forties, it proved to be the vital means through which the present technological mutation came about.

This bureaucratic state capitalism was encumbered in its organic constitution by a powerful *concentration-camp* deformation. It would be to misunderstand the nature of the concentration-camp phenomenon to consider it as a simple institutionalized form of repression. The concentration camp was the expression of the generalization of relations of compulsion in the social organization of labour. It was hence a symptom of a profound regression of the whole of society. This is its universal sociological significance. It was not at all consubstantial with state capitalism, following the development of an organic logic; nor even with its bureaucratic social embodiment. This is why we have to describe it as a *deformation*. This deformation was imposed on the Russian bureaucracy, as on the German bourgeoisie, by the world-wide capitalist recession. The domain of the concentration-camp phenomenon, which was considerable, indicates Russia's degree of integration into the world market. This trait was hence neither marginal nor accidental. It appeared, on the contrary, as an organic characteristic. The concentration camps appeared as one of the constituted ingredients of bureaucratic society; it represented the impact of the world conjuncture on its genesis, as the essential consequence of the historic impasse. But precisely because they were a foreign body to state capitalism, because they were in effect a result of the disintegration of the productive forces, the camps were to become a major obstacle for the development of bureaucratic society in the 1950s, when this same world conjuncture was reversed, in the sense that an accelerated growth began, through the dynamic of a new integrated system of technology. From this point, relations of compulsion, as the dominant relations of labour-organization, were violently challenged.

In the establishment and in the ruling of bureaucratic society, the only processes in operation were blind ones. The formation of the organs of power was the unique operative field where a systematic, premeditated intervention had any effect.

Three series of factors therefore combined to bring about the establishment of bureaucratic state-capitalist society. The first was the initial and fundamental contradiction of the crisis of capitalism which made the first revolution possible, without however accepting any transcendence of the capitalist mode of production. The inescapable consequence of this was the organic splitting of the proletariat, broken up through the antagonism between the tasks of control and production. This gave the bureaucracy its opening as an autonomous force in the process of production. Then there was the social scale of the proletarian revolution of October 1917 which expropriated the big bourgeoisie and the landed proprietors, thus opening the way to the most highly developed form of state monopoly. The final factor was the world regression of the 1930s which at once isolated and decomposed the revolutionary social forces, drove the rural and urban middle classes into a complete impasse, prevented the reconstitution of the big bourgeoisie, and accelerated the retreat into the national arena of the forces of production, in this way providing the bureaucracy with economic support and social reinforcement. This integration of the capitalist crisis into the world arena acted directly on all those mechanisms and processes which affected the establishment of the bureaucratic society. Let us take, as an example, the backwardness of the nationalized industrial sector which we know as the determining factor of the socially explosive tension between town and country. It did not take on its true dimension except in the context of the dislocation of the world market.

The national impasse, from which in 1927 began the growth of productive forces which NEP set in motion, was in no way a simple consequence of the inadequacies and incompetence of the bureaucracy. Even if Lenin had lived, and Trotsky had remained on top of things, it is more than likely that the *economic facts* would have scarcely permitted anything substantially better. Certainly Trotsky, as early as 1923, had been analysing the scissors crisis with great foresight and appreciated the danger of the ruptures it would bring in its wake. But between seeing, predicting and preventing there is a world of difference: the world of genuine, usable methods. The measure envisaged by the opposition against bureaucratic idiocies would without doubt have improved the situation, but they would not have enabled fundamental difficulties to be overcome. State industry needed capital which it could not raise by itself in sufficient quantities; it was hence forced to raise it from the private economy, in essence in the countryside. No one in the state leadership opposed this; the differences between Zinoviev and Preobrazhensky dealt only with the methods to be applied. But Zinovievists, Stalinists and trotskyists were caught in the same contradiction. They wanted to leave private accumulation to develop, because it was a vital recourse for the state, and at the same time contain it and slow it down, because its social impact represented a dangerous threat to power. If a less heavy, more understanding administration had allowed the level of productivity to rise, the managing intelligentsia of the left, in spite of its talents — given the state of available machinery and of the work-force — would still not have been able to facilitate this miracle: to produce enough to satisfy the needs of the peasantry so that the black market could have neither strangled nor seized those considerable capitals which it was draining away from official circuits. Also, the monopoly prices for state profit which Preobrazhenski was demanding could not on their own have had much effect on the conjuncture.

According to all the evidence, there was no other way out than massive foreign aid. With the revolution thrust aside (and the international arena was the only terrain where the Left Opposition could, if it had retained power, have brought about an effective balance), the necessary effort could only come from the world bourgeoisie — whether it had supported, up to and including the use of arms, its natural allies the kulak and the NEP-man; or whether, judging the risk to be too great, it had approached the bureaucracy and accepted Stalin's proposal to intervene by granting concessions. The crisis of the 1930s left room for neither. The world market, in a state of disintegration, far from allowing a way out of the national impasse, brought it on all the more strongly. With all external escape-routes blocked, the bureaucracy was forced into civil war. Stalin expropriated the peasantry and the urban middle classes by military violence. The state bureaucracy appropriated the entire means of production, because it could not do otherwise. The expression "compelled by circumstance" takes on its full meaning. The bureaucracy acted blindly under the joint pressure of the internal situation and the international conjuncture. This submission to events, this constraint imposed by the world capitalist crisis, set new mechanisms in operation. Reflex reactions are not neutral. Their effects reacted powerfully on the genesis and composition of bureaucratic society.

The kulak was officially designated the enemy. In fact, the entire agricultural and urban middle classes, rooted in capitalist private production and private commerce, were involved. The official objective was the collectivization of the countryside within the briefest possible period. If one takes this term in the marxist sense, this was by all accounts an absurdity. Collectivization assumes a high technical level of exploitation. It is not and cannot be the throwing-together of plots of land and their rudimentary machinery. Co-operatives and freely contracted agreements can, at this level, only improve the conditions of labour and harvesting. The socialization of agrarian production depends on a generalized industrialization of agriculture at a high level. Only in the United States was this level *technically* approached. The USSR of 1970 was far from achieving it. In 1930 it was absolutely meaningless. State industry was not even capable of providing the villages with sufficient tractors and fertilizer. It was precisely because of this absence that arms had to be used. None of the leaders was ignorant of this fact. The opposition harped on this constantly and Yakovlev, charged by Stalin to carry out the collectivization, explained in 1928 that the kolkhozy could, for many years be no more than "oases in the middle of innumerable small plots of land". The real objective was the violent seizure of those reserves which had accumulated in the countryside and the direct control, at source, over the surplus product of agricultural production, through the statization of peasant exploitation. These Draconian measures were imposed by the world impasse. They had a double aim: the expropriation of a socially dangerous adversary, and securing investment indispensable to the growth of state industry. In parallel, it was necessary to integrate the networks of free exchange, whether clandestine or not, into state circuits, and in consequence to lay hold of the masses of floating capital which up till then had escaped the administration bureaux. These objectives were not utopian. They corresponded to a real situation and real means of intervention. They were, however, difficult to attain because of the organic weakness of state capitalism and its primitive technology. They were partly compromised by the simultaneously incoherent and uncontrolled character of the military operation. State capitalism in its poverty was incapable of carrying out the direct integration of agrarian production (the soukhozes). Military action confronted an objective, material, insurmountable barrier. The bureaucracy was compelled to adopt a private form concentrating the ownership of the means of production outside the hands of the state: the kolkhoz. This concentration of agrarian property, on the margin of state property, facilitated the seizure of the surplus product. In principle, it regulated the difficulties inherent to the enclosure of diverse tracts of land by concentrating the means of labour. This was the appropriate way in which the state bureaucracy could realize the advantages of large areas of land. In principle, it then permitted a rationalization and a scheme of development in accord with the laws of centralized administrative control. Only in principle, for the obvious reason that the necessary industrial support could not be provided.

This administrative absorption of agriculture was the Achilles' heel of *bureaucratic* state capitalism. Forty years after the kolkhozy were created, persistent technological inadequacy continues to provoke a generalized distrust of them. This struggle is confirmed by the constant lag of production behind needs by the vast role played by the free market; and by the repartition of real labour time between the exploitation of the kolkhozy and the exploitation of private allotments.

Independently of this fact, fundamental in its significance, the development of the institution of the kolkhoz during the course of these forty years was thoroughly uneven. Under the impact of multiple factors (endowment of rich or poor land; local culture; variations in the quality of the work-force in part due to the attraction of better salaries and better services, variable availability of credit, nearness to urban centres, etc.), considerable inequalities appeared between the kolkhozy which revealed their varying fortunes. These inequalities were revealed in an uneven distribution of surplus value among the kolkhoz bureaucracy.

The appearance of an agrarian bureaucracy was, without doubt, the major social fact of collectivization. Three factors affected its constitution: the private concentration of the means of production; the extension of administrative methods of control to agriculture; and global integration into a state-capitalist economy. The bureaucracy was historically that social force which was substituted for the middle classes of private capitalism. The agrarian bureaucracy belonged to the ruling class; but it was an economically differentiated layer of it whose immediate interests could be, and in effect were, divergent. In the same way as the bourgeois society of small merchants considered itself to be exploited by the big bourgeoisie, the industrialists by the financiers, and the small enterprises by the monopolies, the agrarian bureaucracy considered itself deprived through the general repartition of surplus value by the state bureaucracy. It is clear that the existence of a powerful agrarian bureaucracy was the fundamental organic trait of bureaucratic Russian society. It is more or less obvious that we can neither ignore nor underestimate it, if we wish to understand the dynamic of this society.

12 The advent of bureaucratic society

THE SECOND civil war was neither foreseen nor prepared for by the bureaucracy. It was totally improvised. The lact of preparation and the recourse to action dictated by circumstance explains the uncontrolled violence of the operation and the scale of the destruction. Reflex reactions had effects which took on a historical scope.

Improvisation stares us in the face from central directives. On 7 November 1929, Stalin's first instructions were published in an article in *Pravda*, "The Year of the Great Crisis". The order of combat was laid down by a second article by Stalin on 27 December, "To hell with NEP!" Two months later, on 1 March, the bureaux drew up the first balance-sheet: more than 14 million peasant allotments (precisely 13,264,000) had been constituted as kolkhozy. The next day public opinion, the cadres, and the local and regional authorities, knew that retreat had been decided on, through a third article by Stalin: "Dizzy with Success". Fifteen days later, a second balance-sheet was made: the kolkhozy included no more than 5,778,000 allotments. In two weeks nearly nine million families had recovered their plots of land. The inconsistencies leap to the eye. The retreat was transformed into a debacle, and the war resumed in December 1930.

On the ground, the lack of preparation took on nightmarish proportions. No one knew what a kolkhoz was. The statutes were published after the event, far too late. No one was either politically or technically prepared; up until the eve of the war the kulak was still considered an ally; and it was thought that the exploitation of allotments would be safe from interference for many years to come. Collusion between the peasant middle classes and local functionaries was clearly in evidence.

The widest conceivable disorder preceded the launching of operations. As soon as the rumour began to circulate that there would be large-scale confiscations the peasants started hoarding their goods: machinery, cattle and seeds. Military operations were accompanied by a clandestine liquidation of resources which rapidly took on fantastic proportions.

Under these conditions the disaster was so great and so rapid, the lack of breathing-space and the reorganization so complete, the bankruptcy of the local authorities abandoned to their own devices so total that typhus and scurvy appeared in the richest region, the

Ukraine. Only one recourse remained: to finally deprive any peasant who possessed anything. In the absence of a plan, of elementary rules of conduct under a programme, the militia, the shock troops and impromptu delegations in the administration confiscated pell-mell horses, cows, sheep, pigs, fish and children's boots. Amid total confusion, private pillaging went to fantastic lengths. Work was interrupted, land was abandoned; entire regions were returned to fallow. Russia was gripped by famine in 1931 and 1932. Rationing was reimposed in the towns. It is estimated that six million died of hunger in the Ukraine. In certain regions of the Ukraine and White Russia, 30 per cent of the population was decimated by famine. According to other estimates, deaths from hunger in the Ukraine and in the Northern Caucasus rose to eight millions. Abandoned children became a national disgrace.

The country was racked by a profound economic crisis. A major part of the stock of agrarian goods, which the bureaucracy had wanted to seize, was partially wiped out. Not only were 25 million peasant allotments ruined, but the means of production were half destroyed. The statistical records more or less cover the extent of this catastrophe. 55 per cent of all horses were killed. There were an estimated 34.6 million in 1929; there were no more than 15.6 million left in 1934. These losses were irreparable: mechanical traction was still very weak, tractors were scarcely in existence and industry was incapable of filling the gaps. The number of horned animals diminished by 40 per cent (from 30.7 million to 19.5 million); the number of pigs by 55 per cent; the number of sheep by 66 per cent. In 1928 the production of sugar approached 109,000,000 pounds; it was now no more than 48 million, a reduction of more than a half.

Industry suffered severely with the reverberations of this disaster. Raw materials no longer arrived. Molotov officially recognized that industrial production in 1932 rose by only 8 per cent instead of the 36 per cent envisaged by the planners. The work-force was severely disrupted by a return to unbelievable conditions of existence. It again assumed an extreme fluidity. Absenteeism, machine breakages and malfunctions increased sharply. The rate of return on labour fell by 11.7 per cent in 1931.

It is harder still to try to measure the human losses which the civil war caused. In 1929, that is to say in the period of uncertainty where the decision to undertake mass repression had not yet been taken, in the Russian Republic alone, the Ukrainian and Caucasian republics arose. Sentences pronounced by the tribunals rose to 1,216,000 (as against 955,000 in the preceding year) and death sentences rose by 2,000 per cent between 1928 and 1929. In the year 1930 alone, it is estimated that two million were deported, a figure which was to reach four to five millions in 1932. Furthermore, in certain places the whole population of villages, cantons, and even districts was transferred to the Arctic and far Eastern regions.

This civil war was imposed on the bureaucracy by the world conjuncture: as was its savagery, the extent of destruction resulting from the lack of preparation of its leaders confronted with the necessity of confrontation, from their political myopia, from the gross behaviour and brutality of their agents, from the absence of any perspective, from fear and from an elementary defence reflex which demanded rapid progress and the annihilation of the enemy without consideration. In this respect, this second civil war was a faithful mirror of the bureaucracy and its agents. Having disencumbered themselves of marxist culture, both found themselves the heirs of Tsarism. Exceptional circumstances acted like a chemical photographic developer. But this did not force their behaviour upon them. There were to be many examples of this, right up until the Second World War. This said, if the bureaucracy had been of a different character, it could have conducted this war otherwise: but it could not have avoided it. The Left Opposition in 1930 maintained that: "Under satisfactory internal and international conditions, the material and technical situation of agriculture could be radically transformed in ten or fifteen years, guaranteeing collectivization a base in the process of production. But in the course of the intervening years Soviet power could be overthrown several times." Soviet power had been overthrown a long time before; while conditions were in no way satisfactory. The only force which saved the bureaucracy from the growing pressure of the middle classes was the military. In the short, in the long and in the medium term, it was economically condemned. The use or otherwise of arms became a question of its very existence, since its attempts at accommodation with the world bourgeoisie had been blocked.

The central importance of the second civil war relates to the fact that it was the formative process of bureaucratic society. Not only because the bureaucratic class, in seizing the whole of the means of production, turned itself into a ruling class; but also because the fundamental facts of the period of collectivization created organic structures, determine the administration of labour in the production-process, and, in consequence, determined the functional relationships between classes. In the last analysis, at the heart of this violent birth process, it evolved what was to be the iron framework of power.

The rural middle classes were eliminated as a class. They were removed from production but without *the material conditions* of the production–process having changed. This contradiction engendered, as a result of its social substitution, an autonomous agrarian bureaucracy. Through its intermediary, the state monopoly exercised its grip on the whole of the national economy. *But it did not possess an adequate technology of control.* This contradiction became the principal contradiction of state-capitalist bureaucratic society. The divorce between the total concentration of the ownership of the means of production in the hands of the state and the primitive level of techniques of control created a situation of permanent objective violence (in the sense that control procedures perpetrated violence on the forces of production), which in its turn maintained an organic instability. This instability is at the heart of the political crisis which continued uninterrupted until the elimination of Beria, and manifested themselves as a series of waves of mass repression.

This fundamental divorce expressed itself through the economic growth process in the chaotic way that development occurred, and in organic splits. For example, the up-to-date industry which was created during the 1960s was a closed system in relation to the rest of the economy. This organic split, not only in its rhythms of development but in the inherent modalities of its growth, represents today the major problem for bureaucratic state capitalism.

The difficulties inherent to administrative techniques of control (in their primitive state) were considerably aggravated by the near-collapse of the agrarian sector caused by the scale of destruction. It so ravaged the land that fifty years later its effects are still recognizable.

This situation in the countryside, and its economic and social repercussions in the towns (the disruption of the work-force) combined with the reflux in world productive forces, led inescapably to the generalization of coercive relations at work. The acquisition by the state of an enormous mass of exiles provided the basic work-force for the institutions of concentration-camp society.

In this crucible, a state wage-earning class was formed within a decade.

13   The genesis of concentration-camp institutions

The stalinist concentration camps arose out of the civil war of the 1930s. They were the first sign, on the world arena, of the profound decomposition of society.

Concentration camps were neither marginal nor episodic in the genesis of bureaucratic society. On the contrary, their dynamic proved to be extremely powerful. It revealed a considerable creative power. They intervened as a determining factor both of diversification of the state bureaucracy within the structure of power, and in the extension of the relations of compulsion into the work-process (to the extent of introducing profound and persistent deformations into the formation of a state wage-earning force); and they left their powerful imprint on the fundamental juridical work of the decade 1930 to 1940.

The concentration camps drew their importance from their origin in the world regression of the forces of production, and from the permanent organic instability of bureaucratic society. They derived from the same social process which brought about the transformation of the bureaucracy into a ruling class; events hence turned them into a new important material element, an ingredient and an objective fact which entered spontaneously into the elaboration of the new social relations, at the same time and in the same way as the elimination of the middle classes from the production-process. The primitive nature of administrative techniques led to their empirical use as a lever of the state monopoly in the economy. The disintegration of the world conjuncture — taken as an insurmountable obstacle, hindering technological growth — transposed their circumscribed and experimental application as a model (in the sense of *pattern*) for the global administration of the work-force, because of their effectiveness, which was confirmed on an economically and socially barren terrain.

It hence appeared that, from the viewpoint of the historical analysis, the stalinist concentration camp should be situated as an aggregate in the construction of the society. The same institution appeared in Germany as the expression of the disintegration of an advanced industrial society. This is a confirmation of the fundamental fact that the advent of bureaucratic society was an adaptation to worldwide regression.

A witness of the first phase in the enterprise has provided an excellent observation of both the initial impact of events (the improvised, non-deliberate side) and the altogether objective, totally unpremeditated mechanism, which led to the initiation and generalization of the first empirical solution which made the concentration-camp institution into a teaching, in other words from this point, a concerted policy. The American engineer, John G. Littlepage, remarked on the basic difficulty which the NKVD faced in the existence of an enormous mass of prisoners: "The police could not resolve the problem of managing so many people at once, at a time when reorganization was taking years to accomplish."[34] This was a judicious observation with a double meaning. The NKVD was caught with an unforeseen consequence of an ill-prepared war. The course of events worked itself out as we have observed, as a blind process. It is a confirmation also of the numerical scale of the repression. Now, the quantitative factor is not a neutral one. By their nature, large numbers modify the social effects. From the point of view of the science of society this is an essential fact. Numbers appear as an indispensable criterion in the definition of the concentration-camp phenomenon. The decimation of the oppositionists; the arrest, imprisonment, and deportation of Zinovievists, the trotskyists, the rebellious cadres in the factories and the majority of the leading intelligentsia would populate the prisons and the isolators, but would not provoke the concentration-camp mutation; for this it was necessary that a certain numerical quantity should be attained. This norm operates as part of the German as well as the Russian experience.

The objective boundary between a *revolutionary crisis* of society and its *violent disintegration* becomes manifest: the expropriation of the big bourgeoisie and the landed proprietors did not unleash the concentration-camp process.

John D. Littlepage[34] gives evidence of the results of administrative successes of the concentration camps. Littlepage was a technician without political culture, even of a rudimentary type. He seems completely foreign to Russia, in the same way as a westerner in a primitive tribe. The introduction in his own country of the procedures which he had observed in Russia would have seemed both stupid and inconvenient to him. Nevertheless, he had no hostility to the Soviet régime, in fact the contrary was the case, as long as it remained a Russian régime. He was curious and interested in the manner of an ethnologist. He had known Russia neither as a tourist, nor as a journalist, but as an engineer. It was the organization of labour which he had experienced crossing the whole country for many years in the very period which from our point of view is most interesting. His lack of experience in political culture often deprives his generalizations of real interest, as when he risks committing himself to political judgements. His judgement on the well-being or otherwise of public life or daily life must also be understood and treated with reserve. In fact, he never had the idea of comparing conditions of life in Russia with those of America or Canada, in the same way that this idea never occurs to an observer of African society. But as regards everything concerning life-styles, work, and technical questions, he is an irreplaceable observer:

> To my mind, it is not merely a coincidence that those Soviet enterprises directly controlled by the police fulfil their quota much better than the others. When the economy is directed in the way which has been started in Russia, the type of control exercised by the police over all the managers, engineers, and workers becomes necessary. When the Soviet police undertakes the construction of a dyke or a railway it can draw up its plans years in advance and events conform with them. It exercises total control over its workers because they are prisoners who cannot leave work through discontent, as can those of other industries. The police possesses sufficient influence to obtain the necessary raw materials promptly, so that it does not run the risk of late deliveries, as often happens with other industries. Soviet journals often hire the police because of their effective methods of construction, and I recognize that these police enterprises are those where planned economy can best be studied. If one desired to introduce completely controlled economy into Soviet industry and wanted to operate this temporarily and regularly, I think that a control similar to that exercised by the police in its own factories would become necessary.

The practical man in fact, can see through the eyes of a manager of the bureaucratic state. He states that the inescapable counterpart of mediocre control techniques, in the context of the state monopoly, is compulsion; that the internal logic of the system tends to be generalized as a fundamental work relation; that not only was compulsion in its highest expression (police repression) not counter-productive, but that it posed many advantages which were multiplied by the position of the repressive forces of the state.

Littlepage merely makes his observations. He does not make any interpretation or any deduction; but he does not gloss over the ex-perimental facts established. The privilege of the police force, as an *entrepreneur*, is that of not being submitted, as an *employer*, to the labour market, whereas other state trusts must be so. He states this clearly: "It exercises total control over its workers because they are prisoners who cannot leave industry through discontent, as can those of other industries."

Under state-capitalist bureaucratic society, the economic monopoly of the state is still subject to some dependence on the market, in one specific sphere: the labour-market. The bureaucracy was obliged to undertake the military expropriation of the middle classes because it did not possess the *economic means* for the regulation of this divorce between industrial crisis and agricultural crisis which Trotsky had defined as the "scissors" crisis. The laws of the market, even when controlled, were operating *socially* against the interests of the bureaucracy. The relative slowness of the growth of state industry partially emptied the measures of control of their economic effectiveness. The complete appropriation of the means of production did not, however, liberate the state monopoly *economically* from the constraints of the market. On the contrary, the growing major destructions carried out during the second civil war aggravated general impoverishment; such that the state was not in a position to attract and maintain qualified workers in prioritized employment, from the point of view of defined objectives by offering higher wages. Hence the state, once more, had to control the market by *other than economic means*. This was the foundation of relations of compulsion at work. From the moment that this situation began to spread, compulsion became institutional: because, as Littlepage quite justifiably says, it is the only way to "properly and regularly manage". In the same way that the intense preparation for war in Germany and in the United States provided the forces of production, confined in a national framework, with the base of a new growth, the massive destructions of the civil war of the 1930s multiplied elementary demand, which was already immense, and opened a vast period of expansion once order had been re-established. The forces of production, which took on this expansion, ran up against the heavy grip of the authoritarian and centralized administration. It was not at all a question of incompatibility of kind between state control and the capitalist production-process. It was entirely a question of the degree of evolution. The state monopoly could only bring about progress, that is, raised productivity, in the private monopolies that it controlled, through a highly evolved technology where automatic systems were extensively used. This was the price of a more homogeneous and extended rationality (but not of a complete rationality; if the state monopoly did permit the resolution of a certain number of contra-dictions and conflicts in the framework of the national market, it exercised a decisively limited influence on the world market; it remained in all ways under the constraint, in the last resort, of production for the market.) Through the concentration of the private ownership of the means of production and through the powers of prediction, planning and control which it exercised, the state monopoly had a powerful economic lever. It was capable of giving (under the restrictions imposed by the antagonisms of the world market) a powerful impulse to the forces of production. On the other hand, deprived of the vital technology, it was forced in carrying out its plans to use a human work-force. The introduction of officials at all levels of transmission weighed heavily upon the apparatus of control, brought about enormous depredations in the work-force, provoked bottlenecks, and undermined the economy with considerable false costs. This was the more so, because the intervention of various offices was *social*, not at all purely technical, and hence carried with it the search for, and defence of, more or less privileged living conditions. At this level of development an antinomy appeared between the powers of conception and planning, and the powers of execution. This antinomy expressed itself in practice as a permanent violation of the expansive tendencies of the forces of production, manifested by discontinuities, distortions, and disequilibria. The state monopoly hence oscillated in a permanently unstable way between accelerations which it launched, and the brakes which its executive apparatus imposed. The tensions which were thus created, and which the exorbitant social costs they gave rise to made explosive, introduced an organic *social* instability into the global system and into the interior of the ruling class. They hence introduced a repeated, chronic use of repression as a means of regulation, on a scale which it extended to the whole of society. This regulation, in its turn, guaranteed stability and the reinforcement of the concentration-camp institution, through a renewal and constant enlargement of its room for manoeuvre for the expansion of its subjugated work-force.

In effect, between 1930 and 1940, we can observe a constant numerical progression in the operation of the concentration camps. Although global calculations are difficult, the phenomenon as such is undeniable. The 1930s opened with massive deportations of peasants, who constituted the initial work-force of the system. The period called "Yezhovchina", which began after the assassination of Kirov in December 1934 and reached its height with the liquidation of Yezhov in 1938, marked a fantastic extension of the terror. The concentration camp then went into a phase of consolidation. At the same time the juridical structure of the state wage-earning force was elaborated. The stalinist concentration camp exactly like its nazi homologue became a European institution. The Polish and the Baltic people were concentrated, between 1939 and 1940, principally between Archangel, Kotlas, and Murmansk and the deported exiles of Bessarabia and Bukovin in central Asia, many of them at Karaganda.

The real dimensions of the institution are impressive. In Russia, it had space at its disposal which Germany did not, and it had a time span which the nazis did not enjoy. Its weight alone necessarily brought about profound structural deformations in the bureaucratic society. I will give only a number of examples. In a system of camps which in 1941 covered the whole country, eighty concentration-camp complexes were recorded. Each was a functional ensemble with the dimensions of a vast region.

The concentration-camp complex of the north-east (the Sevostlag) was typical. It was situated between Yakutsk, Nogayev, and the mouth of the river Kolyma. Its administrative centre was at Magadan on the banks of the Okhotsk. In 1934 (two years after its creation) it comprised 350,000 exiles, rising to 500,000 in 1935 and around three million in 1941. This in itself indicates the dynamic of the system. The Baltic White Sea complex (the Belbaltlag) contained 300,000 exiles and the Dimitrov complex (the Dimitlag), dedicated to the construction of the Volga-Moscow canal, had 500,000 in 1938.

Concentration-camp economic enterprises first of all became implanted in the activities of the economic infrastructure. They were extended — under the impulse of the reclamation of virgin land — to the entire system of production and exchange: opening new roads, setting hydraulics works in motion, and controlling the flow of rivers, the extraction of minerals, but also to the creation and control of factories, of agricultural exploitation, and transport and the commercial exchange of products. The enlargement of the base of its monopoly completed by the reinforcement of its autonomy is exemplified by the success of the NKVD in constituting its own census of fundamental applied research. This policy of discrimination in favour of highly qualified specialists was written into administrative procedures. The organs of the gulag (the central administration of the camp) did not possess even a nominal file on prisoners. The section dealing with census and distribution, the uro, worked only on anonymous statistics based on the nature of the sentences pronounced. This lack of differentiation did not contradict the NKVD's labour policy, because in its eyes quantity was in general worth more than quality. Making good use of the work-force was left to the competence or otherwise of the local administrations. The nominal dossiers on the prisoners were held by the regional organization. This often led to inextricable difficulties in tracing an exile. As long as transport was a permanent feature of operations, the transit camps were themselves numerous. There was however one exception to this rule. There was a central file concerned with the scientific intelligentsia and highly qualified and technical cadre in Moscow, in order that the NKVD could mobilize for its own use researchers who would otherwise have been lost in the mass of exiles. Some camps and prisons were turned over to scientific research and, quite evidently, enjoyed a privileged régime. A camp of this nature was situated on an island in Lake Saguier, in the region of Kalinin. There was another at Kutchino in the suburbs of Moscow. The German physicist Otto Maar was employed there temporarily in 1949, before returning to an ordinary camp. Solzhenitsyn described this camp in his novel *The First Circle*.

The place and role occupied by concentration-camp production are indicated only through the succinct testimony of the work accomplished in twenty years by the gulags.

Kolyma. The exploitation of gold in the upper reaches of the river Kolyma by the concentration-camp work-force of the Dalstroi mining trust began in 1932. The area was six times that of France. It was at that time a desert. Winter lasted eight months. The temperature went down to minus 65°C. The sea froze over. Summer was torrid, with murderous horseflies. The deportees who worked in the marshes had burnt backs and frozen legs. The balance-sheet fifteen years later: a port, Madagan, had been built. It had its own central electricity generating station, several factories, several scientific institutes, well-equipped laboratories, technical schools, a house of culture, a theatre and a cinema. Its population was estimated at 70,000 people. A very large motorway linked Magadan to Yakutsk, on the Lena. In the south-west it led towards the Aldan, the distributary of the Lena. Five sovkhozy (state farms) were created: Dultscha, 10 kilometres to the north-west of Magadan; Ola, at 25 kilometres; Talon, at 185 kilometres; Elguen, at 540 kilometres; Susuman, at 700 kilometres. Five extremely important enterprises for fishing, and preserving fish, were organized: they dealt with herring, salmon, whales and walrus. Also: an electric motor factory at Atka, a metallurgic factory at Orotukan (rich in iron deposits), etc. This astounding fifteen-year work was entirely the product of concentration-camp labour, organized through its own administration.

The concentration-camp complex of Nirolsk. Balance sheet: the town of Nirolsk, at the estuary of the Yenissei, to the extreme north-west of the Siberian plateau; an industrial centre of the first order, which exploited the richest nickel deposits in the USSR. Population: by the end of the war, 30,000 inhabitants; in 1953 between 300,000 and 400,000.

The concentration-camp complexes of the republic of Komis in the extreme north of European Russia. The concentration-camp enterprise started up in the 1930s. To the north of the republic there was the concentration-camp complex of Ukhta-Petchorlag. It exploited oil-fields. Its importance was to become central after the occupation of the Caucasus by the German army. Production: 1937, 100,000 tons; 1940, 200,000 tons; in the middle of the war, 1,200,000 tons; in 1950, 800,000 tons. The concentration-camp complex of Vorkouta. Coal. The first mine was inaugurated in 1930. This basin became the first centre of coal production of the USSR. A secondary centre was opened at Inta, near Vorkouta. Global production (in millions of tons): 9 in 1932; 120 in 1937; 273 in 1940; 2,349 in 1945; 8,688 in 1950; 13,153 in 1955. The cost in workers was enormous. A former inmate of Vorkouta, Bernhard Roeder, writes: "It was reckoned that on the railways there was one death per crossing and in the pits, two deaths for every metre dug." This railway, it has been said, went to the furthest point in the world.

A striking illustration is thus given of the powerful dynamic of the system. Dalstroi is an extremely remarkable instance. Starting from the extraction of gold it became a giant enterprise of colonization. At the start, Dalstroi's authority extended only to the gold-mines of upper Kolyma and over the land traversed by the road linking it to the coast. It finally extended over the whole of north-east Siberia, from the Lenoy in the east to the Aldan in the north. Its monopoly was both *economic* and *administrative*. In this immense region, Dalstroi substituted its administration for that of the state. It was not content to own economic instruments; a mining trust, a powerful commercial organization, an autonomous fleet linking each factory to Vladivostok. It also had a political department, a department of agriculture, another of communication, etc. Its jurisdiction was equally extended to freed prisoners, to free workers, and to functionaries. Cards carried the legend: "territory under the direct jurisdiction of the NKVD".

The constant growth of its work-force, the absolute discretion it exercised over employment, the advantages in terms of efficiency of its authoritarian administration, the penury of financial means and the technological poverty turned the concentration camp into *the linch-pin of the industrialization of the distant and underdeveloped regions*. The huge wealth created was the basis for the NKVD's autonomy in the state *as a distinctive power*.

It is hence insufficient for an understanding of its specific function — economic, social, political, the three terms indissolubly linked — to assume that the commissariat of internal affairs constituted itself, in the bureaucratic society, as a powerful trust. Its total power has to be grasped through this fundamental fact: the NKVD as an organ of repression had sovereign disposal of a huge reserve work-force. The deportees, as a work-force, belonged to the state; but the state delegated the exercises of its right of property over them to the NKVD. This is so true that the trusts, and more generally, all the factories, had to turn to the central administration of the camps, the gulag, when they needed a labour-force. Now — and this is a key point — the trusts, which were hence also part of the state did not possess free right of disposition over the concentration-camp work-force. By virtue of the contract, they had to pay a rent to the gulag. This royalty, like the considerable profits which the concentration-camp enterprises made, constituted the due possession of the repressive apparatus. The NKVD furthered the surplus-value of concentration-camp labour, a consequence of the expansion of the institution. Arising from this, the process ceased to be blind and became a deliberate policy.

The function of the NKVD in the process of production reacted on its internal structure and introduced an organic anomaly into the composition of the high bureaucracy: the NKVD apparatus accumulated an exceptional quantity of exorbitant political privilege. This double trait constituted an essential factor in the exercise of power.

Within the NKVD two effects of crucial significance should be delineated. The central leadership was considerably reinforced. Internal technical diversification (the distribution of tasks) was changed into a polarization of power. The apparatus charged with the administration of the penal work-force in production acquired precedence as a right and enormous privileges as a fact. The administration of the forced collective-labour camps, the gulags, were constituted as an autonomous apparatus, entirely independent of the Ministries of the Interior of the federated republic, uniquely responsible to the central leadership of the NKVD. This independence vis-à-vis the security organs of the federated republics, which themselves occupied a pre-eminent position, led to the complete independence of the gulag in relation to all other administrations. So the concentration-camp complexes were implanted in regions where their effect was that of a foreign body, an outrage to normal law, with their own rules, and their own functionaries responsible to their autonomy alone. Thus the political path of a camp was not integrated into the party hierarchy, as it should have been, through the intermediary of the region. It worked uniquely through the political direction of the gulag, itself directly subordinate to the Central Committee. The Cheka section of a camp was not placed under the authority of the local organs of the state security; it was not at all accountable to them; on the contrary, it could give them instructions and use their resources in case of necessity. The courts and tribunals which tried both the prisoners *and the free personnel* employed by the camp were outside the jurisdiction of the regional judicial organization, which had no right in relation to their activities, nor appeal in relation to their decisions.

The gulag hence became the dorsal fin of the repressive forces. To break the concentration-camp institution — to withdraw from it the delegation of property rights which was its key — was to lead inescapably to the disintegration of the NKVD's power. Experience only confirms this analysis.

The first fundamental effect of the intervention of the concentration-camp factor was hence a powerful accentuation of the heterogeneity of the ruling class. It is not at all the consequence of the repression as such. No matter how extended was the use of terror, it could not have led to an organic modification of this nature. The autonomous implantation of the concentration-camp apparatus in the production-process alone had the capacity to disturb events. The same mechanisms which produced the agrarian bureaucracy came into being. In these two cases, the private ownership of the means of production is revealed to be a determining factor. That this appropriation takes the formal nature of a delegation of ownership in no way changes its real nature.

The delegation of property rights made to the benefit of the NKVD permitted it to lay hold of the surplus-value generated by the concentration camp. The enormous difference between the cost of the work-force invested (substituted for non-existent mechanical tools) and the rent drawn from the enterprises created (mining, agricultural, industrial, and commercial) and from services (the administrative control of new territory) guaranteed it considerable revenues and turned it into a social power within the state.

The NKVD as a repressive apparatus was a political corps integrated into the political bureaucracy. As a result the effects of its autonomous roots in the production-process, reacted in the sphere of state sovereignty. Differentiations came about in the heart of the upper bureaucracy; they intervened directly in the workings of power and extended, because of this, into the organization of labour and the elaboration of the law.

14 The dynamic of society and the institutions of central power

WE CAN HENCE observe a primary and fundamentally new phenomenon, of great significance, whose real effects were amplified because it developed at the same time that the bureaucratic state-capitalist society was being constituted and under the same historical constraints. Thus, it appeared as an organic deformation of this state capitalism as a whole, a major result conditioned by the profound regression of the 1930s.

The procedures followed were taken in the throes of necessity. The interference of deliberate choice appears as the consciousness of necessity, in the sense that with the terms of the equation given, the chosen solution is the only one possible. To appreciate what was happening, we must first grasp clearly the three basic facts of the situation, that is, the terms of the equation.

Accelerated industrialization was imposed as an imperious necessity. The problem was no longer posed within the perimeters of 1935 to 1939. The civil war had just delivered the entire economy, momentarily, over to private appropriation by the bureaucracy. Up until this point it possessed only one sector of this economy. It had now seized the totality of the productive forces. This seizure had a military and a political character. Although the rural middle classes were dispossessed, agricultural production was not, for all that, state production. This appropriation of the whole economy transformed the bureaucracy from a differentiated class into a ruling class; but its historical social consolidation forced it to give juridical appropriation its real foundation in the production process. In other words it had to proceed to a rapid expansion of state industry, industrial monopoly being the armour of the economic monopoly of the state. The obligation to industrialize hence took on the order of a necessity. The resulting consciousness acquired by the bureaucracy was like the reflex reaction of a living organism and its representation came about in terms of allocations, profitability, immediate needs, and extreme poverty. Industrialization clashed with obstacles at two levels: the organic weaknesses of nationalized industry and the absence of an adequate infrastructure. The second kind of difficulty was the most serious: in effect, it called into question the very possibility of industrial expansion. As a consequence the implantation of a national

182

infrastructure was the key to every undertaking. It was the indispensable material basis for it. The rhythm of execution of these basic essential works determined the general pace of industrialization. Concretely, industrial expansion — in this first phase — signified at one and the same time the refurbishment and rapid development of means of communication over land and water on a continental scale; and the exploitation and rendering productive of natural hydraulic and mineral resources. Two factors completely dominated this programme. Its realization called for the mobilization of considerable resources and colonization at a highly developed level. The exploitation of natural riches meant opening up vast, distant and inhospitable regions and creating new industrial complexes next to sources of energy and reserves of primary materials within the shortest possible space of time. All of this demanded massive population transfers. The initial plan could only be realized in extremely rough living conditions and by means of extremely arduous labour. At this level two decisive factors intervened. The state possessed neither the essential developed technology nor the necessary financial means. It was hence necessary to run entirely on human labour. Lack of capital resources meant it could not follow a policy of paying salaries high enough to attract and stabilize a workforce. And finally the international conjuncture of the 1930s (the organic crisis of world capitalism) stopped it finding the financial and technological support it needed in the external market.

The third objective factor was social violence. The second civil war produced a very high level of social violence. The chronic instability of the state's economic monopoly constantly gave rise to tensions which generated permanent social violence. This instability was due, as we know, to the fact that the dynamic impulse which the integrated capitalist state monopoly gave to the forces of production was unceasingly counteracted by the weaknesses of an excessively top-heavy system of control which brought in its wake a succession of repressive and corrective measures on a grand scale. Social violence created a mass of prisoners, which was constantly being replenished. This penal population, torn from its jobs, was available for forced labour.

The co-existence of these three fundamental facts unleashed the process of transformation of this latent labour-force into a servile and active work-force. Within the working class a concentration-camp type of proletariat was formed. (It is sociologically interesting to observe that ten years later under similar objective conditions brought about by the war, the same metamorphoses occurred in nazi Germany.)

The functional mutation of the mass of prisoners into a subject work-force transferred the monopoly of repressive control of the NKVD* into an act of appropriation of a powerful work-force.

It was a *qualitative* transformation. The NKVD's de facto — but tacitly acknowledged — ownership of a work-force of considerable size brought on the *autonomous* process of routing the repressive apparatus in the production-process. The direct exploitation of this work-force, its hiring out to state trusts and the appropriation of the resultant surplus-value created the economic monopoly of the NKVD. The industrial sphere where it became implanted (setting up the economic infrastructure, exploitation of sources of energy, colonization) was *decisive from the point of view of the global dynamic of the forces of production.* It conferred on this monopoly a central structural position in the economy in terms of primary development. Its leading role in the administration of labour was confirmed legally by the laws and decrees promulgated from 1932 to 1947.

Under the impact of its direct intervention into the production-process, the NKVD operated a discrimination within the state bureaucracy which worked to its advantage. This differentiation was expressed, as the facts reveal, as an exorbitant privilege with respect to laws and regulations, and through an effective pre-eminence in all other administrations and state institutions. (When the leading coalition wanted to emancipate itself completely from the tutelage of the MVD after the assassination of Beria it had to break the autonomous implantation of the gulag and transfer the administration of the corrective-labour camps to the jurisdiction of the minister of justice.)

The NKVD as an organ of repression was a political institution. Its fundamental function (guaranteeing the security of the established régime) was political. Its introduction into the production-process and the economic activity which resulted were not substituted for its political mission. On the contrary, its economic function developed as a consequence of its political function and remained entirely integrated into it in such a way that the pre-eminence over other state administrations was expressed *as a political pre-eminence.* In practice this led to the subordination of the party (the political

---

* For convenience I refer to the repressive apparatus as the NKVD, although in fact this institution changed its name several times. In 1941 the NKVD was divided in principle, into two commissariats (the NKGB, state security, and the NKVD, interior). However, this reorganization only came into effect in April 1943. In 1946 the commissariats became ministries: the MGB and the MVD. The MGB inherited the NKVD secret police. In March 1953 the MGB and MVD were reunified into a single ministry (the MVD) headed by Beria.

administration of the ruling class in society) to the repressive apparatus.

These mechanisms explain the objective process, the elementary social mechanisms which underlay the exorbitant power of the political police. They also explain, how, why and in what respect, the factor of the NKVD played an essential role in the structuring of power.

Analysis reveals that this complex process was indisputably a result of the material historical conditioning of the production–process and its social armour, and that as a consequence it appeared as a objective necessity. This is amply confirmed by the inverse phenomenon (but a phenomenon of the same kind) which first occurred at the end of the 1950s and in the first half of the 1960s, when the higher technological level produced by a world–wide change around 1940 began to have an effect in Russia. Administrative compulsion — as a regulator of production — was rejected by the new technical infrastructure. The introduction into the factories of up–to–date equipment and advanced norms of accountability proved to be objectively incompatible with the generalized usage, as a regulator and as a stimulator, of coercive relations developed through the experience of a subject work–force. It became clear that the system inherited from the 1930s and codified from 1932 to 1947, was a heavy shackle. The concentration camps began to disintegrate from within. This dislocation of such a powerful institution in its turn unleashed social violence (strikes and armed insurrections in the camps). Their central place in the state was confirmed by the fact that their elimination was accompanied by a rupture in the structures of power (the Beria crisis) and a prolonged calling into question of the status of the upper bureaucracy, (the political leaders of the state). This status had permitted it to usurp for its own profit the exercise of the right of property (the struggle of the reformers against centralized authoritarian planning and for autonomy in the factories). The determining role of administrative constraint in the work–process (the rules which regulated a sub-servient work–force contaminated the totality of protetarian relations in production) can also be gauged by the extent of obstacles which the law reform initiated with official destalinization encountered, and by the scale of resistance to the increasing recourse to contractual collective agreements.

Another no less original phenomenon takes on equal significance. The gulag, powerful as it was, was strictly subject to the central authority of the NKVD. Although it was independent, in law and in practice, the security service under the jurisdiction of the federal republics, it was closely attached and subject to the commanding heights of the NKVD. This rigorous subordination was exercised at all levels, as much on giant concentration-camp complexes as on the smallest units of labour and "camp points". The "Chekist operations section" or "third section" was responsible for constant, universal and suspicious surveillance. It was implanted deep in all the institution's activities and had the right to subject all personnel, detained or free, civil or military, to inspection and searches. The constant exercise of this discretionary control paralysed every tiny step towards autonomy and emancipation of the specialized personnel who controlled economic enterprises. It guaranteed by compulsion the organic fusion of repressive functions, economic tasks and military missions.

The administration of the corrective labour camps was immense and complex. It involved several million people with an enormous economic potential and covered vast, often almost inaccessible regions, huge enclaves of closely supervised inhabitants, and a network of railway and maritime transport spanned the whole national territory. This administration was combined with tasks of general supervision and security, which included guarding the frontiers, and therefore necessitated a powerful autonomous military force with numerous officers, modern armaments, and high mobility. The gulag constituted the economic base of support for this army, with an independent command and recruitment. The absolute pre-eminence of the concentration camp over other state administrations was extended to a privileged social status for its military cadre: a commander of security forces had the same rank and enjoyed the same prerogatives as a brigadier-general in the army, and a colonel corresponded to a divisional general. The social force of the NKVD comprised an organic combination of its own economic power, its autonomous security system and its recognized preponderance which gave it rights (without legal limits) to supervise and intervene. The basic task of the third section was to maintain the internal coherence of these factors. By consulting the security of the gulag and maintaining its tight connection with the central administration of the NKVD, the third section guaranteed the hierarchic pre-eminence of political personnel and in this way the respect for the dominant political nature of the institution. In return this politically validated acquired privilege gave the upper hierarchy of the NKVD an exceptional specific weight at the heart of the Central Committee, which was in principle the highest decision-making body. The third section hence fulfilled a major function (doubtless more automatic than deliberate) which now became clear: *it channelled the enormous power of the institution as a whole by concentrating it in its summit.* Thus the heads of the NKVD (Yagoda,

Yezhov or Beria) became, through mechanisms completely independent of their intentions, the exclusive controllers of a power superior to that of all other pressure groups, the Central Committee and the general staff included. This power was in no way a function of the personality concerned. It was exclusively related to his post in a rigid hierarchy reinforced by controls which were themselves hierarchical.

Officially and in practice the combined administrations of the NKVD and the gulag were subordinate only to the orders of the hierarchic chief, the chief of the NKVD. They were accountable only to him and their functions received sanctions and promotions only from him. The fact that Yagoda, Yezhov and Beria in succession were equally able to exercise this identical power in spite of their tragic ends clearly confirms that it was attached to their function and not to their person. Officially and formally the NKVD was under the authority of the Central Committee. In reality this was a legal fiction. When the Political Bureau and the Central Committee wanted to ensure a collegiate succession to Stalin, they had to eliminate Beria physically and to launch a limited but violent military action against his principal collaborators. This throws into sharp relief the real status of the head of the NKVD and the inanity of the legal regulations.

The enormous concentration of power at the head of the NKVD was incorporated by the Secretariat; that is to say by the only real organ of power to survive for a quarter of a century. The NKVD found itself dispossessed to the exclusive advantage of the General Secretary. On the level of the Secretariat a change came about: power ceased to be attached to a function and became an attribute of a person. At this level the chief of the NKVD was thrust into the same position of insecurity as a subaltern official. The enormous effective power controlled by Yagoda and then by Yezhov, did not shield them once Stalin had decided on their fall. On the contrary it was Stalin who each time took over their function. *The Stalinist dictatorship was founded on the incorporation of the power of the NKVD into the Secretariat.*

I have analysed the way in which objective circumstances (the proliferation, diversity and complexity of tasks) and deliberate calculations (factional struggles) gradually established the ascendancy, which was eventually to become absolute, of the Secretariat over the party and over the state. It is hence sufficient to emphasize two principal processes.

The procedure was technically dominated by the *principle of nominations*. From the outset this was one of the politically neutral attributes of the Secretariat. From 1923 to 1929 Stalin made this the basis of a nascent despotism. The Secretariat became the preponderant base for social and political operations. On the secretariat depended, through the mechanism only of appointments, promotions, and sanctions, the career of the higher officials of the party and the state. Through this Stalin exercised an effective professional and material control over the upper bureaucracy. Interests and opportunisms would polarize around the Secretariat; lodged itself in the centre of all intrigues. The integration between the party, the state and the economic monopoly transformed this negotiating influence into a diplomacy of power. The Secretariat spread its action throughout the state. Simply through the mechanism of discretionary choice of appointments, Stalin could disperse his adversaries, destroy their cohesion as a faction and render their opposition vulnerable. The identification of the party with the state transposed this factional, tactical superiority into a preponderance in the conquest of power. The Secretariat became the nucleus of a new power in the process of formation; not only because of the deployment of its activities, but because of the credit that it drew from it. In the social crucible of the civil war the Secretariat acquired a *deliberate* mutation: it concentrated the totality of effective power. From this point the principle of nomination defined the central procedure for the exercise of absolute power by the Secretariat. This was the technique by which Stalin controlled the upper spheres of the NKVD. Through the manipulation of the relevant section of cadres of the Central Committee the Secretariat manipulated the Chekist personnel. Its ultimate expression was the organization of generalized terror. One of the effective functions of the terror was a manipulation of personnel which involved very large numbers and effected a social replacement. The retroactive consequence was to maintain the integrity of the Secretariat's absolute power. This was confirmed continually until the beginning of the 1950s. Stalin's carefully planned actions then came up against fundamental changes in society. The so-called "white coats" plot which launched a new and bloody purge of the higher cadres and political leaders of the state began. The death of Stalin ended the Secretariat's role as a central organ of power.

This political process was entirely governed by the *principle of identifying Stalin with the social interests of the bureaucracy*. This identification corresponded in the first instance to a real decisively important movement of the bureaucracy. It was further reinforced by the launching of a powerful system of poisoning ideas and mystification.

Many people still remember the insane outpourings of prefabricated propaganda which was churned out obsessively (even though it is possible to forget the degree of stupidity, decadence and flabbiness, and the depth of intellectual depravity which were revealed in the world stalinist movement and which deserve close examination). This gross mystification is rich in lessons as an indicator of social putrefaction. In spite of the vast resources mobilized, its breadth and duration did not appear as a major factor in the process by which despotic power was exercised. On the contrary, to grasp this historically we have to understand the initial phase of free consent.

It was through free consent that the bureaucracy in the first instance recognized Stalin as its head. Without this initial genuine identification the stalinist dictatorship would have not been realizable. It is this — and this only — which gave Stalin the power of representativity. It is from this representativity that the secretariat drew its fundamental powers which permitted it to constitute itself as the unique centre of power and which authorized the personal embodiment of the dictatorship. It is hence a phenomenon of great historical significance.

When this identification came about the bureaucracy was in the process of being constituted. It was locked in the violent class conflicts which accompanied and reflected the disintegration of the first world revolution. These confrontations were projected into the interior of the party which became the sole crucible of power. The bureaucracy in its totality could only intervene in this decisive arena through the thermidoreans. Stalin was the most notable among them. His cynical lucidity, his patience, his cunning, his brutality, his vigorous sense of corruption, and his machiavellianism, made him a formidable adversary. His sharp understanding, gained very early on, of the specificity and immediate interests of the social work-force of the state made him its natural privileged interpreter. His tactical successes demonstrated his efficiency. He became the leader capable of realizing the political fusion of the thermidoreans, of the traditional body of civil servants and of the technical cadre of the statized economy. In the violence of the social confrontations the bureaucracy turned to him to guarantee the defence of its interests. *Freely given identification came about as a free abandonment by the bureaucracy of its political prerogatives.* It dispossessed itself of its potential powers. Stalin was not to relinquish these powers. What was necessary was a mutation of world society following the war in order for the bureaucracy to rid itself of stalinist despotism when this became a major obstacle to its development.

It is because of this blank cheque made out to him by a section of the whole bureaucracy, made out because they turned to him to guarantee their social preponderance that Stalin also had at his disposal means for the sovereign regulation of internal conflicts in the ruling class. This tacitly recognized power of arbitration assured his total ascendancy over the NKVD. The NKVD only represented a particular body within the bureaucracy. Its exorbitant privileges aroused in the party, the army, the administrations, and the enterprises, a hostility which could not be neutralized. However great the autonomous power of the NKVD, it could not prevail against the coalition of all the class forces without jeopardizing the foundations of the system. Now this coalition of forces could only come about at the level of the Secretariat. This is what established its absolute preponderance. Stalin could break the NKVD but the NKVD needed Stalin to defend its privileges.

The all-powerful NKVD was hence subject to the more powerful Secretariat. History provides us with irrefutable proof, even if it is necessary to lay bare the mechanisms. This subordination understood, it still remains the case that the NKVD as an instrument was irreplaceable for the dictatorship. Its power — and the nature of its power — were the only things which permitted universal, permanent terror and ensured that the deterrent fear of its intervention should be equally strong in the commanding heights of the state and at the heart of the Political Bureau itself, as in the most humble village, completely deprived of legal guarantees. This power was entirely based on the institution of the concentration camp, which fashioned its very nature.

15 The formation of the legal system

THE ORGANIZATION of stalinist power was the clearest expression of the regressive violence which rose from the depths of world capitalist society in decomposition between 1929 and 1940. The most developed product of this all-embracing reversal — the concentration-camp institution — made its simultaneous appearance (to within three years) in Russia and Germany. The Stalin régime's economic monopoly, its roots in production, were established some ten years earlier in the Soviet Union, where it took on its broadest scope. This delay is significant. It makes clear the original and unique character of the Russian process, whose effects were central. Basically, it was a result of the fact that the pace of disintegration of the first revolution was more accelerated than the pace of the organic crisis of capitalism. One of the reasons is obvious: the strategic defeats of the proletariat consolidated the bourgeoisie at the same time that the stalemate of the revolution, closing off a possible solution, brought capitalism's internal contradictions to the most critical stage of their development. In 1929 the process of disintegration, having come to fruition, produced its own solution: an organic modification of classes and their hierarchical structure. The process of disintegration of the revolution was thus caught up in a planet-wide reflex at the moment when it found the social solution to its contradictions in the outcome of the second civil war. It was in its constitutive phase that integrated state capitalism was seized by a powerful dislocation of the world forces of production. It was thus out of imperious necessity that the concentration-camp economic model emerged (as a reflex response to immediate needs), with generalized relations of constraint at work. This is why the concentration-camp deformations of the new society were organic. And it was because they were organic that they shaped the structures of power. At this level objective necessity became the basis for a deliberate intervention, which turned it into a system of government. Above and beyond a certain degree of empiricisim, it was its long-term efficacy which led to its institution-alization. The three years 1929, 1930 and 1931 were completely dominated by naked pragmatic violence. This brought about a social earthquake. The carnage took place from 1932 to 1934. The resultant state of things developed into a legal order. It rose out of brute social violence, and was consubstantial with it. From the moment that a system of law existed in its turn it became not only a legal justification for calculated intervention, but its operational tool. It constituted the armoury of the exercise of power. It developed its own logic and strength. This logic and strength were in a certain sense magnified by the exercise of power. The role of calculated intervention was inscribed in the legal code and the procedures for its application, to the extent that the law and the exercise of power must also be considered as objective traits, revealing the nature and the dynamic of the society. So far did their impact attain this scale, that Soviet society in the 1980s would be completely opaque without taking into account the legal work of the thirties and forties, the real exercise of power. The accomplishments of this period, in spite of major changes since, remain a permanent deformation.

No one can underestimate the importance of the night of the long knives in the comprehension of marxism. Episodes of a similar character, whose dimensions were even greater, figured incessantly from 1934 until the beginning of 1953. The Kirov affair introduced the constant extension of terror, which devastated the stalinist bureaucracy. The shock was so profound and so long-lasting that Khrushchev dates the terror to the year 1934. For the first time the stalinists underwent stalinist terror. In reality the terror began during the civil war, in 1930. It struck down tens of thousands of workers and hundreds of thousands of kulaks. Khrushchev only makes a passing allusion to it. For him the grand opening (the terror in all its fullness for him and his peers) was 1934. In his report to the 20th Congress he writes like an SA survivor talking of Hitler's murderous delirium. At the same time he reveals implicitly the role of his bloody past in the formation of the upper bureaucracy (a decisive role for its subjective conduct): the priority which it gave to destalinization; its motivation for the murder of Beria; the deliberate foundation of collegiate rule; and the limits imposed on Brezhnev. The solidity of the new collegiate power would be hard to appreciate without a full understanding of the trauma which the exercise of stalinist power produced in the ranks of the upper bureaucracy. This trauma was experienced by the whole bureaucratic class, as is shown by the prestige of the group formed in 1967 by "the sons and daughters of Stalin's innocent communist victims" with the intention of fighting against any return to stalinism. (Among forty signatories attached to a letter addressed to the central committee on the 24 September 1967 figure the names of the descendants of Bukharin, Radek, Antonov-Ovseenko, Shlyapnikov, Piatnitzky, Serebriakov, Enukidzhe, Kalinin, and many others.) Between 1935 and 1938 a million members of the communist party were arrested, six hundred thousand executed, and four hundred thousand deported. The new phase of the terror which opened in 1934 was concerned with the exercise of power, but equally with the logic of the legal system, since Vyshinsky, the founder of stalinist law, was also the organizer and prosecutor of the great trials; the arrests, condemnations, and deportations applied the new code. In this sense, 1934 undeniably marks an important point of departure (but in a different sense to that attached to it by Khrushchev): *naked violence was transformed into a system of institutionalized law*.

It is remarkable and very illuminating that the first fundamental expression of penal law was the juridical establishment of the NKVD, the discretionary character of its power, and its exclusive jurisdiction in the corrective labour camps — in other words the legalization of the already existing concentration-camp institution. Here, the legal system did not create, it simply registered the lessons of experience and gave them general application. This was all the more necessary, precisely because this was the way in which practical organization had already been widely extended, so that it was no longer intervening in a marginal sector of society, but on the contrary, in a vital domain.

The law of 10 July 1934 created the People's Commissariat for Internal Affairs, the NKVD. The ordinance of the TSIK and of the sovnarkom on 27 October 1934 transferred the corrective labour institutions, until then under the jurisdiction of the commissariat of justice of the republics, into exclusive dependence on the NKVD of the USSR. The law of 5 November 1934 set up the special conference of the NKVD (the sinister OSSO) and authorized the application *by administrative means* of deportation and incarceration in a corrective labour camp.

Directly after the Kirov assassination (which was carefully and painstakingly prepared by Stalin) the decree (repealed by Khrushchev) of 1 December 1934, dealing with the investigation of questions concerning terrorist actions, was the foundation of the complete arbitrariness of the terror. Its role was so great and its effects so tragic for millions of people that we must quote the terms of the code of penal procedure of the RSFSR (articles 466 to 470).

466. The inquiry in matters concerning terrorist organizations and terrorist actions directed against the functionaries of the soviet authorities (articles 58.8 and 58.11 of the penal code) must be finished within the space of a minimum of ten days.

467. The indictment shall be given to the accused 24 hours before the tribunal investigates the affair.

468. The inquiry takes place without the participation of the interested parties.

469. Appeal or commutation is not accepted.

470. Condemnation to the supreme punishment shall be put into

effect immediately after the verdict.

This unmitigated terror had lost none of its vigour in 1952, nearly twenty years after its legal codification, the machinations around the alleged doctors' plot heralded new amalgams at the summit, preparatory to a new bloody purge. The motives for a coup d'état by a majority faction of the upper bureaucracy against the NKVD were thus clear. To destroy the NKVD it could not have been enough to eliminate Beria and some twenty-nine of his close collaborators. The instrument had to be broken to render it unusable. Its social power had thus to be smashed by uprooting it from the process of production, by undoing its economic monopoly. Its jurisdiction in the camps was taken from it and given over to juridical institutions. Its economic enterprises were confiscated and redistributed to the competent ministers. These were decisions on questions of principle, which were certainly not easy to apply or rapid in execution. They implied such changes in the jurisdiction of personnel that the private interests at stake were both very large and very complex. Thus it seems (although what happened remains very obscure) that the dismantling of the giant complexes forming the basis of the monopoly had already been undertaken. Withdrawal from the NKVD of the delegation of its property cut it off from the real, objective sources of its power. It was also necessary to abrogate the law which gave legal foundation to its exorbitant privileges and which guaranteed it an effective pre-eminence in the political apparatus of the state. A decree on 1 September 1953, which was not made public, suppressed the OSSO. On 11 September the military tribunals of the NKVD were dissolved. These measures were completed on 20 April 1956 by the abrogation of the famous articles 456 to 470 of the code of penal procedure. A coup d'état always calls for popular approbation: the decree of 28 March 1953 announced a broad amnesty (limited however, in its essentials, to common law) and announced a forthcoming revision of the penal code.

Thus we are really dealing with a coup d'état, and not at all one of these violent changes of leading personnel which abound from 1934 onwards. This coup, through the scope of the measures it took and the even larger scope of their effects, confirms the analysis we have made of the structures of central power, its personnel, and the pre-eminent position of the NKVD in its working. It brought with it a new organization of power which, while safeguarding the personal security of state dignatories, by restoring to the upper bureaucracy its political attributes and its sovereignty of decision-making — confiscated by Stalin — weakened its position vis-à-vis other social categories of the bureaucratic class and disarmed it *relatively* in the face of the cumulative pressures exerted by other classes of Soviet society. This is completely confirmed by the major events of the 1960s and 70s.

The new course was neither liberal in the sense that this is understood by bourgeois democracy, nor was it a return to any kind of proletarian democracy. In effect it kept intact not only the private appropriation of the means of production by the state, but also the monopoly of the exercise of this right of property by the political corps of the state; that is to say by the upper bureaucracy. It was limited to a political and structural reorganization of the central power. Although it was voluntarily restricted in its social effects, this change corresponded to certain exigencies of rationalization of state capitalism and contributed to the acceleration of the crisis of bureaucratic society.

Stalin's death — whatever were the circumstances — came at the moment when his exercise of power was being rejected by the basic structure of society, that is by the workings of state capitalism. State capitalism's productive forces conflicted more and more forcefully with excessively functionalized control. This contradiction was all the more insupportable in that a new technology was available on the world market. Systematic and permanent terror thus appeared as the supreme expression of bureaucratic anachronism. This obstacle presented itself as a general danger under the impact of a growing backwardness in relation to the world market, above all due to the accelerated growth of American capitalism. This backwardness was certainly expressed in terms of economic profitability, but was also confirmed in the decisive domain of basic research. Whether in physics or in genetics, the terror sterilized the laboratories at the moment when, in direct relation with the process of production, it was becoming the accelerator of the economy.

Stalinist terror was incarnated in the secretariat and in the personalization of the exercise of power. Beria was the best placed person, as head of the NKVD, to guarantee the perpetuation of this system of government. On the other hand he did not enjoy the representativity which, from the outset, guaranteed Stalin's omnipotence. He fell to a coalition of forces in the bureaucracy. In the struggle against Beria the majority faction of the upper bureaucracy was supported by the whole ruling class. It used this general consent to break the apparatus of terror *only in so far as this apparatus exercised predominance over the bureaucracy*. Thus it opened the breach. But it did not suppress internment camps, nor the political police, reduced as it was to obedience and to its executive role. In the legal arsenal it abolished only those instruments which were a potential threat to it. It left the rest intact. It accomplished only a part of the tasks required by the new historical conjuncture. This was the basic significance of official destalinization. These narrow limits explain the essential data of the new course of the social crisis.

The most coercive institutional dispositions (the 1934 decrees) were not at all foreign to the body of law which was set up between 1930 and 1940. They were an integral part of it: a logical and undeformed product, of the organizing principles of the penal code. These principles remained. Their most general and also most rigorous application subsisted. From the moment that the preparatory discussion on the eventual reform of the penal code opened, this basic problem became clear. The review *Soviet State and Law*, in its second issue of 1956, is explicit in this respect: "Legal theoreticians must clarify the problems of guarantees and means of ensuring legality in relation to the rights and interests of citizens of the USSR; they must overcome the erroneous postulates which exist in the Soviet theory of proof. Precisely such a postulate is that of academician A. Vyshinsky, who denies the need for the tribunal to establish absolute truth in each affair and accepts the possibility of condemning a man solely on the basis of a probability of this or that fact which the tribunal takes into account. . . . Imputing guilt and responsibility for grave offences to this or that person on the sole basis of the personal testimony of the accused themselves — and this is how organs of instruction, tribunals and prosecutors conduct themselves in practice — constitutes a flagrant violation of the principles of socialist legality and the foundation of the theory of law." The principles are thus contested in their most general sense; this is confirmed by the offensive against Vyshinsky's work, which is precisely the key to penal theory in all its strength. The upper bureaucracy was prepared only to make marginal concessions: reducing the penalty for minor offences in common law; the introduction of elementary guarantees for the accused; and more scope for the defence. On basic principles it did not want to concede anything, and it didn't concede anything. It kept in being the intransigence and arbitrariness of stalinist law which was established in relation to political questions: the famous article 58.

Any real judicial reform was dead even before the reform of authoritarian and centralized control was itself suffocated. Here there is an important connecting link, which we must understand clearly. Between the principles of the penal code and the principles of authoritarian centralized control, there is no discontinuity, but on the contrary, an internal coherence. Between the legal reformers, the economic reforms, and the struggle of the intelligensia for "constitutional rights", leaving aside real disparities and the lack of recognized links, there is a causal continuity which allows us an in-depth appreciation of the crisis and its slow but steady radicalization, an understanding that the struggle for legal guarantees has played a role of the first importance in the emergence of political consciousness and hence in the overall dynamic of Soviet society. Thus we can see why the creation in 1970 of a "Committee for the Defence of Human Rights", on the initiative of academician Andrei Sakharov and the physicist Andrei Tverdokhlebov and Valery Chalidzhe, unleashed a socially explosive war machine. Sakharov's letter of 2 April 1971 in support of "the detained political prisoners in the Leningrad Psychiatric prison" who were on hunger strike and who were "defending humanity's intellectual liberty and the future of the human being", the successive internment of General Piotr Grigorenko, the trial of Brodsky, Siniavsky and Daniel, and Ginzburg and Galanskov, Pavel Litvinov and Larissa Daniel's "appeal to world public opinion", the deportation of Andrei Amalrik and many others, show the burning actuality of the penal laws promulgated from 1930 to 1940.

The penal code is the direct expression of the structure of power and of real social relations between classes. A radical modification of its principles would presuppose changes in political procedures which would be not superficial but organic; they would imply, in the context of the present régime – even more than the complete revision of the mechanics of central control envisaged by the reformers — a new distribution of property laws in relation to the means of production. This is why social resistance occurs.

The marxist dictum, which we have already quoted — "law can never be at a higher level than the economic base and degree of social development to which it corresponds" — here finds a new and broad illustration. Law reflects real social structures and the real level of development. It is not, however, a neutral mirror. It also bears witness to the ruling class's consciousness of its social interests. The language of law — of those who make the law — is therefore mystificatory although circumscribed in its intentions (in the statement of its motives); in order to remain functional, the law is necessarily constrained by reality. Penal law is a strong indicator of social tension (of the level of class struggle) and of what it is that the ruling class wants to defend against social aggression. It therefore reveals with stark clarity the class nature of society.

The principal objective of the coup d'état against Beria was to ensure a collegiate succession to Stalin. This was the *private* aim of the upper bureaucracy. It wanted to restore its hold on power collectively. It then converted this recuperation of decision-making power into a monopoly. Its political mastery of the state gave it direct and sovereign control of state property. The other social categories of the bureaucracy (first and foremost the managing bureaucracy in the factories) could not intervene in central decision-making in any way whatsoever. All that was left to them was the exercise of pressure, which they had never been deprived of. The other classes (proletariat and peasantry) were not only unable to participate in economic decision-making (in the absence of necessary institutions), but were also powerless to organize themselves in pressure groups. The trade unions had long been tools of the establishment in the factory, so that the de facto (but not de jure) non-existence of any legal guarantees prevented the formation of any association (corporative or political) outside of the official bodies of the estate.

The upper bureaucracy had to confront two dangers. The extraordinary shortage of goods created a situation of permanent social tension, loaded with risks. The profitable working of state capitalism called for a rationalization of management method. Here lay a serious long-term danger. The salvation of the upper bureaucracy was tightly bound to its ability to create rational conditions of growth for state capitalism. The shortage of consumer goods posed in immediate terms, in a very sharp way, the question of the peasantry. The peasants comprised the labour-force of the agrarian bureaucracy. Securing real returns from them was tied to their acquiring a certain standard of living. On these returns, in large measure, depended the stability and social reinforcement of the agrarian bureaucracy. The combination of these interests transformed this bureaucratic corps into an efficient pressure group. For its part, the ruling class as a whole was demanding that its social privileges be converted into material well-being; it possessed the means to make its demands felt.

The rationalization of management urgently demanded the imposition of new labour relations. Constraint of a generalized, concentration-camp type was turning out to be an anachronistic aberration. In this respect matters were so urgent that on 8 May 1956 a decree abolished the judicial responsibility of workers and salaried staff who left employment irregularly or were over-frequently absent. The same text ordered the immediate release of persons imprisoned for such offences. This introduced, for the benefit of the heads of advanced enterprises, who were handicapped by the poverty of their skilled workers, a more liberal practice on the labour market, and signalled a return to contractual methods and the free play of wage differentials. It was a first, elementary recognition of the demands of the market, necessary for the proper working of state capitalism. In a certain sense, the worker was allowed to deal directly with his or her immediate employer, the head of enterprise. At the same time there was a revision of the statutes concerning heads of enterprise, which until then had been tightly subordinated to the central administration. Rationalization implied a broad re-examination of these statutes. The managerial bureaucracy, through this series of changes, became a powerful pressure group. The reformers made themselves its interpreters and its theoreticians. It was imperative to recognize the need of scientific personnel for freedom of work, of which they had been violently deprived for a quarter of a century. The growth of modern technology and military security (that is to say, the situation of the state in the world arena) demanded this. Now scientific labour is very specific: complete intellectual freedom in all spheres (elaboration of theory, initiative in experiments, inter-pretation of the facts, and the critique of principles) represents a necessary condition which, through freedom of publication, meeting, and international exchanges necessarily implies close co-operation with the world scientific community. Even more, this necessary freedom reacts on teaching, its direction, and its programmes. This was the stumbling-block to the upper bureau-cracy. It found itself confronted with the most difficult problem possible: how to concede those liberties demanded by the growth of productive forces, and hence indispensable, while at the same time placing a well-defined barrier around them. It therefore tried to transform the scientific intelligensia into a *socially isolated privileged caste*. It met with only relative success. The scientific intelligentsia itself became a powerful pressure group and opposition force, at the very moment when its role in the production-process gave it con-siderable security. This produced a double movement. Scientists intervened in the critique of economic control, with all the authority conferred on them by their position. The world-renowned physicist P.L. Kapitza, in 1966, took up the low level of industrial produc-tivity, which he thought could not be simply reduced "to a gap in the field of science between us and the Americans". In April 1970, in a letter addressed to Brezhnev, Kosygin and Podgorny, academician Sakharov, the historian Medvedev and the physicist Turchin made an incisive critique of the economy which ended with a *political* programme of gradual democratization. This was a document of crucial significance, bringing together two movements. Permanent criticism, which is a principle of scientific thought (since it ascribes an absolute discriminatory function only to experience), could not for long be dissociated from fundamental freedoms of expression and association. The meetings of these movements came about in a joint opposition involving scientists, literary figures and artists. Sakharov joined with the cellist Rostropovich when he argued, on 14 November 1970, taking up the defence of Solzhenitsyn: "Every man must be able to say without fear what he thinks." This brings to light the casual relation, which, from the beginning of the 1970s, brought together in a unified social dynamic the disparate oppositions in the domains of law, economic control, and public freedom. The upper bureaucracy could find no more adequate response than to tell Andrei Tverdokhlebov, Valery Chalidzhe and Andrei Sakharov that their "Committee for the Defence of Human Rights" was illegal, as in effect did prosecutor Roman Rudenkov, and to invent psychiatric clinics as an adjunct of selective repression. To resist the coming together of such powerful social pressures, based on such solid support, the post-stalinist upper bureaucracy no longer possessed the preventive mass terror, of which, in the defence of its own interest, it had broken the principal instrument, the NKVD. This is an established fact which must be fully taken into account. It makes it possible, for example, to estimate the real strength of those tendencies which, in the 1960s and 1970s were working towards the re-establishment of stalinism and which, in certain respects very justifiably, caused such alarm for the intellectuals. Such a return to functional stalinism would have pre-supposed that the upper bureaucracy would once more put in the hands of one of its peers a discretionary power over it and over others. After the cruel experiences of 1934 to 1953, it could not take this decision except as an act of desperation, confronted with such a peril that it was convinced that it could not survive otherwise. It would also be necessary to re-establish the NKVD — the pivot of despotic power — with all its privileges. That is to say, it would call for the reintroduction of concentration-camp institutions in the pro-duction-process. Now from all the evidence, this would be to go so much against the social and technological demands of modern production that the risk of disintegration of the productive forces of state capital would become an immediate and catastrophic threat. It thus appears that for such a reaction to be consistent there would have to be not only an extremely critical internal situation but also a violent reversal of the world conjuncture; an eventuality, however, which cannot be ruled out altogether. It thus seems more in conformity with present conditions to suggest that these ultra-react-ionaries, who are recruited above all from the mediocre functionaries of intermediary organs, cannot obtain much more than a toughening of political prohibitions.

The upper bureaucracy was hence obliged to manoeuvre and concede. Acceptable concessions were still very limited. Immediate demands — both from the managerial corps of the enterprises and from the intelligentsia, and also from the peasantry and proletariat — would become much more dangerous if they found political expression. The 1960s undeniably showed an evolution of this order among the intelligentsia. A clear understanding of the risks it was running explains the central strategic principle of the post-stalinist upper bureaucracy, confirmed by all its major actions: keep the oppositionists in a state of complete disorganization. Pulverized, they would remain politically inert. The repression thus had the principal task of preventing any regroupment of forces. It could not achieve this without permanent, generalized preventive control. This control and prevention needed a legal cover in order to deprive the bureaucracy's adversaries of the juridical means to delay and dissuade. *The upper bureaucracy thus found itself under a strict obligation to keep the armoury of the stalinist penal code intact.*

The permanence and the constant application of these ossified laws, after the coup d'état, established the juridical continuity of the régime. The upper bureaucracy thus had all the more need to stress its political discontinuity. It had to obtain the political credit, the same blank cheque which had originally been the source of Stalin's power. It thus had to wash its hands of its historic responsibility by setting aside any deliberate involvement on its part in the crimes of the stalinist era. This is the dominant political sense of Khrushchev's report to the 20th Congress.

16 Khrushchev's theory of Stalin's power

IN NO WAY did Khrushchev maintain that he and his colleagues were ignorant of the scope and methods of the repression. Such a flagrant falsification would not have furthered their aims. All he maintained was that the high dignitaries of the régime were reduced to impotence. This was his central thesis. "Any attempt to oppose suspicions and accusations without foundation," he explained, "would have resulted in the person who came out in opposition becoming a victim of the repression." He indicated that officials such as Voroshilov, Molotov, Mikoyan — that is to say the very highest level — were on the verge of being executed. This thesis could not however remain credible unless its author could demonstrate the unique and sole responsibility of Stalin, not only in general decision-making but also in its particular applications. Khrushchev maintained this consistently. Stalin demanded "absolute submission to his will". Stalin was the originator of the concept of "enemy of the people". It was Stalin who had recourse to "the administrative violence of mass repression". To establish the decisive role of Stalin in particular, Khrushchev used three arguments: direct intervention, hierarchical responsibility, and criminal connivance. "He encouraged the vicious practice under which the NKVD prepared lists of people whose cases were submitted to military jurisdiction and whose sentences were decided in advance. Yezhov sent these lists to Stalin personally in order that he could approve the condemnations." He recalled that Yezhov was Stalin's creature, that it was Stalin who, on 25 September 1936, imposed the replacement of Yagoda by Yezhov in order "to recover from four years' back-sliding in repression on the part of the NKVD". As to connivance, he took Beria, "the enraged enemy of our people, the agent of foreign espionage services", as witness. "The question is posed as to why Beria, who had liquidated tens of thousands of members of the party and of the soviets, was not unmasked by Stalin." He replied: "Because he had very cleverly used Stalin's weaknesses; feeding him suspicions, he helped Stalin in every way and *acted with his support*." (My emphasis.)

The contagion of the terror is presented as the causal chain of successive levels of subordination in the hierarchy. "Whoever opposed Stalin's conception or attempted to explain his own point of view and the basis of his position was eliminated from the ruling cadres and subsequently subjected to moral and physical destruction."

Taking impotence to be similar to non-responsibility, Khrushchev exempted the upper bureaucracy. *He separated it politically* from the crimes which it lived through and carried out. At the same time, with great ease, he exempted the régime from its historic responsibilities. If in fact the enterprise was that of Stalin alone; if this bloody era was due only to a monstrous amplification of his own innate cruelty, then the structures of the régime had always been healthy and remained so. Khrushchev reinforced this idea by locating the beginning of the terror in 1934. He introduced the action of a caesura in the course of the repression. He approved of the struggle led by Stalin against the trotskyists, Zinovievists, Bukharinites, "these enemies of leninism", "who have been long ago defeated in the party". He approved the deportation of the kulaks, that is to say the second civil war and its strategic conduct. He condemned without reservation the regression which began after the assassination of Kirov, "against many honest communists, against the cadres of the party who had carried the heavy load of the civil war and of the initial most difficult years of the revolution, of industrialization and collectivization, *who had actually fought against the trotskyists and rightists for the leninist line in the party*". (My emphasis.)

Thus Khrushchev established *a political distinction within Stalinism.* He reassured the political corps of the state, whose support he sought. By validating the historic work of Stalin in the crucial years from 1929 to 1934, he was able to say clearly that there was no danger, under the pretext of destalinization, of calling into question the enormous social privileges acquired by the state bureaucracy; and the renewed condemnation of the old opposition guaranteed the positions of these who had been the active agents of the repression. In this way Khrushchev avoided a political trial. The liberation of those who had suffered "unjustly", their rehabilitation and their return did not imply any weakening of the positions of the officials still at their posts, who had arrested, condemned and deported them. This was a major and a necessary undertaking, since the upper bureaucracy wanted to gain the confidence of the existing body and its officials.

Khrushchev completed this manoeuvre by suggesting a reconciliation; that is to say the reintegration into the state apparatus of those who had been dissidents up till then, provided they accepted the social status quo. "As for those", he said, "who in the past have opposed the line of the party, there have not *often* been *serious reasons* for their physical destruction. The formula 'enemy of the people' was created in order to physically annihilate these individuals. . . many had worked beside Lenin during his life." (My emphasis).

Official recognition, which could appease their rancour, allowed them to regain their positions and to be integrated (and some in fact spoke at subsequent congresses).

Hence we are talking about a very broad political operation corresponding to a definite interest; but no more than that, and certainly not a serious attempt to explain the past. But no matter how skilful and cunning Khrushchev proved to be, he could hide neither his dismissive attitude to the best-known events, nor the inconsistency of his interpretation. It was not *after* 1934 that the falsification of history opened with the onset of the cult of the personality; it was in 1929, on the occasion of his fiftieth birthday, that the press and state publications discovered that Stalin had been the predigious military chief of the October insurrection, the creator of the Red Army, the closest collaborator of Lenin, and the organizer of victory. Indeed it was at the 17th Congress (in January 1934) that Kirov proclaimed Stalin "the greatest man of all times and of all peoples" (*Pravda*, 2 February 1934). To pretend that the "despotic and capricious character" of Stalin was at the root of everything and that the systematic application of terror during a quarter of a century could be explained by the weakness and lack of character of his entourage ("doubtless the arbitary actions of a single person encouraged and permitted arbitrary actions on the part of others") is by all accounts grievously inadequate. In order that such a flagrant contradiction between the scale of the crime and the alleged causes should remain obscured, it was necessary that those concerned should be constrained by powerful motivation not to pose indiscreet questions. In fact, the decisive argument, which ensured loyalty but was never expressly formulated, was very simple: by absolving the upper bureaucracy of its historic responsibility the entire bureaucratic corps was exempted and the social security of the régime preserved.

On the other hand, the insistent care taken by Khrushchev to make 1934 a year of carnage separating two historical moments of stalinism established the reverse of what he was trying to prove; through revealing the juridical, political and social relationships, the permanence of the institutional infrastructure was confirmed. In fact between 1929 and 1934 the fundamental role of stalinism was accomplished: the establishment and organization of the state bureaucracy as a ruling class. Now in Khrushchev's eyes this was the positive political and social balance-sheet. The terror, which could be and was legitimately condemned, came later. It was precisely that terror and no other of which he proclaimed the end. Khrushchev had no need to elaborate a theory of the ruling class — it was an instinctive reality to him, as he showed by presenting the victims of the terror in order of their social precedence. The political corps of the state occupied the foreground. Out of the 139 members and alternates of the Central Committee elected by the 17th Congress, 98 were arrested and assassinated. 1,108 out of 1,956 at this congress were "arrested and charged with counter-revolutionary crimes". There followed "the first-secretaries of the central committees or party committees of the districts and republics". The military occupied the second rank. Technicians were relegated to third rank (and they had been the first, in 1928, to become the object of this kind of perse-cution and trial). As for the rest, as for "ordinary soviet citizens", workers and peasants, "it is sufficient to say that the number of arrests carried out under the heading of counter-revolutionary crimes multiplied tenfold between 1936 and 1937". The social emphasis was on the cadres. Khrushchev demanded of his social supporters, the qualified representatives of the ruling class, that they give the upper bureaucracy the means of guaranteeing a new stability for established institutions.

The major difficulty encountered by Khrushchev's theses relates to the internal coherence of the laws elaborated between 1930 and 1940 and to the fact that this coherent body of law reflects at one and the same time the *real relations between classes* and the *real nature of power*. By maintaining the armour of the Penal Code in working order — because its efficiency was needed — the upper bureaucracy confirmed that the *fundamental* relations between classes had not been modified and that the relative progress in the running of state capitalism had not substantially altered relations between the social categories of the ruling class.

Khrushchev demonstrated his shrewdness by falsifying history under a guise of revealing the truth, thus covering over the crucial period in which bureaucratic society was born.

The official revelations touched, not on the terror itself as it was lived by millions of soviet citizens, but on the mystification in which it had been dressed up. Khrushchev destroyed the state tissue of lies. He exposed the machinations of the police, the techniques of the provocateurs, the prefabrication of trials. He established the falseness of the accusations and the inanity of the testimony obtained by torture. This was the truthful side.

This truth assumed great persuasive power *because it was exposed by the very régime which had brought about the situation that it was denouncing*. Molotov, Mikoyan, Khrushchev and the others *were* the instruments of the power that Stalin had wielded. Now they kept this same power in place.

The only rupture in continuity was the death of Stalin and the execution of Beria. Khrushchev's central objective was to prevent *a change in the régime which followed*. In order to realize this goal, he carried out a retreat in advance (the decision to make an official revelation) and he used the commotion which this provoked to delineate the boundaries of admitted official truth.

The falsification embodied in this position concerns the causes of the terror, its social structure, and its immense consequences. The terror, in fact, being as we know a product of the disintegration of the first revolution, acted within the world working class, and its effects — for example, on the conduct of the civil war in Spain — worked to accelerate the rhythm of world-wide regression.

Khrushchev's falsification carries with it a profound distortion of Stalin's role.

17 Stalin's cardinal task: organic laws 1932–40

STALIN DEFINED the political foundation of the Law. It was left to Vyshinsky to formulate penal theory, elaborate its principles and define its precise mode of application. Khrushchev's revelations in this area are exclusively concerned with that which is directly due to Vyshinsky. It is remarkable that he does not deal at all, in this field, with the domain with which Stalin concerned himself. A critical investigation of this area would destroy the basis of Khrushchev's falsifications.

Stalin wrote in *Questions of Leninism*:

> The suppression of classes must be brought about, not by the extinction of class struggle, but by its accentuation. *The withering away of the state, will come about, not by a weakening of state power, but by its maximum reinforcement*. This is indispensable to bring about the demolition of the dying classes and to organize defence against capitalist encirclement, which is far from being destroyed, and will not be for some time. (My emphasis).

The theoretical veneer was absurd; the empirical justification was half-truths; the serious and solid nucleus was the reinforcement of the state. Stalin was saying two things, one borrowed, the other true.

His sophism on the withering away of the state was a political concession to the reasoning in use among the Old Bolsheviks and in marxist circles. It was only window-dressing. The allusion to "the demolition of the dying classes" was simply a diversionary tactic. Khrushchev was to reply (but later) that the repression was directed "not against the rest of the defeated exploiting classes, but against honest workers of the party and the Soviet state". This was certainly true after dekulakization. A kernel of truth remains: the maximum reinforcement of the state.

Stalin was the man of the state. His social milieu was the political corps of the state. His instruments for intervention were the services provided by the state. The party itself existed only as a creation of the state. The régime was based on the private property of the state. The exercise of property rights was anchored in state property. Social privileges accorded to state officials were a product of the nationalized economy. The appropriation of this surplus value is only guaranteed to the extent that state ownership of the forces of production is not transformed into socialized property or returned to monopoly capitalism. The social power of the political corps was a function of the political, economic, social and military strength of the state itself. As a consequence, the directive on the maximum re-inforcement of the state *was absolutely* justified from the point of view of the class which *possessed the state*. It was in this sense that Stalin was saying something true.

Stalin considered that the key to the reinforcement of the state *was the reinforcement of the protection of economic ownership and exercise of rights over this ownership*.

Stalin made this strategic choice clear in a way which was brutal — but precise, clear and simple — in the manner of a nineteenth-century mill-owner. His reasoning by analogy — divested of all the theoretical trappings — was done in order to be listened to and understood by those who had a direct interest — those who effec-tively controlled property, who drew from it a substantial and real profit, by those who as a consequence had a very concrete, clearly definable interest in its conservation and reinforcement. Stalin wrote in *Questions of Leninism*:

> The base of our régime is to be found in public property, in the same way that the base of the capitalist régime is to be found in private property. If the capitalists in their time were able to affirm the capitalist régime by proclaiming private property sacrosanct and untouchable, we in our turn, as communists, must with even stronger justification, declare public property sacrosanct and untouchable, in order to reinforce in this way the new socialist forms of the economy in all areas of production and commerce.

The Soviet jurists distinguished state property from public property, the second category covering the property of the kolkhozes and the co-operatives. We know that this juridical distinction was founded in reality. The agrarian bureaucracy disposed of an autonomous basis in the production-process. Just the same, without being integrated into state capitalism, exploitation of the kolkhozy was socially guaranteed by it. Thus said the Law.

The dominant form of property was state property. On this point, mystificatory ambiguity was reduced to its simplest possible expression. It is summarized in this single explanatory phrase: "which is the property of the whole people". The Law said only that the ownership of the means of production belonged to the state. This affirmation corresponded to the facts. If it had said anything else, the Law would have been useless. The Law, on the contrary, did not say — at least explicitly — what state property is. More exactly the Law did not say — explicitly — who the state belonged to. It was the organization of the régime itself which said it. We know that the state in fact belonged as private property to the social corps of the state; that is to say, the bureaucracy. The Law recognized this implicitly. The Law, yet again, was obliged to correspond to the reality of society (which was not necessarily the case for the constitution). Thus we know *what* the Law protected and *who* it protected. In this way we know who *controlled* and who *exercised* ownership. Starting from the given social facts, a reading of the Penal Code reveals a remarkable internal coherence. The state is at the heart of every single protective mechanism. The property of the state, the personnel of the state, power and the exercise of power are protected by draconian legal dispositions and are the *only* institutions so protected. If, on the other hand, state property was in the process of becoming social property (if it belonged to the people as a whole) the Penal Code would necessarily have devoted a large part of its dispositions to guaranteeing the functioning and security of all controls *by society over the state*: to guaranteeing the rights and security of the people who exercised these controls. Now, there does not exist the least trace of such dispositions, for the sole reason that they correspond to nothing real. The Penal Code only recognizes the prerogatives of the state and its administration. It does not protect society against the state. At the same time, if it is asked against whom state property is protected, the response is equally precise. Against evil managers, certainly; but first of all, in the sphere of commerce, against private property, and in state production, against the workers in the enterprises. The Penal Code does not guarantee the workers a single opportunity to exercise their rights. On the contrary it accords considerable protection to the enterprise director against his workers. It grants no guarantees to the state wage-earners against the state as employer; on the contrary, it grants the state discretionary powers over its work-force. In this way the Law described with precision the real relations between classes.

The Law does not have to provide a *proof* of the class nature of the Soviet state. This proof arises from the analysis of its historical development. The Law appears as a statement. It *describes real* relations. This description cannot contradict the model of society which was arrived at through an analysis of concrete historical development. A manifest *incompatibility* results from a reading of Soviet Penal Law according to the criteria of the state with a proletariat as the ruling class (even with the major part of its powers delegated to a parasitic fraction of itself). On the contrary a rigorous *cohesion* is revealed by reading the Soviet Penal Law according to the notion of state property as private property and according to the class antagonisms which this implies.

The organization of the Penal Code rests in its entirety on the law of 7 August 1932 which ensures the protection of the welfare of the state. The official exposition of its grounds takes us back to Stalin's argument: "The TSIK and the SNK of the USSR hold that public property (that is to say, state property, the kolkhozy, and the co-operatives) is a foundation-stone of the Soviet structure, that it is sacred and inviolable and that those who feed parasitically off public property must be regarded as *enemies of the people* considering that a resolute struggle against those who pillage public welfare is the first duty of the organs of Soviet power." (My emphasis.)

Of this law, Stalin wrote: "to allow the theft and dilapidation of public property, whether it concerns state goods or goods belonging to the co-operatives or the kolkhoz, and *proving to be negligent* in relation to such *counter-revolutionary* misdeeds, is to contribute to undermining the Soviet régime which rests on public property as its basis. This was the point of departure of our government when it recently published its law on the protection of public property. This law now constitutes *the basis of revolutionary legality*. The implacable obligation to apply it is the first duty of every communist, of every worker, and every kolkhoz member."

The fundamental character — from the point of view of the legislator's intentions — of the law of 7 August 1932 is clearly spelled out. It constitutes, officially but also in reality, *the basis of legality*. Stalin's commentary links three basic notions: the protection of state property, the social and political security of the ruling power, and the severity of the penalties incurred. Any attack on the integrity of state goods or any negligence in their protection amounts to a direct threat to the established power (and is thus a counter-revolutionary act, that is, a political act); it therefore calls for exemplary punishment (shooting, long deprivation of liberty or deportation to a corrective labour camp). His exposition of grounds introduces a supplementary notion, "the enemy of the people". We saw the role that Khrushchev assigned to this in the machinery of mass repression. This notion appeared in the penal code in 1932 and not after 1934, as an instrument of defence of state property. Khrushchev was careful to avoid mentioning this.

Stalin's political instructions ordained that the 1932 law should be considered the prototype on which legislative work should base itself. It is enough to look through the penal code, the code of penal procedure, and legal writings, to see that in effect the references to his exposition of grounds and his dispositions, are made repeatedly in all articles of the penal code[35]. From the point of view of the penalties prescribed, the 1932 law was extremely severe. The Soviet jurist Kareva, in his book on Soviet law published in 1948, declared: "The law of 7 August 1932 established the application of the severest punishments for the pillage of public property." In fact, through its reference to corrective labour camps with deprivation of liberty, it introduced the concentration camp principle which became the cornerstone of legalized coercion.

The 1932 law — in spite of what Stalin's expression "now" might imply — was not therefore provisory, nor limited to the immediate circumstances (the economic disaster and famine of 1932) which produced it. On the contrary — and this is very significant — it remained a fundamental law, and its coercive provisions were *reinforced* long after the tragic consequences of forced collectivization had been essentially overcome. According to Kareva, the decree of 4 June 1947 (after the Second World War), "On penal responsibility for the dilapidation of state goods and public goods", established "prolonged incarceration in corrective labour camps (*from between seven years and twenty years*, with confiscation of goods)".

The importance attributed to the 1932 law goes beyond the legislative domain. For the first time in my knowledge, repression as such was considered to be a powerful instrument for the transformation of society. Now this is one of Stalin's cardinal theses, one of the keys to his conduct. Repression as an institution became the efficient means of changing the traditional data of society. This remarkable concept is at one and the same time the cornerstone of despotic power and of its consciousness. One can thus consider it as an axiom of any counter-revolution *from above*. It dominated stalinist strategy and gave rationality to the show trials and successive mass repressions.

One of the notables among Soviet jurists, Estrine, in his book on Soviet penal law published in 1935, outlines very clearly this crucial concept: "For the realization of the task which consists in *ensuring the penetration of a consciousness of socialist legality into the heart of the broadest possible masses of workers*, enormous significance attaches not only to the fact of the publication and application of a law prescribing severe punishment for the dilapidation of socialist property but also to the interpretation of this law made by comrade Stalin, in elevating it to the level of a *major principle from the political point of view*."

The field of application of this concept — and hence the lessons drawn from the law of 1932 — in fact covered the totality of social activities. To convince oneself of this it is enough to consult a work published by the Ministry of Justice in 1948 on Soviet military penal law, whose author, a certain professor V.M. Chkhikvadzhe, repeats insistently, on page after page, this lapidary judgement: "We can say *without exaggeration* that Soviet legislation concerning penal military law has played an important role in the gigantic national war of the

Soviet people against German fascism and the imperialism of the Japanese bandits." (My emphasis)

As for the definition of what should be understood by the application of penalties (which is at the heart, as Estrine says, of reaching the consciousness of the broadest masses of workers) the same Chkhikvadzhe says without beating about the bush: "*Just as in penal law*, in penal military law punishment consists in imposing determinate moral and physical suffering on the guilty. As a result it inevitably includes the element of intimidation without which the very notion of punishment cannot be conceived." (My emphasis.)

Thus, to the extent that penal law is organized on the 1932 model, following Stalin's political instructions, it correctly describes the antagonistic class relationships of Soviet society, these antagonisms themselves being caught up in the barbarous recession in world society. *The fact of the concentration-camp system became the creator of the system of law.*

Vyshinsky taught Professor Chkhikvadzhe's generation the corrective role of "moral and physical suffering". The theoretician of Soviet Law and the organizer of the show trials — and thus the most competent expert after Stalin — wrote: "In the system of organs of the proletarian dictatorship, the institution of corrective labour plays a serious and important role, *because it is through them, in summary, that the whole of judicial policy is realized.*"[36]

18 The juridical foundations for the political defence of the state

THERE ARE TWO aspects of the relation between Soviet Law as a whole and the crucially important law of 1932. Its *political* content developed at three levels: defence of state property (offences against state property or against its management defined as a counter-revolutionary crime); defence of the state administration (article 59); defence of the régime and its representatives (article 58). Show trials and systematic repression developed legally on this foundation. The *social* content of Soviet Law developed in three directions: defence of fixed capital and state production (article 128), delimitation of the authority of enterprise directors (law of June 1940); prerogatives of the state as employer and measures of social defence (laws and decrees of 1938, 1940, 1942 and 1947). The outcome was the generalization of legalized coercive relations in the labour-process.

The law of 1932 assimilated attacks on property into political crimes. It stipulated: "These offences are to be placed on the same footing as offences against the state." Its preamble characterized them as "counter-revolutionary misdeeds". Those who pillage state goods are "regarded as enemies of the people". Article 58 defines political crime: "Any act shall be considered as counter-revolutionary which is aimed at overturning, defeating or weakening the Soviet power (. . .) or aimed at the defeat or weakening of the national security of the Union and the economic, political and national conquests of the proletarian revolution."

The defence of state property was thus linked to more than the defence of the state in general. Strengthening its economic monopoly was not only meant to reinforce the social state apparatus. Offences against state property were identified with an attack on state power. This identification shows exactly who exercised the property rights in their full sense: the political apparatus of the state, the upper bureaucracy — those who held sway over the prerogatives of power.

Soviet Law describes, with great precision, one of the new organic features of developed state capitalism: the incorporation of the political factor into the concept of property and its real possession. *It was this conjunction between the private possession of the state and the private appropriation of the means of production which led to and explains the identification between crimes against property and political crime.*

By deliberately confusing the penal significance of crimes against

213

property and assaults on state power, the Law registered the foundation of bureaucratic appropriation.

The mechanism of this appropriation in its turn explains why the upper bureaucracy, which controls the state politically, was able to create for itself — by using its monopoly of political decision-making to acquire the effective exercise of property rights — a position of pre-eminent importance within the ruling class.

The Law made it a ruling class in two ways. As we have seen, it gave juridical expression to the position of the enterprise directors (the managerial bureaucracy). And in the Penal Code it gave over-whelming and in fact structural importance to the direct intervention of political authority, hierarchically and rigorously subordinated to the central power.

The Law reserved a distinct and eminent place for political crimes. Article 46 says: "Offences covered by this Code are divided into: a) offences against the foundations of the Soviet régime, established in the USSR by the power of the workers and peasants. These offences are considered by the same token to be the most dangerous. b) all other offences."

Drawing the logical conclusions of this characterization of "most dangerous", the very same article 46 prescribes limits to the tribunal's capacities. For "other offences", the judge is free to decide how lenient to be, but may not exceed a certain degree of severity. For political crimes the reverse is the case. "For offences in the first category, the Code prescribes the limit *below* which the tribunal has no right to go in meting out measures of social defence and judicial correction. For all other offences, the Code prescribes only the *upper limit* to the penalties which can be exacted by the tribunal." (My emphasis.)

Judged by the severity of the penalties and the degree of blame attached, an offence of a political nature is a qualitatively more serious one.

These provisions conform to the doctrine of Law and its objectives laid down by the political authorities. Vyshinsky was the undisputed "master" of legal theory and was still acknowledged to be so in 1956. His works — *The Theory of Judicial Proof in Soviet Law, The Problem of Evaluation of Proof in Criminal Trials, Basic Issues of Soviet Socialist Juridical Law*, and his *Procedural Manual* — provided the basis and the orientation of official teaching. They served as reference works for all soviet jurists. The legislators took inspiration from them, the judges conformed to them. They were hence essential works.

This monopoly was broken in 1956, to be precise on 22 June 1956. On that day the review *Soviet State and Law* published the proceedings of the 20th Congress. Since then, Vyshinsky's standing has gone up and down with that of his master. His work was at the heart of the flux and reflux of the political struggles between Stalin's epigones.

Soviet Law must be read with Vyshinsky's intentions in mind. In fact this is the only way to read it so as to understand its internal coherence and dynamism. In a study entitled *On Some Problems in Soviet Law*, which appeared in 1957 (that is, within the perspective defined by the 20th Congress), the jurist A. Piontkovsky gives a very clear definition to the fundamental outlook governing the elaboration of Soviet Law: "In order to determine the essence of Soviet Law, he [Vyshinsky] based himself on *'one-way relations between rulers and subjects'*. It is not surprising that this single-minded approach banished any consideration of the subjective rights of citizens from the thinking of Soviet jurists."[37] Vyshinsky, confronted with the tensions between antagonistic classes, as we know full well, took his mission to be the provision of the legal armour needed for the reinforcement, preservation and affirmation of the social conquests of the bureaucracy. The theory of "relations between rulers and subjects" is confirmed by its principle and in its applications as a *theory of new class relations — antagonistic relations — in bureaucratic society*. Since it deals with the definition of social conflicts and the means of resolving them, the theory had to match up to reality as well as the objectives of the bureaucracy. Both the theory of Law and the Law itself have to be seen as objective factors in the appreciation of the class nature of the Soviet state.

The fact that class issues are at the root of the problem is clearly shown by the directives to the tribunals. Article 47 of the Penal Code states that: "The essential question to be settled in each particular case is the social danger represented by the offences."

The real nature of the régime is also revealed by the important fact that the legal texts were drawn up in such a way as to *ensure the greatest possible freedom of interpretation and the most generous possible provisions for the intervention of political authority*. Penal theory and procedure go hand in hand. Here I shall only quote some examples of these legal formulations, chosen at random, which are enough to characterize the system.

The essential role assigned to intent in the assessment of guilt. For example, in the commentary on absenteeism at work:

> If the tribunal establishes that the person concerned has stayed away from work intentionally, with the aim of leaving it without permission, then the case of the accused shall come under the category of having left employment at the factory or establishment concerned, the same applies if the accused has returned to work by the time the tribunal is sitting.

The same applies even to questions of economic management. Article 128 underlines this: "Bad management, flowing from negligence or lack of commitment. . . ." This general rule applies to counter-revolutionary acts, which carry the heaviest penalties. Article 58 stipulates:

> Damage inflicted on the state, transport, commerce, monetary circulation or the credit system, as well as co-operation with or participation in *counter-revolutionary acts*, either by the misappropriation of state institutions and enterprises, or by acts directed against their normal functioning. [My emphasis.]

Now, the code nowhere spells out the concrete nature of these offences. It is left to the discretion of the judge, although subject to the control of the prosecutor.

Obscurity in the definition of offences: This is systematic and deliberate. It allows great freedom both in the choice of offence with which to charge the accused, and in the severity of sentence to be deemed appropriate. Article 47b is a clear example: "The *possibility*, in the perpetration of an offence, of prejudicing the interests of the state and workers, even when the offence *is not immediately directed* against the interests of the state or the workers." (My emphasis.) The text makes it possible to include every type of infraction of the law under the category of crimes against the state, even when the offences concerned have no direct effect on public goods and their control. It is enough that the judge is satisfied that the offences *could have had* this result. The decision is left to his discretion. Furthermore, the phrase "possibility of prejudicing the interests of the state and workers' appeals to a very general concept in Soviet Law which has very serious results. The legislator does not judge the damage done by whether or not there has been any effective consequence of the offence. The formula "has brought about or could have brought about" is widely employed in the texts. The absence of damage is not considered to be an extenuating circumstance.

The principle of analogy. The accused can be condemned for a crime which does not appear in the Penal Code. Article 16:

> If one or another socially dangerous action is not dealt with directly by the present Code, then the basis and limits of the responsibility of the author of this action are determined in accordance with the articles of the Code dealing with offences most closely related to the acts in question.

Collective responsibility: On the question of complicity, Vyshinsky defines official doctrine quite clearly: "The justice of a definition of complicity, as activity casually linked with the author of the crime, is doubtful. To understand complicity what is necessary is not the existence of a causal link, but a *general link with the author of the crime.*"[38] Thus it is not necessary to have acted or connived with the author of the crime. It is sufficient to be his parents, a circle of his friends, or simpy occupational or general acquaintances. This principle has played a considerable role in mass repression.

Confessions considered to be sufficient proof. Vyshinsky developed this thesis at length. He applied it in exemplary fashion in the Moscow trials. It should be noted that it fits in perfectly with the collection of deliberate omissions and arbitrary interpretation that I have just been examining. Under the conditions existing at the time, confessions became the most satisfactory procedure for establishing the truth. Omissions and freedom of interpretation do not, in fact, lend themselves to any more solid system of proof. Elsewhere, Vyshinsky wrote: "To ask the tribunal to pass judgement with reference to absolute truth is impossible under present conditions of judicial activity."[39]

The proof of innocence rests with the accused. If the accused does not confess, he must produce proof of innocence. "While the responsibility of providing evidence rests with the prosecution, the accused must provide the elements of his defence."[40] Given the state of the law and of penal procedure, this task seems very difficult, and almost impossible where strictly political matters are concerned. The most he could hope for is to establish the lack of bad intentions, to escape exemplary punishment. According to the Penal Code: "Measures of social defence of a corrective judicial character are only to be applied to those who have committed socially dangerous acts where these persons have: (a) acted with intention, that is to say understood the socially dangerous character of the consequences of their actions, desired these consequences or knowingly accepted them; or (b) acted imprudently, that is to say without knowing the consequences of their actions; but should have foreseen them, or unreasonably believed that they could avoid the consequences."

Methods of physical coercion: "the use of methods of physical repression by the NKVD" was *legalized* in 1937 by virtue of a Central Committee decision reported thus by Khrushchev: "The CC, of the PC of the Soviet Union (b) considers that physical repression must still be used of necessity as an exception applicable to known, obstinate enemies of the people, as a method which is both justified and appropriate." This practice was in fact the basis of the show trials and the mass repression. From the point of view of theoretical justification, it was the inevitable result of the doctrine which considered confessions to be sufficient proof. Its raison d'être was its efficacy. Khrushchev describes it without any circumlocutions:

> How could it be that people could confess to crimes they had not committed? In one way only — through the use of physical pressure, torture, leading to loss of judgement and a state where they are no

longer of sound mind, depriving them of human dignity. It was thus that the "confessions" were obtained.

He repeated this in relation to the "doctors' plot": "Stalin personally summoned the judge in charge of the investigation, and gave him instructions and advice on the methods of interrogation to be used. These methods were simple: 'batter, batter and batter again'." Physical coercion was the basis of the methods used. It included more refined techniques. Total sleep deprivation over a long period, for example, proved more efficient than blows. The drawback was that it took longer. The use of torture did not run counter to the spirit of the law. The Soviet penal concept was founded on chastisement. Chkhikvadzhe defined punishment (using a formula employed in the schools) as moral and physical suffering. He summed up current thinking when he stated that only moral and physical suffering could provide "the element of intimidation without which the very notion of punishment is not conceivable". Intimidation was indeed made into a powerful educational tool by Estrine. Physical and moral suffering justified the repressive role of the concentration camps, which Vyshinsky took to be "fundamental". He said of these institutions that they embodied "all of judicial policy". In this context, regardless of its functional necessity, it would have been illogical for that moral and physical suffering which took the form of torture not to preside over the crucial educational phase of penal procedure.

The subordination of the tribunal to the prosecutor. The wide liberty of interpretation tolerated by the texts and exploited by the tribunal, was the subject of tight control by the prosecutor. "The control of the prosecutor over the legality of tribunal judgments and of decisions on matters falling in these categories must be consolidated, so that illegal judgments and decisions can immediately be challenged." The most essential function of the judge — the pronouncement of judgment — is placed under the control of the public prosecutor. The prosecutor is tightly and exclusively tied to the Attorney-General, who is himself appointed by the "Supreme Soviet". Since 1933, the prosecutors of the autonomous and federated republics have been appointed directly by the Attorney-General, and are responsible only to him. Hence they fall entirely outside the powers of the respective executive and legislative bodies of these republics. The Attorney-General of the USSR being the direct instrument of the central authority, this rigorously hierarchic system has become — within the system of judicial order — as powerful an instrument of repression as the NKVD, and for the same reasons. Vyshinsky justified the 1933 decision in his *Course in Penal Procedure* and in his work *Judicial Organization in the USSR*. It is highly significant that the 1955 reform did not change this system. Hence, political authority is imposed directly on the judge via the intervention of the public prosecutor. This situation is justified and amplified by the theory of Law. Vyshinsky expounds it quite clearly: "The tribunal is the direct agent of state policy as expressed in the laws of the state." "The laws of the soviet power are a political directive and the work of the judge amounts not just to the application of the law in conformity with the needs of bourgeois juridical logic, but to the implacable application of the law as a political expression of the party and the government."

Defining the judge's function, Vyshinsky insistently returns to this theme. The judge must be "not only a Soviet jurist, that is to say an expert and a specialist on his judicial work, but also a political worker, rapidly and precisely applying the directives of the party and the government".

Legal theory, the Penal Code and the code of penal procedure, together with the interpretative material and judicial practice, form a coherent totality. It is this unified ensemble, in whole and in part, which constitutes "the basis of legality".

A question which arises is this: did the Moscow trials conform to the provisions of the Penal Code and the code of penal procedure, and to normal judicial practice? In fact the trials differed only in the historic breadth of the accusations. The indictment was founded on articles 58.8, 58.11 and 19 of the Penal Code; the sentences on article 58.2. The investigation procedure followed the directives of articles 466–470, already cited. No matter how rigid and harsh these provisions may have been, they were in no way in contradiction with the principles on which normal procedure was based. All they did was increase the severity of the charges and the penalties. The fact that they were personally directed by Stalin was only an application of the general theory, by virtue of universally accepted and recommended practice. The obedience of the judge to the directives of political authority was by this time a norm, in conformity with received teaching, to the extent that Rodos, the examining magistrate involved in the Kossior affair when interrogated by Khrushchev, replied in the simplest possible way: "They told me that Kossior and Chubar were enemies of the people and, for this reason, my task as directing judge was to make them confess that they were enemies of the people." He added, expecting in this way to absolve himself of all responsibility, "I thought I was carrying out party instructions." In Law and in fact, he was carrying them out. Vyshinsky — as prosecutor in the Moscow trials — respected the rules scrupulously.

If the Moscow trials were also a testament to complete and

deliberate falsification of the truth; if the debates in these trials were prefabricated; if the confessions were extorted and false; and if the condemnations were no more than legalized murder; then we have no need to explain them by "a brutal violation of socialist legality", as Khrushchev called it in 1956. It was on the contrary the product of a coherent system, in conformity with that system. This part of Khrushchev's falsification does bear comparison with the facts.

A final and important question remains. Since the provisions of the Penal Code and penal procedure undoubtedly gave great freedom of intervention to political authority, why was it necessary in 1934 to establish the "special conference" of the NKVD and its administrative procedures? This took up a great deal of time and resources.

The elimination, between 1927 and 1929, of trotskyist, Zinovievist and Bukharinist oppositionists concerned only the political aristocracy of the country: several tens of thousands of militants. The hundreds of thousands of kulaks deported in 1930 were the product of the war. The "trial of the Shashty engineers" of June 1928; that of the "industrial party of Professor Ramsin" in November and December 1930; the "trial of Mensheviks" of March 1931, and the "trial of the saboteurs and spies on industrial energy" in April 1933; these dealt only with restricted circles of technical and scientific cadres. In 1934, the level escalated. The Kirov assassination opened up the period of mass administrative repression. Each word here is used advisedly. The repression was cold-blooded, premeditated, and carefully prepared. It did not correspond — as in 1930 — to a civil war imposed by the conjuncture and conducted blindly. The Kirov assassination was premeditated, with a view to producing carefully estimated effects. Its effects were calculated. From then on, repression was a strategy on the part of the upper bureaucracy. It was an operation carried out by the apparatus which had profound effects on the nation. It affected large numbers and proceeded rapidly. The "Yezhovshchina" found more than ten million victims. In its wake, entire nationalities were deported. From 1934, the million became a unit of account.

On this scale, legal procedure, no matter what the provisions of the law, became a bottle-neck. It was not usable. Administrative procedure offered the most effective method, and furthermore the only one possible. This is why the NKVD, the OSSO and the concentration camps constituted an indispensable infrastructure. When they broke up this triple structure, the authors of the coup d'état made mass repression impossible. Judicial measures based on legal methods were only suitable for selective repression.

From 1955 to 1970, *penal legislation and judicial procedure confirmed and maintained as a "basis of legality" the legal principles elaborated between 1930 and 1940. The continuity of these principles characterizes the fundamental nature of the conjuncture which opened with the carnage of the 1950s.*

The decree of 27 March 1953, which introduced the revision of the Penal Code, was very restrictive. It revealed the hesitations, problems and intentions of the upper bureaucracy. The aim of the reform was to "shift penal responsibility in certain cases relating to the economy, morals and other minor offences, by disciplinary and administrative measures, and to diminish penal responsibility in isolated cases". Successive amendments did not modify principles around which the penal armour was constructed.

The new legislative texts, and the new provisions laid down by the decrees of 1955 to 1970, underline the essential continuity involved. A number of examples should suffice to convince us. Article 190 — in frequent use — stipulates: "The diffusion of false assertions denigrating the Soviet social and political régime; the systematic oral diffusion of false assertions denigrating the soviet social and political régime, as well as the diffusion or publication, in manuscript, printed form or any other form, of writings of the same tenor shall be punished by deprivation of liberty, for a duration of up to three years or a maximum fine of one hundred roubles." This adaptation to new forms of social action respects both the spirit and the letter of the principles elaborated in the 1930s and 1940s. The prosecutor and, under his control, the judge, are uniquely responsible for determining the degree of falsehood and of denigration. And they do it — as before — with respect to the political instructions of the authorities.

Article 70 of the Penal Code of the RSFSR declares: "Agitation or propaganda with the aim of sapping or weakening soviet power, or provoking the commission of particularly dangerous infractions against the state; the diffusion with the same aim of slanders denigrating the soviet social and political régime, as well as the diffusion, publication or possession of writings of the same tenor, shall be punished by deprivation of liberty, for a duration of six to seven years, which may or may not be accompanied by house arrest of between two and five years; or solely by house arrest of two to five years." This article marks a considerable increase in the severity of the penalties incurred and adds to the list of offences the possession of writings considered to be seditious. Article 183 of the penal code of the Latvian SSR punishes failure to denounce infractions by deprivation of liberty of up to two years or up to a year's corrective labour. Article 206 of the Penal Code defines "hooliganism" as "voluntary actions posing a serious threat to public order and indicative of contempt for society". This deliberately ambiguous definition, in the tradition of the 1930s, allows for unlimited arbitrariness in the interpretation of the law. In fact the measures taken since 1966 under the pretext of combating "hooliganism" have shown that any demonstration in a public place can fall under the definition of article 206.

Judicial penal practice confirms this fundamental continuity. Even though administrative procedures can no longer be used for mass repression, they remain in constant use for limited short-term operations. The MVD is always allowed to raid without authority, and to seize documents without the person concerned being present. Solzhenitsyn is the most celebrated case of this. It persists in its moral and physical intimidation of witnesses, without the victims being allowed any legal recourse. A certificate from a practising doctor is enough to commit a recalcitrant intellectual to a psychiatric clinic. Trials since 1950 have followed the same procedure, even with respect to their arbitrariness in the interpretation of the law, as in the 1930s. The judge continues to pass sentence under the vigilant eye of the prosecutor, and accepts the same political subordination. Article 58 is no more restricted to exceptional circumstances than it was before. It continues to feed the prison camps, and what it lacks in quantity, it makes up for in quality. Anatoly Marchenko, after having been deported to the Moldavian labour camps between 1961 and 1966, was re-arrested on 21 July 1968 for having demonstrated his solidarity with the Czechs. He was condemned to a year's deportation for an unproven infraction of the passport laws. On 20 August 1969, as if to confirm the permanence of the old methods, a tribunal locked him up for a further two years for his attitude in the camps. The internal régime in the corrective labour camps, established by Vyshinsky on the principle that the arduousness of living conditions should match the seriousness of the offence, remains in force. Oppositional intellectuals — like Sinyavsky, Daniel, Ginzburg and Galanskov — are, as before, condemned to a "severe régime", the second harshest of the four prescribed by Vyshinsky. Brezhnev's régime no more respects the constitution than the régime based on Stalin's personal power. This is so much the case that implementation of article 125, recognizing freedom of speech, press, meetings and public demonstrations, has become one of the main demands of the intellectual opposition.

I will recount one more significant fact. The police-like elimination of the theories of relativity and Mendelian genetics; the systematic sterilization of research by repression; the extermination of numerous scientists of world standing; and the detention of even larger numbers involved in teaching and research — these are certainly the most revealing expressions of the depths plumbed by the barbarous regression which made stalinism possible, and hence it is one of its two historic expressions (the other being nazism). The wave of terror became a paroxysm between 1929 and 1931. It rose again to a crest between 1946 and 1948. The polemic was again unleashed between 1953 and 1958. The biologist Zhores Medvedev wrote in *The Rise and Fall of Lysenko*: "The conflict with true science, which was not confined to agriculture, did not start with Lysenko. It began under Stalin and continued under Khrushchev. Lysenko was one result of this conflict: he was *the delegate of a kind of science which satisfied the political and tactical objectives of the state apparatus.*" (My emphasis.) Later, he says: "The situation began to evolve in 1965, after the first conference on the peaceful uses of atomic energy, held in Geneva under the auspices of the United Nations. We began to rediscover the existence of other countries."

This continuity of behaviour, in an area which was crucial for the survival of the country, lasted *nearly thirty-five years*. It establishes in the same way as would a laboratory experiment, the permanence and continuity, in and through the 1953 coup d'état, of the fundamental structure of power and its class basis; a continuity of which the Law was only the faithful reflection.

Nevertheless, major changes were going on. But they were in an area which precedes the development of the Law: in the internal relation of forces in society.

19 The new legal system and the new class system

THE MOST fundamental lessons to be drawn from the structure of Soviet Law are not only to be drawn from its social content. It defined the division of responsibility in work organization between the state bureaucracy and the managerial corps in the factories. It defined the position of the wage-earner in production. Hence, it dealt with crucial functions which determined the nature of classes and of society. It did not create: it described and hence confirmed.

Here also penal Law, because it defines transgressions, reveals social *tensions* and, as a result, the underlying *class dynamic*. The nature and extent of sanctions, the nature of penal procedure and the way it is set in motion, by uncovering the object and scale of social conflicts, confirm the existence of exploitation of the work-force (without, however, revealing its mechanisms). In this way we also obtain a remarkable confirmation of the level of development of the forces of production and the degree of civilization.

This essential chapter of penal Law was articulated around the laws and decrees of 20 December 1940 (on the "prohibition of arbitrary departure by workers and staff from enterprises and establishments"); of 2 October 1940 (on the work-force reserves of the state); of 19 October 1940 ("on obligatory transfers"). The laws of 27 December 1932 and 28 April 1933 (on the re-establishment of internal passports) were the necessary prelude.

The Soviet jurists clearly understood that from the point of view of the organic development of legislation, the 1932 law was the driving force, that is to say that there was a causal link between the defence of state property and the organization of work in production. Estrine wrote in his commentary on penal law:

> Comrade Stalin attached prime importance to, and *established the basic principles of*, the tasks of the struggle for discipline at work. To this end was promulgated the law of 15 November 1932 on the struggle against unjustified absences (*proquls*) which entailed the dismissal of the offender from the establishment, the withdrawal of the food tokens and tokens for goods given him by the factory, and his expulsion from the apartment placed at his disposal by the same establishment. *It is in this concrete manner and at the same time with due regard to principles* that in this period comrade Stalin accomplished the task of directing penal policy, as well as directing policy in other spheres. Furthermore, under the direction of comrade Stalin, the struggle for quality in production

> developed and gathered strength, with the publication of the law of 8 December 1933 on responsibility for production of poor or inadequate quality. [My emphasis.]

This text is of great interest and merits our attention. Confronted with a concrete difficulty — the fluidity of the work-force — Stalin took coercive measures, of draconian proportions, to be applied immediately. This was the meaning of the law of 15 November 1932. These elementary measures, of the greatest urgency, were necessarily transitory. They constituted the point of departure of further institutional elaboration, which reached its fully-developed form in the laws and the decree of 1938 and 1940. This process of the development of institutions is a key example. Empirical experience was the guiding principle. Initially, there was neither a philosophy of law, nor a global conception of social relations, but reflex reactions flowing from the immediate problem encountered. This is exactly what set in train the institution of the concentration camps, as we have observed. It was the same process which led to forced collectivization and to the second civil war, which was to turn the bureaucracy as a differentiated class into a ruling class. Hence through a blind historical process, the organic principles of the new society emerged. It is this that confirms its objective and unplanned character.

It is no less remarkable that the law of December 1933 "on responsibility for production of poor or inadequate quality", which represents the same type of reflex reaction, at the same time determined a structure of subordination of the enterprise directors to the state bureaucracy. The relations of subordination were permanent because as late as 1970 they registered the functional relations between these two major social components of the ruling class. The internal organization of the ruling class was brought about at the same time and under the same constraints as the new hierarchic relations between classes. So much is this the case that it would be wrong to speak, as is generally done, of the appearance of a new class as an isolated phenomenon. It must be considered as a feature of the advent of a new class system. This is in conformity with the theory of society.

Stalin's real superiority came from his capacity to draw general conclusions from the tactical lessons imposed by circumstance, in the sense of interpreting the social interests of the collectivity that he represented. As Estrine points out, he gave an interpretation in terms of basic principles to decisions which were dictated by circumstance. Thus it was that Stalin showed himself to be the legislator of bureaucratic society. He knew how to lead the bureaucracy to military victory by employing a violence all the more devastating in that its use was not part of a concerted strategy. With victory achieved, he knew how to give bureaucratic society its legal foundations, by means of the brutal and barbaric defence of property and work-discipline. This was the undeniable historic role of Stalin which was masked — for obvious political reasons — by the other side of Khrushchev's falsification.

The law of 22 August 1932 against speculation offers a further significant confirmation. Its immediate object was the social consolidation of the military victory of 1930. Its goal was to prevent the reconstitution of the middle classes which had been eliminated from the economy. Stalin explains it very clearly in his presentation to the Central Committee in January 1933.

> We have succeeded, in the course of this recent period, in completely eliminating from the commercial circuits private business people, merchants and intermediaries of all kinds. Obviously, this does not exclude the possibility that, in accordance with the law of atavism, private merchants and speculators will reappear in the commercial sphere, using the most convenient avenue to do so: that is, kolkhoz commerce. Even the kolkhoz members themselves are sometimes inclined to launch into speculation, which obviously does not bring honour to them. But to combat these unhealthy phenomena we have the law recently published by the soviet authorities on the suppression of speculation and the punishment of speculators. You are evidently aware that this law is not characterized by its leniency.

This law confirms the fact, by now well-established, that forced collectivization corresponded to regulation *of a military character*, in which armed force was substituted for non-existent economic methods. Because the impasse was *technological* in character, force of arms could not in its own right modify the *material* conditions of the production-process. As a result there remained a material basis for the reappearance of the dispossessed middle classes. The unexpected "law of atavism", if it is to make any sense at all, could only be the social atavism of the capitalist production-process which had been maintained. We know that military violence, by modifying the *social* terms of the process of production, passed on the natural side-effects of capitalist mechanisms to the agrarian bureaucracy. Just the same, we are compelled to note that this law remained a burning reality during the sixties some forty years after its formulation. The prime role of speculation and its new breadth is evident in all the various forms the economy has undergone in the post-Stalin period. The persistent validity of this law in a profoundly different conjuncture demonstrates — as would an experimental observation in a laboratory — the cardinal role of the market. At this level the law offers an even more fundamental verification of the inadequacy of coercive administration and of the growth in the productive forces of state capitalism. Hence it illuminates the *historical conditioning* (the dominant effect of the world conjuncture) of the inauguration of this administrative control.

If we really want to take full account of the provisions made during 1933 in order to punish bad management, and of article 59 concerning "particularly dangerous offences against administrative order" although "not tending directly to the overthrow of soviet power" but threatening nevertheless "to disturb the normal operation of the administrative organs of the national economy" (whose object was hence to muzzle collective action in pursuit of claims) — it must be accepted that this period, immediately following the second civil war, should be considered as the matrix of all the bureaucracy's legislation. It is no less important to observe that the law of 20 December 1938 establishing *work pass-books* was promulgated through (and as a legal conclusion of) the very large-scale repression conducted by Yezhov. This underlines one of the principal functions of the terror, which Khrushchev deliberately overlooked. This is all the more striking in that we are dealing with the period after 1934, which was the subject of Khrushchev's revelations.

The re-establishment of internal passports (laws of 27 December 1932 and 28 April 1933) was the first institutional generalization of the policy of administrative constraint. Stalin in fact used, remodelled and adapted the tsarist precedent.

Lenin criticized the institution of internal passports under tsarism, when the undertaking was merely a cottage industry: what would he have said about Stalin's undertaking, which was on the scale of a mass industry?

> The social democrats call for the complete freedom of movement and freedom for the people to change jobs. What does "freedom of movement" mean? It means that the peasant must be free to go where he wants, to choose the village or town he wants without having to demand authorization from anyone. This means that internal passports must be abolished in Russia (they have been abolished long ago in other countries), so that no gendarme, no Zemsky can be authorized to prevent a peasant from staying or moving where he wants. The peasant remains enslaved by officials to the point where he can no longer settle in a new village or region.[41]

Izvestia of 28 December 1932 clearly defined the social objectives being pursued:

> We should not consider the passport as a simple formality, as a new piece of paper to be added to other documents. From now on the passport must be a powerful weapon in the hands of the proletarian dictatorship, to control and organize the population, to reaffirm its links with production, and to cleanse our towns of socially dangerous elements.

The internal passport had two general kinds of effect. By setting up a tight surveillance network, it played a fundamental role in security. By rooting the work-force in a single place, it became an instrument for imposing labour discipline at the point of production.

The law of December 1932 was not just a legitimation of transitory and short-term measures. It institutionalized them. It established a unified defence of the power of the régime, reinforcing both its political power and its power as employer (that is to say its exercise of its property rights.) It constituted an operational base for a global policy of coercive administration.

In order to invest the internal passport with its political role, the law made it into "the basic document establishing the identity of a citizen of the USSR". Its main objective was to register individuals *socially* and localize them. Hence it became obligatory to hold one from the age of sixteen years onwards. Younger children had to be noted on the passports of those in charge of them. All changes of residence had to be registered on the passport, along with any change of job or sackings, and any marriage or divorce. Landed property-owners or administrators were obliged to notify the authorities within twenty-four hours of any new arrivals. Other inhabitants were to inform on any contravention. Counterfeit, false declarations or the use of another person's passport came under the heading of article 72 of the Penal Code which prescribed severe penalties.

The emphasis was placed firmly on the need to register every move precisely and with the date recorded. In certain agricultural zones exempted from these provisions, the status of the peasant actually got worse. Without this essential item of documentation, it was now impossible to travel.

The extent and density of this network, combined with a card-index system, made it possible in principle to ascertain at any time the place of residence, professional situation, and relations of any suspect, and the places he visited. This facilitated efficient repression. Detailed lists could be created, and desired arrests carried out with great speed and certainty. This infrastructure was just as useful for mass as for selective repression. *This is what explains the fact that in 1970 — forty years after its promulgation — the law remained in force*. To ensure that the state could intervene, in its role as employer, in the job market, "enterprises and institutions are obliged to ensure that all citizens taken into employment present their passports or provisional certificates, and must note on the passports or provisional certificates the date of commencement of employment." In certain cases the worker's situation became worse. In his commentary on *Labour Legislation*, published in Moscow in 1947, the jurist Goliakov enumerated those professions (arms industry, coal-mining, banking, savings banks) in which the management retained the passports of its wage-workers and salaried staff.

In 1970, article 198 of the Penal Code declared it a criminal act to violate the provisions of the passport laws. If the violation involves visiting somewhere without a passport or without registering with the police, and if the miscreant has already been punished twice for the same violation, then the penalty is up to one year's deprivation of liberty, or corrective labour for the same length of time, or a fine of up to 500 roubles. Of course there is no legislation which cannot be evaded. The passport provisions certainly are evaded, as we shall see later. Their formal and real rigour of application is a permanent incitement to corruption of security and administrative personnel. But the beneficiaries of this fraud are precisely those who must have the means to carry it out: status or money.

The creation of a "labour pass-book" (law of 20 December 1938) considerably extended the role of coercive and administrative control in the production-process. The commentary in *Izvestia* throws light on the *intentions* of the legislator. The legal text actually *describes the condition of the workers*. "The labour pass-book is bringing order to the control of the cadres and is becoming a powerful lever for reinforcing labour discipline and putting a stop to mobility in the work-force."[42]

The existence of a labour pass-book — throughout the territory of the Soviet Union — made it possible to set up an individualized social and professional file on wage-earners. This individual file is organized by the employer. It follows the worker throughout his working life. Without the pass-book, work is impossible. On the other hand the pass-book cannot regulate the actual operation of the labour contract. It provides the employer with the occupational, social and political identity of the worker. Since the questionnaire is filled in by the director's personal staff and counter-signed by him, what it offers is the opinion of the previous employer. This value judgement is not only technical: it is also social and political. This aspect is pointed out by *Izvestia*, which explains that in this way one can detect "suspect individuals" and "hostile elements". The employer (the enterprise director or the state department concerned with labour) obviously draws enormous advantage from this information. It renders powerful means of curtailment, intimidation and sanction.

The text of the law confirms this interpretation. Article 2 makes it obligatory to: "carry in the pass-book the following information relating to the owner of the pass-book: family name, forename and father's forename, age, level of education, occupation and information on previous employment, transfers from one place of employment to another, reasons for the transfer and any certificates or recommendations received". Article 10 prescribes that "pass-books are to be filled in by the administration of the establishment and the institution". In paragraph d) it stipulates that amongst information on previous employment must appear reasons for discharge from job. Article 6 stipulates: "Workers and staff taken into employment must present their pass-book to the administration of the enterprise." Paragraph f) of article 10 states: "When a worker leaves his job, all information on the worker, certificates and recommendations registered by the enterprise must be confirmed by the signature of the enterprise director (or a person specially mandated by him) and by the seal of the enterprise (or institution)." In order that the reasons for any lay-off can be clearly interpreted, it is stated that "reasons for discharge must be in conformity with the labour laws or must refer to an article of this Code." The pass-book is obligatory also for temporary and seasonal workers (article 8).

The worker is hence subject to double control by the central administration. In his activities outside work, he is subject to the passport legislation. In the work-place, his social and occupational conduct are registered in the pass-book. The recognition he receives from the bosses — over which he has no control — determines his possibility of promotion, his wage-bracket, and his chances of obtaining better-paid work. The law describes a situation which gives the employer wide powers over his work-force; which deprives the wage-earner of any legal defence; and which hence gives rise to a fundamentally unequal relationship between the two parties on the labour-market.

The decree of 26 June 1940 introduced administrative coercion into the heart of the production-process by subordinating the labour market to it. Here is the key section:

> 3. Departure *without authorization* from co-operative, public or state-run enterprises or establishments by workers and employees is forbidden, as well as any unauthorized move from one enterprise to another or from one establishment to another.
>
> Leaving an establishment and an enterprise or moving from one enterprise to another and from one establishment to another can be authorized solely by the head of the enterprise or of the establishment.

The passport legislation registered the work-force on the spot, making it administratively difficult to move from one town to another, or from one region to another. The pass-book legislation created a particularly advantageous situation for the employer, as much from the standpoint of the organization of work in the work-place as from the standpoint of the negotiation of the labour contract. It established a *major inequality* between employer and wage-earner. These two series of legal provisions *limit the free disposal of labour power by the labourer*. The fundamental condition of the wage-earner is that of being obliged to negotiate with his labour-power in order to exist. The conjunctural situation of the economy weighs on the labour-market in favour of one or the other party. Trade-union organization, by grouping and organizing the process of negotiation, ameliorates the unequal terms of the exchange. The soviet worker has already been deprived of trade-union organization. The trade union has become a weapon of the state in production. The worker is thus forced to negotiate individually with the centralized administration of the state employer. In this exchange, his real position is known to the opposing party thanks to its administrative dossier: the pass-book. Hence the inequality is reinforced.

The decree of 26 June 1940 opened up a new stage. Its article 3 deprived the worker of the free disposal — however limited it may have been — of his labour-power. The state seized administrative control over it. An authoritarian distribution of labour-power was substituted for ordinary legal contractual provisions.

What was involved was not just a *worsening* of the legal provisions, but a qualitative change. Up to this point the measures taken were in a certain sense marginal. They reacted with the production process from the outside. Now, administrative coercion was affecting the production-process from the *inside*, by changing the *mechanisms* of the labour-market. For this reason it acquired great power to change things organically. It had become part of the social dynamic.

To be precise, the law of June 1940 did not suppress the labour-market. The principle of exchange remained. The worker remained a *wage*-worker. What actually happened was that the *state assumed control over the terms of the market*. It *alone* fixed the overall wage level. It settled *only* the overall division of the labour force between one branch of industry and another, or one region and another. Hence, administrative coercion defined the dominant relations in the labour-market. Relative inequality between the two parties became absolute.

In 1947, Goliakov confirmed that the immediate aim was to tie the work-force down as securely as possible. He wrote:

> Certain workers, seeking to profit from the absence of unemployment in our country, have *interpreted the right to work as the right to choose their own employment*, without taking into account the interests and needs of the state. They have interpreted it as the right to move from one factory to another according to the principle "I shall go where I please". It is against these fly-by-nights, who create an intolerable instability in their pursuit of fast money, that article 3 of the Law of 26 June 1940 is directed. [My emphasis.]

The wage-worker was thus, without doubt, deprived of his right to use the workings of the labour-market to his advantage, and to hire out his labour-power to the highest bidder. To achieve this, the state-employer used repressive measures to force the worker to stay in his factory, and took over the determination of the terms of the market. These two actions were combined in effect, but not identical in nature. In the former, the state was taking administrative control over the labour-force. The worker was dispossessed of his only natural property — his labour power — which became state property; he ceased to be a wage-earner. He was in a state of servitude. The penal (concentration-camp) work-force was a model for this enslavement. On the other hand, control over the terms of the market maintained the existence of its function. Its free workings were certainly suspended. In fact the pressing needs of the economy expressed themselves as a powerful force, which became indirectly substituted for contractual negotiation. The state determined the overall salary totals. Different branches of the economy competed with each other for the division of the budget. The heads of the trusts and the enterprises, obliged by the plan's objectives to find labour of a given quality at a fixed remuneration, fought to obtain investments and financial instruments which they deemed indispensable. The worker, eliminated from the negotiation process, reinserted himself through the pressure which he exercised on the enterprise directors. The wage-earner, although shorn of his power, remained a wage-earner.

Hence, there existed a certain antinomy between these two series of legal measures, even if they worked quite well together in practice. This antinomy, expressed in the Law, serves to demonstrate both the extent of social regression and the extraordinarily primitive character of this administrative control.

The state's conquest of the terms of the market was a *political* operation, *guaranteed* by its penal powers. The steps taken were apparently simple: the state subjected the two contracting parties to its authority. This was the *appearance* of the new juridical situation. In reality, it was nothing more than a fiction. The labour legislation maintains the fiction:

> In the determination of remuneration, *agreement between the parties plays only a subordinate role*. Any agreement reached cannot be in contradiction with the Law and must fall within the strict limits decreed by the Law — for example, in determining the precise salary level in cases where this level is defined by a clause such as "between . . . and . . ."; or in deciding the salary level of employees occupying a plurality of posts, etc. [My emphasis.]

In his 1950 commentary, Pacherstnik gives his definition — remarkable for that time — of the principle governing these authoritarian contractual relations. He puts it in the same perspective:

> The particular character of juridical labour relations originating with those laws governing work assignments, consists first of all in the fact that they arise not from the initiative of the contracting parties, but on the initiative of those organs of the state charged with establishing obligatory labour relations between the parties concerned, but *which do not themselves participate in these relations*. The character and place of work are in this case determined not by the parties, *but by the body at whose disposition the worker is placed*.

Pacherstnik's proposed definition is a statement of principles. It is no longer tied to the pursuit of strategic objectives, in the style of Goliakov's commentaries. Pacherstnik is forced to give theoretical coherence to twenty years of practice: that is, to an established institutional system. He continues:

> Thus, as we have said, the general principle expressed by article 12 of the constitution of the USSR, which says that each must be used according to his ability, is fully applicable to the assignment of labour. The non-observation of this principle will strike at the national economy as well as the personal and material interests of its citizens, because socialist production requires an efficient, rational, and well-planned division of labour. Hence the body which decides the character of work to be undertaken by the person assigned to the work is governed above all by a general principle of social order.

Article 12 of the Constitution says:

> Work in the USSR is, for each able-bodied citizen, a duty and a question of honour. It is governed by the principle: "he who does not work, does not eat." In the USSR, the socialist principle "From each according to his abilities, to each according to his labour" is applied.

This attempt at theoretical justification on the part of Pacherstnik — which links together the obligatory assignment of labour with the conception of rational centralized planning — encompasses the logical consequences of the decree of June 1940: consequences which it is convenient to look at before going into more fundamental issues.

The Law of 2 October 1940 on the state reserve labour-force introduced a new extension of authoritarian administrative control into the production process. It provided the basis of obligatory labour assignment. It was a response to one of industry's major needs. It brought a solution which conformed to the general nature of the established system, its low level of development, and the shortage of available financial instruments.

The preamble defined the objectives in the field of centralized planning:

> The task of further industrial development demands a continuously renewed influx of workers for the factories, pits, transport, manufacture, and mines. Without uninterrupted complementary growth of

> the work–force, satisfactory development of our industry is impossible. Under these conditions, a new task confronts our country: the organized preparation of new workers recruited from the heart of the youth in the villages and kolkhozy, and the creation of labour reserves, vital for the development of industry. We consider as indispensable the formation of state industrial reserves of the order of 800,000 to 1,000,000 men.

Hence, what was involved was the provision of permanent investment for the state in the shape of a reserve labour-force. This poses three key questions. How was this to be achieved? Who would have the right of disposal over this labour-force? And under what conditions and for what length of time would the labour-force be assigned? The answers to these questions define the system.

Recruitment was obligatory and was carried out by the authorities. Articles 8 and 9 are unambiguous: "The presidents of the kolkhozy are obliged to choose each year" a given number of young people from 14 to 15 years of age "with a view to their mobilization for professional schools or the railways". "The soviets of workers' deputies in the villages *must* choose. . ." etc. When the Law gets to the procedural details, there is no criterion given for choice. The kolkhoz presidents and the workers' soviets are free to decide arbitrarily, Pacherstnik justifies this procedure quite simply: "Under socialist society, private interests are inseparable from public interests."[43] Offenders are liable to severe penalties. "Students in the technical schools, in the emergency schools and in the FZO schools, who leave their educational establishment without permission or who are guilty of gross or systematic violations of school discipline, are liable, on judgment by the tribunal, to detention in a labour colony for one year." The school directors are obliged to "inform the prosecutor in their area of the facts relating to any unauthorized departure or violation of discipline *the day after or at the latest the following day that the facts are established*". The prosecutors must complete their enquiries within five days. The tribunals must pronounce judgment within a further five days. Officials who have covered up for adolescents, who have hired them or who have given them certificates when they have committed such violations, are themselves liable to disciplinary or penal measures. Parents who are "accomplices" are subject to "the appropriate measures to influence them through the intermediary of the social organizations of the enterprise, institution or kolkhoz in which they work". At the same time "persons who try to avoid working in the enterprises or institutions to which they have been directed after finishing higher education, are subject to subsection 1 of article 5 of the decree of the Supreme Praesidium of the USSR of 26 June 1940". *The centralized administrative procedures adopted were hence authoritarian and coercive.*

Article 6 defines *who*, legally, has *free disposal* over the reserve labour-force: "The state labour-reserves are at the direct disposition of the Council of Commissars of the People of the USSR and cannot be used by the Commissariats of the People or establishments without government authorization." This exclusive right applies first of all to the decision to make use of the labour-force. Article 7 states: "The right to call up annually, 800,000 to 1,000,000 people is reserved to the Commissars of the People of the USSR." Hence it is the central state apparatus — the upper bureaucracy — which exercises property rights (free disposal) over the reserve labour-force.

Article 10 — in relation to the third question — is very important. "All those individuals who have finished their apprenticeship — in technical schools, railway schools or factory schools — *are considered to be conscripted* [This does not exempt them from their allotted military service — *D.R.*] and must work for *four years* for a state enterprise under the direction of the Administration of Labour Reserves, and under the general guidelines given by the Commissars of the People of the USSR, their salary will be established in their place of work according to general principles."

First observation. The law of 2 October 1940 was a logical extension of the decree of 26 June. Compulsory labour assignment was only the extended application of the basic principle which tied the worker down to the work-place. In both cases, he is entirely subordinated to the officials. The central administration decides the place of work and the nature of the employment. The appropriate agencies decide the salary level. The head managers evaluate the conduct of the employee and punish any deviations. The Law provides for countless judicial measures against recalcitrant workers or students. It offers a complete arsenal of disciplinary and penal sanctions. *It does not offer a single means whereby the student or worker can appeal against the administration.* This makes it clear why the impunity of the central administration came to be at the heart of the incisive critique made by the reformers during the sixties.

Second observation. This causal link between the decree of 26 June and the Law of 2 November is made clear by the judicial status of the wage-earner once his period of compulsory labour-service is over. He does not by any means recover his freedom to work where he wants. He remains attached to the factory. Pacherstnik explains this very well:

> The rules which compel young specialists and former pupils of state reserve schools to work for three or four years respectively in enterprises and institutions, under the direction of the appropriate state body, do not imply that once this period is over, the parties can

terminate the juridical relation between them simply because the specified duty has been discharged, even if the labour contract is of a specific and limited duration. Once the specified period has elapsed, young specialists and young workers must continue to work in the enterprise or institution concerned on the same basis as the other workers and employees.

This is a result of the decree of 26 June, which is of general application. As Pacherstnik explains:

The discharging of a young specialist or a young worker by the enterprise administration after the period of compulsory service has expired would be illegal; so would their unauthorized departure from their jobs. Neither party can terminate the relationship laid down by the labour laws except on the basis of the general principles laid down by laws governing the work of workers and employees.

These general principles are the content of the decree of 26 June.

Third observation. The Law confirms the fact that authoritarian administrative relations structure the labour-process. The legal description of these relations corresponds to a stable infrastructure and not to a temporary and circumstantial situation.

The decree of 19 October "On compulsory transfers" generalized the principle of authoritarian assignment to the whole of the labour-force. In order to establish what is stated in the above sentence, we have to make clear what are the needs of the economy that are inherent to a system of rigid planning.

"The task of guaranteeing qualified workers" for the economy "necessitates a judicious division of engineers, technicians, supervisors, staff and workers between different enterprises, up to and including transfers from enterprises with a surplus of qualified personnel to enterprises suffering from shortage." A law which did not permit compulsory transfer would be a "fetter on the development of the economy". As a result, article 1 lays down: "The Commissars of the People of the USSR are accorded the right of compulsory transfer between enterprises of engineers, civil engineers, technicians, supervisors, designers, accountants, economists, planners and qualified workers of the sixth grade and higher, regardless of the location of these enterprises." Article 5 stipulates: "Individuals guilty of disobeying an order of the people's commissars in relation to their compulsory transfer. . . shall be considered to have left their work-place without authority and will be referred to a tribunal" by virtue of article 5 of the decree of 26 June 1940. Article 5 lays down that the promulgation of this law nullifies contracts made under the previous laws, in the sense that the People's Commissars are authorized "to keep the said engineers, staff and qualified workers in the enterprises where they are working under contract". This piece of legislation clearly codifies the regulation of the wages of workers who have been silenced.

The decree of 19 October — building on that of 26 June — took on a permanent character. Compulsory transfer and compulsory confinement to a single place of work were without legal time-limits. They entered into common law. This common law encompassed, from 19 October onwards, all qualified personnel: that is to say, the aristocracy of labour. The law of 8 October 1942 introduced these new relations into agriculture. Authoritarian administrative procedure now organized the whole of the labour-process. It provided the skeleton of the social armour of the production-process. It took on a global meaning.

20 Institutions: the society as characterized by its laws, 1930–70

SOVIET PENAL Law *describes* a class society of a new type. State appropriation of the means of production was its juridical foundation. The dominant antagonism between classes was expressed as a confrontation between the state apparatus and the productive labour-force.

The violence of this conflict was expressed legally as a continual reinforcement of the *inequality of exchange* on the labour-market.

The Law describes the status of the state apparatus in the *act of exercising its rights* as a ruling class. It and it alone enjoys the free disposal of essential property. In effect, it decides its investments for itself, and settles how they are to be divided. It exercises sovereign disposal over the labour-force. It and it alone fixes the rate of surplus-value. It alone decides where it is to be allocated, by reserving for itself the definition of the volume of reserves, the mass of re-investment, salary levels and their distribution by category. It alone assumes general control over the workings of the economy. Its juridical instruments are: the size and scope of the penal sanctions applicable to crimes against property, its management, the workings of the enterprises, and the integrity and quality of its products; penal sanctions in the production-process; the centralized and authoritarian administration of production and exchange; and the disciplinary and penal sanctions to be exercised against the obstructions which its potential opponents can create. The security of the state and of its apparatus are *socially* guaranteed by the rigour of the Law.

The Law describes the state apparatus as a ruling class of heterogeneous organic composition. It expresses this heterogeneity in its functional attributes. The Law *prescribes* that the agrarian bureaucracy is the benefactor of a *delegation of property rights*, giving it a distinct role in the process of production, guaranteed by the general juridical provisions governing state property. The Law *prescribes* that the enterprise directors benefit from *a delegation of power* in the technical and social control of the productive apparatus. The Law *confirms* that the free and full exercise of property rights is reserved, in practice, for the political apparatus of the state; that is, the upper bureaucracy.

The Law describes in full the exercise of property as a function of the full *exercise* of the power of political decision-making. Another

238

reading of the Law defines the *possession* of property as a function of *the possession* of the state. The Law hence implies a distinction between the title to property and the exercise of the attributes and privileges which attach to it.

The Law makes a distinction between the status of state property and all other forms of property. It interprets this difference as an antagonistic relation. The positive provisions of penal law protect state property against social tendencies to reprivatize it. In spirit and in fact, by virtue of its positive and negative provisions and by virtue of those provisions which are missing, penal law guarantees state property also against any attempt to socialize it. The Law rejects as incompatible any process, whether institutionalized or otherwise, which leads towards the withering away of the state. The Law treats state property as a stable institution in the process of reinforcement. In practice it describes it as private (as opposed to socialized), as strongly *integrated and concentrated* (in contrast to the relative concentration of classical monopolies).

The Law assimilates the reinforcement of state property to the reinforcement of the state apparatus. In accumulating decrees and provisions which render ineffective any element of social control by the classes which constitute the work-force of the production-process (industrial and white-collar workers, technical staff, and peasants) over the exercise of property rights, it confers a monopoly of control on the state apparatus; a monopoly which is confirmed and strengthened by the positive provisions of the Penal Code. The Law provides rigorous guarantees for the social security of this monopoly. It does not offer a single legal recourse against its aggressiveness.

The Law hence describes the status of a ruling class founded on the *identification of the appropriation of the state with the means of production*. The structure of this appropriation necessarily corresponds to the structure of property: it is integrated and concentrated. Appropriation is hence *private* (it is the right of a definite class and not at all of the whole of society) and *collective* (it is the right of the class as a whole and not at all of any of its individual members). Surplus-value is extracted *collectively*. It is carved up unequally within the ruling class as a result of its lack of social homogeneity.

The Law describes the exercise of property as a transformation of political decision-making into power of control over the economy. In this way, the Law defines the political nature of the state apparatus and shows that this role is not reduced just because the state has seized control of the means of production. It does this by integrating the two functions and incorporating the political factor into the ownership of property. The Law *defines* the situation to be thus, and to some extent legitimizes it; but only within certain narrow limits. Property belongs to the state. It is collectively apprehended by the state class. Property rights belong to the class as a whole. The Law frees the state apparatus from the exclusive use of decision-making powers conferred by these property rights, in the shape of a functional assignment of tasks, articulated around the concentration of property. The prerogatives and privileges which the upper bureaucracy draws from this are hence not based on property alone, but on the context of a specific structure for its control (rigid, authoritarian and centralized planning). Hence these privileges are by their nature conjunctural and transitory. There cannot be an integrated state capitalism without integrated state property; but there can be an integrated state capitalism without rigid and authoritarian control.

The Law describes the juridical and social status of the directorial apparatus of the enterprises as a *foundation of authority*. It lays down a rigid subordination of the enterprise directors (the managerial bureaucracy) to the political apparatus of the state (the upper bureaucracy). The enterprise directors do not participate — as responsible parties — in the elaboration of the centralized plan. They intervene neither in the definition nor in the overall allocation of investment. They decide neither the total amount of salaries nor its distribution by categories. They determine neither the volume nor the quality of production by their enterprise, nor the intensity of labour, nor the sale price of their products. They must organize work in such a way as to make the result conform to rigid directives; without being able to change a single one of the decisive factors involved. On the other hand, they are accountable for the fixed capital in their factory, for the use made of invested capital, for the work-force employed, for the quantity and quality of the goods produced, and for security in the work-place. Article 128 of the Penal Code fixes the legal extent of this responsibility, and the severity of the penalties incurred for violations.[44] From the time when these coercive constraints began to be relaxed, this strict subordination became the central theme of the conflict between the directors and their interpreters, the reformers.

On the other hand, the delegation of power transfers the principal productive function of capital to the directorial apparatus. This apparatus incarnates the hold of state capital. *It determines, in each enterprise, what is to be the organic combination of capital and labour*. This prerogative is assigned it by law. The Penal Code specifies severe penalties for those who contravene the management directives.[45] The workers' professional life, social conduct, and conditions of existence are — principally through the device of the pass-book — subject to tight and discretionary control by the manager. Article 3 of the decree of 26 June 1940 gives the director sole right to authorize or refuse permission to a worker wishing to leave the enterprise or take up employment in another. At the point where classes meet, in the labour-market, the Law defines the attributes of the enterprise director as *based on the power of the ruling class.*

The official description of the process of negotiation between classes in the labour-market involves *three parties:* the bodies of the central administration "charged with establishing obligatory labour relations between the parties, but not themselves participating in these relations"; the employer (the manager) and the wage-earner, who represent the only real contracting parties. The Law effectively ensures that the "two parties" play only a "subordinate role", *as Pacherstnik emphasized.* The Law makes it clear that this description is in fact a *juridical fiction*, this fiction being of course a political requirement. This is an abuse both in the Law and in practice which draws a dividing line — as if they were two distinct entities between the enterprise directors and the upper bureaucracy. The directors are the base of the administration's power and carry out its instructions. To consider them as two distinct juridical entities and as socially aut-onomous in the negotiation process *between classes* is like asserting that the government and its appointed diplomats are two distinct powers in an international conference. The qualified official representing the central apparatus, and the manager constitute between them a *single interested party*. In negotiations with the work-force, there are only two parties: the state, in its function as employer, and the wage-earner. In this negotiation the wage-earner bargains *on his own* and can effectively play only a narrowly sub-ordinate role.

It is true that differences of opinion (and interest) can (and do) divide the political apparatus of the state from the enterprise directors. But these differences depend on the nature and scope of the powers to be allocated to the enterprise directors and ultimately on the degree of initiative the director is allowed. That is to say, the differences are located within a strategy whose principles are common to all parts of the ruling class. The wage-earner can, of course, profit or lose from these disagreements. But at root the situation is unchanged. The director embodies the function and power of state capital in the enterprise.

The Law describes the working class as a class of state wage-earners. In its positive provisions, it establishes that the proletariat is completely deprived of any social control over state property and its administration. Hence it defines a situation where the producer is *socially separated from the means of production*. It describes characteristic labour relations in the enterprise, which turn the productive unit into the basic structure in which this social separation is accomplished. The situation described by the law is in conformity with the general context of state property based on the Law. It defines the fundamental condition of social exploitation to which the work-force is subject.

In conformity with this context, the Law describes a system of organization of the labour-market which is essentially based on *inequality of exchange*.

The Law establishes a situation of *absolute* inequality. The wage-earner is excluded from the negotiation process. The state-employer exercises total control over the determination of wages. It distributes the labour-force by means of arbitrary assignment. The Law defines a situation where the wage-earner is completely deprived of *political* control over the political leadership of the state; where it is deprived of its trade-union and corporate organizations; where it is reduced to individually-conducted negotiations, tightly controlled by a centralized state employer.

This condition is not based on the institution of state property. It resulted from the historical combination of an economically and socially regressive world conjuncture, and the emergence of a social structure adapted to it: *rigid* and *coercive* centralized state planning. The working of state capitalism involves inequality of exchange in the labour-market, but in no way implies *absolute* inequality. Thus what was involved was a transitory and conjunctural phenomenon. Since 1955, the recognition of market mechanisms has restored a less unbalanced system of unequal exchange on the labour-market. The wage-earner recuperated a degree of elementary control over his labour-power, thanks to the effect of salary differentials; the competitive struggle for profit by the enterprises; the greater degree of initiative for the enterprise directors; and a relative slackening of authoritarian constraint on the part of the central administration. These measures were imposed by the new world conjuncture and the growth, under its influence, of the productive forces of state capitalism.

In the early seventies, nevertheless, the wage-earners remained completely deprived of any trade-union or corporate organization, and of any autonomous political expression. Pressure for changes in the conditions of work expressed itself as an elemental unorganized force. The absence of legal and institutional provisions for contractual relations between the classes (which would themselves be a recognition of an independently structured, politically and socially autonomous representation of the proletariat) creates permanent organic instability.

Within the broader sphere of state capitalism, the Law *registers* a *solution of continuity* which closer analysis shows to be a break in the technological infrastructure of the production-process: that is to say, a factor of instability in the foundations of the system of management. The Law *describes* the agrarian system as an entity which is economically and socially — that is, *functionally* — a foreign body within the state-capitalist system. The Law makes it clear that the hold of state capitalism over agriculture is primarily based on its social preponderance (by means of political and military administration) and thus confirms that the lack of integration is entirely due to technological backwardness (to the relatively low level of the productive forces). It is relatively simple to understand the lines of force. The Law expresses the uprooting of the traditional middle classes and penal law provides for their re-insertion into the process of production. The Law identifies the agrarian bureaucracy as the social form of this replacement and guarantees its dominant role.

The Law establishes the kolkhoz as the predominant social form of both collective and private property. The law confirms that the link between state industry and kolkhoz-based enterprises is subordinated to the laws of the market. In recognizing and legalizing the delegation of property rights, the Law expresses the technological weakness of state capitalism, confirmed by the relatively limited extent of the sovkhozy. The Law describes and confirms the peasantry as the labour-force of the agrarian bureaucracy in the production-process. Beyond this point, complex and contradictory provisions, constantly being added to, express the permanent inadequacy of reliance on antagonistic procedures. Private small land-ownership lives on, constantly fluctuating in both its actual existence and its legal expression, but always a source of considerable revenue. The form of revenue (whether in the form of a wage or otherwise) is persistently complex and persistently incoherent.

The roots of the kolkhozy in private ownership bring them into constant conflict with the extension into agriculture of rigid and centralized authoritarian administration. Private accumulation brings about profound differences within the agrarian bureaucracy (rich and poor kolkhozy). Private appropriation of the agrarian surplus creates social differences, which give rise to individual concentrations of wealth in the agrarian bureaucracy. The co-existence of a state market, a kolkhoz market, and a black market, and their extension into speculative networks including the village, the enterprises and the industrial trusts (as made obvious by the provisions of penal law) confirm the existence of permanent social fluctuations in the rural world, which — in the shape of economic disorder — threaten to grow into a chronic source of instability in the working of state capitalism.

The Penal Code thus expresses the inability of the bureaucracy to control market mechanisms *economically*. It makes it clear that — short of acquiring better technology and accumulating the necessary capital — the upper bureaucracy, in the interests of its social preservation (i.e. for the defence of the immediate and long-term interests of the state class), is obliged to try to surmount the workings of the market by means of authoritarian administrative decision-making. The Penal Code defined coercive and restrictive decrees which put this strategy into practice. By virtue of their number and scope, these decrees clearly structure the social armour of the production-process. Because it expresses institutionalized coercion as an economic function, the Law refutes Khrushchev's interpretation of the repression. In doing so it interprets and reveals the real level of the productive forces and the real extent of civilization. Not only was there no question of *surpassing* the capitalist mode of production, but the actual *control of integrated capital* ran up against the slowness of technical progress, which was in its turn aggravated by social resistance to its diffusion.

The society described by the Law elaborated during the 1930s and 1940s is the same in its social *dynamic* as the society of the 1970s. Functionally, all that has been changed is the use of constraint on such an extensive scale that it conflicted with the powerful expansion of new technology and the high level of integration of the world production-process.

21 The experience of power: continuity and legitimacy

THERE WERE thus two interlinked aspects to repression. Repression acted on the production-process as a factor of *impulsion and cohesion*. The circumstances which conditioned it make it seem like an objective force. Historically, its appearance coincided with the breakdown of the world system of the 1930s. Its appearance in Russia and Germany (that is to say, in different national contexts, but as part of the same world-process) and its rapid and cancerous extension into the labour-process, confirm this view. It reached its limits in equally objective changes in the overall conjuncture. Repression is being rejected from the production circuits by the integrated relations of the new technology, with its changed labour-skills, in the same way that an antibody rejects a graft. The stronger the resistance of its sources of social support, the more explosive are the tensions generated.

Repression acted as a *political function of the exercise of power*. In this sense it was much more profoundly the result of deliberate choice, and its effects reverberated in society like so many shock-waves. For over a quarter of a century, trials served as the detonator of waves of mass repression. In conception, preparation, and execution they corresponded strictly to a premeditated scheme. Their final product — the accelerated substitution of one generation for another and, as a corollary, a change in the social origin of the hierarchy — was an automatic consequence. The scale of the consequences changed the nature of the goals pursued. The element of deliberate choice loses its relevance on such a scale. The terror ceased to be the prerogative of those in power and became an ingredient of the dynamic of class struggle. The final product of the show trials was the raw material of the society of the 1970s. This analysis completely refutes Khrushchev's thesis.

To produce results which were so organic in character, the terror could not be simply episodic. On the contrary, it had to become normal procedure. I have already analysed the central structure of state power (the Secretariat); its principal coercive institution, the NKVD and its juridical armour, the Penal Code. It remains to examine the exercise of power. Such an analysis is necessary for understanding the system of terror.

The political trial was the means by which power was exercised.

To be precise, it was the central element around which everything else was brought together and assembled. The trial was not an occasional exercise inspired by exceptional circumstances. Nor was it a marginal phenomenon of little impact. The trial was a regular procedure resorted to in the course of the exercise of power, and efficiently adapted to suit widely different circumstances.

For this reason it indicates not only *how* power was exercised but also *why* it was exercised in this way. A trial was a carefully premeditated exercise. Its concerted character is exposed by the methodical preparation which went into a trial and by the choice of objectives. Setting a trial in motion always brought together two techniques.

The amalgamation of the *accused* enabled the prosecutor to secure the confessions or capitulations he required. Vyshinsky pushed this method to its limits. This police procedure, as a means of fabricating lies, took its inspiration from the spicy dishes prepared in Stalin's kitchen.

The amalgamation of *objectives*, on the other hand, revealed the political intentions of the Secretariat. Stalin's attack was always oblique. The publicly-stated intentions of the trial always concealed the principal goal of his machinations, which only became clear through its results. The more complex the ramifications, the better-founded were they on calculation and premeditation. These crab-like moves of his always led towards his eventual goals.

Thus the act of accusation, in all its obvious falsehood, exposed the real preoccupations of those in power and make it possible to grasp the real danger as the Secretariat saw it. The trials were hence highly indicative of the real nature of society.

We can get to the heart of the issue via an apparently secondary affair in a minor trial: the trial of the Mensheviks in 1931. The Mensheviks had been without any real political weight for a long time. Putting them on trial on the basis of a limited set of accusations, as with other trials which took place that year, was part of a plan to intimidate technical and scientific layers. The policeman-like inclusion of Ryazanov in the ranks of the accused, an apparently ill-conceived move, was to have profound repercussions. Accused of holding back documents of the Russian Social Democracy in the archives of the Marx-Engels Institute, Ryazanov — who did not appear before the tribunal — was condemned to deportation for treason. His works were destroyed and his editions of Marx and Engels were banned. The Marx-Engels Institute was incorporated into the Lenin Institute. Such are the facts, briefly summarized.

This is a typical example of a lateral operation without any consistent link with the main question at issue, but which bears on a much more significant objective. The results were two-fold: Ryazanov was deported and the archives which he controlled passed into Stalin's hands. The second step explains the first.

Who was Ryazanov? Ryazanov took part in all the major debates of the international workers'movement before the 1914 war. He rejoined Lenin in 1917, at the same crucial moment as Trotsky, Yoffe, Lunacharsky, Manuilsky and many others. He was one of the founders of the railwaymen's union. He disagreed with Lenin's strategy at Brest-Litovsk. In 1922 he condemned the introduction of the death penalty into the Penal Code. In the discussion about the trade unions, he gave intransigent support to the view that the function of the trade unions was exclusively to defend workers' corporate interests and their wages. During the NEP debate he reproached Lenin with the authoritarian procedure by which he took his decision. He denounced the bureaucratization of the party and the state. He was well-known for his sarcasm. For example, he would frequently and wittily recall that Lenin treated the "Old Bolsheviks" like "old imbeciles". He was a long-established revolutionary, as well as a world-famous scholar. He belonged — along with Lenin, Martov, and Trotsky — to the intellectual generation of the eighties. As editor of posthumous works of Engels and Marx, he founded the scientific centre which carried their names, and directed its work. In 1930 — several months before his arrest — the Soviet press described him, on the occasion of his sixtieth birthday, as the "greatest Marxologist of our time". It described him as having devoted "his active life to the workers' cause for more than forty years". Having lived among its leaders, he had an intimate knowledge of the history and origins of Bolshevism. He intervened in all the debates, but his independence of judgement led him to be regarded as "beyond factions". His open and obstinate hostility in 1926 led Stalin to declare of him "Ryazanov is nostalgic for Turkestan". Nevertheless, he was not exiled or deported in 1927 or 1928. Being "beyond factions" also put him out of the picture. This eminent revolutionary soldier had constantly exhibited a firmness of character which excluded the possibility of taming him by threats or of corrupting him.

The social relation of forces established in 1931 by the civil war removed any possibility of a change in the historic conjuncture. The war itself — which Stalin had always considered to be dangerous for the régime (which to a certain extent explains his retreat from politics in 1941, to which Khrushchev persistently refers) was not a short-term likelihood. All the oppositionists, both right and left, were "out of the picture".

Ryazanov was the most respected and eminent authority on all aspects of the study of the works of Marx and Engels, the movement of socialist ideas, and the theses and history of Bolshevism. He controlled archives of great historical and theoretical value. This sector now acquired crucial political importance.

The *functional* consolidation of the régime — nationally and internationally — demanded the creation of a mystificatory ideology. Its foundations — the theory of socialism in one country — had to be completed with a new theory of the state. The theory of the strengthening of the state had to be substituted for that of its withering away. It was this new thesis which in effect dominated the elaboration of the Law. A new historic justification of the exercise of power was needed.

This justification was undertaken on two distinct levels. In the most general sense it had to affirm the social continuity of the October revolution. On this point, Stalin followed a characteristic course of action. He enshrined the identification of the bureaucracy with the proletariat. He announced the disappearance of classes (all that remained were the "vestiges" of hostile classes) and their replacement by socio-professional *categories*. He proclaimed entry into the higher phase predicted by Marx, so that "Communism" was substituted for the period previously called "socialist" and, as an inevitable result, the *dictatorship* of the proletariat (that is to say, its class domination) disappeared. More specifically, he identified the personalization of the exercise of power with the Leninist model in the revolutionary epoch.

The bureaucracy as a whole was in solidarity with this general mystification process, because of its fundamental interests. Like all ruling classes, it had to *deny* its class nature in order to *mask* the mechanisms by which surplus-value was being appropriated. Stalin's insistent remarks on the new function of commodity categories in the economy, on the new character of the wage and on the need to reinterpret the overall meaning of *Capital*, all tended in this direction. The bureaucracy, on the other hand, was more reserved, because it was less directly and collectively involved in the personalization of power.

The prestige of the October revolution — which survived its destruction — constituted a political force on a world scale of inestimable value to the bureaucracy. The identification of the bureaucracy with the first world revolution guaranteed its organic implantation in the world proletariat; it assured its political ascendancy in the parties and trade unions; and it gave it an initial position of strength, both military and diplomatic, in its relations with other powers. There is a mass of evidence to confirm this.

The historical origin of the bureaucracy lies in the nature of its property, which gave rise to a real ambiguity embedded in its very essence, lending great power to the bureaucracy's mystificatory ideology. It is undeniable that the bureaucracy was a social product of the October revolution. It is essential to reveal also that it arose as a result of an organic split in the proletariat. Hence, it is obvious that the private state ownership of the means of production serves to integrate a collective structure. (Property is private to the decisive extent that it belongs to a class which exploits the work-force to its exclusive benefit; but it is collective in so far as none of the members of that class enjoys any personal roots in the production-process, and therefore property titles cannot be handed on.) Furthermore, under integrated state capitalism the wage becomes a dominant instrument for the private distribution of profit. The *social* mode of promotion becomes an essential factor in the hereditary transmission of privileges. To put it another way, the gradually increasing complexity of the social mechanism of exploitation, which by the nineteenth century was already far more difficult to understand than the relatively simple forms of slavery and serfdom, gave the slow evolution of monopoly its apotheosis in the monopoly of the state. These fundamental ambiguities explain the powerful grip of the mystification process. The real workings of society, its legal codification, real relations between classes, political institutions, and basic strategy (axised on the social pre-eminence of "cadres") formed a coherent whole in flagrant contradiction with the mystificatory ideology. What is difficult to grasp are the processes by which social exploitation is carried out, and not the exploitation itself, which is patently clear.

In order to achieve a successful conclusion to such a contradictory but vital enterprise Stalin, its instigator, had to shut away scientific research and seal the archives. Ryazanov held the key to this undertaking. He could establish, with irrefutable evidence to support him, the deformations and travesties of the theses of Marx and Lenin. He could prove that history was being falsified. He could be neither corrupted nor manoeuvred. The trial of the Mensheviks was used to lay a charge against him which would compromise his status *as a thinker*, by asserting that he had used his knowledge and control over the archives to manipulate them for partisan and political ends. This provided the justification for the measures taken against him and against his works, and for the seizure of the archives. This oblique operation, apparently secondary in character, was in fact part of a major historical scheme.

The fundamental incompatibility between ideology and the facts was most clearly expressed at the level of the exercise of power. Stalin never made a separation between the social interests of the bureaucracy and his own political interests.

The establishment of the bureaucracy, first as a distinct class and then as a ruling class, came about simultaneously with the organization of Stalin's despotism. The political and social victories of the bureaucracy culminated in the dictatorship of the Secretariat, which had been its instrument. In the same way the continuity of the October revolution was conceived by Stalin as having a direct link with the personalization of power. The transfer of authority from Lenin to Stalin hence became the key to everything — from Stalin's point of view — and even the raison d'être for the falsification. Stalin was obsessed by his Biography. Khrushchev, confirming Boris Souvarine's view, saw this as a result of Stalin's megalomania. But this obsession in fact corresponded to a major political concern for continuity. The Biography was an essential basic ingredient in the mystificatory enterprise. Its purpose was to seal Stalin's reputation as Lenin's closest companion and collaborator, his designated political heir, and his historical successor.

Although the general level of mystification surrounding the social origins of the bureaucracy and the structure of its property created an objectively useful ambiguity, the myth had no basis in reality. It was in obvious conflict with the truth. Every fact known about Lenin's real role made this all the more obvious. Lenin was equally accepted as a leader of the party, head of the state, and a leader in the sphere of theoretical elaboration. For him, these were not separate but complementary activities. To establish his historical descent Stalin had to succeed Lenin in *all three spheres*. Stalin was hence compelled to effect a complete disfiguration of Bolshevik history. For this purpose he used all the coercive apparatus of the state. In effect, he had to control access to the archives; scrutinize the list of banned documents; withdraw from circulation those histories of the party and those memoirs which did not conform with his needs (Enukidzhe, Krupskaya and Gorky were to rewrite their memoirs); organize well-publicized launchings of hagiographies prepared according to his instructions and read and annotated by him; censor reviews; and exercise tight surveillance over personal accounts and testimonies.

Now, the past history of the thermidoreans was the revolution. All of them of any importance had played various roles as actors in the revolution. They knew the truth, some even its darkest corners. If they contributed to its falsification, they did it consciously; because their interests lay in doing it or in letting it be done. At the level of power, Stalin could not count on these interests remaining stable. Interests changed when the Troika broke up, Zinoviev and Kamenev found there were advantages in giving up its secrets. The thermidoreans — those who counted — were hence potential enemies in Stalin's eyes. His comrades from when he was young — Mdivani, Enukidzhe, Ordzhonikidze, his most recent associates — Gorky and Yagoda — and the members of the narrow circle who knew the exact nature of his relations with Lenin — Zinoviev and Kamenev — were not to survive. Now we can discern the central problem of the repression. Two questions provide the key. What was politically dangerous about the archives? Who could draw political advantage from them?

The break between Lenin and Stalin was accomplished in December 1922. The old disagreements became irreconcilable. The activities of Ordzhonikidze in Georgia precipitated an official expression of this break. It was hence on the (politically and consti-tutionally crucial) terrain of nationalities that this struggle manifested itself. No compromise was possible.[46] The notes dictated by Lenin on 30 and 31 December are of rare violence. Even the episode in October 1917 which Stalin was to use to such effect against Zinoviev and Kamenev, was not at the same level of brutality. Lenin dealt with Stalin in terms which he had hitherto reserved for class enemies. He asserted that "as far as the Georgian question is concerned, this is a characteristic example of the need for a truly proletarian attitude and demands of us a redoubling of care, foresight and flexibility". Of Stalin he says:

> The Georgian who looks contemptuously on this aspect of the affair, and who disdainfully throws about accusations of "social-nationalism" *(although he himself is not only a true, authentic "social-nationalist" but also a brutal Great-Russian bully)*; this Georgian is in reality an obstacle to proletarian class solidarity, since nothing holds this back more than national injustice. There is no more sensitive issue among the oppressed nationalities than the feeling of equality and the violation of this equality.
>
> It hence goes without saying that Stalin and Dzherzhinsky must be made politically responsible for this profoundly Great-Russian nationalist campaign.[47]

In describing Stalin as a "brutal Great-Russian bully", Lenin was making a political judgement. He made a *precise social and historical* judgement on the directives of the General Secretary, as applied in Georgia by his envoy Ordzhonikidze and his inquisitor Dzherzhinsky. In characterizing this policy as anti-proletarian, chauvinist and coercive, he was identifying the *real social natire of the state*. Thus Stalin's policy, far from appearing as a deviation from the norm, confirmed on the contrary the *persistent contradiction between the state which emerged from the proletarian revolution, and the revolution itself*. In the last days of 1922, in his description of the state, Lenin sharpened the definition which he had already given in introducing NEP and drew close to the thesis developed by Rakovsky in 1930. Taking up the central theme that it was "absolutely necessary to unify the apparatus", he asked what state apparatus was being referred to. He replied:

> That which we call a state apparatus is still *profoundly foreign* and represents a hotchpotch of bourgeois and tsarist survivals, which it would have been impossible for us to transform in five years without the aid of other countries, and which could not be done, preoccupied as we were with military matters and with the struggle against famine. Under these conditions, it is altogether natural that "freedom to secede from the union", which we use as a justification, appears as a bureaucratic formula which cannot defend Russia's allogens against an authentic Russian invasion: *from the Great-Russian, from the chauvinist, from the scoundrel, from the oppressor which the typical Russian bureaucrat is at heart*. There is no doubt that the genuinely sovietized workers, who are a tiny proportion, will drown in this ocean of Great-Russian chauvinist rabble, like a fly in milk. [My emphasis throughout.]

Lenin thus held that the social corps of the state (this "ocean of Great-Russian chauvinist rabble") was the foundation of a great-power chauvinism of which Stalin, as General Secretary, was the political instrument. From this point onwards — and precisely because of it — the document of 31 December 1922 took on a significance which remained socially explosive in the 1970s.

The relations between classes, and the world conjuncture, had changed profoundly since 1922; but this change took the form of a *major reinforcement of the social factors brought to light by Lenin's lucid analysis*. Lenin certainly did not foresee the final fixed form of the class produced by this society; but he discerned and analysed its main constituent elements. It is for this reason that the problems he was dealing with were of burning immediacy, because they related to the organic growth process of the society, to its class dynamic. The significance of the problems grew in proportion to the power conquered by the bureaucracy. Lenin's critique, in this light, takes on new historic significance. This is because Lenin grasped — above and beyond the abstract concept of the workers' state — the functional reality of the state; because he detached the social determinants of this functional reality; because his creative imagination thus provided the clarity needed to comprehend their underlying tendencies; and because his critique touched directly on a historic context which was not at that time clearly identifiable. This was why the archives represented such a danger.

It is remarkable that Lenin broke with Stalin over the question of Georgia, and that twenty-five years later one of the last repressive campaigns run by Stalin, the last before the doctors' plot, once again decimated Georgia (the Mingrelian nationalist pseudo-plot of 1952).

Meanwhile, Ordzhonikidze's brutality had developed into the massacres conducted by Yezhov, and the collective deportations of minority nationalities of the 1940s. There had been a considerable change in scale.

If Khrushchev, in taking up Lenin's remarks about Stalin's brutality, reduced it to a question of character traits, it was because he had to hide the *political continuity* which dictated that Khrushchev should play the role of a "brutal Great-Russian bully" in Hungary, as his successor Brezhnev did in Czechoslovakia. Hence Lenin's notes were not only useful ammunition for the Ukrainians and for the Crimean Tartars in the 1960s, but also for the Roumanians, Czechs, Poles, Cubans and the Yugoslavs.

Lenin writes, "It is necessary to distinguish between the nationalism of an oppressed nation and that of the oppressor nation, between the nationalism of a large nation and that of a small nation"; he affirms: "Internationalism for the oppressor nation or for the 'large' nation (even if, like a bully, it is only large through violence) must consist not only in respect for *formal equality* between nations, but also in a compensatory inequality on the part of the oppressor nation, on the part of the large nation, an inequality which must be manifested in a practical way. Whoever has not understood this has not understood the truly proletarian attitude to the national question." With these words, he places himself quite naturally at the heart of the debate which dominated economic and political relations between states in the bureaucratic world sphere; and at the centre of the conflict which has embroiled the international communist movement since the start of the 1950s.

With brilliant foresight, Lenin evokes the "hundreds of thousands of people in Asia who will in the near future take the stage of history following us", and the immense prejudice which national politics could engender "if on the eve of this eruption in the East and at its first awakening, we lower our authority in their eyes by the slightest brutality or injustice towards our own nationalities". He asserts that it is not at all sufficient "to make a common front against Western imperialism" but that it is necessary to avoid using this common front in order to gain a position of strength, because "it would be another thing entirely to *become engaged ourselves*, even on minor questions, in *imperialist relations* with the oppressed nationalities, and thus awaken suspicion as to the sincerity of our principles, and as to the principled justification for our war with imperialism"; in saying this Lenin could well be describing the Chinese crisis, the Sino-Soviet conflict and the tensions between Moscow and the revolutionary vanguard in Latin America, Africa and Asia. It is certainly significant that Lenin saw nothing in the existing state of affairs which hinder the Soviet state itself from becoming involved in "imperialist relations".

Lenin's major writings of this period — his notes on the national question, his "Testament", his programmatic article "Better Fewer, But Better", his interventions on the monopoly of foreign trade, his enquiry into bureaucracy, and his project of turning the workers' and peasants' inspection into a weapon of war against the bureaucracy's power — all these completely refute Stalin's allegation that Lenin was simply a sick man who had fallen under the influence of women (Krupskaya and his two secretaries); an allegation which was made at a meeting of heads of delegations to the Twelfth Congress. On the contrary, this last work of Lenin (whose unity and value must lead us to consider the entire text to be his Testament) reveals a political imagination which retains intact its scope and creative capacity. It is necessary to read the daily reports of his secretaries to understand what this meant in terms of effort of will, resistance to the periods during which he lost his lucidity, and the permanent tension between this solitary illness and a hostile entourage which never disarmed itself. It also shows us his total identification with the revolution. It is because Lenin knew that his death was not far off — although he understood clearly that the time left to him could not be predicted — that he made such haste to get to the heart of the matter. During the last months, he concentrated on a single question: the leadership of the party and the state: both in their historic breadth and in their detailed working. In "Better Fewer, But Better," he wrote:

> The system of international relations is now such that in Europe one state, Germany, is subjugated by the victors. Furthermore several states, amongst them some of the oldest Western states, find themselves, following victory, in a situation from which they can profit by making certain concessions to their oppressed classes; concessions which, although only half-measures, hold back the development of the revolutionary movement in these countries by creating an appearance of "social peace". On the other hand a large number of states, including those of the East, India, China, etc., precisely because of the second imperialist war, have found themselves thrown out of the ring. Their evolution has definitively placed them on the general path of development of European capitalism. It is now clear to the whole world that they have been launched on a course which can only add to the crisis of world capitalism as a whole.

It is worth quoting the whole of this.

> The outcome of the struggle depends ultimately on the fact that Russia, India, China etc. form the vast majority of the world population. And it is just this majority of the population which, for several years, has been drawn with incredible rapidity into a struggle for its emancipation. . . .

But what interests us is not at all this inevitable victory of socialism. What concerns us is the tactic which we must follow — we, the communist party of Russia, in order to stop the counter-revolutionary states of Western Europe from crushing us. In order that we can survive until the next military conflict between the imperialist West and the nationalist and revolutionary East, between the most civilized states of the world and the backward countries like those of the East, which now form the majority, *this majority must have time to civilize itself. We no less are not civilized enough to pass directly to socialism, without the requisite political premises.*

These political premises must therefore be safeguarded.

We must realize the maximum economy in our state apparatus. We must abolish from it all traces of great excesses bequeathed by Russian Tsarism together with its capitalist and bureaucratic apparatus.

By dealing with the question of leadership at this historical level, the appropriate context is also given for the struggle of Lenin against the "brutal Great-Russian chauvinist bully", the Georgian. The rapid progress of the break between Lenin and Stalin is striking. From this assertion: "things are going badly with our state apparatus, if they are not yet detestable", to its consequence: the need to "replace Stalin" by a superior and different man — his conclusion of 4 January — Lenin moved over to a complete personal and political break on 5 March. Here we find ourselves a long way from Khrushchev's interpretation. But to be sure, we are talking about 1923 and not 1934.

The "Notebook of Lenin's Secretaries (21 November 1922 to 6 March 1923)" was not published in the Soviet Union until 1963 and did not appear in the complete works until 1969.[48] The dates — November 1922 to March 1923 — delimit the last months of Lenin's political life. On 7 March a new attack left him completely paralysed until his death on 21 January 1924. When the Notebook opens, Lenin had been at his post at the Kremlin since October; but he knew that by now he was at the mercy of the disease. Compelled in December 1921 to interrupt his governmental activities ("insomnia", he wrote at the time, "has taken on frightful proportions"), incapable of speaking and even of moving for two months after the attack which he survived in May, the improvement in his condition in July did not fool him. Nor did it fool the narrow circle of the leadership. The period of December 1921 to October 1922 was decisive from the point of view of the exercise of power. Power had effectively been concentrated in Lenin's hands. With Lenin paralysed, the Political Bureau took over his position. Once Lenin's days were numbered, the imminence of the question of succession provoked the clandestine coalition of the Troika; that is to say, the creation of a majority in the Political Bureau which made it possible for the

Secretariat (i.e. for Stalin) to take hold of all effective power. Trotsky was isolated.

When Lenin returned to Moscow in October 1922, he remained a potential danger for Stalin, *but he had in reality lost power*. This is the first central point which the Notebook confirms completely. Lenin was politically disarmed because in the eyes of the Troika he was living on borrowed time. Lenin knew this. He knew that he could seriously count on nobody but Trotsky. The decisions he took and the letters he wrote are irrefutable proof of this. Lenin was isolated at the summit of the apparatus. This isolation was effective because power had been completely absorbed into the closed circles of the upper bureaucracy. The prestige and authority of Lenin in the party were only limited by the interests of an already bloated clientele. Prudence dictated that his isolation should be made total. *Stalin used medical prescriptions to turn Lenin into a political prisoner.* Lenin knew this and organized his intervention clandestinely. The Notebook contains a formal proof of this. On 18 December, the Central Committee took an extremely important step: it put Stalin in charge of Lenin's medical régime. Stalin could thus deal *legally* with the doctors and secretaries. The tight, rigorous medical surveillance to which he was subjected was aimed at depriving Lenin of information and seizing his writings. The secretaries, who were brought from the Council of Commissars of the People and from the Commissions of Labour and Defence (L. Fotieva and her assistant M. Volodicheva), were long-standing militants and deeply attached to Lenin. They were constrained to obey Stalin by the discipline of the party and by virtue of the decision of the Central Committee of 18 December. As they also had to pass on to him the information they recorded, they reflected Stalin's orders and responses. It is for this reason that the Notebook — destined for the archives — was of such inestimable political value. The quiet but deadly conflict is taken straight from life. The hypocritical use made of the doctors and the administrative procrastinations exasperated Lenin and speeded up the effects of the illness. This is clearly visible in the daily annotations. The Notebook is hence also an extraordinary human document. In a completely sober tone — but not a dry one — it reveals an extraordinarily powerful human spirit. I know of no other document which brings one as close to Lenin. To see it is to see his entourage, and hence to understand him. This daily piece of transcription is the living record of a tragedy which foreshadows and ushers in (all the players having already made their entry) the tragedy of the show trials. Even the doctors are there, ready to reappear with Yagoda, and to make their final entry when death came to take Stalin in his turn. Before the long night of blood begins, the central figure is Lenin. His destiny has already struck him down. At the very source of power, but already its prisoner, fighting against his physical disability and against his jailers, he tries to outline the coming dangers. History as a stage director is a genius. The secretaries record the drama as it proceeds. On 30 January, Fotieva notes:

> On 24 January, Vladimir Ilyich asked for Fotieva and charged her with asking Dzherzhinsky or Stalin for the dossier of the commission on the Georgian question in order to study it in detail. On Thursday 25 January, he asked if this dossier had arrived. I replied that Dzherzhinsky was not coming until Saturday. On Saturday, Dzherzhinsky said that the dossier was with Stalin. "I have sent a letter to Stalin and he was away from Moscow." Suddenly the truth comes to light: Yesterday on 29 January, Stalin telephoned to say that he could not release *the dossier without the authorization of the Political Bureau. He asked me how it was that Lenin was up to date with what was going on, if I was not telling him useless things.* For example, his article on the workers' and peasants' inspection *shows that he knows a certain amount of detailed information.* I replied, "I have told him nothing and I have no reason to believe that he is keeping up with what is going on." Today, Vladimir Ilyich called me to ask for the reply and told me that he was going to fight to get hold of the documentation.

Lenin, in order to win support for his struggle against the bureaucracy and against his imprisonment, sent a demand to the central office of statistics on 5 February (transmitted by his collaborator Glasser) to supply him with details of the census of functionaries in Petrograd, Moscow and Kharkov, which was at the printers. Two days later, he asked once again for the galley proofs. Fotieva noted, on 7 February, "*I told him that for this he must have Stalin's authorization.*" On 3 February, returning to the Georgian question, Fotieva noted:

> He asked if this question had been discussed by the Political Bureau. I replied that *I did not have the right to speak to him about it.* He asked me, "You have been forbidden to speak to me precisely and particularly about that?" I replied, "No, in a general sense, I do not have the right to talk about current events." "Is this then a question of current events?" I realized that I had blundered. I repeated that I did not have the right to speak to him about it.

Lenin was forced to find ways of escaping this permanent sequestration. In relation to a letter addressed to Trotsky, cementing their agreement on the question of the defence of the monopoly of foreign trade which Stalin was trying to dismantle by subterfuge, Fotieva wrote on 5 December 1922:

> Lenin asked for Fotieva and gave her a letter written by him for Trotsky, charging Fotieva personally with typing the letter and sending it, keeping a copy in a sealed envelope in the confidential archives. He had many bad things to write about. He said I should destroy the

original, but it is together with the copy in the confidential archives. On 24 December, his other secretary Volodicheva records:

> On the day after (24 December) between 18.30 and 20.00, Vladimir Ilyich called for me again. He drew my attention to the fact that the things he had dictated yesterday (23 December) were absolutely confidential. He stressed this several times. He asked for all his dictated material to be stored in a particular place, under my specific responsibility and to be kept absolutely secret. At this point he added further instructions.

This concerned the Testament. In his supplementary instructions, Lenin stipulated that the sealed envelopes could be opened by no one but himself and, after his death, by Nadezhda Constantinovna, his wife. On 30 January Fotieva recalled this exchange: "On 24 January, Vladimir Ilyich said to me: 'Before we go further, on this "confidential" matter, I know that you are not telling me the truth.' When I assured him that the contrary was true, he said, 'My opinion is written down there.'"

And finally, on 12 February, this last and crucial observation by Fotieva:

> Vladimir Ilyich is getting worse, he has a violent headache. After Maria Ilyichna, the doctors put him in such a bad mood that his lips were trembling. In the evening, Forster said that reading newspapers was categorically forbidden, as well as visits and political information. When he asked what was meant by this, Forster replied: "Well, for example: you have been taking an interest in the census of employees of the soviets." The fact that the doctors were so well-informed seemed to drive Vladimir Ilyich out of his mind. Overall, Vladimir Ilyich seemed to have the impression that it was not the doctors who were giving instructions to the Central Committee, but the Committee that was instructing the doctors. He spoke to me incessantly of the three habitual topics, all the while complaining about his headache.

Maria Ilyichna Ulianovna was Lenin's sister; Forster was a German professor of neurology consulted by Lenin's doctors. The three subjects were Georgia, his Testament and his article on the workers' inspection.

Lenin's haste is evident in his instructions to Fotieva on 14 February:

> Vladimir Ilyich called me at 12. He did not have a headache any more. He said that he felt fine. He said his illness was nervous in origin, so that sometimes he was in perfect health, and that his head felt fine, but that at other times he felt worse. This was why we had to hurry with the tasks he had given us, because he wanted to put something very important and relevant to the Congress, and he hoped to be able to do it. But if we were slow and messed things up, he would be very disturbed. The doctors arrived and he had to stop talking.

The same day in the evening, Lenin decided to ally himself with those Georgians who were enemies of Stalin. Fotieva noted under "Notes from Vladimir Ilyich": "Make Soltz (member of the Praesidium of the Central Control Commission) understand that he (Lenin) was on the side of the offended parties. Make someone among them understand that he is on their side." On 5 March, he dictated two letters to Volodicheva. One was to Trotsky, asking him to take up the defence of the Georgians. The other was to Stalin, breaking off all personal and political relations with him. On 6 March, he dictated a letter to the Mdivani group stating that he was preparing an intervention in favour of the Georgians. Volodicheva notes that he re-read the letter addressed to Stalin "and demanded that it be given to him personally and that the reply be brought directly to him". She adds:

> He was ill. Nadezhda Constantinovna asked me not to send the letter to Stalin, and I acceded to this request throughout 6 March. But on the 7th, I said that I had to carry out Vladimir Ilyich's instructions. She had a conversation with Kamenev, and the letter was sent to Stalin and Kamenev, and then to Zinoviev, when he came back from Petrograd. Stalin wrote his reply straight after receiving the letter from Vladimir Ilyich (the letter was personally delivered by me to Stalin and it was I who took Stalin's reply). The letter was not given to Vladimir Ilyich because he was getting worse.

The contents of the archives totally destroyed the myth that Stalin was the faithful companion, heir and interpreter of Lenin and leninism.

The profound break between Lenin and Stalin which is brought to light by this evidence — a break which was in effect a transfer of power from one class to another — is hence confirmed, and its political and personal meaning clearly proved by these items in the archives, whose existence was known outside Russia from 1927 onwards, but which were officially published in Moscow, in the reference edition of Lenin's works, only in 1969. It is notable that it took sixteen years for Stalin's epigones to publish this information, and even then they did it discreetly. Khrushchev allowed himself only a number of allusions to it. These items (and without doubt many others like them which are still locked up) do not only demystify the Stalinist myth, but they also destroy the Khrushchevite interpretation. This interpretation is still useful and necessary for the bureaucracy in the 1980s.

The archives explode Stalin's *revolutionary* legitimacy. They remove all credibility from the official theses of continuity in the *personal* exercise of power. They introduce an element of weakness into the theory of succession and hence into the effective organization of the dictatorship. It took the Second World War and the accession of the generation of "men without a past" to the top leadership, before the state could project a self-image in which it identified itself closely enough with Ivan the Terrible or Peter the Great to supplant the gilded icons of Lenin and Stalin. The archives were therefore sealed, the witnesses were smeared, compromised and killed.

22 The massacre of the Thermidoreans

THERE CAN BE no doubt that Stalin pushed falsification to ridiculous limits. The crude megalomania attributed to him by Khrushchev certainly plays some part in episodes like his condemnation of the historian Karaiev for misunderstanding the role which he claimed to have played in the workers' movement in Baku. There are numerous such examples. But megalomania is not the root cause. The central fact is that Stalin considered historical fact as dangerous to his *exercise of power*. Stalin's crimes hence result from a carefully considered political strategy.

What real threat was there to Stalin's power and how could it come about? Through his traditional opponents, the Zinovievites, Bukharinists and Trotskyists? Certainly not. They were eliminated in 1927. Imprisoned or deported, they were reduced to complete impotence. Successive calculated attacks had deprived them of all moral and political weight. The second civil war completely annihilated their class base. The proletariat, pushed back into and repressed in the factories, had been joined by a massive influx from the villages. The new arrivals were lacking in any political or trade-union consciousness or experience. The proletariat was incapable of giving any weight to its most elementary class demands, let alone trying to overturn the régime. The middle peasantry was split up and scattered as an autonomous social force. The poor peasants — without leadership, without unity, without initiative and without authority — had fallen under the yoke of the agrarian bureaucracy. The technical intelligentsia — encouraged in its expectations by the government legislation of 1935 — was deep in intrigue for position and honour. Preoccupied with enjoying life and starved of privileges, it knew that the true measure of its success was a basic political in-difference. Its conventional wisdom regarded any involvement in affairs of state as folly. The revolutionary generation of October 1917 — in all its tendencies — was so near extinction that, from 1934 onwards, it seemed like an anachronistic survival, without the slightest purchase on society. It was divested of its intellectual prestige, at one time so immense, by frequent and humiliating public calumny; it was morally degraded by its infamous prostitution; it lacked any political consistency. Stalin knew all this perfectly well. He had done everything to bring this situation about. The most pusillanimous man in power had nothing to fear from these phantoms.

The oppositions which appeared in the 1950s and the 1960s confirmed the fact that this hiatus was of historic breadth. They were *sui generis*. Their roots lay in the situation created by the Second World War. (Stalin had been prophetic in this respect also, even if the precise way things worked out was different from what he imagined and had taken longer to develop.) They arose from the world crisis of state capitalism. They were nurtured by spontaneous criticism of the intolerance and disorder of bureaucratic management. Their criteria were elaborated in conformity with the main global course of scientific and technological thought. The discontinuity between the revolutionary marxist generation of the 1920s and the oppositionists of the 1950s and 1960s was infinitely greater in Russia than in the rest of the world. Trotsky's world prestige, the creative power of his international activity and the resurgence of trotskyist organizations during the 1960s, conceal the situation in Russia itself. Outside of Russia, the revolutionary heritage could be transmitted via teaching, in publications, in free study, in a certain continuity of organization, albeit weak and sometimes clandestine. In the Soviet Union the brick wall surrounding the archives and the state of generalized terror which accompanied it, created a profoundly different situation. The break between generations relates to their *knowledge of history as it actually happened* and to the *development of the science of society*. The falsification that was imposed everywhere by the state as truth, censorship and a wall of silence brought into being an inevitable and very basic ignorance. Dogmatism and scholasticism at one and the same time denatured marxist methodology and deterred the new generation, formed in the new world school of science and technology, from studying it.

On the other hand the systematic distortion of the history of the revolution maintained its prestige, which was politically useful and necessary for consolidating the ruling class and its strategic world interests. It did so to such an extent that a true knowledge of the revolutionary period would still have been socially dangerous even in the 1970s. For example, consider the impact of the Khrushchevite rehabilitations — circumspect and calculated though they were — on the groupings of sons and daughters of previously eminent figures who had been deported or executed. Brezhnev's hope of maintaining rigorous censorship, and strict secrecy, the reinforcement of legal repression against publications, and the dispersal and seizure of works not bearing the official stamp, show that the upper bureaucracy understands full well what would be the consequences of freedom of scientific enquiry. This veto on research, the banning of publications, and the stifling of discussion which resulted, of course, hold back not only the study of history but of science itself.

Sakharov tells us that "Roy Medvedev has devoted an analysis of a thousand pages to the evolution of Stalinism"; that this study "was conducted in a marxist framework" but that it was not published "in spite of its great value and its profound vision".

The clandestinity into which science has been forced to retreat perpetuates profound ignorance. The prestige of the revolution hence gives great power to the work of historical criticism, without however recreating a living feeling of continuity between the revolutionary generation of the 1920s and the awakening of oppositional sentiment which took place in the 1960s. In conformity with this profound discontinuity, criticism of Stalin's role in the Second World War (began by Nekrich in 1965, amplified by the 1966 controversy which followed the seizure of his book *The 24 June 1941*, and which Medvedev took up in April 1969 in his pamphlet *Should Stalin be Rehabilitated?*) found a wider audience and had a greater immediate impact than the issue of the rehabilitation of Zinoviev, Bukharin or Trotsky. At the same time, the major dramatization of the Moscow trials appeared; it concerned the post-war generation less than the trial of Tukhachevsky behind closed doors.

This political and social destruction of the revolutionary generation was clearly understood by the thermidoreans in 1934. They were fully conscious of what had happened. The 17th Congress was entitled the "Congress of Victors". This was not just because of the ostentation of the new arrivals. It also expressed a kind of balance-sheet, the official consecration of an irreversible conquest. Stalin, now proclaimed "greatest leader of all times and of all peoples" gave expression to a unanimous feeling of security when he announced to the enthusiastic delegates: "At this congress there is nothing left to expose, no one else to fight." The letters of submission and allegiance of the last resisters — Sosnovsky and Rakovsky — signified total victory. The accompanying repression which, since 1933, had eliminated more than 340,000 party members, had cleansed the party of the scars of the second civil war. The new society had elaborated and promulgated its own laws. The Secretariat became the supreme organ of the autocracy. The central power, the administration of the state, control of the economy and the unions were tightly in the grip of the thermidoreans and their clients. The thermidoreans constituted the only legal political body and the only one which was effectively organized. These were the foremost and irrefutable *facts* of the situation.

The 17th Congress opened in January. In December 1934, the course of the terror — which had been suspended for eleven months — resumed. Stalin personally placed his signature and seal against more than 350 lists of names of people to be arrested and shot. On these lists appeared 40,000 high officials of the party and the state. This selection of names reveals the central object of the repression. These premeditated measures, between 1935 and 1941, led to the arrest and execution of *more than a million stalinists* (holders of party cards or members of the Young Communists). These million political officials — arrested, deported, killed or lost in the depths of the camps and prisons — was Khrushchev's official balance-sheet of the Russian night of the long knives. It signalled the destruction of the thermidorean apparatus and its leading figures, and of the clientele linked to it in the exercise of power. The mechanisms by which the regression was generalized extended it into all social categories (industrial enterprise directors, kolkhoz cadres, scientific researchers, historians, intellectuals, military personnel, engineers, public works contractors, railwaymen, salaried staff and workers, often outside of any party) following the associations of work, family or amalgamations of local and particular interests. The scale reached in this sphere was several millions (probably between seven and eight million). This generalized action signalled the physical and social annihilation of a generation. These events constitute the second irrefutable *fact*.

The institutions which were affected by this bloody purge are typical. The real seat of power — the Secretariat — was the only one to remain intact. The Central Committee which emerged from the 17th Congress — the Congress of Victors — was decimated. We know that out of 139 members (full and candidate members), 110 were executed. From 1936 to 1938, more than 90 per cent of the functionaries of the central committees in the republics, regions and towns were exterminated. From 1937 to 1938, the personnel of the Central Committee of the Young Communists and the majority of their functionaries were annihilated. Almost all the political dignitaries of the régime were imprisoned, deported, killed or had vanished: six presidents out of seven from the executive of the soviets, and the bulk of its full and candidate members; about nine out of ten of the Commissars of the Peoples of the Russian and Federated Republics went; almost all the Control Commission members; nearly all 80 members of the council of war set up in 1934; the principal heads of the NKVD and many retired Cheka members; nearly all members of the commission charged with overseeing the constitution and the commission for overseeing the revision of the history text-books; and a large contingent of top-ranking diplomats. Sixty per cent of the officials of the Communist International — those who, after the Seventh and last World Congress (the one which adopted the "popular front" line in 1935) were designated as honoured stalinists, all of whom made their careers witch-hunting trotskyists and then Zinovievists — all these were liquidated. Three hundred of them featured on a single list signed by Stalin. The officer corps of the army were ravaged. More than 80 per cent of the higher-ranking officers were shot. Tens of thousands of lower-ranking officers were arrested, imprisoned or deported. The official list given by Khrushchev numbers: 14 army generals out of 16; 66 divisional generals out of 199 ; 221 brigade generals out of 377; 8 admirals out of 8 ; 11 army commissars out of 11; 25,000 superior and subaltern officers — nearly half of those in the service.

Khrushchev, in his report to the 20th Congress, furnished a striking illustration: "During this period, the leading cadres who had acquired military experience in Spain or the Far East were almost completely liquidated." He made it clear that the repression went "literally from the level of batallion commander up to the highest military circles". In the state apparatus, the party, and in the army, it was the socially strategic nerve centres which were prioritized. Every component of the hierarchic armour of the bureaucracy which took part in the process of control (concentration and diffusion) was attacked. In other words, all possible points of convergence for social forces. This is the third irrefutable *fact*.

These three well-established facts give us a historically-based answer to the question: "Who?" We know that there existed more than 350 lists signed personally by Stalin. We know that these lists contained more than 40,000 names of high dignitaries, who were supposed to be, and in fact were, arrested and shot. We know that Stalin directed the enquiries and accusations. We know that all the key posts in the state, party, and army suffered a turnover of personnel of between 80 per cent and 90 per cent, and sometimes even 100 per cent. We know that the arrest, imprisonment and execution of these 40,000 high dignitaries led to the arrest, execution or deportation of more than a million subordinate functionaries, all party card holders. We know that the personnel of regional and provincial political apparatuses and the party committees down to the level of villages and city districts, together with all associated organizations, was almost totally replaced. From our knowledge of how the bureaucracy worked, we know that this personnel was tied by its functions to the 40,000-strong aristocracy by a network of services rendered, protection, and favouritism in promotion; that it was divided into clienteles attached to various important people or various groups in the central apparatus, conducting themselves in the last resort as coalitions around common interests. (This phenomenon, as I have indicated, was already quite extensive in 1923. Ten years later, it was the central pillar of the state administration.) These assumed or open ties of solidarity, these overt or covert compromises provided the basis for the first logical generalization of the terror. The 40,000 logically became a million. This million in its turn logically became the point of departure for a universal extension of the terror which reached its culmination in 1937.

The concentration of the property of the state resulted in a tight interlocking between the political apparatus of the state and the managerial apparatus of the economy. The network of clienteles and their interests tied ministries to enterprises and touched upon every single relation between the central administrations, the corresponding bodies in the federated republics and the managerial apparatus of the industrial and commercial trusts, of the factories, the kolkhozes and the co-operatives. This complicity among the various parts of the bureaucracy on promotion, division of the spoils, and the conduct of professional duties, laid the logical basis for the ultimate expansion of the terror. The provisions of the Penal Code, which we know of, justified in advance every repressive measure, including the most extreme. This total generalization of the terror was at once deliberate and blind. It was a concerted operation in two senses. First, in the objects pursued: the purging of the intelligentsia (historians, scientists, economists, teachers, writers), the massive deportation of national minorities and the annihilation of Jewish writers and their freedom of cultural expression. Secondly, in its finality: the complete destruction of the links between the political aristocracy which was the initial target of the repression, and its ramifications in society.

The terror progressed blindly. It dealt with large numbers. Careful individual selection of targets was impractical. The technique of percentages necessarily supplanted it. The creation of pass-books and internal passports offered the technical basis for this operation. There were plenty of local arbitrary acts. At the end of 1938 these inevitable excesses, which had thrown up countless flagrant scandals, enabled Stalin legally to suppress his notorious collaborators, who were extremely compromising for him. *The several million victims were the logical consequence of the 40,000 who were shot.*

These 40,000 are the key to the enterprise. This is underlined by the care which Stalin attached to their selection, his decision to follow the affair personally, the attention he gave to their charges, the high positions which the majority of them held in the party and in the state, and the repercussions in the ranks of the bureaucracy of their arrest and of the testimonies extracted under torture. It becomes quite clear that Stalin wanted to destroy the group which constituted the upper levels of the political corps of the state. Now this layer consisted precisely of the thermidoreans. They belonged — through their leading cadres — to the Bolshevik "old guard" of 1917. Many of them had been close collaborators of Lenin. Every one of them had a *biography* — that is to say, an authentic revolutionary past. Without them and without their definite support Stalin could not have risen to power in the party or in the state. They embodied the resistance to change of the institutions which had arisen out of the revolution and the subsequent social mutation of the state. In the disintegration of the first world revolution, they had been the political catalyst of bureaucratic society.

In conformity with the real goal which Stalin was pursuing, — again drawing attention to the concerted and co-ordinated character of this enterprise and hence to its function — Stalin destroyed the official organizations of the "old guard" and prepared the way for the non-party functionaries. This highly significant step is in total contradiction with Khrushchev's interpretation of events. In May 1935 he dissolved the Society of Old Bolsheviks. On 1 June he dissolved the Association of Former Political Prisoners; in February 1936 the Communist Academy. The brusque promotion of the non-party functionaries corresponded to a double tactical aim. He hoped to mobilise public opinion against the thermidoreans and the big party chiefs (he conducted a tacit plebiscite against them) and to bring about a complete changeover in the state personnel by opening the way to the men without a past. He took the occasion of a toast to the army, in May 1935, to condemn the intangible dogma of the primacy of the party: "to the health of all Bolsheviks, within the party and without it. Yes, without it. Party members are only a minority. Non-party men are the majority. But in their ranks, are there not true Bolsheviks? Two days later, in a speech to the military academy, he raised the stakes: "these days we speak too much of the merits of the leaders, of the chiefs. Everything is attributed to them, nearly all our achievements. This is obviously inexact and untrue."

The answer to the question "Who?" is to be found in these irrefutable and precise facts. Zinovievists, Bukharinists, and trotskyists played their tragic parts in the opening scenes of the trials. Certainly Zinoviev, Kamenev, Smirnov, Bukharin, Rykov, Radek, Piatakov, Mrachkovsky, Sokolnikov, Tervaganian, Evdokimov and Rakovsky were not in any sense present only in fiction. By nailing them to the pillory of abject confession and in executing the most eminent among them in the Lubianka dungeons, Stalin destroyed the generation of October. The revolution had long been annihilated, and was assassinated once again in the humiliated bodies of Lenin's party. So much so that the Kafkaesque parody of the trial itself took on a historic and emotional aspect which masked its real purpose. Stalin set up Lenin's collaborators as decoys. The real purpose of the trial — its political result — was the annihilation of the Thermidor generation. The real targets of the trials were to be found on 350 lists and numbered 40,000.

The thermidorians represented an inescapable danger for Stalin, because they were his familiars, because they formed his entourage, and could approach him at any time and because they had lived by his side through the same events. They therefore held the keys to the mystification process. The embargo on the archives could not deprive them of their past. As a result, they could re-establish the facts, either partly or almost in their entirety. That is to say, they could destroy the falsification on which the legitimacy and inheritance of power was based, because they themselves were in the running for the top job. They had authentic revolutionary credentials. They knew how to make good use of their former association with Lenin. (In the midst of his polemic on the Georgian affair, when he was demanding "exemplary punishment" for Ordzhonikidze, Lenin added: "I say this with all the more regret since I counted him among my friends and struggled side by side with him abroad, in exile.") They thus had the chance to present themselves as Lenin's faithful heirs. They controlled the whole network of the state, with the sole exception of the Secretariat. They disposed of numerous and widespread networks of clients. They were without scruples, which was precisely why Stalin had been able to make such good use of them: but it could also lead to his downfall.

A potential danger only becomes real under circumstances which make it so. The conjuncture of 1934 was tailor-made to encourage such ambitions:

Because the régime was securely established. The peasantry was still recovering from a crushing military defeat. It had been dispossessed of its goods, and all its work had been despoiled by the state. Its bases of resistance had been destroyed and its cadres killed, deported or dispersed. The industrial proletariat was without any class organization: the trade unions had become repressive organs of the state. Its political leaders, who had been so powerful in the 1920s, were excluded from the leading trade-union bodies, wiped out from the factories, imprisoned and executed, or had become agents of the régime. Even the composition of the working class had altered to the advantage of the bureaucracy through the influx from the villages, which lacked any trade-union or political tradition. Immediate demands found no organizational support and no leaders capable of interpreting them. They could only be expressed in savage, unco-ordinated actions which led nowhere. Pillage was substituted for trade-union struggle. Wages were miserable, but unemployment was avoided by the arbitrary maintenance of a factory work-force with no real employment. More profoundly and more decisively, antagonistic classes had become irreversibly caught up in the new relations of production. The peasantry was trapped in the kolkhozy, and the dispersed rich peasantry had been replaced in the fields by the agrarian bureaucracy. The urban petty bourgeoisie was making a career in the administration. Its intelligentsia had been incorporated into the privileged managerial circles in the factories, the co-operatives, teaching and propaganda. The régime's solidity was so great that in spite of the immense ravages of the terror, it was to pass the crucial test of the Second World War. In spite of a tremendous weakening of the army, disastrous defeats, gross, costly and repeated errors, the régime emerged from the test strengthened, and with its class support reinforced on a world scale. The cost of this victory was excessively high, but was nevertheless accepted. The bureaucracy — as a ruling class — had proven that it was at least as stable as the Western capitalist régimes. The war gave bureaucratic society its diploma in historical longevity.

In 1934 the thermidoreans were very conscious of this basic security. The Congress of Victors expressed a well-founded satisfaction. Irreversible class stability freed the private interests and ambitions of those who benefited from it. It was now possible to struggle for the exercise of power, since this would no longer call into question the safety of the society itself.

Because the functional difficulties of the economy — in this securely established régime — were beginning to predominate. The bureaucracy, secure though it was, remained — as did the bourgeoisie — subordinated to the dynamic of the productive forces. Their growth brought them into conflict with a management system integrated into state capitalism. This contradictory dynamic created a permanent organic instability in the system. The proliferation of functionaries coincided with centralized authoritarian planning, in a world context where an advanced technology of substitution was missing. This obstacle could not be overcome by purely technical means, and so could only be surmounted through a radical change in the administration of the economy. Centralized authoritarian planning is not the only possible way to run state capitalism. Autonomy for the enterprises and a wider recourse to market mechanisms are perfectly compatible with it. A shortage of investments is not irremediable in the way that a lack of technology is, although both are obstacles to any weakening of coercion. On the contrary, autonomy implies a change from the delegation of authority to the delegation of property, in other words, the generalization of the status accorded the agrarian bureaucracy, to the advantage of the directors of industrial enterprises.

Because of the integration of property through the state, the right of control (that is to say, the free exercise of the right of property) is incorporated into the right to make political decisions. The bureaucracy, as the collective owner of the state, does not take part in its entirety in the process of political elaboration. The political corps of the state (the upper bureaucracy) created its role in the form of a monopoly. Authoritarian centralized planning allowed it to extend this monopoly into an exclusive exercise of property rights. This double aspect is the basis of the upper bureaucracy's pre-eminence within the ruling class. Effective autonomy of the enterprises would therefore open a breach in the privileges acquired by the political corps of the state (in this case, the thermidoreans). Furthermore, access to political controls on the part of new layers of the bureaucracy, which is necessarily implied by such changes, would have plainly posed the question of power.

These functional difficulties — precisely because they express permanent and fundamental problems — show that around 1934 bureaucratic society became fixed in place. It had its own dynamic, which developed its own specific contradictions. We must therefore analyse these contradictions in their proper social context, and not according to criteria relevant to other social formations or to models which do not correspond with this reality. The mechanisms which were set in motion accentuated the heterogeneity of the bureaucracy, as by analogy, the growth of monopoly capitalism diversified the organic composition of the bourgeoisie and aggravated the conflict between different sectors within it.

The Congress of Victors expresses very sharply the clear vision which the ruling class had of its own stability. It was expressed in daily life as a more and more impatient attitude on the part of the new arrivals; an impatience for ownership to be transformed into comfort and enjoyment, and for privileges won to be properly based in law. This is clearly shown by the measures taken in 1935. Food restrictions were abolished. The free market reappeared. The Kolkhozes were allowed to sell the produce of small-scale production at its market price. The government decided to cancel kolkhoz debts to the state. Piece-work wages became the rule. Stakhanovism widened the range of wages (by a factor of up to ten). The role of the cadres was extended. Fashion journals, banned up till now, reappeared. Paris couturiers were invited. Elegance in clothing was officially recommended. The state organized a trade in perfumes, lotions, creams, and make-up. The reformed Civil Code limited divorce, sanctioned paternity suits, prohibited abortion and re-established family honour. This did not stop the leading figures from divorcing to marry actresses and daughters of the bourgeoisie or of the aristocracy. At the Kremlin, banquets and champagne receptions proliferated. Stalin returned to Tiflis and had himself photographed with his mother, whom he had not seen for years. There were dances everywhere. Escape in all its forms became legitimate: sport, sailing, arctic exploration, expeditions into central Asia. Patriotism became a daily slogan. Decorations and distinctions mushroomed. The army reintroduced grades, medals, and marshals (suppressed since Kutuzov). The Commissariat of the Interior was awarded uniforms and distinctive symbols. The cossacks were re-established. The pedagogic innovations of the revolution were annulled. Traditions and routines from the tsarist epoch were revived: the authority of the managers and the magistrates, rules, punishments, rewards, school reports and dossiers, notes, examinations, diplomas, grades and university degrees. The uniform school system with the right to free school materials and meals was abolished; homework, private tuition, entrance examinations and final examinations, punishment notes, etc., were all revived. Russia's past was exalted through the personalities of Saint Alexander Nevsky, conqueror of the black knights; Ataman Ermak, conqueror of Siberia; Prince Pojarski, the scourge of the Poles; Field-Marshals Suvorov and Kutuzov, Ivan the Terrible and Peter the Great. The constitution adopted in June 1936 substituted a parliament (the Supreme Soviet), elected by universal suffrage, for the soviets. It consolidated private property rights already established, and recognized the right of inheritance without restriction. Stalin proclaimed: "Life is better, comrades. Life has never been so enjoyable." This was the climate under which the mass repression burst forth.

This thirst for good living, to have the means appropriate to one's rank and to satisfy one's ambitions, ran straight up against the poverty of resources available for this purpose. Blockages in production ceased to be the domain of the experts and became the subject of bitter complaints by the propertied classes. Wives, daughters and sons besieged managers, engineers, cadres and officials with their recriminations. The managerial apparatus turned on the central administration. The upper bureaucracy became worried and began to ask how well-founded the practices of the General Secretariat were. The clans became active. Mole-like opposition opened the way to political intrigue. The thermidoreans developed tendencies to rake over the past, to remind the Secretariat how indispensable they were to it and that they deserved some weight in decision-making. Now that the régime was solidly established, this layer no longer indulged in self-effacement out of fear of the outcome of social conflict. The question of the exercise of power, its structure, and its possible collectivization was implicitly on the order of the day. The thermidorean heads were Stalin's Barons. The massacre of the Barons could be discerned in outline during these months of 1934.

Stalin triumphed. The thermidoreans were eliminated. Men without a past succeeded them in the leadership positions. One generation took over from another. The political emancipation of the upper bureaucracy was set back nearly twenty-five years. The victory was achieved without concession or compromise.

Out of all the questions raised by such massive events, one particular enigma leads us to the heart of the mystery of this society. How was Stalin able to achieve such complete victory over 40,000 privileged and well-known political figures? These were people steeped in the atmosphere of the civil war. They were people who for fifteen years had been party, to a greater or lesser degree, to all the intrigues of the state. They had taken over the posts of their fallen opponents. They could flatter themselves with having been able to plot the downfall of some of Lenin's most prestigious collaborators. They had built the state up themselves, filling all its highest and most strategic positions. They knew their leader better than anyone. They knew his deviousness, his cunning, his duplicity and his cold-blooded vengeance, because they themselves had served him devotedly in both small and great matters. How was Stalin able to arrest, imprison, deport and kill these 40,000 people, their families, and their allies — more than a million people, the whole state apparatus, the élite of the ruling class? Contemporary history does not offer any comparable example. Hitler's night of the long knives is just a minor episode when compared with such facts. It must be clear that this victory is the key to the innermost secrets of this society.

The passivity of those classes which were socially antagonistic served Stalin as well as the thermidoreans. He would never have become involved in such a dangerous enterprise if he was not certain of the stability of the régime. Stalin took no delight in risks. He struck, knowing exactly what he was doing. When he was unsure of his ground he would manoeuvre and compromise. His prudence and caution in the defeat of the Left Opposition shows this quite clearly. It was not enough for him to have the adversary in his sights. He had to be prepared against any possible counter-move. He was better equipped to deal with the situation than his entourage.

The revolutionary credentials of the thermidoreans were only dangerous for Stalin's exercise of power as a result of the ruling mystificatory ideology. The bureaucracy — like the French bourgeoisie — was able to justify its existence in the mythical past. The origin of the bureaucracy was hence to be found officially in the proletarian revolution. Thus the bureaucracy denied its existence as a class. It defined itself as one social category among others in a classless society. This is what allowed it to claim that obvious social differences were purely functional and not the result of a new system for organizing the exploitation of the labour-force. This veil drawn over the real nature of the ruling class was aimed at politically disarming the socially antagonistic classes. Mystification thus played a cardinal role. It was second nature to the bureaucracy. But it was a restrictive second nature. It meant that in the struggle for power, phrases about continuity and loyalty had to be used constantly.

By this logic, the credentials of the thermidoreans had indisputable value. Stalin, however, was in fact at a considerable advantage. The double falsification he had effected, concerning the social role of the bureaucracy and the legitimacy of its exercise of power, was carried out to his advantage, on his initiative, under his directives, and with the consent and collaboration of all the thermidoreans. Their surrender of sovereignty to the "inspired leader" in a moment of intense crisis had started a consistent political tradition. Stalin, who had set himself over the party and the state, drew effective power from this myth-making. He became the recourse of the "non-party men".He was able to make good use of the divergent forces which he brought together against the upper bureaucracy. Bukharin — lucid even in the act of prostituting himself — interpreted Stalin's intentions quite clearly (too clearly in spite of his servile tone). "Everyone wants to touch him," he writes, "to feel the force of this powerful spirit, this will which radiates from him, this astonishing and beloved man." When we recall the contempt which Bukharin had for the man (although he was wrong to despise everything about him), when we recall the lengths to which Stalin went to distance himself from the crowds which he feared, and in what execration, moderated only by fear, he was held by his entourage, then we realize that this portrait of an icon is a cruel and savage mockery. Bukharin explicitly stressed the political purpose of the hyperbole when he added: "Human waves follow in his wake. What a demonstration of unity! What an unforgettable scene of indestructible unity!"

Stalin looked for a confirmation of his legitimacy in a referendum-like ratification. He wanted to establish his independence from the party and the state: that is to say, his personal power. Certainly, what was involved was a half-real, half-fictitious referendum. He did not go to the lengths of institutionalizing it. He limited it to a kind of shadow-play. Against the thermidoreans, he mobilized the lower personnel of the party, and the impatience of the non-party men. He gave support against the upper bureaucracy to all the diverse forces of discontent, ambition and deceit in the ruling class, and he made a coalition with them. His repeated declarations on the role of the non-party men, on their place in the state from which they were still excluded, and his promises of a "happy life" had this meaning. This key aspect of stalinist strategy in these crucial years is very little known or studied. But it was decisive. Stalin could not have succeeded without something to replace those he removed.

The massacre of the thermidoreans was a highly concerted enterprise. The exploitation of Kirov's murder — itself deliberate — was premeditated. The violent shock provoked by the murder and its disturbing effects were intended and were carefully evaluated. The choice of the accused (Zinoviev, Kamenev, Bukharin and Trotsky) corresponds to a calculated diversion to mask the real objectives of the trials, deceive the real adversary and conceal the real objectives. The world prestige of these people was used to transfix the public's attention and it had the desired effect. The steady expansion of successive trials until their final climax, and the mass repression, were carefully co-ordinated. Nothing, neither in the increasingly complex preparation of false testimony, nor in the extension of the repression, was left to chance, least of all its overall direction. Fear itself, in its constantly increasing intensity, was seen as a spur which would incite the thermidoreans, in the vain hope of survival, to denounce each other and precipitate their own destruction. This murderous enterprise is prodigious enough in its results, but the extent of its preparation is just as staggering.

This fact is the more revealing because in other similar matters, Stalin proceeded in a completely different way. He had previously acted in spite of himself, under the pressure of events, and without anticipation, to undertake forced collectivization. He led the second civil war by following his nose, without any strategy at all. He attributed this lack of foresight to "the dizziness of success". He legislated in the same way. The organic laws of the society always started off as emergency decrees, issued in the heat of the moment. It was not until later, on judging the results, that they were generalized and were rooted in basic principles. The conduct of military operations at the start of the Second World War was so beyond his grasp that for a whole period he refused to take the slightest decision, leaving his perplexed generals and commissars to take the responsibility — and making them pay dearly for the prestige of their success. But in contrast, when power was *politically* threatened — when it had to be taken or defended — Stalin intervened with the power of foresight and prediction of a chess master. He was only efficient when the bureaux had a grip on society. As soon as social forces escaped them, Stalin lost control. He either tailed events or went to earth. He did not conquer power, he usurped it. He succeeded only because he already occupied a position in power and knew how to reap the benefits from it. In many respects the mass repression must be considered his masterpiece. In it, he deployed exceptional cunning, and all the ferocious determination of his maturity. He acted, to be sure, with great economy of means.

23 Mass trials and administrative repression, 1934–9

THE KIROV murder was the key to the whole operation. Everything was organized around it. It was the chief instrument of the trials and the administrative repression.

Kirov was killed on 1 December 1934, in his office at Smolny in Leningrad. He was killed by a bullet from a revolver fired by the communist Nikolayev. The body of the victim, the weapon, and the assassin: these are the only facts which cannot be disputed. The circumstances and motives of the crime remain obscure. All the rest was fabricated. Judicial procedure was no more than an instrument (although an essential one) in a strategic whole. Enquiries and trials are only methods of action. The fact that at the outset 100,000 inhabitants of Leningrad were deported shows clearly that this judicial procedure and administrative repression were together part of a unified system. Its construction was all the more complex, given that it was completely artificial.

The accused were not the real target. They were world-renowned political personalities. These two aspects of the same fact proved the principal problem for the instigators of the trial. A switch of identities was the key to the enterprise. It allowed Stalin to surprise and destroy his real adversaries, in the process eliminating the last vestiges of the past. Furthermore, to achieve a successful outcome, Stalin could not explain the reason for the switch even to his closest collaborators. It was necessary for the interested parties (the thermidorean leaders) to believe that the terror would once again strike the decimated ranks of the old oppositions. When they became aware of the truth, things were already so far advanced that fear and the simple desire to survive rendered them powerless. The personalities of the first set of defendants (the whole Political Bureau of the revolution with the sole exception of Lenin, who was dead, and Stalin, who was living) perfectly suited the diversion which Stalin was seeking. On the other hand, so clear was the contrast, that it laid bare the false politics involved. However, that which disgusted international opinion could not awake the suspicions of the entourage, who were fully familiar with such practices. More worrying for these people was the public denunciation by the Prosecutor of methods and ambitions which were attributed to Trotsky (whose role in the fictitious plot was crucial). This attribution was plainly absurd, and was obviously a serious attempt to cast suspicion on other people and to raise the spectre of other palace intrigues. To make sense of all this would be a difficult task. In fact, political coherence was never achieved. Strategic co-ordination, on the other hand, was quite clear, although hard to achieve. The progressive revelation of the list of accused was aimed at maintaining the initiative. It ensured that repression could be prepared in advance. Every stage introduced a new factor which could only be understood later in the light of events. The solution to the puzzle could only be found once all the accusations had been made. The whole thing was like a detective novel whose logic, hidden by apparent confusion and successive sudden changes, only becomes clear in the last chapter. It is significant that the conduct of repressive operations determined the progress of judicial operations. This order of priority in conception and this precise combination in execution demanded rigorous initial planning. The rationality of Stalin's crimes is clarified by the ends attained.

Three periods can be discerned in the preparation of the repression. The first was the preparation of the crime. It is to be seen in the rather strange circumstances in which the murderer was executed. It will doubtless remain largely obscure until the sealed archives become accessible. The second stretches from December 1934 to July 1935. It was a preparatory phase. This was to a certain extent a phase of public preparation. The trial of Kamenev which certainly played an important role in setting up the police intrigue, was held in camera. The third period opened in August 1936 with the show trial of Zinoviev and Kamenev and reached its conclusion in March 1938 with the trial of Bukharin and Yagoda. This was the final phase of judicial preparation and initiated the mass repression. Hence, it took a year (August 1935 to August 1936) of intense and secret work to fit the pieces of the puzzle together.

From December 1934 to July 1935 there were five trials. They appeared to follow each other without any relation of cause and effect. Each one opened up territory which it left unexplored. On 5 December — four days after Kirov's murder — the military tribunal of the Supreme Court condemned 71 "White" terrorists to death. 104 were shot. It was asserted that these people had entered the country secretly through Poland, Lithuania and Finland, with the intention of committing assassinations. Nothing else was said. Not a word on the eventual complicity, the reasons, foreign support, or involvement in the assassination of Kirov. On 24 December the Tass News Agency announced the arrest of fourteen former Zinovievists. Kotolynov, Kamenev and Evdokimov were amongst them. The new release added that in the absence of sufficient evidence no proceedings were to be taken. On 28 December the trial of Nikolayev opened. A lot must have been expected of it: the assassin was in the dock. The only information was that a foreign consul had offered Nikolayev Trotsky's good offices. The tribunal's enquiries went no further. On 2 January 1935 the Soviet authorities revealed that the Lithuanian ambassador Bissiericks was involved. The fourteen accused were condemned and executed. The principal actor disappeared from the scene. Eleven of those who were shot had protested their innocence.

On 16 January the first trial of Zinoviev and Kamenev took place. Zinoviev confessed "political responsibility for the former anti-party Zinovievist group and the assassination that had just taken place". But his was a very general responsibility, rather abstract, and completely separate from the execution of the crime, with no relation to the Lithuanian ambassador, the "White" terrorists, or Trotsky. The tribunal was only interested, it seemed, in the circumstances surrounding the murder. In this respect three new elements appeared: the prisoners were working for the "re-establishment of capitalism"; they were organized from a centre whose clandestine base was in Moscow; they had not struggled as they ought to have against the moral decomposition engendered by opposition to the party; and it was precisely because of this decline in morals that "a band of brigands could be formed and could commit its crime". In a certain sense, the sentences pronounced kept the accused "in reserve". Nineteen of them were given 137 years of exile between them. On 23 January — three weeks later — there was a theatrical coup: Mevded, head of the Leningrad NKVD and eleven of his co-workers were indicted. The accusation was exceptionally grave. "Being in possession of information on an attempt being prepared against Kirov," notes the Prosecutor, "they manifested an attitude which was not merely careless, but amounted to criminal negligence. They did not take the necessary steps. . . even though they had every possibility of doing so." The opportunity was open to drag the circumstances of the murder from the obscurity in which they lurked. It was not grasped. The penalties were to be light — from two to ten years in prison. Such unexpected clemency and the Prosecutor's suggestive little phrase ("even though they had every possibility of doing so"), leads us to suspect that an underhand deal was involved. This would be quite an illuminating deal, because it concerned nothing less important than the execution of the crime itself. Like so many others, it was not to be honoured. Mevded and his colleagues were executed in 1937. One year later, they would have been able to tell us something about Yagoda's testimony. Of Kamenev's trials, which opened in camera on 27 July, we know nothing.

So, here in the summer of 1935 we have the pieces laid out on the chessboard, as difficult to interpret as the stone figures of Easter Island. We have the White Guards, a Lithuanian ambassador, some eminent Zinovievists, Trotsky, and some high officials of the NKVD. This was a strange cortège for an executed assassin. They seem to be pieces abandoned by justice lost in the night. With the trials over, the puzzle completed, they appear the exact opposite. After the trial of Zinoviev and Kamenev in August 1936, the complementary trial of Radek and Sokolnikov in January 1937 and the prodigious achievement represented by the trial of Bukharin and Yagoda in March 1938, they can be seen in their correct sequence as the essential, necessary, initial data of the whole work. Their unwonted appearance at the start of the proceedings was calculated. It set up a scenario whose complex outgrowths were to compromise the widest conceivable circles in a unified plot aimed at the destruction of supreme power. This scenario was written with the sole aim of allowing the repression to strike to the heart of the state and into all parts of Soviet society.

It had been planned in advance that Trotsky should be the inventor and the co-ordinator of the whole plot (a role which certainly matched his renown but which also made use of the fact that no other member of Lenin's Political Bureau was living abroad). So it seemed certain that his role would feature from the start of the proceedings, without it being possible to say anything further about it, since the decisive details of the intrigue had not yet been settled. Since Zinoviev and Kamenev had to be responsible for unifying the oppositional groups and to take major responsibility in building up terrorist networks, the Zinovievists had to figure among the first to be accused — both from the point of view of verisimilitude and because of their necessary part in the intrigue — and the Moscow centre, destined to go through such a fabulous extension, had to figure amongst the first discoveries. Since the assassination of Kirov was nothing but the prelude to the murder of Stalin, and since in the execution of the former and the preparation of the later, so many and such diverse participants had to be involved, no precise charge could be brought before all the loose ends of the intrigue had been tied up. However it was possible and in fact useful to show without delay what were the political interests of the plotters and to expose the moral degeneration which would explain why they had become fascists and assassins, brought down by their lust for power. This scenario exalted the irreplaceable role of Stalin in the defence of the Soviet fatherland — thus underlining the enormity of the proposed crimes, so that the violent anger of honest citizens would demand terrible penalties in retribution. This explains the appearance on the scene (like in classical Chinese theatre) of skilful and lucid henchmen of imperialism, hiding behind cynical masks. This is why there had to be zealous intermediaries, sources of money, and supplies of arms lurking in Trotsky's shadow. They had to figure in the dirge sung at Kirov's funeral. Thus the White Guards and the Lithuanian ambassador, at first unwonted, became the modest heralds of much more powerful incarnations of evil.

Nevertheless in this sphere more than any other the stage director had to guard against making clear the incredible extent of the plot too early on. On the contrary, he had to maintain the suspense, because the story was to lead to the annihilation of most of the state apparatus, and thence to the decimation of the army. More than in any other part of the drama the judicial process was run in the interests of repression. The approach was indirect and calculated to delay. The final mission of the Lithuanian ambassador and his cronies had already been planned in 1935.

In August 1936, in the course of the key trial of Zinoviev and Kamenev, Stalin's intentions became clear. A single forgery among the hotchpotch of others signalled the condemnation to death of Tukhachevsky and his colleagues which was to astonish the world a year later: an apocryphal letter from Trotsky to Dreitzer. It was signed "the old man" (a familiar and friendly appellation used at that time in the ranks of the oppositionist youth abroad). An agent of his son Sedov was supposed to have given it to Dreitzer's sister in Warsaw, and she was supposed to get it into the USSR. Its tenor was as follows, quoted from memory at the trial: "Dear Friend, We have a problem to resolve. We must hasten the assassination of Stalin and Voroshilov. In case of war, we must take a defeatist position and profit from the disarray: we must organize cells in the Red Army."[49]

It was envisaged that in the last act Yagoda — who in fact played such a role in the actual murder — was to accuse himself of the crime in order that the real accomplices could be executed. Mevded's trial was to furnish the arguments needed in an act which was not to ensue for three years. The Yagoda affair has the interest of being the only one where the fiction had any relation to reality. It demonstrates more clearly than anything else what calculation, what cunning, what foresight, and what premeditation was needed for Stalin's success. In its end results, this success proved a majestic one, both because it had an infinite number of difficulties to surmount and because of the unparalleled scale of the crimes perpetrated. Today it is clear that when Kirov was killed, Stalin already had his plan worked out. He put the first pieces on the chessboard in line with the dictates of the plan and the play which he had conceived. But no one except him knew the plan. Stalin was the author of the major theme, but he left others to fill in the details. The long process of fabrication has been known for a long time. What is important is to understand that the use of these techniques was in no sense an accidental aberration. They suited the objective conditions and were in fact the only ones possible. They are the only ones which suit the established system and follow its rationality. This is why it is illusory to propose to change them. Khrushchev's protestations on the immorality of the methods used by the NKVD are absurd, because Khrushchev defended the validity of the system. The procedures used were functional and highly efficient because they were part and parcel of the structure of power and its exercise. The Attorney-General and the heads of the NKVD — charged with the details of the operation — had been given a task which was out of the ordinary. They had to invent everything without jeopardizing their freedom to invent. The outlines provided by Stalin had to be followed. His directives were precise and strict. All that remained was to fill out the details. This required consummate skill because nothing could be changed, either in the organization of the theses or in the progress of the drama, and because verisimilitude had to be respected. The major theme — the plotting of Stalin's murder — if it was to produce the desired political effect, had to be presented as a world-wide operation and had to implicate all Lenin's companions (Zinoviev, Kamenev, Trotsky and Bukharin), the élite of the October revolution (Piatakov, Rakovsky, Radek and Rykov), the officers of the Red Army who fought in the civil war, Yagoda, obscure provocateurs, agents of the tsaristokhrana, the Gestapo, Rudolf Hess, the intelligence service, and "the Chiefs of Staff of Japan, Germany and Poland".

It was necessary to transform these former oppositionists — about whom every detail was known including their life-histories, what they had done, the posts they had occupied, and whose books were publicly and widely available — into assassins without ideology. It was necessary to satisfy the formula which Vyshinsky used at the beginning of his inquisition: "These are not political men, but a band of common criminals and assassins." They had to be so power-hungry and so convinced that only murder would give them access to it that they would be prepared to sell off "the Ukraine, Byelorussia, the Republics of Central Asia, Georgia, Armenia, Azherbaidzhan, and the maritime provinces". The accusation specifies "that the criminal activities of the bloc were carried out under the immediate supervision and under plans established by the Chiefs of Staff of Japan, Germany and Poland", and that Trotsky in his negotiations with Rudolf Hess "had promised, should a trotskyist government come to power in the wake of the defeat of the Soviet Union, to make a series of political, economic and territorial concessions to the detriment of the USSR going as far as ceding the Ukraine to Germany, and the maritime provinces and the region of Amour to Japan".

For the same pressing political motives, the intrigue had to be constructed in such a way that Trotsky would appear as the central figure. This made it necessary for the decisive episodes where the plot was concocted to be placed abroad. This was to be the location for co-operation between secret services and the terrorist centre. These were the essential outlines provided by Stalin. No one had the right to change them. The Attorney-General and the NKVD had, on the contrary, to determine their roles according to this scheme. Their obligation to situate important scenes abroad multiplied the dangers and seriously increased the risks being run. They were caught red-handed in their falsification. False interviews, false journeys, false letters, and false intermediaries have to take account of plausible places, plausible timetables, real visas, real hotels, and real visits, in short, a mass of verifiable data. Vyshinsky did not succeed. The affair of the Hotel Bristol is well known. The prosecution asserted that in 1932 there was an important meeting in the vestibule of the Hotel Bristol in Copenhagen, whose aim was to prepare an interview with Trotsky to which many important questions were linked. Now the Hotel Bristol can be found in many old editions of Baedeker. But in 1917 it was destroyed. Even if Vyshinsky did make a mistake in the end, he had certainly done his best. We know that at the beginning of November 1936 the GPU organized the theft of Trotsky's personal archives which had been left in the Institute of Social History in Paris. They comprised personal notes and private correspondence. It was nevertheless impossible to use these items, because the discrepancy between what was really written and what should have been there according to the story was so great.

It was enough to affirm imperturbably that "Trotsky had been linked with the German Secret Service since 1921"; this would be understood by naive imbeciles, corrupt politicians, and cynical sophists. But a hotel is a material fact, as is a visa, or the dates of the visit. Thus what happened in the trials to the material evidence in general was the same as what had happened to the letter attributed to Trotsky which we have already cited. This letter was famous for its momentous effect. After receiving it from his sister in Warsaw, Dreitzer sent it (for the purposes of the intrigue) to Mrachkovsky, who was several thousand kilometres away in Kazakhstan. Mrachkovsky identified the handwriting and was then so kind as to destroy it "to comply with the rules of the conspiracy", which fortunately made it unnecessary to produce it. The tribunal was hence reduced to knowing of the letter only thanks to Dreitzer's effort of memory — a highly commendable effort, to be sure, since the Chief of Staff would be shot for it. The Prosecutor could only bring in pieces of evidence relating to the intrigue if he could make them disappear as soon as possible in order to give sufficient consistency to the evidence.

These already great difficulties were aggravated by Stalin's desire to keep his real aims hidden until he was sure of success. Thus it was that when they received instructions insisting that the murder of Stalin had to be prepared by the assassination of several of those close to him, (in order that the real murder of Kirov should not seem too isolated) the Prosecutor and the NKVD were naturally led to choose the personalities most in favour with Stalin and were cruelly deceived through their ignorance of the real intentions of their master. Thus it was that Kossior and Postyshev appeared among the victims designated by the accusation of 1936. Unfortunately, things developed so that it suited Stalin in executing his secret plan to have Postyshev and Kossior arrested in 1938, judged, condemned, and executed for criminal activity which in their testimony took place on the same dates as those on which they were supposed to have been victims of the terrorist centre according to the imprudent version of 1936 — the same terrorist centre of which they were supposed to be members.

Eventually these grand trials provoked others, more anonymous, but more numerous. They were needed for generalized repression, in which tens of thousands of Soviet citizens were arraigned for having tried to kill Stalin. How could the clerks of the local prosecutors and NKVD bureaux work out the best possible story to condemn each one of them? This story was needed because administrative procedure itself had to fit its dossiers together, to give its arbitrariness some basis in supposed evidence. To some extent these difficulties were external. But there were others which faced the judicial enquiry. Not all material proof could be made to disappear as easily as Trotsky's apocryphal letter. The pursuit of fictitious truth is subject to the same restrictions as the pursuit of real truth, when it aspires to verisimilitude. Internal logic which is unable to resolve its problems, when faced with the real facts — because it has no base of support in reality — must seek for its coherence in a supplementary effort of imagination. These tens of thousands of men who were interrogated were all supposed to be terrorists. Terrorists use arms. Arms have a material existence. If a single one of them ever possessed arms, the presiding judge was obliged to establish where they had gone. They could not simply disappear. Now, these arms existed only in fiction. The prisoner knew it, the judge knew it. But here fiction is the real world. The prisoner had to say what he had done with them. This pursuit of a suitable imaginary solution could last several weeks, could result in great physical and moral suffering to the prisoner, create many problems for the judge and overwhelm him. If in despair he had to write in the record that the guilty person passed his arms on to a confederate, then the police had to make new arrests, new interrogations, and once again invoke the power of imagination. It was obviously better to discover among his real relations an inveterate bachelor, without a family, who was dead and could be made the last repository of these cumbersome arms. The judge could then leave off and the prisoner could get a bit of peace in his cell. Both well deserved respite; it was not so easy to obtain. These objective difficulties were inherent to the fiction that was the key to the system. They did not leave any choice in the means employed. There was only one type of convenient procedure. Its rationality lay in its efficiency; that is to say in its conformity with the institutions of power.

The principle was quite simple. The accused had to dream up facts which would establish their own guilt. (Their fictitious life, in order to give a semblance of consistency, had to be based on real life, and no one knew this better than the accused themselves.) This general rule governed everything. Co-operation between the prisoner and the judge was the basis of the procedure. Physical brutality and the regular use of torture had the goal of encouraging the prisoner to participate in this collaboration and of awakening his imagination. In certain cases, infrequent ones, it must be said, haggling could produce the same result. Confessions were nothing more than the application of these rules to judicial procedure.

There has been much speculation in relation to certain of Bukharin's declarations during his trial that there was a bargain struck between Stalin, Zinoviev, Kamenev and Bukharin. These have not been proven but seem quite probable. The testimony relating to Raik provides another equally tragic example. For his part Khrushchev brought official confirmation of this haggling. Citing the case of Rosenblum, who was arrested in 1937, he explained that after suffering "terrible torture", "he was then taken to Zakovsky's office and the latter offered him his freedom on condition that he would give the tribunal false testimony which had been fabricated in 1937 by the NKVD." He cites what was proposed by Zakovsky: "The NKVD will prepare you a draft giving details of each of the centre's branches. You must study them carefully and remember every question which could be put to you by the tribunal. . . If you do your job, you will save your skin and you will be fed and clothed at government expense until you die." Khrushchev also reports the protest made by Ikhe, who was shot in February 1940: "Being unable to endure the tortures inflicted on me by Uchakov and Nikolayev, who knew that my broken ribs had not yet mended and were causing me violent pain, I was obliged to incriminate myself and others. The bulk of my testimony was suggested or dictated to me by Uchakov and the rest came from my personal recollection of NKVD documents from Western Siberia. If certain parts of the story which Uchakov fabricated and which I signed did not tally, I was compelled to sign a new version."

Judges and policemen were responsible for carrying out this work. Each bureau had its designated cases, which it had to deal with. Their career, often their liberty, and perhaps their lives depended on success or failure. They had to deal with the case without knowing exactly how their piece of the puzzle was supposed to fit. Nevertheless the case as a whole had to hang together. After the web had been woven it was left to the prisoners to invent the details. Each was working in ignorance of the others. The examining magistrate had the duty of correcting the inevitable discrepancies and ensuring that the prisoners dreamed up stories which fitted. On the prisoners' inventive ability depended the career, liberty and sometimes the life of the judge or Cheka member. It is one of the most striking features of this procedure, which was fully exploited by Stalin. It was clear that this dangerous dependence would not incline judges and policemen to mercy, but would on the contrary tend to make them see the prisoners as the perverse cause of their probable downfall. This is why they found respite in the constant use of violence. The functional rationality of the system is again expressed in the use made of the inevitable errors which resulted from the procedures used. They served as pretexts to arrest the real accomplices, judge them in their turn and execute them. Their legal death would contribute to the elimination of all traces of the crime.

Thus, the cardinal principle of the system becomes clear (the key to the exercise of power): individual fear was the basis of collective terror. It was therefore necessary for the success of the terror that no one should be free from fear. The fall of Yagoda and of Yezhov taught every NKVD functionary that if his all-powerful chief was mortal, so much more so was he. Now it is well known that gut fear for one's life very often leads to moral cowardice, the abandonment of any resistance, and frequently to a frantic search for security in the frenetic obedience of orders — in an excess of zeal. Fear hence figured in the exercise of power as a deliberate factor, whose use was carefully planned. This was the complementary reason which led Stalin to kill Lenin's companions; and to kill them publicly, creating the biggest possible splash.

Their fall from grace spread terror among the thermidoreans. The massacre of the thermidoreans themselves warned against any aspirations to independence on the part of the men without a past; this guaranteed Stalin his hold on power. If Stalin dared that which even his seasoned entourage recoiled from, it was not folly but rational calculation. Audacity in crime was the supreme expression of his art of government.

Stalin ordered the assassination of Kirov. We certainly have no direct proof of this, but the evidence we have shows it irrefutably. The murder was not a surprise, nor a spontaneous blow. It had been prepared. The Cheka arrested Nikolayev for the first time a month and a half before the crime. He was prowling around Smolny. He was arrested a second time. A revolver was found in his towel. He was released both times. The police gave him back his revolver and his towel. On the day of the crime this suspect, under close surveillance, managed to place himself in the corridor that Kirov used to use. The head bodyguard, breaking both his habits and the strict and permanent orders to which he was subjected, was keeping out of the way, far behind Kirov. Nikolayev could not miss his man. The NKVD set it up for him. This is not everything. Stalin, Molotov, and Voroshilov met several times to interrogate the chief bodyguard themselves. This man was responsible for Kirov's security. He was killed during his transfer. According to the official version, he died in a traffic accident. The chauffeur's story — as told by Khrushchev — tears this version to shreds. The NKVD actually used a lorry in place of one of its normal vehicles. Why? It was clear that a closed lorry would be more suited to a discreet execution. Khrushchev observed: "Everything had obviously been prepared in advance, even the details."

Two members of the NKVD were inside with their colleague the chief bodyguard. A third was sitting in the cabin next to the chauffeur. At a specific moment in the journey, he took hold of the steering-wheel and caused the lorry to veer towards a house. The bewildered chauffeur regained control, and the lorry struck the façade with its bumper. No damage, no one wounded but the head bodyguard was dead. Khrushchev concluded that this was a "premeditated crime". The two NKVD functionaries in the back of the lorry, who had thus been witnesses to the fatal accident, were shot without explanation. Khrushchev said: "Someone must have needed to suppress them, to cover any trace." Who? These unambiguous facts, which Khrushchev released in 1961, were known to Stalin at the time. Was it not the case that in depriving him of the most crucial witness that he wished to interrogate, a major obstruction was created for a vital enquiry? How could he be satisfied with the idiotic official version of the accident, unless it suited him down to the ground? This attention to detail, which Khrushchev found so striking, carries his trade-mark. Stalin prepared a murder as others did a hold-up.

Mevded and his collaborators were, as we know, arrested. Of their execution in 1937, Khrushchev was to say: "We may think that they were shot, to cover up the last traces of the organizers of Kirov's assassination." In 1938 Yagoda testified that not only was he aware of, but that he prepared the murder of the second-in-command in the NKVD in Leningrad through an intermediary. The validity of his confession is subject to doubt because, as with all these testimonies, it was extorted. What is certain is that from the start he was well abreast of Nikolayev's suspicious movements. Mevded's first hope was, after the fashion of his colleagues, to cover himself administratively. He did not release Nikolayev. He did not give him his weapon back, he did not let him into Smolny. He did not instruct the chief bodyguard to keep out of the way, without having received precise orders. Such orders, leading to the murder of a member of the Central Committee, could only be given by Yagoda, all-powerful chief of the NKVD. But Yagoda himself was surrounded by spies in the pay of Stalin. He knew this. The question which Khrushchev posed in relation to Yezhov ("could Yezhov, for example, have arrested Kossior without Stalin knowing it?") is equally valid for Yagoda and Kirov. Even if one admits that, with the help of intrigue, Yagoda had decided to take such huge risks, it would certainly not have been worth it for this provincial murder, which could lead nowhere except to his certain downfall. He would have then tried to kill Stalin, who had constant meetings with him. Hence it is obvious that Yagoda consulted Stalin and that he did no more than carry out instructions. Stalin ordered Kirov's assassination.

Khrushchev gives us two complementary accounts of the crime. The first — the more summary account — is given in his secret report to the 20th Congress. The second — which is more detailed — is given in his public intervention in 1961 at the 22nd Congress. Each time, he designated Stalin as the culprit, without however naming him. He hid behind enquiries in progress (enquiries which no one speaks of any more. Why?). Why, since he was charging him with such a huge crime? Because the murder of Kirov occupies a special, exceptional place. Because Khrushchev retained only that part of the truth which was politically useful to him. If many details which are missing in the version given in his secret report, appear in his public intervention of 1961, it is because at the 20th Congress, Molotov, Malenkov and Kaganovich were allies who had to be taken account of (they were members of the commission of the Central Committee which published the text of the Resolution of 30 June 1956 denouncing the personality cult). But at the 22nd Congress, they were the defeated adversaries of the anti-party group. At the 20th Congress it was necessary to unify the collective leadership and prevent any recidivism of the Beria type. At the 22nd Congress, Khrushchev tried to enlarge his own base by implicating the more or less concealed supporters of the anti-party group with new and compromising revelations on the role of Voroshilov, Malenkov and Molotov in Stalin's crimes. He also had to ward off the grudges which were already accumulating against his control (Brezhnev and Podgorny had already entered the Secretariat in the spring of 1963) by making it clear that the resources of the archives had not been fully used. Stalin's crimes were exploited in the factional struggle. At the 20th Congress the report was both very prudent (the revelations were circumscribed and circumspect) and explosive (because of the official recognition of the major facts which were known but not admitted), secret and yet publicized. It was a top-level operation. It was a measure taken by Stalin's heirs to guarantee their physical and political security. They had to be secure against palace intrigues. This life-insurance only makes sense because the legitimacy of the collective leadership was itself called into question, opening a crisis of the régime.

It was therefore necessary to say enough to make any retreat difficult, but not so much as to lose power. Khrushchev's revelations resulted from a compromise. It was a compromise between conflicting needs and between men who knew each other to be temporarily paralysed adversaries. Khrushchev developed his famous double interpretation. The despotism and its crimes were the result of character disorders on Stalin's part, the result of his corruption through the exercise of power, disorders which led him to madness at the end of his life. During these excesses the leninist nucleus of the Central Committee kept going against all odds. It resisted as much as it could. It was never compromised by the treachery and torture. It was the victim of it. Stalin, Yezhov, and Beria were the only culprits. Khrushchev only retained that part of the truth which conformed to his theses and his objectives. However, a document known only to a few initiates in the closed circles of the upper leadership can be neutralized and rendered ineffectual. In order that the report should not be merely a useless scrap of paper, it had to be publicized. This publicity alone created the desired irreversible effects. But the publicity had to avoid compromising the stability of the régime. The apparatus had to be informed of it, because it was in the apparatus that plots were hatched. It was necessary not to tell the population too quickly or too completely. Now the apparatus, already frightened, had the greatest possible interest in discretion. The report was therefore not to be published throughout the party, but read out in front of selected audiences. Copies of the texts were to be kept in selected archives. However, such a sensational operation could not be kept quiet for long. Public disclosure was hence to be carried out abroad in a roundabout way, through organized defections and the American agencies. In this way, the effect could be neutralized and the time gained could be used to consolidate the leadership. It is remarkable that Stalin's epigones used methods so close to those which he used against Tukhachevsky.

The struggle against Molotov, Kaganovich, Malenkov and Voroshilov constrained Khrushchev to take another small step towards the truth. The myth of the uncompromised Leninist nucleus was exploded. At the 22nd Congress Shelepin, who was then directing the KGB, declared: "The assassination of Sergei Mironovich Kirov was used as a pretext by Stalin, by Molotov and by Kaganovich, who were his closest collaborators, as a pretext to settle accounts with undesirable people." He made this more precise: "Numerous documents in our possession show irrefutably that members of the anti-party group participated in the massive and illegal waves of repression against numerous militants in the party, the Young Communists and the army soviets, and that these collaborators bear direct responsibility for their physical liquidation." Molotov, Malenkov and Kaganovich were expelled. The plenary meeting of the Central Committee of February 1964 was dedicated mainly to this question. In his introductory report Suslov wrote: "Our party has destroyed the anti-party group of Molotov, Kaganovich, and Malenkov. This group oppose the liquidation of the cult of personality, mainly because some of its members bear responsibility for the massive repression against innocent people when they were leading the country beside Stalin. On several occasions, as we have already said, Molotov tried to be more religious than the Pope. On one of the documents condemning a group of women workers to a heavy prison sentence, Molotov wrote beside one of the names on the list: A.H.P.P., which means Apply the Heaviest Possible Penalty." Khrushchev continued to burn his bridges. On 30 October 1961 he made the Congress pass unanimously a resolution removing Stalin's sarcophagus from the Lenin mausoleum. He removed Stalin's name from innumerable towns, squares, streets, and buildings. But he still spoke of *using* Kirov's murder, making it known that the last word had not been spoken and that many things "have still to be fully elucidated". Khrushchev was forced by measures which were liberal in effect (to the extent that they were a feature of this period) to rally the support of the post-war intelligentsia: an intelligentsia which was already close to the enterprise directors and which could transform live social discontent into political opposition. He met with powerful resistance from the state apparatus and the administrative corps of the state. He used the dossiers as blackmail against his adversaries. Leaders of greater or lesser stature, who had served Stalin and who survived in their leading positions, who had committed reprehensible acts, out of prudence, inertia, or ambition, were disqualified by these acts. Whoever held the dossiers controlled the men. Khrushchev therefore used them carefully. The police dossiers became the basis of political arguments. The ever-present danger was that of going too far in this game, which was not without peril for the régime. Thus when Brezhnev came to power he did not use such explosive methods publicly against Khrushchev, (whose dossier is without doubt in keeping with his career). He would have had to open a new and this time more dangerous stage of liberalization. Recalling what Khrushchev had had to do in his climb to power and what he had had to accept, undertake, and invent in order to safeguard his position and his life, this would have meant no more and no less than opening a trial of the official destalinizers. Given the stage to which Khrushchev had taken things, it would have been a dangerous leap into the unknown to have called him into question as an attentive and docile servitor of Stalin (which he undoubtedly was). Khrushchev had played a central role in the 20th and 22nd Congresses and it would have been necessary to have laid bare the social reality of Stalin's role. Not only was Brezhnev not disposed to such an adventure, but he was determined to put an end to this scabrous use of the past. The dossiers were closed once more. He was more concerned to reinforce Khrushchev's prudence than to follow him like the sorcerer's apprentice. Explicit recognition that Stalin had ordered the assassination of Kirov would add little to his crimes, but would destroy the circumspect explanation which Khrushchev had given.

This interpretation remained — well after Khrushchev — the corner-stone of official world destalinization. It was an interpretation which Brezhnev made much use of, because it allowed him to appear faithful to the 20th Congress (but not to the 22nd), all the while encouraging a discreet and partial restoration of Stalin's historic work. He had a pressing need to consolidate and justify this work because of its value for the exercise of power. Since the Kirov murder was the hub of the whole trials and repressions, to identify correctly the author of this crime would make so clear the extent of premeditation and intrigue leading up to these events that the thesis of megalomania and creeping madness would be discredited.

It is highly significant that the crime was no surprise to Stalin and that he allowed it to be prepared and gave the order for its execution. It illustrates one of the fundamental resources required for the exercise of power.

The true facts surrounding Nikolayev remain completely obscure. He was able to operate as an NKVD agent on special commission. He pleaded guilty under orders. The price of his loyalty was death, as was that of Mevded and his collaborators, the bodyguard of Kirov, his executed colleagues, of Yagoda himself, and many others. In principle, a dead official is a silent one, but this is not entirely true. It is clear that the NKVD committed an error in leaving the lorry driver alive. Accepting the hypothesis that the young communist Nikolayev, revolting against the permanent violence of the bureaucracy, wanted to follow living revolutionary socialist tradition by making an example of Kirov, who embodied the repression in Leningrad, the first arrest has a precise meaning.

If we accept the hypothesis than Nikolayev was an NKVD agent, the arrest was not implausible. It was clear that his special mission was not known by local agencies, with the exception of one of the high dignitaries of Leningrad. As a result the local units would have received orders not to get mixed up in the affair at this first stage. At the point of the execution, after the second arrest, a certain degree of collaboration was necessary. Ignorance on the part of local units offers a perfect explanation of the known anomalies. It is interesting to note that this was to be the thesis put forward at Yagoda's trial. This version is completely coherent, with the sole reservation that Yagoda would never have taken such an initiative on his own. Thus the hypothesis than Nikolayev was an agent of the NKVD cannot be dismissed.

Once the local NKVD had been alerted (this would involve the security of the principal official representative in the town) it would be obliged to transmit its suspicions to the central administration. When Yagoda was informed he would have had to send a note to the Secretariat which by reason of its tenor would have had to be read personally by Stalin. Poskrebyshev, his secretary, was there to scrutinize. Once again the principal concern of the NKVD officials was to cover themselves administratively. Furthermore, as we know, these steps correspond to the established facts. Stalin was thus in possession of a dossier one and a half months before the murder. His agents controlled the actions of the suspect. He had the situation in hand. He had time to weigh up the pros and cons. It was thus in full knowledge that he gave the order which allowed the murderer to act. Whether Nikolayev, was an agent of the NKVD or a terrorist, or manipulated like the man who set fire to the Reichstag building, the decisive facts are the same. Whether Stalin took advantage of the occasion which presented itself and authorized the assassination, or whether he took the initiative, it is quite clear that he was able to use it to his advantage. He had already made his plan and the designated victim suited him.

The order to execute Kirov proves that Stalin had decided in principle, before December 1934, on the massacre of the thermidoreans, and that he had decided the outline of his strategy. The events which followed the murder show that he conceived of it as the detonator which he needed. For Kirov, once dead, was to play his role so well, it must have been preconceived. The murder of Kirov is a fine example of a provocation calculated for its effects long after it takes place. In fact Stalin often used provocation, either to trap his opponents, or to initiate a carefully-prepared scheme. He had made an efficient technique of it over the years (trying it out in the factional struggles which ravaged the party and the state apparatus from 1923 to 1929). However, until now, its field of application had been limited. The fact that he was able to use the murder of Kirov as the first act of the drama which brought down the thermidoreans shows the power of his foresight and cunning. In a less important area, although a crucial one, in the complex machinations against Tukachevsky, he also demonstrated this remarkable faculty which is rarely present to such a degree.

Why Kirov? Even if Stalin did take advantage of the occasion as it presented itself, in failing to stop the murder he went ahead because he found that Kirov suited his aims. The choice is thus instructive. At first glance this provincial official does not seem very suitable. It is not clear how the assassination of Kirov would facilitate the murder of Stalin. Kirov's position did not open any direct road to power. The moment it is clear that Yagoda — whose function made him part of Stalin's close entourage — was to be involved in the plot, the affair seems so absurd that anyone with the least awareness could not see it other than as a trap and a provocation (as indeed it was). This feeling is so strong, and such an obstacle to the coherence of the scenario that Vyshinsky became preoccupied with it and made Zinoviev say: "It is not enough to knock down the oak, it is also necessary to fight the saplings growing around it." This would satisfy simple spirits. Stalin in his cunning could not ignore the obstacle. Hence if he accepted this weakness in the scenario it was because in reality Kirov's murder, though awkward for the story being constructed, served his real purposes admirably.

Stalin was not trying to convince the high dignitaries of the régime of the reality of the plot. All he wanted to do was to conceal his intentions from them for as long as possible. On the contrary he wanted to persuade public opinion, the depoliticized mass of the population, the bulk of the administrative foot-soldiers of the party, the élite of the enterprise-directors and technicians far from the real centres of power and ignorant of its intrigues. Now, Kirov was marvellously convenient for this double purpose. His marginal position — in relation to the Secretariat — the modesty of his career, which kept him far from the narrow circle of Stalin's entourage, to which he could gain access neither through his past nor through family alliances: everything which made his assassination so difficult to square with the fiction being concocted, reassured thermidorean leaders, who had to be reassured. One can easily imagine how the murder of one of them perpetrated under such troubled circumstances, would have alerted them. It is obvious, for example, that Molotov and Voroshilov, who were summoned by Stalin to conduct the interrogation of the head of the bodyguard with him, would not for an instant believe the official version of the accident. We know how worried they were twenty years later, knowing the past as they did, when the Kremlin doctors were arrested. We can assume that if death had not providentially intervened they would have gone looking for it (as they did later in relation to Beria). Now, in 1930, there were many more audacious people around in the corridors of power than the Molotov clan. The mediocrity of the person killed helped Stalin assuage their fears.[50] The choice was thus a good one. It was to prove even better in its second function, which was to create a profound disturbance in public opinion from which Stalin would profit. This person, neither too unimportant nor too important, was made to measure for the destiny which Stalin gave him. At the heart of the whole machination Stalin set a trap. The whole operation's success depended on its successful working. Zinoviev, Kamenev, Trotsky and Bukharin, were, as we know, intended to conceal the real accused. They played the role of decoy but they could only play this role effectively if Kirov played his. It was essential that there could be no doubt over Kirov's loyalty to Stalin. In fact it was irreproachable. The apparatchiks knew this. The public also knew it, although only for a short time. This devotion was publicized from the Tribune of the Congress of Victors where this stalinist notable lauded his master as the greatest leader of all time. The publicity surrounding this opportune proposition dragged Kirov from the obscurity of the apparatus to put him at the top of the bill which never lost its perennial attraction. It was not difficult to convince simple people, but also those (the great majority) who only saw the palace intrigues from afar, that by killing Kirov the assassin was trying to get at Stalin. The vast apolitical bulk of the population was prepared to believe it. Deliberate mystification had done its work. The thermidoreans were hoist with their own petard. They knew it and they were isolated. To be sure, Stalin worked very hard for this. His attacks on the cadres were directed towards this. The popular view was that responsibility for the misery and repression did not fall on Stalin but on his bad advisers and leaders.[51] This was also a common conviction amongst the middle layers of the ruling class. Khrushchev was to use it against Beria and it has an echo in Stalin's daughter's memoirs. In addition, the remark attributed to Bulganin was not just an evasion. Replying to pastor Gottschalck-Hausen, a Danish conservative parliamentary deputy, who asked him why the leaders did not get rid of Stalin, (adding: "You knew how to do it, didn't you?") he replied: "Legally there was nothing that we could have done at any point. There were ample reasons for executing him but the people would simply not have understood." We know that many humble people (and not just the servants in his dacha) cried on his death. The mystification of "the bad leaders" had immense effects. Stalin was able to appeal to the most backward layers of the population. He was careful to keep himself in with them, knowing that it is dangerous to raise demons. This covert plebiscite was one of Stalin's greatest triumphs. It is also a measure of the profound depoliticization of this society, a tangible result of the systematic destruction of its political and trade-union cadres. We know how far this destruction had gone by the end of NEP. In his actions Stalin, making use of this political illiteracy, drew great benefits from the indifference of the villages and factories towards the state political apparatus which was alien to them, and from their hostility to privileged local administration, which was restrictive and often incompetent. This blind connivance is a striking confirmation of the class nature of the state. Stalin retained the element of surprise. It was completely effective in the political milieu whose downfall he was seeking. It was a characteristic technique of Stalin's to advance and surprise someone, and then to exploit to the full the disarray created. Rapid and unexpected action, which had been a long time in preparation, drew its impact from the full use of provocation. Stalin attributed his own intentions to his adversaries. He condemned and executed them for wanting to do what he had done. The exploitation of Kirov's assassination is a good example of this strategy. He created the pretext: the murder of Kirov. He prepared the massacre of the thermidoreans by attributing to his adversaries his own techniques — the plot and the use of terror. To add still further to the confusion he invented false culprits in order to strike his real targets better. The murder of Tukhachevsky provides another remarkable illustration. Stalin ascribed to the General Staff his own intention of reaching an accord with Hitler. He made use of the execution to facilitate his negotiations with Berlin and conclude the Soviet-German pact. We cannot underestimate the art involved in such machinations.

He counted on the stupefied incredulity of the majority of thermidoreans and used their lack of comprehension to destroy them, and he won. He made full use of the widespread, profound, and almost ineradicable conviction that Stalin would not attack tried and tested stalinists. It seemed unimaginable that Stalin would order the downfall of those who had faithfully and constantly served him. Proofs abounded. The political apparatus was still completely organized around the struggle against the traditional opposition. Victory did not change their intellectual armour. Nothing had prepared them for such a complete about-turn in the situation. This is why surprise had such great effect. Stalin essentially exploited disturbance and disarray. He drew a kind of objective credit from it. Since treason by Stalin was inconceivable, the suspicion grew that behind apparently senseless accusations there must be some truth. This meant that fear had already turned the arrested people into terrified, uncomprehending and self-accusing people. Suspicion fed on isolation. The prisoner was intellectually paralysed by stupefaction. He proclaimed his innocence but also his loyalty. He addressed plea after plea to Stalin to confound his calumniators. To those people who did not belong to Stalin's immediate circle, it seemed they could only be victims of a faction struggle going on around Stalin. They therefore addressed themselves to the supreme arbiter, ignorant of the contempt in which he held them. Yakir wrote to him: "I am a loyal soldier, devoted to the party, to the state, to the people. I have been so for years. All my conscious life has been devoted to loyal work, filled with self-abnegation, in full view of the party and its leaders. . . I am loyal in every one of my words, I shall die speaking words of love for you, for the party, and for the country, with an unsullied faith in the victory of communism." In reply, on this letter are pencilled the words "scoundrel and prostitute" in Stalin's handwriting. Khrushchev added: "In his intervention to the Congress, comrade Shelepin told you how the best representatives of the communist party in the Red Army were repressed. He has also read you comrade Yakir's letter to Stalin and quoted the resolutions on this letter. It should also be added that at the moment of his death, Yakir cried out: 'Long live the party! Long live Stalin!' He had such confidence in the party, and such faith in Stalin, that he would not even allow himself to think that the illegal measures against him were the result of conscious planning. He thought that enemies had infiltrated the organs of the Commissariat of the People. On the eve of his death, his conduct was reported to Stalin, Stalin reviled him."

Stalin turned this blindness into a formidable weapon. He got the time he needed for decisive action: two years. He used it effectively to prevent any resistance coalescing. He took his enemy unawares and kept him dispersed and divided. Then he could win. Duplicity took on great tactical importance. Kirov discharged his duty by his death. The sixteen people who were shot in the 1936 trial opened a new stage. Naked terror took over. Zinoviev, Kamenev, Smirnov, Evdokimov, Bakayev, Ter-Vaganian, Mrachkovsky, and Reinhold — just to name the most well-known — were executed. The effect was terrifying. By killing them, Stalin made it known that he was prepared to go to any lengths.

24 Repression as a norm of government

STALIN constructed a model of repression which he used to define a normal technique of government. This is what must be grasped. Our attention is first of all drawn to the phase of very high intensity between 1936–38. This is what led to the judicial murders, summary executions, and hundreds of thousands of arrests, imprisonments, and deportations. As a result the fascinated observer is inclined to see nothing beyond these three years and to conclude that without being in any way accidental, the repression was nevertheless exceptional. This takes no account of a number of important structures: the arsenal of laws (and its corner-stone, the Penal Code), the apparatus of the NKVD and its central position in the state. Without these instruments the most intensified phase of the repression would have been completely different, closer to a pogrom, but in fact the repression was an ordered phenomenon. It was directed. It was planned. In its greatest and most expensive excesses it was calculated and centrally controlled. Its structure was that of a top-level operation, organized by the apparatus. The episodes in question should not be isolated from their administrative and political context. The repressive process was an integrated one.

However, there is one important fact: the repression was used in profoundly different successive conjunctures. There is a unity in the procedure used in each of these distinct situations. It is abundantly clear that the resort to repression was used each time to promote a policy. Detached from its immediate circumstances and its emotional effects, repression appears as an invariant in the exercise of power. Finally, chronology is significant in this domain.

From 1928–30 — the founding years when the power of the secretariat was definitively established and society took on an organic consistency — until 1953 when Stalin's death changed the composition of the government bodies, a period of twenty-five years elapsed. In a quarter of a century certain invariants can be discerned. Furthermore, the Second World War was such a caesura that any procedures which were retained beyond it are clearly permanent in character.

From 1928–1933 — a period of five years — the second civil war developed into a selective repression centred on the literary, scientific and technical intelligentsia, but which applied a first purge to the ranks of the party thermidoreans. It was an integral part of the process of administrative and social stalinization. It was articulated around four trials: "the trial of the Schachty engineers" in June 1928; "the trial of the industrial party from November to December 1930; and "the trial of the saboteurs of the energy industry", April 1933.

From 1934 to 1941 — seven years — the use of repression was continuous and systematic. The instrument of repression became a lever for radical change in the composition of the political corps of the state. This period began with a respite of eleven months (January to November 1934). We now know that Stalin used this period to develop the repression from its initial crude forms and to turn it into a scientific system. The three show trials prepared, as we know, from December 1934 onwards, opened the final phase. The trial of the "Trotskyist-Zinovievist Terrorist Centre" (Zinoviev, Kamenev, Evdokimov, Smirnov etc.), 19-24 August 1936; the trial of the "Trotskyist Anti-Soviet Centre" (Piatakov, Radek, Sokolnikov, etc.), 23-30 January 1937. The "trial of the Bloc of Rightists and anti-soviet Trotskyists" (Bukharin, Rykov, Yagoda, Rakovsky, etc.) 2-13 March 1938. In 1937 and 1938 the Yezhovshchina burst upon the country.

The year 1937 brought in a new usage for the repression. The trial of Tukhachevsky in June inaugurated a vast strategic operation whose final result was the Stalin/Hitler pact. Repression was the main lever in its launching. The repression diversified its political role and enlarged its domain of application. A great number of foreign communist notables were killed. I cannot analyse here the repression of foreign communist cadres, which was of considerable social and political influence. It opened on a large scale in 1936 in Spain. It was conducted in close liaison with the new diplomatic orientation. Above all it struck at the Polish communist party and the German and Yugoslavian communist parties; also affected were the Greek and Finnish communist parties, and to a lesser extent the Bulgarians and the Italians. The procedure relating to the legal communist parties was more indirect (expulsions, slanders, etc.) and more circumspect. Members of the Austrian Schutzbund who took refuge in the USSR were "liquidated".

Between 1937 and 1941 repression ravaged the army. Military cadres from the chief of staff downwards were exterminated. This process reached down to the level of battalion and company commanders. An enormous number were arrested, deported, or executed. The repression was more selective during the war. The soviet jurists already cited provided the theoretical basis for this repression.

In 1941 500,000 Germans living on the Volga who had constituted an autonomous republic, were collectively deported (decree of 28 August 1941). The NKVD put them in the provinces of Omsk, Novossibirsk, and in the Altai region.

In 1943 the Karatchis, a Turkish people of the Muslim religion from the western Caucasas (75,000) and Kalmuks, a mongol people of the Buddhist religion who had been settled to the north-west of the Caspian Sea, from the beginning of the seventeenth century (190,000), were deported and their republics dissolved.

In 1944 the Chechen-Ingush, a Muslim people from the Central Caucasas, comprising around 500,000 people (407,000 Chechen and 92,000 Ingush, according to the census of 1939) and the Balkars, a Muslim people numbering 75,000, were "deported to far-away places" and their republics disappeared. The Crimean Tartars: 300,000 were deported to Siberia and their republic struck off the map. Khrushchev was to say: "The Ukrainians only avoided this because there were too many of them and there was nowhere to send them. If not they would have been deported too." He observed: "These deportations were not dictated by the slightest military considerations." He notes that for example the decision to deport the Karatchis was taken at the end of 1943 "when there was a breakthrough on every front of the great patriotic war to the advantage of the Soviet Union".[52]

Between 1948 and 1952 writers in the Yiddish tongue were exterminated. In 1948 the so-called Leningrad affair erupted. Close collaborators of Stalin — Voznezhensky, first vice-president of the Council of Ministers, Kuznetsov, Rodionov, Pokov and others were the victims. The exact character of the charges is not known. Khrushchev simply notes: "As has now been established, this was a coup." He stresses that "those whose lives were sacrificed" included "eminent and competent leaders", who "had at one time been very close to Stalin". He adds: "The facts prove that 'the Leningrad Affair' was also a result of the absolutism which Stalin had tested out against the party cadres."

From 1951 to 1952 Georgia was once again the site of a new centre of repressive activity. The official pretext was the "Mingrelian conspiracy". Khrushchev refers to two resolutions adopted by the Central Committee, one in November 1951 and the other in March 1952. Their text has never been published. The press has never given any information on "the Mingrelian organization" which is supposed to have existed in Georgia. Khrushchev specifies that its declared object "was the liquidation of Soviet power in this republic, with the aid of imperialist powers". He says that the resolutions were "personally dictated" by Stalin and that the Central Committee "adopted them without any previous discussion on the Political Bureau". "They contained grave charges against numerous loyal communists. . . a certain number of leading militants in the party and the soviets were arrested as a result. As was subsequently proved, nothing more was involved than smears against the Georgian party organization." As a result "thousands of innocent people were victims of stubbornness and anarchy. All this came about under the 'brilliant' leadership of Stalin, the 'first son of the Georgian nation', as the Georgians liked to call him."

On 12 January 1953 Stalin accompanied by Malenkov, Beria, Voroshilov and Khrushchev went to a grand Polish gala organized with a competition of orchestral singers, choirs and the ballet of the Poznan Opera. On the next day, 13 January, *Pravda* published the following communiqué: "During the proceedings, the state security services unmasked a group of terrorist doctors." The text of the communiqué was accompanied by an even more revealing commentary:

> During the proceedings, the state security services unmasked a group of terrorist doctors whose aim was to end the life of active militants of the Soviet Union. This terrorist group comprised Professor Vovsi, Professor Vinogradov, Professor M. Kogan, Professor B. Kogan, Professor Yegorov, Professor A. Feldman (oto-rhino), Professor Etinguer, Professor A. Grinstein (neurology), and Doctor G. Mayarov. From the documents, and scientific research, the conclusion of expert doctors and the testimony of the culprits, it has been established that these criminals, enemies hidden from the people, had cut short the life of their patients by faulty treatment. . . These criminal doctors hoped to sap the health of the leading military cadres of the Soviet Union, to put them out of action, and hence to weaken the defence of the country. They tried to put out of action Marshal A. Vassilievsky and Marshal Govorov, Army General Shetmenko, Marshal Konoev, Admiral G. Levchenko and others, but their arrest disturbed their criminal plans and the criminals did not achieve their aim. It has been established that all these doctor assassins, who have become monsters of the human race, who have soiled the sacred banner of science and profaned the honour of men of science, were agents in the service of foreign spies. The majority of participants of the terrorist group, M. Vovsi, B. Kogan, A. Feldman, A. Grinstein, Etinguer and the others, were tied to the Jewish International Bourgeois Nationalist Organization "Joint", created by the American espionage service to give material support to Jews in other countries.
>
> In fact, this organization, under the direction of the American espionage service, is conducting widespread terrorist and espionage activity in a series of countries, including the Soviet Union. The accused Vovsi declared, during the enquiry, that he received from the United States directives "for the extermination of the leading cadres of the USSR" from the organization "Joint" through the agency of the doctor Shimelovich and a well-known bourgeois nationalist, Michoels. The other participants in the terrorist group — V. Vinogradov, M. Kogan and P. Yegorov — were agents of the English espionage service. The

enquiry will shortly be over.

The Kirov operation was beginning once again. Even the basic details were the same. The commentary in *Pravda* specified: "comrades A. Zhdanov and A. Shterbakov fell victim to this band of ferocious beasts with human faces. The criminals have testified that, taking advantage of comrade Zhdanov's illness they had intentionally hidden the fact that he was suffering from a miocardial lesion and had prescribed him a régime which was contra-indicated for this grave illness, thus provoking the death of comrade Zhdanov. These doctors also shortened the life of comrade Shterbakov, and brought on his death by using very powerful contra-indicated medicaments and prescribing harmful treatment for him. These criminals have done their best in the first place to destroy the health of leading soviet military cadres. . .". The foreign secret services reappeared in the guise of an international Jewish bourgeois nationalist organization ("Joint") which was "a creation of the American espionage services". Members of the terrorist group were "paid agents", "sold body and soul" to the Americans. *Pravda* denounced "an atmosphere of placidity and blissful optimism". The testimonies were recorded. They were distributed to the members of the Political Bureau. Vyshinsky, Minister for Foreign Affairs, returned to the juridical scene. He presented to the Law Institute of the Soviet Academy a report revising and enlarging the concept of offence. Propaganda was mobilized and produced the desired results. In France *L'Humanité* of 23 January 1953 published a declaration signed by ten French doctors, appealing to the French medical corps to support the action taken by the Soviet government.

Everything was in position. The affair was of the highest importance. This is shown by the solemnity of the preparation, the world audience being looked to, the nature of the charges, the powerful instruments assembled, the considerable role which was insistently attributed to foreign espionage services. The choice of the Kremlin as location for the criminal plot; the choice of the two first victims from the ranks of the top leaders; and the attention focused on the leading army cadres show as clearly as is possible that the intended target was for the second time the state leadership. Faced with the necessity for a radical change in the Political Bureau and the high administration, Stalin quite naturally resorted to tried and tested techniques elaborated twenty-three years earlier, and thus gave definitive proof of the role it occupied in his art of government. The members of the Political Bureau were Malenkov, Beria, Molotov, Voroshilov, Khrushchev, Bulganin, Kaganovich, Mikoyan, Saburov and Pervukhin. Alternate members were Shvernik, Ponomarenko, Melnikov, and Bagirev.

On 4 March 1953, the Tass News Agency reported that on the night of the 1-2 March Stalin had been the victim of a cerebral haemmorrhage. The doctors were by his side. "Treatment was conducted under the continual surveillance of the Central Committee and the Soviet Government." On 6 March Stalin's death was announced.

This chronology shows that for a quarter of a century the use of the technique of repression in affairs of state was an invariant. The Second World War changed nothing. The enumeration of the questions dealt with shows that Stalin used it to solve every problem — some of them of international scale — even though their nature was profoundly different. The last enterprise which he was hatching on the eve of his death shows irrefutably that he still considered repression as the principal basis of every major political objective. With this confirmed, it becomes quite clear that repression had been institutionalized. It was the permanent cornerstone in the conduct of affairs of state. It lay at the heart of the exercise of power.

25 Governmental procedure and the underlying society

FROM THE point of view of the nature of the state and the exercise of power the most important fact is this: after a quarter of a century and a world war, the machine of repression was in motion again, at its highest level, missing nothing, precise and efficient. It was no more a question of Tartars or Jews or eminent functionaries of the provincial administration, but the Political Bureau. That is to say, eminent members of the régime, in principle wielding complete executive power. The majority of them had taken part in the massacre of the 1930s and all of them had lived through it. They knew what was coming and they felt threatened.

Events provide an experimental confirmation of theoretical analysis of the instruments of power and its exercise. We can observe the way in which the state's nerve-centre functioned. At this level the extreme concentration of personal relations was highly significant. These represent a reflection of the methods and objectives of the decision-making process. Before our eyes is the most advanced stage of a transformation of the instruments of power, whose first symptoms were clear in the eruption of the conflict between the party and the trade unions on the eve of the NEP. Now, the relations we are describing, in their essentials, still remain at the heart of the régime's problems in the 1970s and at the beginning of the 1980s. This means that if we cannot identify them, then the most recent changes in Soviet society will be incomprehensible. The majority of the Political Bureau was condemned. It knew it. The legal titulars to the highest state functions were incapable of saving not only their positions but also their lives. This is the first crucial observation to be made. The majority knew what was in store for it before the doctors' affair exploded on the scene. Thus it was not taken by surprise; it had had the necessary time to prepare for this eventuality. However, it had done nothing to help itself in this period. When Khrushchev says "Stalin, on all the evidence, had the intention of doing away with all the former members of the Political Bureau", he was referring not to a lesson drawn from what happened, but to a prior certainty. The indications of Stalin's intentions were numerous and unambiguous. He repeatedly asserted that "members of the Political Bureau should be replaced by others". The first clear indication was his unwarranted attack on Molotov and Mikoyan. In his speech to the

Plenary Session of the Central Committee which took place shortly after the 19th Congress, Stalin let it be understood that these two very close collaborators had been guilty of "crimes", without saying anything more precise. No one was fooled, the interested parties least of all. Molotov had been party to the machinations of 1934. Mikoyan and Kaganovich had replaced Zinoviev and Kamenev on the Political Bureau. Khrushchev owed his own advancement (his nomination to secretary of the Ukrainian Communist Party and his position as alternate to the Political Bureau) to the liquidation of Kossior. Furthermore when he observed, "It is not out of the question that if Stalin had remained alive a few months more, comrades Molotov and Mikoyan would not have spoken to this Congress", he said nothing which, from the outset, was not known to initiates.

The second indication, no less clear, was Stalin's proposal to raise the number of members of the Political Bureau (which was now the praesidium of the Central Committee) to twenty-five. It was an old procedure, employed frequently since 1923. It was adapted to the functioning of the apparatus. The number of Political Bureau or Central Committee members was raised to neutralize those that the General Secretary wished to eliminate. Stalin's epigones used it whenever necessary. Thus Khrushchev, with the knowledge of a specialist, understood that the object of this measure was "the future elimination of original members of the Political Bureau", and their replacement. Vyshinsky was among the new members.

Finally, we have the attack on Voroshilov. Stalin said openly that he suspected him of being a British agent. The NKVD bugged his apartment.

The opening of the doctors' affair only showed them that the last stages of the operation were beginning. All the more so since Stalin — always at his most dangerous when smooth-tongued — declared, after presenting the testimony of the doctors: "You were as blind as kittens. What would happen without me? The country would fall before you could recognize the enemy." They knew then that it was an absolute political condemnation, and that the penalty could only be death. In the scenario which they knew so well, charges of incompetence were the prelude to those of complicity with the enemy. However, they remained paralysed. It is true that we don't know exactly how Stalin died. It still seems quite probable that his cerebral haemorrhage was providential. It is however quite plausible that medical surveillance by the Central Committee would not have bothered much about curing him.

We can see in this rare case how a group of leaders, in principle wielding considerable power, and fully cognizant of what was in store for them, are incapable of taking the most elementary steps to save their lives. This extraordinary paralysis was an obvious effect of the absolute preponderance of the General Secretary. Khrushchev only wanted to see the most superficial expression of this preponderance. He emphasized the pathological aggravation of Stalin's capricious, irritable and brutal behaviour after the war. He stressed that his suspicious nature degenerated to the point of obsession, of a persecution complex. It caused all the more harm because he settled everything unilaterally, without consideration for anyone or anything.

Without doubt, exercising power for a quarter of a century without reference to persons or institutions, and ruling in a completely arbitrary way, would create mental problems. The isolation implied by such total authority would make things worse. His judgement would become impaired. It is no less undeniable that the extreme concentration of governmental powers would weigh his personal intervention very extensively, without any limits. But no matter how valid these considerations are, they leave open the crucial question: how was Stalin able also to subjugate the state's leaders? We know that far from being deranged, he always pursued his desired objectives with great concentration and lucidity. Even if he had degenerated as Khrushchev claims, his madness would still not explain how he managed to exercise power.

A story about Tito provides us with a striking insight into what went on. (The anecdotes in Khrushchev's report are taken straight from life.) Stalin confided to Khrushchev — and certainly not without the intention of frightening him — "It would be enough for me to lift my little finger and Tito would be no more, he would collapse." This was an imprudent prophecy, as it happened, but it was only a premature generalization of a practice which up till then had been continual and efficient. Thus one can easily imagine Khrushchev's fears, since why should Stalin have wanted to remind him of what his whole entourage had known for years? We are reminded of these fears by the fierce resentment which took possession of Khrushchev so long afterwards and which led him to say during this memorable meeting of the 20th Congress: "If I lift my little finger Kossior will be no more. I lift my little finger once more and there will be no more Postychev nor Chubar. I lift my little finger once more and Voznessensky, Kuznetsov and countless others will disappear." Khrushchev's long diatribe, although carefully calculated to achieve specific aims, was nourished on still-burning hatred and humiliation. This violence, which lurked in chance remarks and sarcasm (for example the allusion to "stupid Georgians"), is also a fact to be remembered, and even an important fact for understanding what took place in the most tightly-knit circles, between these men officially in charge of everything. Khrushchev recounts one of these humiliating scenes which Stalin delighted in, in a passage which was struck out of the official version. Taking Tito on one side (in 1945), Stalin said to him, in a voice loud enough for everyone around to hear:

> "What a pity you are not always here with me. You are an intelligent and sensible man, you should have been my collaborator. And you have to leave soon, look who I'm going to be left with. Look, look at him (pointing to Bulganin), this parakeet, this uniformed dandy who takes himself for a military man, and even a strategist. In reality he can hardly shuffle around the floor. Or look at him here (pointing to Molotov). His brain is as petrified as his face is stony. He understands nothing about the simplest things. He can't even find a country on a map and he messes around with foreign affairs. (Hearing this, Molotov paled and became silent.) Or look at this malign *khokhol*★ (designating Khrushchev); he has already outstripped his tiny abilities. He keeps on climbing, and he wants to push himself even further forward. Do you see who I'm left with? Alone and no one to rely on. . . ." Then Stalin shouted to me: "Come on, khokhol, dance the gopak." Well, I danced. Recently, after the meeting with comrade Tito, he recalled this scene to us.

This contempt for men went with a complete contempt for rules. Stalin took it on himself to expel Voroshilov from the Political Bureau and excluded him from this body for several years, long before he suspected him of being a British agent. He forbade him to take part in the meetings. Voroshilov could find no response. When he learned that the Political Bureau was to meet he telephoned Stalin to ask for permission to turn up and Khrushchev notes: "Sometimes Stalin would let him, but he never failed to show his annoyance." A remark of Bulganin (a remark made in confidence which Khrushchev repeated) goes even further: "It sometimes happened that someone would come to see Stalin, at his invitation, as a friend. And when he sat down beside Stalin he would never know where he would be sent afterwards, whether he would be sent home or to prison." Thus when Stalin said, "If you don't get a confession from the doctors, you'll lose your head," Ignatiev, whom he took on one side, knew that his head would roll.

It is easy to tell many other illuminating anecdotes. It is sufficient to cite Khrushchev. His conclusions are clear, precise, and irrefutable. The real exercise of power took no account of the constitution, the party statutes or administrative rules. The preponderance of the Secretariat was absolute. Members of the Political Bureau and

---

★*Khokhol*: a pejorative term for a Ukrainian.

the Central Committee — and hence of the highest political authority in the régime — had no effective guarantee of their security. The total and permanent insecurity in which they lived paralysed them but assured the complete independence and untrammelled power of the General Secretary. This complete subordination of the supreme bodies of power to the Secretariat was in no sense temporary. It was not limited to any particular period. It lasted for a quarter of a century. The functional value of fear was as great in 1953 as on 1 December 1934. There is no other example in history of an advanced industrial country where there was such a complete and utter submission of the leading circles to the arbitrary dictates of a single person. Even fascist dictatorships can show no equivalent. Hitler himself could not dispose of Goering, Goebbels or Himmler in the way that Stalin got rid of Ordzhonikidze, Yezhov or Voroshilov. This resurgence of discretionary power over the most eminent members of the régime, like the asiatic despotism of strong states, is highly significant. These rigorously established facts lead to the crucial question: *how (by what means) could terror hold such complete sway over the leaders of the political corps of the state?*

It is clear that the first — limited — answer is to be found in the choice of men. That is to say, in his deliberate conduct of the 1930s massacre, Stalin carried out a certain selection. He did not kill indiscriminately. He preserved docile mediocrity. This selection is historically important, because it determines the *subsequent* composition of the higher bodies of the state, such as its administrative political apparatus, the party. As we have seen, this mediocrity, by virtue of its consistency, became an important political factor. It was not just the result of blind chance. It was intentional.

At the beginning of the present cycle — the five years of the sharpest phase (1934) — the closed circle of thermidorean leaders was not homogeneous. Whilst it is difficult to distinguish two clear groups, there are two types of background: the faction which allowed Stalin to seize power but which owed him nothing, and the phalanx of those whose career was in essence created by him. Molotov, Kaganovich, Voroshilov and Mikoyan were the most notable among the latter. In this milieu Khrushchev represented the ambitions which Stalin drew out of the depths of the apparatus. Stalin made use of their mediocrity, their docility, and their desires. In his eyes they could be used as instruments. He first used them to divide the thermidorean forces and to destroy what had to be destroyed. Of the others, those who by virtue of their past considered themselves Stalin's peers, Ordzhonikidze is without doubt the most eminent and the most representative. He belonged among Stalin's closest intimates, to the nucleus of friends of his youth. His powerful personality, his long friendly association with Lenin, and his former role in the leadership of the party gave him a privileged position. This leader of the thermidoreans was a presumptive successor to Stalin. The party Control Commission gave him a powerful means of intervention. Whilst decimating the Left Opposition he was able to rally its deserters. Piatakov, whose collaboration he had retained, was the first and most brilliant of these protégés. Ordzhonikidze was perfectly capable of gathering a competent general staff around him. He had the run of the Kremlin. Of course, he had to submit to control by the security service, as did anyone close to Stalin. He did not have the right to carry arms. However, his personal ascendancy could have guaranteed him accomplices. In public he worked for Stalin's supremacy. In private he guarded his tongue and maintained his independence.

In 1929 (at the beginning of what has become known as "the cult of personality") *Pravda* devoted a complete issue to the celebration of Stalin's fiftieth birthday. Ordzhonikidze's article was entitled "The Granite Bolshevik". Among other things we find in it: "Today the whole world is writing about Stalin. In future he will be much written about. It could not be otherwise. After the death of Vladimir Ilyich, Stalin confronted us in all his grandeur. It was under his leadership that the struggle against trotskyism and the rightists was led. Their victory would have driven Soviet power to ruin. The world enemies of communism pronounce his name with hatred. For our part we wish Stalin the best of health, the greatest possible success in socialist construction in the USSR, and the victory of the proletarian revolution the world over under the flag of Leninism."

It is said that in 1936 Ordzhonikidze went into a violent rage when he learnt of the arrest of Piatakov, whom he had made his adjutant. From then on he knew he was threatened directly. His reaction was highly significant: he set about counter-attacking. In 1937, after the condemnation of Piatakov and Radek, he is said to have addressed the following remarks to Stalin: "You are mad. I know it now. I have been watching you for a long time. I will tell the party that you can no longer be our leader, because you are mentally ill." He died suddenly several days later on 18 January 1937. According to Khrushchev, Stalin forced Ordzhonikidze to kill himself and had his brother executed. Khrushchev imputed the assassination of Ordzhonikidze and his brother to the influence of Beria. This appears to be a convenient myth. In such an important and personal matter, Stalin would have decided on his own. His whole family fell to the repression. Stalin exterminated this faction. He did not even spare his childhood friends. The most intimate of them, Budu Mdivani, was arrested in Tiflis, and executed in July 1937. Enukidzhe — for fifteen years Secretary of the Executive of the USSR Supreme Soviet — was shot in Moscow at the end of the same year. Stalin deliberately eliminated the most capable, audacious and firm thermidorean leaders in the process of selection that accompanied the massacre. He allowed only mediocre and servile leading cadres to survive. The 22nd Congress provides us with several testimonies to this servility. We know that on the letter addressed to him by Yakir he wrote: "Scoundrel and prostitute". Voroshilov added: "A completely justified description"; this was countersigned by Molotov. Kaganovich wrote: "This traitor, this scoundrel. . . [followed, we are told, by an obscenity] deserves one single punishment: death." On 9 June 1937, on the eve of his execution, Yakir wrote to Voroshilov: "In memory of many past years of loyal work in the Red Army, I ask you to take charge of looking after my family who have been left destitute and who are completely innocent. I ask you to help them. I ask the same of Yezhov." Voroshilov annotated this: "I distrust the loyalty of a man who was in general disloyal", signed and dated 10 June 1937. The family, which belonged to the régime's upper circle, was to be arrested and deported. We can thus see how the lack of character of those who Stalin selected to live left them open to the effects of fear. He used them, up to the moment when he judged it useful to dispense with them. This is what he was preparing to do in 1953. However, this does not explain how Stalin was able to carry out this selection. It does not explain how these leaders, informed by years of experience, warned by clear omens, and knowing themselves to be condemned, that is already dead in Stalin's eyes, were reduced to impotence. Shortly after Stalin's death they showed that they were fully capable of acting decisively in order to survive. Therefore there must have been some means of neutralizing them other than fear.

The organization of the Secretariat provides the decisive answer. The key to Stalin's exorbitant power was the legislation which integrated the NKVD into the Secretariat. The direct subordination of the NKVD to Stalin provided the requisite mechanism. My analysis of the double structure of the Secretariat and the NKVD and of their mode of operation can be verified rigorously by examining the way power was exercised. If this chapter is re-read it will be seen how the facts which have been presented above support this idea, and how they become coherent in its light. Thus we can understand how Stalin's death was not and could not have been anything other than the first stage in the emancipation of the upper bureaucracy. The decisive step was the execution of Beria. Stalin's death and Beria's murder are two indissociable moments of the same political process.

This arrangement also explains Stalin's remarkable economy of means. To carry out his immense long-term enterprise, with all its complexities and historic significance, Stalin made continual use, in the key positions, of only four people: Poskrebyshev, Vyshinsky, Yezhov, Zhdanov. (It is true that because of the risks taken by Stalin and the calculations he made, Yagoda, Yezhov and Beria succeeded each other as head of the NKVD. But it was always the same post that was involved.) Hence four collaborators were enough for him to govern for a quarter of a century with prodigious efficiency. Of course all his objectives were not attained. For example, events intervened to prevent him realizing the diplomatic policy for which he had prepared by the decapitation of the army. But it still remains true that the political corps of the state was changed from top to bottom and that the organic basis of the resulting society remained essentially unchanged at the beginning of the 1970s. It is also true that the basic system of law which he promulgated and the instruments of intervention which he created served as a model for the constitution of European bureaucratic society.

The actual organization of the work of the government in no way corresponded to the constitution, the party statutes, or to the division of administrative responsibility. It conformed closely with the concentration of power in the hands of the Secretariat. Poskrebyshev was Stalin's personal secretary. He understood the most intimate missions. He was the direct instrument of the Secretariat. He had an extensive knowledge of the secrets of power. An hour after Stalin's death, he was dead too. It is not known from what cause.

Vyshinsky was responsible for the cardinal task of this period: the elaboration of its organic laws and the organization of the massacre of the thermidoreans: that is to say, the complete reshaping of the political corps of the state. Yagoda simply brought to bear the decisive strength of the NKVD, and Yezhov and Beria played this role in their turn. They occupied the decisive strategic position in the state. Zhdanov, who followed Kirov, fulfilled a role which is often underestimated, but was nevertheless crucial. His task was to deepen the work of deliberate mystification into an official dogma. This was largely from the point of view of the continuity of power; it was not an academic exercise. He used dogma as did the Inquisition, to control, tame and administer the intelligentsia. Thus he intervened in a political sector that was very sensitive for the ruling class. He had to prevent the formation of an opposition to the régime in the only social mileu which possessed the necessary means to conceptualize immediate demands and hence organize them into a programme. It was quite natural that his interventions should grow in number and become increasingly important after the war. The effects of his work can still be felt long after his death, at the beginning of the 1970s.

Stalin's enterprise was thus just as concerted in the organization of the work of the government as in the premeditated organization of long-term objectives. The real division of labour ensured that the Political Bureau and Central Committee were no more than rubber-stamp bodies. They could not acquire any importance. Stalin never gave them any more than the fiction of power. The choice of men is no less striking. Poskrebyshev, Yezhov, Beria and Zhdanov emerged from the obscurity of the apparatus. They were men without a past. Vyshinsky, whose principal mission was to lay the keystone of the organization of the régime, was an opportunist politician, and a right-wing Menshevik and sworn opponent of the Bolsheviks before the revolution.

The high degree of efficiency of this system of government shows how well suited it was to the structure of the society. The effective exercise of power — like the charges in the show trials — is a very authentic record of social institutions and their workings, and thus shows up the class nature of the state. Administrative manipulation as a permanent technique was used by Stalin in small as well as great matters. He had set up the execution of 40,000 high functionaries. He had paralysed the general staff in the same way. His methods were so successful that the political apparatus of the state was completely recomposed and the officer corps decapitated. It is scarcely credible that he should have done this with such economy of means, but it was so. Administrative manipulation lends itself to secrecy. One has to be very well versed in the art of intrigue and to be fully aware of the interests of the people concerned to guess at what lies behind a movement of personnel. For this reason personnel movement was well suited to Stalin's strategy. Who could have foreseen the significance of the almost simultaneous nomination of Yezhov and Vyshinsky, even though these long premeditated promotions (Stalin did not improvise such a decisive move) marked a crucial phase in setting up the trials and the massacre? Nikolai Yezhov was at that time fourth secretary of the Central Committee. He became president of the Control Commission in place of Kaganovich, who moved to the Ministry of Transport where he succeeded Andreyev, who replaced Yezhov who knew that Yagoda's position was open and that Yezhov was destined to hear his confession. Enukidzhe left the presidency of the Executive of the Supreme Soviet for that of the Soviet of the Transcaucasus. Attorney-General Akulov replaced him and the assistant prosecutor Vyshinsky took Akulov's place. Three months later, Enukidze, who had been expelled for a breach of norms, was shot. Who — apart from Poskrebyshev — could have foreseen that with the key piece in position the trial could begin?

On 12 April 1937 the news broke of Marshal Tukhackevsky's nomination to Commander of the Volga military region. Who could see in this evident disgrace the first step towards making this most eminent military leader into a German spy, to be shot? Who could imagine on learning that General Efumov replaced Tukhackevsky on 10 June in his position on the Volga, that on the day after, the ill-fated 11th, charges would be published, and sentence pronounced and executed? Who could have foreseen that Marshal Egorov was nominated to the Commissariat of Defence in place of Tukhackevsky in order that he could pronounce the death sentence and send him to the firing squad for the same reason as, and directly after, the lowly NKVD agents who were compromised in Kirov's murder?

It could have been foreseen by some of the very high dignitaries — Poskrebyshev, Vyshinsky, Yezhov, Voroshilov, and a small number of discreet collaborators who set the whole thing up — but certainly not the astonished Central Committee, nor the Officer Corps, even though it was forewarned by the suicide of Cramaruik, Assistant Commissioner of War and head of the political leadership of the Army. According to the official Moscow version a military council was held in Voroshilov's office (Defence Commissar) from 1 to 4 June. Voroshilov made a report on "the secret counter-revolutionary band of spies and conspirators in the Red Army". According to information given by Walter G. Krivitsky, an eminent Bolshevik, highly placed in the Soviet secret service in Western Europe, there was to be no trial. The military men present were simply to have appended their signature to the sentence. Out of nine military judges, seven were shot: Marshals Egorov and Blucher, Generals Alksnis, Belov, Dybenko, Kashirin and Goriachev.

Who could have conceived — even among the most informed circles — that the murder of Tukhackevsky, Yakir, Uborevich, Kork, Iedeman, Feldman, Primakov and Putna was paving the way for the execution of nearly 30,000 officers? There were of course certain signs which could easily be interpreted. The fact that Vyshinsky, in the 1936 trial, had slipped Trotsky's apocryphal letter into the dossier — the letter on the need for work in the army. This would be the first sign that Stalin was preparing an action against the military. The fact that Radek had mentioned the name of Tukhachevsky, almost inadvertently, in reply to a question by Vyshinsky during the audience of 24 January 1937, whilst he was denouncing General Putna, military attaché in London. This clearly indicated the imminent downfall of the Marshal, since the slightest reference would be significant. Krivitsky explains this very well. While reading the record of the session of 24 January, he suddenly started. He said to his wife: "Tukhachevsky is done for." It is, however, remarkable that his wife, who belonged to the circle of people in the know, hesitated to accept his judgement. He had to insist: "Do you believe for a second that Radek would have dared on his own let slip Tukhachevsky's name in front of the tribunal? No, it is Vyshinsky who put Tukhachevsky's name in Radek's mouth, and it is Stalin who pushes Vyshinsky. Do you not understand that Radek speaks for Vyshinsky and Vyshinsky for Stalin? I tell you again, Tukhachevsky is dead."[54]

What is in fact surprising, is not Krivitsky's clairvoyance, but on the contrary the fact that he had to argue to make himself believed. This was the beginning of 1937 — the culmination of the repression. For two years the operation had been following its spectacular course. Krivitsky held such a position in the secret service that there was nothing he did not know about the techniques of the apparatus. The Krivitsky family, because of Walter's rank, was received "throughout Moscow" and was on close terms with the highest circles in the régime. In meetings with these people, or even better, with the Kremlin entourage, rumours were born and spread. Opinion was made. No one would have been overly astonished to learn that Yagoda had poisoned Gorky. People knew that since his return in 1932, Gorky had become intolerable through his habit of playing the moralist, the conscience, and the preacher. No one doubted that his new wife Mara's imperious demands for money played a major part in his decision to return to "his father's house". They had learned that Stalin had finally become irritated by the insistent demands of the writer who wanted to return abroad on health grounds, and that their relations were strained.

It is not improbable that Yagoda eliminated his predecessor Minzhinsky, and that he believed this was Stalin's instruction, nor that he gained from the assassination of Peshkov, whose wife he is said to have desired. Already in 1932 these same people in the know had wanted to see in the suicide of Nadezhda Alleluyeva the dark hand of a murder perpetrated by Stalin in a fit of anger. If Raskolnikov denounced the charges against Yagoda as scandalous lies, it was because he was of a different moral stamp and saw further than the milieu confined to Moscow to whom anything seemed possible now. Now, it was precisely these latter people, completely accustomed to the use of crime in politics, regarding it almost as a norm, who were for a long time reluctant to believe that such eminent figures in their society as Tukhachevsky, could end up as miserably as the fallen heroes of an already distant past. If this was the judgement of informed people in Moscow, how much more reason was there in the provinces, far away from the centre of the intrigue, to be totally unprepared for what was coming, even as late as 1937.

It is necessary to take account of this daily reality, to understand the importance of secrecy and the effect of surprise in the execution of Stalin's plans. Of course, Gamarnik's suicide was a more explosive event, and easier to decipher than a furtive allusion in the record of a trial. But in those days political suicides were so commonplace that it became difficult to see what each one in particular signified. There was the suicide of Tomsky, former member of the Political Bureau and former President of the Council of Trade Unions; that of Skrypnik, Commissar of Public Instruction in the Ukraine, of Lominadze, former Secretary of the Georgian Central Committee and the young Communist International, of Khandzhian, Secretary of the Armenian Party, Cherviakov, President of the Executive Committee in White Russia, of Lyubchenko, President of the Committee of Commissars in Ukraine, and many other notables. Finally, even if it were possible to foresee the fall of some eminent personality, as did Krivitsky, and to know which institution was going to conduct the next repressive action, it was impossible to work out how broad the sweep of each operation would be. The secrecy of the administrative preparation and the high degree of efficiency of the small resources they used make it impossible. The extent of the action was hence always a total surprise. We have to conclude from the results achieved by Stalin that this strategy was perfectly suited to its victims. The upper civil and military bureaucracy was caught in the trap of the cloistered and hierarchic state organization. The pyramidal construction of the administration, the watertightness of the system of command and the one-way control from top to bottom, reinforced by overt and covert control mechanisms at every level, gave rise to a dispersion of forces, and a division of means, and brought about a loss of initiative which is difficult to overcome. It is true that the thermidorean chiefs often possessed very wide networks of clientele. But they used them as if they were private capital. These clientele were formed out of the conflict between individual careers. They served particular interests and were not created for any other purpose. The links and relations formed on the fringes of professional activity remained hierarchic and personalized. At the same time as it completely destroyed the ability of the social corps of the state to intervene, the state's rigid framework imposed an extreme functional concentration of initiative and of means at the summit of the apparatus. Only the Secretariat held universal effective power.

Stalin respected this reality and used it as a powerful lever. It is remarkable that he did not destroy the party at the same time that he annihilated its cadres. The party was not only the political administration of the ruling class in society, but was also the bureaucracy's instrument for social recruitment. The bureaucracy — like all ruling classes — renewed itself by integrating into its ranks social layers whose origin was foreign to it. This transfer was brought about by co-optation. This method of renewal is in itself a test of the class nature of the state. The party was the instrument of this co-optation. This was one of its essential functions. Stalin kept this up at the height of the repression. He used it to speed up the passage from one generation to another. Now, this rapid substitution was one of the major political conditions for the success of the enterprise. The care which Stalin took to preserve this instrument of social continuity right through the massacre is a highly significant supplementary confirmation of the co-ordinated nature of the enterprise.

The double effect of the complete destruction of forces, division of means, and concentration of initiative and capacity for intervention at the summit — which was a natural, not a deliberate phenomenon, a spontaneous product of this kind of structure — completely determined the objective data (the technical context) of the struggle for power within the ruling class. We know that the bureaucracy (like all classes) is of heterogeneous social composition. We know that this heterogeneity implies the existence of divergent social interests. Finally we know that when the socially dominant position of the class in power remains solid, but at the same time is encountering grave difficulties from the growth of the productive forces, that its internal heterogeneity can be accentuated and clashes of interest within its ranks can be aggravated to such a point that a deep crisis opens at the level of the state. The violence which accumulates through this process has to find an outlet. The technical nature of this outlet does not depend at all on the protagonists. It is imposed by the nature of the society. The nature of highly organized bureaucratic society creates an alternative technique: the "palace coup" or "palace revolution". Stalin's palace coup took on the scope of a coup d'état.

The charges made in the show trials bear witness to the striking authenticity of this analysis. Of course we know nothing (since the archives are still sealed) of the intrigues in the ranks of the thermidoreans and of how advanced they were. We do not even know if they went beyond the stage of minor disagreements between dignitaries. It is certain that Stalin was one step ahead of them. It is probable that his intervention was pre-emptive, to prevent discontent from surfacing as intentions. But this is not the problem.

Stalin's instructions were not arbitrary. Vyshinsky's procedures were not utopian. The charges made corresponded closely with the real state of society. They were a faithful image. The real organization of the state was a solid base of support for the fiction. The imagined dangers were actually possible. This is the authenticity which makes itself felt so strongly. The prosecutor's false accusations outline the methods which a genuine subversion would have had to use, because the state or organization of society, in its material reality, lent itself to such techniques but eliminated others. A palace conspiracy is what would be involved. The state's leading circles would have to be a base of support for such a plot. It would have to be articulated around centres grafted on to the administration. It would have to make use of terror. Vyshinsky, speaking through the mouth of one of the accused, Rygold, explains the use of terror in a very interesting way: "Zinoviev justified the need to use terror, saying that, although terror was irreconcilable with marxism, it was now necessary under these circumstances to reject such arguments, since there were now no other methods of struggle against the leadership of the party and government since Stalin united in his person all the strength and firmness of the party leadership. This is why, in the first instance, Stalin had to be suppressed." The terrorism described in the charge is a *terrorism of the apparatus*, profoundly different in its methods from classical terrorism arising from the depths of a people deprived of their rights by despotism. The conspirators — as Voroshilov so well describes it — had built "nests" in the apparatus. More accurately in the summits of the civil and military apparatus. The dates cited in the official record of the cross–examination are themselves highly significant. According to the charges the first contacts were made during the summer of 1932. The centre was definitively established at the end of 1932. Clandestine action began in earnest in the last months of 1934 — that is to say when bureaucratic society had been constituted organically. What emerges from the prosecutor's choice of dates is that the plot became operational when the society created by the second civil war had been definitively established, and that it worked on the terrain established by this society. It is no less remarkable that the only notable difference between the technical option chosen by Stalin and that attributed to his adversaries lay in the scale of the means utilized, not in their nature. A palace coup and a palace revolution rely on the same social support. The charge-sheet of the show trials was a faithful image of society.

The economy of means used shows that Stalin's intervention was an operation on the apparatus. This is indisputable. It amounted to the arrest, deportation and execution of 40,000 top–level civil functionaries and 30,000 officers. It was a complete reconstruction of the leading elements in the state apparatus and a thoroughgoing shake-up of the army. Furthermore, by a process of contamination these violent measures eventually involved several million citizens from all social spheres. The social scale of the results was immense. In this precise sense they attacked the elementary interests of all classes in society. This is the second indisputable fact. The disproportion between the initial means and the results achieved is extraordinary. It is even more extraordinary that the state leadership and the army submitted passively to the massacre which ravaged them.

Such an obvious disproportion is a major event, and a vital experimental datum. No reasonable interpretation can ignore it or leave it out of consideration. The only way to understand it is to accept that administrative relations and their restrictive outgrowths organized the whole of society. This extension in its turn is only intelligible if we accept that coercive administrative relations determined the social structure of the production–process. That is to say that they controlled the social dynamic in its formation, in the matrix of the productive forces. This necessarily presupposes private appropriation of the means of production by the social corps of the state. The hypothesis of a parasitic bureaucratic formation imposed on the proletariat is in reality completely refuted by the facts. The theory of the bureaucracy as a social class — and a ruling social class — is the only way to account for this crucial experience.

26 The fundamental dynamic continuity, 1930–70

THIS QUARTER century opens with the second civil war. The state bureaucracy, through an extremely violent military confrontation with the rural and urban middle classes, established itself as a socially autonomous ruling class. This fundamental change modified the composition of classes and their functional hierarchy. The new social identity which had been established furnished itself with a legal status. This was the crucial work of the 1930s. It was achieved through a permanent confrontation with the obstacles which arose out of the conjuncture. Administrative organization was improvised in a pragmatic effort to resolve immediate difficulties in the search for solutions which conformed with the functional originality of the society. The organization of labour became the initial task and the one which generated all other social relations between classes. It introduced administrative relations as the social armour of the production–process. But this did not take place freely. On the contrary it was subordinated to the world conjuncture. The dominant world-wide regression compelled administrative relations to become integrated into coercive structures. These imposed technical necessities, because they were acting at the heart of the process of formation of the productive forces, in the matrix of the production-process, creating their own social relations. Through the intermediary of corporate interests, coercive relations ceased to be simply techniques and became social factors of great power. The internal divergences within the ruling class, provoked by this complex process, produced a crisis in the exercise of power. This led to unparalleled violence, a violence of the apparatus, whose epicentre was to be found within the upper bureaucracy. The absolutely fundamental, immense work of these years ended with the appearance of a global dynamic of a profoundly new society. The second decade, the 1940s, under the impact of the Second World War, consolidated the new class system in the most striking and decisive manner through its world-wide expansion. The crisis of capitalism, combined with an organic regression in the revolutionary capacity of the proletariat, laid the basis for a major extension of bureaucratic society in Europe and Asia. Its basic structures, and its dynamic, taking due account of inevitable historical differences, conform to the model elaborated in the 1930s.

There is no break between the society of the 1930s and international bureaucratic society with its present contradictions, as it now appears in the 1980s. There is an organic continuity. The break which the Chinese theorists see in the mid-1950s does not exist. Nothing real corresponds to the placing of brackets around the twenty-five crucial years of stalinist control which preceded the Khrushchev school. On the contrary, experience shows that there has been a dynamic continuity. The only historic rupture which took place was before then. NEP is the principal point of departure of this break. It came about economically, socially and politically, as the decomposition of the first world revolution. The second civil war opened a new historical period which is not yet over.

This continuity is organic and dynamic. But it develops in a profoundly different world context than that of the 1930s, and this, of course, is crucially important. Since around the 1950s, bureaucratic society has embarked on a world-wide confrontation, provoked by technological change. It is confronting the second world revolution. But it is confronting it with its own structures, the original result of twenty-five years of stalinism. To misunderstand this would make it impossible to understand the real nature of contemporary crisis and all its relevant manifestations: economic, social, political and strategic. It would thus lead to errors of judgement whose predictable and unpredictable effects could be enormous.

This continuity is not passive, but dynamic, because its heritage is itself dynamic. The work of the 1930s and 1940s was a constant adaptation to a changing world situation. But it conformed to the decisive aspects of bureaucratic society. And this is the most important thing, and has been since 1950. Of course the exercise of power is not so brutal. A relative equilibrium has been achieved at the heart of the state leadership. But this relative amelioration has left intact the functional armour of the state and of society. The physical security of the upper bureaucracy was acquired through a palace coup in complete conformity with the stalinist example. On 11 July 1953 a communiqué from the Central Committee announced that Beria had been arrested. On 26 December 1953 a second communiqué revealed that Beria had been judged by a special court between 18 and 23 December, and that sentence was carried out on the 23rd. The official procedure was at one with that invented by Stalin. Furthermore, the requirement that Beria should have been an agent in the pay of foreign espionage services since 1920 conformed scrupulously with Vyshinsky's typical scenario. It is remarkable that at the very moment when he was denouncing these myths, and in relation to the same thing, Khrushchev used them against Beria. In fact Beria was already where he could do no harm on 28 June 1953.

On that day the leaders who had blocked together made a spectacular sortie, without Beria. When the delegation from the French Socialist Party returned from its stay in Moscow, a version of Beria's death was circulated without naming those responsible. Khrushchev had confided to a member of this delegation (to its head) that Beria had been killed by a bullet in the neck as a meeting of the Political Bureau broke up. It was probably Mikoyan who did the deed. The judicial process would have taken place straight afterwards. The details are of secondary importance. The arrest of Beria and his closest collaborators and the execution of the majority among them constituted a palace coup of considerable force against the NKVD.

But the Political Bureau remained a rubber-stamp body. Classical procedures of manipulative administration, which were used in 1953 against Malenkov, and then again in June 1957, and in October 1964 against Khrushchev, were identical to the 1930 version. The renewal of the small leading team was carried out as before (except for the blood, which was not unimportant for the interested parties). In November 1962 the eight-member Secretariat became twelve. Six months later it numbered fourteen, with the addition of Brezhnev and Podgorny. The meaning of this operation became clear in March to April 1966 when the 23rd Congress carried through a political condemnation of Khrushchev, expelled him from the state apparatus, and exiled him to a comfortable but isolated dacha. It is not without interest that effective power was distributed through a small collective of high officials (Brezhnev, Kosygin, Mikoyan, Suslov, Illyichev, Pomarev and Shelepin), or that it was concentrated in three of them, or that of this troika, the balance inclined to favour Brezhnev. But it changes nothing essential in the exercise of power. Nor does Kosygin's personal antipathy towards Malenkov, nourished on memories of Leningrad, although not negligible in the ruling-circle intrigues, tell us anything significant and new about the present mechanisms involved in the exercise of power. In essence, these have not changed.

Of course mass repression has given way to selective repression. This has become very important with respect to relations of force within the ruling class and within society. But the monopoly of political power rests in the hands of the upper bureaucracy and the means which guarantee its preservation remain unchanged. It is not an accident that, in February 1962, under the pretext of celebrating his seventieth birthday, *Pravda* rehabilitated Zhdanov, who died in 1948 (one of the putative victims of the Kremlin doctors). Continuity in this crucial sphere (the political and social control of the intelligentsia) was as rigorous under Brezhnev as under Khrushchev. The principles of censorship and the secrecy of the archives, the institutional key to the exercise of power, are firmly and thoroughly maintained. At the beginning of the 1970s Zhores Medvedev wrote: "Until the death of Stalin, everything destined for publication had to be censored three times: first in manuscript form, then in typescript form and then in printed form before distribution. Since 1956, censorship of manuscripts has been stopped, but the two other stages are just as much in force."[55]

Of course, coercive relations in the organization of work — which the world level of technology has rendered archaic and dangerous to the growth of the productive forces — have given way to collective agreements, although limited by the absence of an independent representative of labour. But centralized and coercive administrative relations still govern the administration of the economy. To such a point that since 1955 they have remained at the heart of the crisis which is gripping European bureaucratic society. Finally the intellectual heritage of the 1930s, and the accelerated changeover of generations, is still in the 1980s an important factor in the organization of social forces.

With the basic elements of this society analysed and located it is now essential to take up once again the examination of the dynamic of the class struggle. It is necessary to understand bureaucratic society in the process of confrontation with the second world revolution.

Notes

1. "Resolution on the Russian revolution", in *Fourth Congress of the Third International*, November 1922.
2. Leon Trotsky, *History of the Russian Revolution*, part 4.
3. Karl Marx, *Critique of the Gotha Programme*.
4. Marx, *Wage-Labour and Capital*.
5. V.I. Lenin, *State and Revolution*.
6. Trotsky, *Permanent Revolution*.
7. Marx, *Critique of the Gotha Programme*.
8. Marx, *Capital*, vol. 1, section 2.
9. These quotations are taken from Lenin's speech to the Fourth Congress of the Third International on 13 November 1922, just after his first attack of illness; they were to be his last intervention before the International.
10. These figures apply only to industrial workers, not to domestic or artisan labour. See Salomon Schwartz, *Workers in the Soviet Union*.
11. Lenin, *Collected Works*, vol. 33.
12. ibid.
13. *Inprecor*, no. 31, 1928.
14. *Pravda*, 26 November 1928.
15. The complete text can be found in *Communist Bulletin*, second year, no. 24, 9 June 1921.
16. These quotations are taken from a speech given by Trotsky to the "Transport Conference" and published in the *Communist Bulletin*, second year, no. 4, 27 January 1921.
17. Speech to the Communist group of the Central Pan-Russian Council of Trade Unions, 15 March 1920.
18. Speech to the third Pan-Russian Congress of Soviets in the Public Sector, 27 January 1920.
19. ibid.
20. "Documents and materials", in Lenin, *Complete Works*, vol. 25.
21. ibid.
22. On the other hand, we also find it clearly stated in the same text: "Communists working in the factories enjoy no privileges in relation to other workers; they merely have higher duties."
23. The phrase "concentration camps" must be understood here as what are more usually referred to as "internment camps".
24. Trotsky, *The Communist International after Lenin*.
25. Trotsky, *My Life*.
26. Lenin, op. cit.
27. "The peasants. . . are to some extent owners, and to some extent workers. Property draws them towards capitalism." See Lenin, op. cit.
28. Speech to the plenary assembly of the Soviet of Regional Committees of the Communist Party and the Moscow Trade-Union Council, 6 November 1920.

29. Lenin's report to the Tenth Party Congress, in *Communist Bulletin*, 14 April 1921.
30. It would be difficult to call Ryazanov a thermidorean. Nevertheless it was he who wanted to prohibit "elections on the basis of platforms" at Congress. He drew a vigorous reply from Lenin: "We cannot deprive the members of the Central Committee of the right to address themselves to the party." But that point had already been reached. In this climate, the decision to publish a discussion bulletin and special periodicals was like trying to cauterize an artificial limb.
31. "Politics is concentrated economics. In the present stage, the economic question in the Soviet Republic must more than ever be resolved from the political point of view." Trotsky, *The Deformed Revolution*.
32. Lenin, op.cit.
33. Trotsky, *The Deformed Revolution*.
34. John D. Littlepage, *Searching for the Siberian Gold Mines, 1927-8*.
35. For a more detailed analysis of the texts, see David Rousset, "A propos des changements qui auraient lieu dans la société soviétique", in *Saturne* no. 4, November 1955.
36. *Prisons as Educational Establishments*, a collection of articles under the general editorship of A. Vyshinsky, Moscow 1934.
37. *Izvestia*, 1 March 1957.
38. A. Vyshinsky, *Basic Issues of Socialist Juridical Science*.
39. A. Vyshinsky, *The Theory of Judiciary Proof in Soviet Law*.
40. op. cit.
41. Lenin, *Complete Works*, vol. 5.
42. *Izvestia*, 22 December 1938.
43. This was certainly not the view of everyone, since he writes: "These days, it sometimes happens that certain people, once their studies are over, try to avoid being sent to the appropriate job and make their own choice of work, that which seems most convenient to them. These facts are referred to in the press. They most frequently take the form of a refusal to leave the home, neighbourhood, or circle of friends and relatives. Such people sometimes work in fields different from their speciality, at a lower salary, or even refuse to work at all, in order to avoid being assigned to another locality. There can be no doubt that such facts point to a dishonest attitude towards social duty."
44. Knowledge of these articles of the penal code is necessary to understand the nature and importance of the demands which, from 1957 to 1970, fuelled the polemics on authoritarian and centralized control. Article 128 condemns enterprise directors to two year's prison or a year's corrective labour for "bad management" or "negligence or lack of conscientiousness". Article 128a assimilates unfinished products and production of poor quality "which does not match up to compulsory standards" to an "offence against the state equivalent to sabotage". Penalties prescribed: from five to eight years' imprisonment (decree of 16 November 1949).
45. The directorial apparatus which exercises this function of authority is equally obliged to respect the directives of the central administration.

Article 6 of the decree of 26 June 1940 stipulates: "Directors of enterprises and of establishments who fail to submit to the tribunal's judgment persons guilty of unauthorized departure from work, will themselves be sent before the tribunal." The same applies to directors "Who have admitted persons sheltering from the law, after they have abandoned an enterprise or establishment without authorization".

46. The first stage of this conflict was the very severe criticism which Lenin made of the "Draft resolution on relations between the RSFSR and the independent republics", presented in September 1922 by Stalin. In a letter dated 27 September and addressed to the Political Bureau, Lenin envisages a profoundly different solution from that of autonomy, founded on complete equality of right.

47. Ordzhonikidzhe allowed himself to strike an opponent. We can thus imagine what Lenin would have had to say about the mass deportation of national minorities and the military expeditions into Hungary and Czechoslovakia. On Dzherzhinsky, Lenin had this to say: "I also fear that comrade Dzherzhinsky, who went to the Caucasus to enquire after the 'crimes' of these 'social-nationalists' was himself distinguished by his one hundred per cent Russian outlook (we know that Russified allogens constantly bring their Russian-ness to our attention) and that the impartiality of this whole commission is well typified by Ordzhonikidzhe's taking the law into his own hands. I think for Russians to take the law into our own hands cannot be justified by any provocation, or by any outrage, and that comrade Dzherzhinsky has committed an irreparable error in resorting to such measures so lightly."

48. It was published for the first time in the review *Voprosy Istorii K.P.S.S.* no. 2, 1963. It was included in volume 42 of the complete works published in Moscow in 1969. This text corresponds exactly with the version cited by Trotsky in his letter to the Historical Institute of the Party in October 1927 (see *The Deformed Revolution*). In the Notebook Lenin's secretaries took down the instructions that he gave them, the visits that he received, the problems which preoccupied him and a number of his remarks as well as the course of his disease. The Notebook is in handwritten form. It contains four columns: the date, the secretary's name, the instructions received, and notes on their execution. On the flyleaf is written, "Please write in this notebook all instructions received and all the relevant facts relating to the period of attendance, with any material relevant to the carrying out of the instructions, 21 November 1922."

49. Alexandrovich Dreitzer was an officer in the Red Army during the civil war. He took part in the fighting against Kolchak and in the war against Poland, and was twice given the Order of the Red Flag. The chief of Trotsky's bodyguard, he was thrown out of the party at the fifteenth congress. He broke with the Left Opposition in 1929.

50. There is a wealth of evidence for this. I had occasion to see this myself during the course of some very instructive conversations which I had with some very simple young Russians in the nazi camps. One of

them, who had been a very young child in 1932, explained the huge famine which must have seared his imagination in these terms: "At that time there was a bad leader in charge of the Ukraine. . ." This was certainly not a universally-held opinion. One day whilst speaking to some more educated young Russians, I told them that after the war they should go abroad and that it would be a good idea to end the restrictive passport policy. One of them said to me, "Stalin is not a communist." A glacial silence fell over our group and I was not able to resume the interview. This boy must have been 17 or 18 years old. He must have been repeating something he had heard in his own circle before being deported.

51. Sergei Kirov was born in 1886. He joined the Bolshevik Party in 1904. After the revolution he held positions of responsibility in the Caucasus and in Azerbaidzhan. He joined the Central Committee in 1923. In 1926 he became the Leningrad Party Secretary. He led the struggle against Zinoviev and his group. In 1927 — after the expulsion of the oppositionists — he was elected as an alternate to the Political Bureau. He became a full member in 1930. In 1934 he was nominated Secretary of the Central Committee. His career was that of a typical middle-level thermidorean. He belonged neither to the thermidorean élite composed of those who had exercised central responsibilities in Lenin's time (during the revolution and after) nor to the clan of childhood friends (the Georgians who had been linked with Stalin during his adolescence).

52. Khrushchev omitted to mention the Volga Germans and the Crimean Tartars.

53. Aleksandr N. Poskrebyshev joined the Bolshevik Party in 1917. He was a Lieutenant-General, became an alternate member of the Central Committee in 1934 and a full member in 1939.

54. Walter G. Krivitsky, *Stalin's Agent*.

55. Z. Medvedev, op. cit.

Index